Exploring the
METROPOLITAN
COMMUNITY

Exploring the
METROPOLITAN
COMMUNITY

EDITED BY

John C. Bollens

UNIVERSITY OF CALIFORNIA PRESS

BERKELEY AND LOS ANGELES · 1961

UNIVERSITY OF CALIFORNIA PRESS
BERKELEY AND LOS ANGELES, CALIFORNIA
CAMBRIDGE UNIVERSITY PRESS, LONDON, ENGLAND
© 1961 BY THE REGENTS OF THE UNIVERSITY OF CALIFORNIA
LIBRARY OF CONGRESS CATALOG CARD NUMBER: 61-7536
PRINTED IN THE UNITED STATES OF AMERICA

CONTRIBUTORS

John C. Bollens   Werner Z. Hirsch
Scott Greer   Carl A. McCandless

Henry J. Schmandt

Preface

THIS BOOK is intended for a wide audience—everyone concerned
about metropolitan areas. It is the product of the efforts of five
persons whose common experience was service on the staff of
the Metropolitan St. Louis Survey, which conducted an extensive
series of studies of the St. Louis City-County area. Although
the book is based on research in one metropolitan area, it contains both findings and methods that should be of value in many
other heavily populated concentrations.

The book is novel in two important respects. First, its scope
is broad, covering many major facets of metropolitan development from the vantage point of specialists in several social science disciplines. Second, all its contents should be understandable
to various types of specialists, public and private civic leaders,
and interested citizens, because of the language and the style of
writing. It is important that researchers not only assimilate but
also communicate. A conscientious endeavor has been made,
through writing, editing, and rewriting, to see that this publication meets this test.

The Metropolitan St. Louis Survey, organized under the joint
auspices of St. Louis and Washington universities, had three
principal purposes. They were to undertake integrated research
on the most important governmental, political, social, and economic aspects of the local metropolitan area, disseminate its results, and train persons in appropriate methods of inquiry.

The Survey was initially financed by grants of $250,000 from

the Ford Foundation of New York and $50,000 from the Mc-
Donnell Aircraft Corporation Charitable Trust of St. Louis. Subsequently, the Ford Foundation made a supplementary grant of
$25,000 for the preparation and publication of this book and
for a separate case study of the work and deliberations of the
official City-County charter commission, the Metropolitan Board
of Freeholders, and of the ensuing campaign that preceded the
1959 election on its plan of governmental reorganization.

The Survey functioned with full-time research personnel from
June, 1956, through August, 1957. The regular research group
consisted of eleven full-time and thirteen part-time persons;
twelve of the latter were graduate students of the two local universities. This corps was supplemented periodically by interviewers (at one time as many as sixty) for the survey of citizen
participation and opinion and by local and out-of-area consultants. After completion of the service of the full-time researchers,
the Survey maintained an office, staffed by a secretary, until July,
1959, to facilitate the distribution of its two public reports and
to make available to the Metropolitan Board of Freeholders any
data that had been assembled by the Survey.

The board of control of the Survey consisted of Father Paul C.
Reinert, president of St. Louis University; Ethan A. H. Shepley,
chancellor of Washington University; Thomas H. Eliot, chairman of the Department of Political Science, Washington University; and Paul G. Steinbicker, chairman of the Department
of Political Science, St. Louis University. Professors Eliot and
Steinbicker served as codirectors, thus assuming final responsibility to the Ford Foundation and the McDonnell Charitable
Trust for all activities conducted under Survey auspices.

The full-time staff, headed by an executive officer–director of
research appointed by the board and drawn about equally from
the St. Louis area and other parts of the nation, was composed
of four political scientists (one of whom concentrated on public
finance, with special emphasis on the study of factors affecting
expenditure levels), five sociologists, and two economists; one
part-time researcher was an urban planner.

In deciding upon the nature of its work, the Survey had to
determine what aspects of a metropolitan area needed to be re-
searched thoroughly in order to gain a solid foundation for sound
public and private decisions about its development. Looking at
a few governmental fault lines or a few slices of metropolitan
life without regard for other pertinent facts, it was judged,

would provide neither an adequate basis nor a proper perspective for understanding and decision-making. Contributing to a fuller comprehension of the functioning of a metropolitan area (and conceivably of other metropolitan areas as well) thus became the criterion for determining to proceed with each project.

More specifically, the decision to carry out most individual research projects rested on the apparent relevance of each to better knowledge and insight about the area's governments, especially the adequacy of their organization and processes. Two reasons prompted undertaking most research within a governmental context. First, such a context provided an integrating focus for the numerous phases of the work, to which the particular techniques and the orientation of persons trained and experienced in different social sciences were applied. Second, this context gave the Survey's research immediate practical value, as petitions were already being circulated to form an official charter commission, responsible for formulating a plan of City-County governmental reorganization. (The imminence of the establishment of this charter commission forced the Survey to operate within a tight time limit.)

The principal research investigations of the Survey centered on

the governments: functions, territory, structure, finances, personnel, operations, and relations

the people: characteristics; interest, attitudes, and formal and informal participation concerning public affairs; opinions of community leaders

the economy: past development, locational factors, current features, internal interdependence, and projections of growth

Many of the results of these inquiries appear in this book.

Dissemination of the Survey's research findings and methods and of information about its activities and objectives was carried out orally and in written form. Oral communications were composed of a large number of talks before local and out-of-area groups and forums, including five presentations to the official City-County board of freeholders; approximately twenty-five appearances on local television and radio (mostly the former); repeated contacts with local newspaper personnel; interviews by writers for nationally distributed publications (one series produced a feature article in the August 24, 1957, issue of *Business*

Week) ; and consultations with study groups and interested individuals of other areas. The written efforts consisted of not only
this book but also two reports, *Background for Action* and *Path
of Progress for Metropolitan St. Louis,* designed primarily for
the local public and published in February and August, 1957
(the latter won one of the first three national Fruin-Colnon
awards for outstanding contributions to the solution of problems
of urban and metropolitan areas), and a study of drafting and
campaigning for and against an officially prepared area reorganization plan. In addition, the Survey's research will receive further distribution through articles and monographs written singly
and jointly by various former staff members.

The Survey engaged in two types of training activities aimed
at increasing the supply of persons competent to carry out research in this field of rising importance and concern. Under
staff supervision, a total of twelve graduate students from the
two local universities participated on a half-time basis in numerous phases of the research projects. A graduate seminar in
metropolitan research was organized especially for these students. Accredited by the two universities and conducted by eleven
persons associated with the Survey who were then or who recently had been on the staffs of seven universities and colleges,
the course was interdisciplinary in content, drawing extensively
on the theories and methodology of several social sciences. A
detailed syllabus was prepared for use in the seminar.

Each part of this book was written expressly for the volume
since the completion of the participants' full-time work with the
Survey in late August, 1957. Since that time the five contributors have been involved in other full-time activities at widely
scattered geographical locations. Moreover, some sections of this
book are based on further analysis of data collected during the
initial fifteen-month period. In particular, Scott Greer undertook extended analysis of certain sample survey data.

The contents of the book and their order of presentation merit
brief explanation. Part one presents the major social, economic,
and governmental characteristics of the St. Louis City-County
area. It provides the background for all other parts and indicates the environment—some of the major working materials—
of the Survey. The final chapter of part one is concerned with
the means by which the City-County area, in the absence of
comprehensive governmental reorganization, thus far has been
able to avoid public problems of catastrophic proportions. Then

follows, in part two, a detailed and candid consideration of the factors that resulted in the Survey's recommendations at the local, metropolitan, and state levels. (To my knowledge, this is the first instance in which any metropolitan study has publicly presented the rationale of its decisions.)

Part three focuses on participation in local government through voting for officials, citizen relations with local governments, and opinions about the desirability and possibility of governmental change in the area. These three matters are considered in terms of the people of the central city and suburbs (both together and as two categories) and of their personal socioeconomic characteristics. Part four begins with the methods and results of two inquiries about factors affecting expenditure levels and minimum standards of adequacy for selected services. For many readers the central interest of these two inquiries will be the various elements included in making the determinations. It concludes with a means of analysis that reveals the relationships of sectors of the local metropolitan economy and with a discussion of several methods of forecasting that may aid in better comprehending certain needs and resources of the future.

A few words should be said about several matters of style, capitalization, and terms. Much of the writing is cast in the present tense and the facts, unless otherwise noted, are as of 1956–57, the time of the Survey's full-time research. "City" and "County" are used consistently to refer to the city of St. Louis and St. Louis County, respectively, thus avoiding confusion with suburban cities in the County (generally identified along with County towns and villages as municipalities) and the county offices existing in the City. Phrases such as "at the time of the Survey's research" and "while the Survey's work was in progress" pertain to the June, 1956, through August, 1957, period when a full-time research staff was in operation.

In my view, this book and the research of the Survey have been an adventure. And they have been an adventure in several ways—the pioneering nature of a number of the lines of inquiry, methods of investigation, and research results, the interaction and broadening knowledge and insights of researchers from different backgrounds of training and work, and the striving to develop common communication and understanding among these individuals. Without question, it has been an adventure and an education for me to direct the work of the Survey and to take part in writing and editing this book and the two public reports.

And the same, I feel sure, can be said for this book's other contributors and for additional members of the Survey staff.

If these endeavors have been successful beyond mutual education for those directly involved, this book will provide a revealing portrayal of a metropolitan area and will be a worthwhile exploration for you.

Acknowledgment is gladly given to a number of individuals and organizations for their assistance in the development of this book. The Ford Foundation and the McDonnell Charitable Trust made generous grants that permitted the establishment of the Survey, and the former's supplemental grant facilitated the production of the book. Thomas H. Eliot of Washington University and Paul G. Steinbicker of St. Louis University, who were resourceful and understanding members of the Survey's board of control, reviewed the entire manuscript. Several of my associates in three departments at the University of California, Los Angeles—Wendell Bell, Dwaine Marvick, and Charles M. Tiebout—and two former staff members of the Survey—Walter C. Kaufman and G. Ross Stephens, now of Wayne State University and the University of Connecticut, respectively—offered helpful suggestions about particular sections. Appreciation also is expressed to the many researchers and interviewers who contributed to the arsenal of facts that undergird this volume.

Special words of gratitude go to Henry J. Schmandt, now of the University of Wisconsin at Milwaukee, who was a strong right arm in the work of the Survey (and in a later similar study of the Dayton area) and in appraising many sections of this book.

J. C. B.

Pacific Palisades, California

Contents

PART FOUR
MEASUREMENT AND ECONOMIC STUDIES

Part One
THE SETTING
OF THE SURVEY

1

The People

THE ST. LOUIS metropolitan area, which is in the heart of the nation, contains 2,520 square miles and is situated on the west side of the Mississippi River in eastern Missouri, midway between the state's north and south boundaries, and on the east side of the river in southwestern Illinois. It extends westward and northward from a bend in the Mississippi River, where St. Louis City is located, into the higher land of St. Louis and St. Charles counties and southward into the hills and rugged terrain of the south sections of St. Louis County. On the Illinois side of the Mississippi River (the East Side, as it is known), the metropolitan community stretches over industrial and agricultural lands and along forty miles of river flats from the bluffs of Alton in Madison County to the marshland of St. Clair County.

Throughout this volume the term "St. Louis metropolitan area" refers to the standard metropolitan area as defined by the Census Bureau. At the time of the Survey it consisted of St. Louis City (which lies outside St. Louis County), St. Louis County and St. Charles County in Missouri, and St. Clair and Madison counties in Illinois. The term "City-County area" refers to the territory encompassed by St. Louis City and St. Louis County. The City-County area, which contains about three-fourths of the population of the St. Louis metropolitan area, was the focus of the research work of the Metropolitan St. Louis Survey.

The population of the metropolitan area has increased with every decennial census, from approximately a half million in

1880 to more than three times that number today. However, although growth has been steady, it has been for some decades
below the average for urban areas in the United States and there
is a justifiable feeling that it is falling behind. Local leaders find
it difficult to forget that the St. Louis metropolitan area has
been surpassed by the urban complexes whose central cities are
Boston, Chicago, Detroit, Los Angeles, Pittsburgh, and San
Francisco–Oakland. While the area has been declining in relative

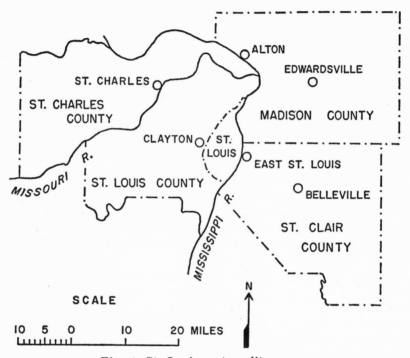

Fig. 1. St. Louis metropolitan area.

size, the City's proportion of the population of the total metropolitan area has also been declining. Thus, within a context of
steady growth, there has been public concern for the rate and
kind of growth, and there has been fear of decline; one local newspaper several years ago featured a series of articles entitled "Progress or Decay?" suggesting that a slower than average rate of
growth might eventually lead to stagnation.

To be sure, there is decay—structural decay at least. The
East Side includes miles of slums interspersed among the plants
of heavy industry; a blue-collar workers' area, it stretches along

the east bank of the Mississippi without pattern, center, or civic integration. The city of St. Louis also includes an enormous slum; in one-fifth of the census tracts dilapidated housing, mixed land use, and lack of open spaces produce a "blighted area" that houses one-fourth of the labor force.

The City, however, is cognizant of this condition and has made a frontal attack on some of the most dilapidated areas; 6,200 units of public housing have been completed and 3,000 more units have been authorized by the national government. Urban renewal and redevelopment projects affecting more than 700 acres are in progress; the largest one is in the Mill Creek area in the central section of the City. The downtown business area has not seen a new office structure rise in more than twenty years; only fourteen structures are less than thirty years old and more than 75 per cent of them are more than fifty years old. Ten per cent of the space in downtown office buildings is vacant; a considerable portion is used for warehousing. In 1957, 37,600 fewer people but 4,700 more automobiles came daily into downtown St. Louis than in 1950.

Beyond the concentration of worst housing in the City lie many pleasant neighborhoods of tall row-houses shaded by old trees, ancient parks, and a homeowning population. Such neighborhoods lie mainly west and south of the midtown shopping and entertainment center, a large development halfway between the river and the city limits.

In suburban St. Louis County, neighborhoods range from the tract developments housing blue-collar workers to the commuter suburbs of the upper middle-class, large houses with wide lawns and arching trees. In the center of the County a pleasant commercial development is rapidly expanding around the County courthouse in Clayton to exploit the rich suburban market in consumer goods. Other large shopping centers, such as Northlands in the northern section and Crestwood in the southern, have recently been constructed. Thus the picture in the City-County area is one of rapid growth at the peripheries, stagnation at the center, and stability between.

Although the St. Louis City-County area is unique in many of its characteristics, its experience of rapid growth and change is paralleled in every great metropolitan center in the United States. Both uniqueness and general similarity are revealed through considerations of its past, the broad processes that have affected the City-County area, and its social geography.

THE PAST

The St. Louis metropolitan area is an old urban center, one that was founded and became metropolitan before twentieth-century technology began to change the shapes of cities. The central city of the area is far more densely settled than are the centers of most newer metropolitan areas. Its density averages 14,000 persons for each square mile; this is three times that of the city of Los Angeles.

Growing up in the age of coal and steam, the older portions of St. Louis City reflect the high premium placed on land near transportation facilities. Until recently, the most important facilities were the river and the railroads. Location of industry in such sections brought about the construction nearby of extensive, crowded residential districts to house the labor force. Another heritage from the age of coal and steam is the thick film of grime covering many of the aged buildings in the downtown commercial center. This discoloration creates the impression that the older part of the City is even older than it is; only in the past two decades has the municipal government been able to suppress the use of fuels that once gave downtown St. Louis a dusky, evening aspect at noontime.

The crowded housing near the downtown section remains in use, and congestion has been increased by the conversion of single-family residences into multiple-family dwellings. Today, twenty-eight census tracts near the river which have about one-fourth of the dwellings in the City, contain over half the overcrowded dwellings and more than three-fourths of the substandard housing. New properties, however, have been continuously developed in the outlying sections of the City and in the County for the higher income classes, which have the time and facilities to travel longer distances to work and shop.

The total urban population on the Missouri side of the river was for many years largely contained within the geographical boundaries of the city of St. Louis. During the 1920's the last of the large areas within the geographical limits of the City was built up; there remained little space for new residences except outside its corporate boundaries. (Ninety per cent of the dwellings in the City, as of 1950, were more than twenty years old.) At the same time, the extension of paved roads and the growing use of automobiles made many more suburban districts practical as residential neighborhoods for those who worked in the City.

In this way, residential population in the County accelerated rapidly after 1920. In that year St. Louis County had 100,737 residents; by January, 1956, the number had increased more than fivefold to an estimated 571,000.

In contrast to the County's rapid increase, the population of St. Louis City has remained virtually constant from 1930 to the present; the current estimate is approximately 850,000. The Second World War caused a temporary cessation of new residential construction in the suburbs and also prevented the redevelopment of aging neighborhoods within the City. At the same time, the war economy brought full employment and the demand for a larger labor force. The population of the area continued to increase, with migrants entering City and County, expanding the productive labor force and the consumer market, and creating new pressures upon already inadequate housing accommodations and governmental services.

While a considerable amount of housing in the City has become more inadequate and obsolete, the suburban ring nearest the City has also been aging and increasing in density; today, several of the larger inner suburbs (University City, Maplewood, Wellston, and Pine Lawn) have average densities of 10,000 or more persons per square mile. In effect, the social fabric of the city of St. Louis has extended beyond its governmental limits into the County; the same processes that have changed the structure and population of neighborhoods in the City are continuing beyond its boundaries.

SOCIAL CHANGE AND THE CHANGING POPULATION

To understand the nature of the people and the problems of government in the area, it is necessary to consider the rapid social changes that in the last half-century have created a predominantly urban America. Three kinds of changes have been most important: the sheer expansion of urban population, the rise in the socioeconomic level of the people, and the great alterations in the style of life of urban citizens.

EXPANSION OF POPULATION

The population growth of the Missouri portion of the St. Louis metropolitan area (with which the remainder of this section focusing on the people will be chiefly concerned) has taken place

almost entirely in suburban St. Louis County.[1] This, in turn, is
the result of both large-scale in-migration and natural increase.
Net in-migration—the excess of people moving into the County
over those leaving—accounts for about two-thirds of the growth.
Natural increase—the excess of births over deaths—produces
the other one-third. Because a large proportion of the County
adults are young married people, the birth rate is high and the
death rate is unusually low, and continuing high rates of natural
increase are to be expected.

Although the growth of the total population of the City-County
area has resulted largely from growth in the County, there has
been a large movement of people into both the City and the
County. Twenty-six per cent of the adults in the city of St.
Louis and 25 per cent of those in St. Louis County have been in
the area less than twenty years. A substantial part of the present
adult population has been in the metropolitan area less than ten
years—12 per cent in the City and 13 per cent in the County. Less
than one-half of the adults in the City-County area in 1957 were
born there: 38 per cent in the City and 48 per cent in the County.
As in many other metropolitan centers, the greatest portion of
growth has derived from migration of people from the small
towns and rural areas. This movement has resulted in a population with widely varying social and cultural backgrounds.

Regional origins and rural-urban background. Similar proportions in County and City were born in St. Louis City, and
over half the population was born outside the area (see table 1).
In both City and County a large proportion (one-fourth) of all
adults were born in other counties of Missouri or in Illinois,
but in origins outside these two states there is a sharp difference.
Many more City than County people were born in the Southern
states, but many more in the County were born in non-Southern
states.

A great many of these migrants to the City and County have
rural backgrounds. In central city and suburbs alike, many people
have come from open country farms as well as from small towns
and other great urban centers. Almost 17 per cent of them were
born on a farm and a further 37 per cent had lived on a farm.
Their way of life and their definition of the community and its

---

[1] The data for the following profile of the people of the City-County area
were gathered in 1957 by the Metropolitan St. Louis Survey through a
large-scale sample survey in which 1,800 respondents in the City-County
area were chosen by systematic random sampling as a dependable cross-
section of the total population.

TABLE 1

PLACE OF BIRTH OF THE ADULT POPULATION OF ST. LOUIS CITY
AND ST. LOUIS COUNTY, 1957

	Place of birth					
Present residence	St. Louis City	St. Louis County	Other counties in Mo. or Ill.	Southern states	United States other than South	Foreign
St. Louis City	38.6%	1.6%	26.0%	22.1%	5.6%	6.0%
St. Louis County	39.2	8.1	25.5	8.8	12.7	5.6

NOTE: Percentages derived from sample survey data have been rounded in tables and consequently do not always total 100 per cent.

problems differ from those to whom the City-County area is a native habitat.

Characteristics of migrants. It is appropriate to present certain comparisons of the natives of the City-County area, the old migrants who have resided in the area at least twenty years, the wartime migrants who have lived locally between five and twenty years, and the new migrants who have been settled in the area less than five years. Particular attention is given to similarities and differences between migrants to the City and those to the County.

In both City and County the largest proportion of each type of migrant was born in other Missouri counties or in Illinois. A difference between City and County residents has increased with the influx of the wartime and newer migrants. During these migration periods, the City has consistently drawn most of its outside (non-Missouri and non-Illinois) population from the Southern states, while the County has increasingly attracted people who had resided in non-Southern states.

In City and County alike, the largest proportion of the natives of a particular nationality background consists of persons whose families originally came from Germany. The proportions are very similar for the two areas. The largest components of each class of migrants, however, is the "Old American," comprising persons from the British Isles and northern and western Europe, except Germany. Migration into the County has been disproportionately Old American compared with that into the City. The City migrants, in turn, regardless of whether they are the older, wartime, or newer migrants, are more often Negroes. Although the high point of Negro in-migration was during the Second

World War, judging from those who remained in the area and
were enumerated in the sample survey, Negroes are still a substantial proportion of the newest arrivals. (The small sample
of new migrants in the City does not allow for confidence on
the exact proportion.)

In both the City and County, 16 per cent of the total adult
population was born on a farm. None of the three classes of migrants who live in either City or County, however, has less than
23 per cent rural-born. The various classes of migrants do not
differ markedly from one another or between City and County
in proportions of rural birth.

Similarly, the differences in religion are not very pronounced
between City and County migrants. Far fewer migrants than
natives in the City are Catholics. (Fifty-one per cent of the City
natives are Catholic.) In the City more older migrants (about
one in four) than wartime or newer migrants are Catholics, but
this is not the situation in the County where approximately the
same proportions (about one in five) of individuals are Catholics in each of the three migrant groups.

In contrast, differences in education are quite evident. The
natives of the County are less than twice as likely to have had
some college education than those of the City. Migrants to the
County from outside the City-County area, however, are from two
to three times more likely to have been to college than migrants to
the City. Furthermore, the newer the migrant to the County, the
more likely he is to have had some higher educational training.
More than one-half of the new migrants to the County have had
at least some college education. Each class of migrants who have
settled in the City is more apt to have had not more than an
eighth-grade education than its counterpart in the County. In
fact, City migrants are more likely than natives to have had not
more than eight grades of schooling.[2] In the County the wartime
and new migrants are much less likely to have such low educational achievements. Thus, continued migration into the City has
tended to lower educational levels, while migration into the
County has raised them.

If the difference in the kinds of population moving into City
and County continues, it will result in an increasing proportion
of the City being made up of Southern Negro migrants with lower
educational levels, while the County will include a larger propor-

---

[2] The new migrants into the City are excluded from the comparison because the sample involved only a small number of them.

tion of Old Americans from the non-Southern states who have considerable educational training. Such statements are not conclusive, of course, for numerous recent migrants into the County could move on to other areas and the size of the sample of new migrants into the City is too small to lodge much confidence in it. If these trends are extended, however, they doubtlessly will have profound effects upon the service needs of various parts of the City-County area and probably upon the chances of successfully instituting area-wide governmental changes in future years.

Nationality background. Although the foreign-born are a small and declining proportion of most urban populations in America (and are less than 5 per cent of the adults in the City-County area), a great many people are descendants of recent immigrants. In fact, a majority of the adults in St. Louis County (51 per cent) and a substantial minority in the City (41 per cent) are three generations or less removed from foreign origins. The Old American of Anglo-Saxon origins is a minority in most great metropolitan areas.

The variations in length of native background are particularly interesting in connection with the original nationality of the family. Each American metropolitan area has its own blend from the population sources that fed the tremendous national growth of the nineteenth century. The kinds of nationality groups and the degree to which they occupy a special position in the social and cultural milieu of the urban center varies tremendously, with concentrations of Poles in Detroit, Mexicans in Los Angeles, and Jews, Italians, and Puerto Ricans in New York City.

TABLE 2

NATIONALITY BACKGROUND OF THE ADULT RESIDENTS
OF ST. LOUIS CITY AND ST. LOUIS COUNTY

Nationality origin of family	City	County
German	24%	33%
Irish	12	13
Other northern or western European	16	16
English, Scottish, Welsh	11	20
Italian	5	2
Russian	*a	3
Other eastern and southern European	4	6
American Negroes	23	2
Don't know, refused to state	5	5

a In all tables an asterisk denotes an entry of less than one-half of 1 per cent.

The St. Louis City-County adult population is a somewhat unusual ethnic fabric (see table 2). A majority in City and in County are north European in background, and German nationality is the most common family background. The Irish are a substantial population in each area; English, Scottish, and Welsh are a very small minority in the City and about one-fifth of the population in the County. Southern and eastern European origins are relatively rare.

Religion. The nationality background of the population is closely related to religious preference. Over 90 per cent do profess a preference. A majority of the adults in the City-County area prefer a Protestant denomination, as would be expected in a population of predominantly north European origins, but a sizable minority, 34 per cent in the City and 32 per cent in the County, are Catholics. Those with a Catholic preference tend to have German, Irish, or Italian background. A small minority, chiefly those of Russian background in the central part of the County, prefer the Jewish religion.

Color. The population of the City, as reflected in the sample survey, is more than one-fifth Negro. In the suburban county, in contrast, Negroes are less than 2 per cent of the population. Negroes are more likely than others to have moved into the City-County area during the past two decades, 39 per cent having come since 1937 as against 22 per cent of the non-Negroes in the City. This reflects the tremendous demand for industrial manpower during the war effort of the 1940's. For the past ten years, however, Negroes have entered the area at approximately the same rate as have non-Negroes; 13 per cent of Negroes and non-Negroes have lived in the City-County area for less than ten years. Although there is a gain in the Negro proportion of the population of the City (from 18 per cent in 1950 to 24 per cent in 1957), this probably reflects the higher rate of natural increase of Negroes compared to the non-Negroes, for the Negro population of the City is younger than the remainder of the population.

In summary, the growth of the City-County area has resulted principally from a high rate of in-migration, particularly in the 1940's. This influx of people from other areas has produced a population that is extremely heterogeneous with respect to region of birth, rural versus urban experience, nationality background, ethnicity, color, and religion. Comparatively, the St. Louis area is not an extreme case; its rate of in-migration and growth is certainly no more than is usual for American urban areas in recent decades.

Only 65 per cent of the adults of the area are whites of native parentage. Many of them are in-migrants; only 31 per cent of the total adult population is made up of white adults of native parentage who were born in the metropolitan area. And of this 31 per cent many are Catholics. Consequently, the Protestant whites of native parentage constitute only 14 per cent of the adult population in the City-County area.

RISING SOCIOECONOMIC LEVEL OF THE POPULATION

The elevation in the socioeconomic level of urban populations in America is attributable to three developments that are basic and continuing in the larger American society. They are the growing productivity of the economy (outdistancing additional consumers), the rising educational level, and the increasing demand for skilled and technically trained labor, accompanied by a steady decline in the need for unskilled manual laborers.

The increase in household income, which has resulted largely from the increased productivity of the economy, is apparent in table 3, which shows distribution of incomes for 1950 and 1957 in

TABLE 3

HOUSEHOLD INCOME DISTRIBUTION, ST. LOUIS CITY-COUNTY AREA

Year	$0–1,999	$2,000–3,999	$4,000–6,999	$7,000–9,999	$10,000 and over	Not ascertained
1950	28%	33%	21%	4%	3%	11%
1957	11	18	37	15	9	9

SOURCES: 1950 Census of Population; Sample Survey of 1957.

the City-County area. Clearly the tendency has been for the lower income brackets to include a drastically shrinking population, while the middle income groups include a larger proportion. In the County, the upper brackets include a very substantial proportion of the people. Although inflation occurred between 1950 and 1957, it could not possibly account entirely for these broad shifts.

The sharp increase in average educational levels is pointed out in table 4, which shows achievements of adults aged 25 and over as of 1950 and 1957. Although, in 1957, a substantial portion of the adults in the area had less than a high school education, the proportion is considerably smaller than it was in 1950. This

TABLE 4

EDUCATIONAL LEVEL OF ADULTS AGED 25 AND OVER,
ST. LOUIS CITY-COUNTY AREA, 1950 AND 1957

Year	0 to 8th grade	Some high school	Completed high school	Some college or more
1950	54%	15%	18%	13%
1957	39	21	24	16

SOURCES: 1950 Census of Population; Sample Survey of 1957.

change is owing to the nature of in-migration in the seven-year
period, and, more importantly, to the rising levels of general
education.

The smallest change has occurred in occupational level (see
table 5). Socioeconomic status has been increasing among the
population, but income and education have risen much more rapidly than occupational level. Today blue-collar workers have more
education and are better paid than in 1950. On the average, however, they do not necessarily have a much more skilled or responsible job.

TABLE 5

OCCUPATIONAL LEVEL[a] OF ADULTS, ST. LOUIS CITY-COUNTY AREA

Year	Upper white collar	Lower white collar	Upper blue collar	Lower blue collar
1950	19%	27%	15%	40%
1957	22	21	21	35

SOURCES: 1950 Census of Population; Sample Survey of 1957. The two sets of data are not strictly
comparable, as the Census includes all employed persons, while the survey only interviewed persons
21 years of age and over.
    [a] The occupational levels are defined as follows: upper white collar includes managers, proprietors,
and officials plus professional, technical, and kindred workers; lower white collar includes clerical
and sales workers; upper blue collar includes foremen, craftsmen, and kindred workers; lower blue
collar includes all others with the exception of farm managers and proprietors. These two categories
were omitted from the total and do not affect the percentage base.

CHANGES IN THE STYLE OF LIFE OF URBAN CITIZENS

Although almost as high a percentage of adults in the City as in
the County have come from outside the metropolitan area, the
population of the City has remained virtually the same since the
1930's. The reason is the "two-step flow"; many in-migrants move
first into the City and then to the suburban county. Such movement toward the suburbs is general in American metropolitan

areas. However, as table 6 indicates, the growth of St. Louis County does not all result from this two-step flow. New residential

TABLE 6

Last Previous Residence before Present Residence,
St. Louis City and St. Louis County, 1957

Present residence	Person moved to present dwelling from			
	St. Louis City	St. Louis County	Other	Not ascertained
St. Louis City	84%	5%	9%	2%
St. Louis County	43	44	12	1

opportunities in the County draw population not only from the City but from other parts of the County and from outside the metropolitan area as well. At the same time, there is some movement from the County back to the City, particularly by older couples.

Those who move to suburban neighborhoods are not a random selection from the population of the City. They are usually home-owning and family-centered, although they range in occupational level from blue-collar workers to executives and professionals. The increase in the County's population has resulted from both lack of space in the City and the increasing number of families that have adopted a style of life that emphasizes child-raising and homeownership—in short, a "familistic" way of life. In the City only 39 per cent of the units are owner-occupied and only 46 per cent of the households include one or more children. The corresponding figures in the County are 84 per cent and 61 per cent. Fifty-two per cent of the owner-occupied homes in the City are mortgaged as compared to 66 per cent in the County.

One important result of these selective movements of residential population within the urban area is the differentiation in the age and sex composition of the central city and the County. Figure 2 shows the age composition of the City and the three sections of the suburban county, as estimated from the sample survey of 1957. (Although it is not shown here, the Negro age distribution in the City is very similar to that in the County as a whole; the remainder of the population in the City is the oldest and has the fewest children of any large area population studied.)

In the City the proportion of females to males is higher than in the County as a whole. This results primarily from the greater proportion of older people in the City (for women outnumber men in the older-age groups) and the greater number of employment opportunities for single women there. The City has a larger proportion in the older-productive-age group (45–64) and in the old-age group (65 and over). The County, in contrast, shows a heav-

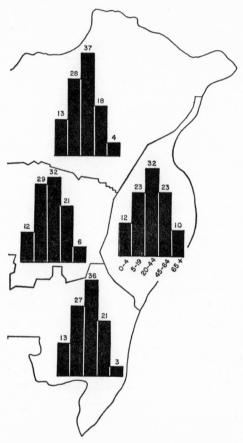

Fig. 2. Age composition in St. Louis City and three sections of St. Louis County.

ier concentration of the younger, dependent population, particularly in the group ranging in ages from 5 through 19, and in the young-adult classification—20 through 44. The people of the County thus tend to be members of younger families with dependent children, living in their own homes for which they still owe substantial mortgage payments.

SOCIAL GEOGRAPHY OF THE CITY-COUNTY AREA

Over-all comparisons of the suburbs and central city tend to obscure the great variation within each. To make the description of the population more precise than is possible through a general comparison, data organized by census tracts were analyzed by means of three indexes. The social rank index measures the socio-economic status of the neighborhood as a whole. The urbanization index measures the style of life common to the neighborhood, whether it is family-centered and home-centered ("low urbanization") or whether it is a neighborhood of apartment houses with few children and many women working outside the home ("high urbanization"). The segregation index is based on the proportion of Negroes and other segregated populations in the neighborhood, compared with the proportion of these populations in the urban area as a whole.

Today, the governmental boundary between St. Louis City and St. Louis County is nowhere a social boundary between a rural or semirural county and urban city. Nor is it a line between the urban "poor" and the suburban "prosperous." Instead, the City limits now run through neighborhoods that are essentially similar in social rank on either side of the boundary. Such neighborhoods, made up mostly of people employed in blue-collar jobs or lower-level white-collar jobs, now constitute the broad middle range of the population in most American cities. Middle-rank neighborhoods contain approximately 70 per cent of the population in the City and in the County.

The neighborhoods in which the other 30 per cent of the population resides differ greatly between the suburbs and the City. Those in the County, which are concentrated in the central area, are of high social rank; those in the City, which are near the river and in the central portion, are very low social rank.

There is a more consistent difference between the City as a whole and the County as a whole when style of life of the neighborhood populations is considered. The County tends to be child-centered and family-centered, regardless of social rank; neighborhoods of single-family dwelling units that contain many children and few women working outside the home predominate. The City is more urban in its characteristics, with more neighborhoods that have apartment dwellers, few children, and many women working outside the home. However, there are only a few census tracts in the City where an extremely urban way of life is the rule. They

are of two kinds: the skid-row area in the downtown district, and
the upper-rank apartment house and hotel districts to the north
of Forest Park on the western edge of the City. In the County no
neighborhoods are extremely urban, but along the City boundary
in the older parts of the County are populations as nonsuburban
as most of those in the central city.

The segregated populations are mostly in the central city, as is
common in American metropolitan complexes. In St. Louis they
are usually Negro, with a few small enclaves of Italians and eastern Europeans. They are found in the older neighborhoods of low
social rank, which are situated near the river. In recent years, as
the Negro population of St. Louis City has expanded, the segregated neighborhoods have been extended toward the north and
west. However, the few ethnic neighborhoods in St. Louis County
are not the result of invasion from the City. Instead, they are
chiefly small enclaves of Negroes, who are long-term residents in
various parts of the County, and the one segregated tract in University City contains mainly ethnic populations of Russian and
central European Jewish origins.

It is apparent that the City-County area contains neighborhoods of the greatest diversity; the heterogeneity, produced by
the large-scale movement of people into the area, the wide range
in occupational and educational achievement, and variations in
styles of life, makes it difficult to compare the City and the County
as meaningful wholes. There are, however, certain important differences: the poor are concentrated in the City (although in only
one large segment of the City), the wealthy are concentrated in
the County (although mainly in its central portion), and the
County is in most parts predominantly suburban in life style.

Yet the City and the County are parts of a single interdepend-
ent structure, the metropolitan area. Their separation by a governmental boundary is a historical accident, and the image of
"suburban county and blighted central city" obscures more than
clarifies. Many wealthy residents of the central portion of the
County are dependent on the labor supplied by the poorest sections of the City, and the populations of average social rank are
an overwhelming majority in the City, the County, and the City-
County area as a whole.

2

The Economy

HISTORICAL DEVELOPMENT

Location on some of the most important land and water routes of the nation contributed much to the early and subsequent economic development of St. Louis, one of the oldest Midwestern cities. The explorer Pierre Laclede Ligueste perceived the geographical advantages—accessibility to trappers, hunters, and Indians, as well as convenient transportation—when he selected the site in 1764 as the nucleus of a fur-trading empire.

As the westward movement gained momentum, the fur-trading post became the major supply center of the expanding American frontier. Commercial activities increased, especially in food, dry-goods, and hardware. The location of St. Louis became even more important during the steamboat era extending from the 1830's to the 1860's. Because of the deepening of the Mississippi River channel at St. Louis, the City became an important transfer and bulk-breaking point. Consequently, the functions of a warehousing and reshipping center were added to those of a trading center and supply base.

Although the steamboat stimulated commerce in St. Louis, it stifled industrial development, which had been struggling against deficiencies of capital and labor since the town's pioneer period. Easy and cheap transportation increased dependence on outside manufacturers at a time when inadequate roads and transportation facilities impeded transactions between the farm and local industrial markets. The railroad would provide the solution to this problem. St. Louis businessmen, however, were preoccupied with profitable commerce and overconfident of the supremacy of the steamboat. Few of them invested in manufacturing or railroads before 1860.

During the Civil War it became apparent that the economy of St. Louis was too closely associated with the Mississippi River. A better balance needed to be acquired by developing a comprehensive railroad system and by expanding manufacturing activities. After the war, connecting railroads were built from St. Louis to the west, southwest, and east; eastern railroad routes necessitated the spanning of the Mississippi River. Despite legislative, financial, and engineering difficulties, Eads Bridge was completed in 1874 and St. Louis proceeded to become a prominent railroad center. Unfortunately the delay cost St. Louis its markets in the rich Upper Mississippi Valley and Chicago became a more prominent railroad and distribution center.

Large-scale manufacturing was initiated locally during the Civil War.[1] Among the early industries were shoe and clothing manufacturing, meat-packing, brewing, the manufacture of chemicals, and the products of foundries and machine shops. The value of production increased 400 per cent from 1860 to 1880 and it more than doubled in the following decade.

The territory that now comprises the St. Louis metropolitan area began taking urban form in the last quarter of the nineteenth century. When St. Louis City was legally separated from the County in 1876, the County was primarily rural and contained only five incorporated places. During the remainder of the century growth was quite rapid in the City and moderate in the County. Cities in Madison and St. Clair counties were carved out of farm land, and some heavy industries of St. Louis sought more favorable locations for fuel and transportation on the east side of the Mississippi.

At the close of the last century, St. Louis had an urban industrial economy and was the manufacturing center for the Midwest. Since then, the economy of the St. Louis metropolitan area has expanded at a pace quite similar to that of the United States in general. Its growth in population, labor force, commercial and industrial activity, and per capita income, however, has been less extensive than the expansion of most of its competing metro-

---

[1] In the early half of the nineteenth century there were small manufacturing establishments in St. Louis. Most of them, however, were operated on the handicraft basis rather than the factory system.

politan areas.[2] There have been numerous opportunities in the St. Louis area, and in some instances these opportunities have been seized upon to build successful companies and stimulate major industrial development. In other instances, conservative thinking has deprived the area of some of the greatness and economic eminence it otherwise might have attained. Nevertheless, through the course of technological developments, cyclical fluctuations, international warfare, and postwar expansions of the twentieth century, the St. Louis area economy has experienced a quiet and constant development as it has adapted to the changing world.

PRESENT STRUCTURE AND ACTIVITIES

The St. Louis metropolitan area is the ninth largest in the nation. The city of St. Louis, which is the industrial and economic core of the metropolitan area, is a mature center in which practically all the land has been developed for a number of years. A few years ago it was called a decaying city in danger of losing its productive population and its industrial and commercial opportunities because of slums, inadequate facilities, and lack of open land. Recently efforts have been under way to halt this decay and inject new vitality into the economy to create a climate more appealing as a place to live, work, and do business. Approximately 45 per cent of the total population of the metropolitan area resides within its boundaries.

St. Louis County, which adjoins the City, is a rapidly growing area that recently has experienced extensive residential, commercial, and industrial expansion. The many municipalities in the County vary in economic activity from strictly residential communities to a few, such as University City, Clayton, Webster Groves, and Kirkwood, which have considerable commercial or industrial development or both. Relatively little land in the County is devoted to industrial use, however. Of the approximately 8,000 acres in such use, one-third (2,600 acres) is utilized for heavy industrial purposes and two-thirds (5,300 acres) for light industry. Almost 30 per cent of the people of the metropolitan area live in St. Louis County.

St. Charles County has rich farm land and is predominantly

---

[2] Metropolitan areas considered as economic competitors of the St. Louis metropolitan area are those whose central cities are Atlanta, Chicago, Cincinnati, Cleveland, Dallas–Fort Worth, Detroit, Kansas City, Milwaukee, Minneapolis–St. Paul, New York, and Pittsburgh.

agricultural, although in recent years a few large industries with government contracts have located there. The population has remained relatively stable and now includes less than 2 per cent of the total of the metropolitan area.

Madison and St. Clair counties in Illinois contain industrial and agricultural developments. Their principal economic activity is heavy manufacturing, with emphasis on primary metals and foods. Both have experienced moderate population growth in recent decades; each has approximately 11 per cent of the metropolitan population.

The hinterland of the St. Louis metropolitan area is the mid-American region, which is more agricultural than the United States as a whole.[3] This region affords the local metropolitan area a vast labor force reservoir as well as markets, raw materials, water, power, and fuel supplies.

Numerous economic activities in the central city and the four counties of the St. Louis metropolitan area are closely interwoven. This is especially true of St. Louis City and County. Most of the major financial institutions, daily newspapers, radio and television studios, retail establishments, cultural centers, and general hospitals are located in the City but serve County residents as well. Still more significant is the large number of people who live in one community and work in another. For example, approximately 80 per cent of the employed residents of St. Louis City work in the City and 14 per cent in the County. On the other hand, 37 per cent of the employed residents of St. Louis County work in the County while 52 per cent are employed in the City. The remaining employed residents—6 per cent in the City and 11 per cent in the County—work in St. Clair, Madison, and St. Charles counties.

LABOR FORCE

In mid-1957 the total civilian labor force of the St. Louis metropolitan area numbered 845,500 persons, almost 96 per cent of whom were employed. Women wage- and salary-workers constituted over one-fourth of this labor force.

A more detailed analysis of the composition of this labor force must be based on the 1950 census. Almost four-fifths of the males

---

[3] The mid-America region refers to the state of Missouri and the eight adjacent states of Illinois, Iowa, Kentucky, Tennessee, Arkansas, Oklahoma, Kansas, and Nebraska.

over 14 years of age were either employed or seeking employment. In the City 36 per cent of the women were members of the labor force, but in the County only 25 per cent worked outside the home. This is typical of many metropolitan areas. The core city offers interesting employment opportunities in its offices and plants which attract young single women from the hinterland. The residential suburbs with a heavy population of young families have few women in the labor force.

With minor exceptions the occupational composition of the local labor force resembles that of most other metropolitan areas. Many area residents earn a living employed as operatives (operators of machinery, such as welders, truck drivers, and seamstresses), craftsmen, and clerical workers. Locally there is a slightly larger percentage of laborers and a smaller percentage of professionals, technicians, and sales workers than in some metropolitan areas, such as Chicago, Cleveland, Dallas–Fort Worth, Minneapolis–St. Paul, and New York. This distinction is owing in large part to the heavy industrialization and the relatively large Negro population of the St. Louis metropolitan area.

There is a distinct difference between the occupational distribution of the labor force that resides in the City and County. The City has a higher concentration of operatives, clerical workers, service workers, and laborers. The higher income occupations are more predominant in the County than the City; the County has a higher percentage of professionals, technicians, managers, officials, sales workers, craftsmen, and foremen.

ECONOMIC COMPOSITION

The St. Louis metropolitan area has a good representation of large firms and small employers offering opportunities for workers in the community. Approximately 30 per cent of the employed labor force work for the 159 large firms that have 500 or more employees. Another 15 per cent are employed in establishments that contain between 100 and 150 employees. The remaining 55 per cent work for employers of less than 100 persons.

Manufacturing is the most important element of the local economy, employing more than one of every three workers. Wholesale and retail trade rank second in employment opportunities; services (for example, personal services, business services, and automobile repairs) are third; and transportation and public utilities, fourth. St. Louis also is a financial center, the headquarters of the eighth federal reserve bank district. In the metropolitan area there are more than 100 banks with total deposits of more than three billion dollars.

MANUFACTURING

The gross product—the output of all sectors of the local economy—exceeded fifteen and one-half billion dollars in 1955. Approximately one-third of this gross product resulted from manufacturing. The leading industries are, in order, food and kindred products, transportation equipment, petroleum and coal products, and chemicals.

Unlike the Detroit and Pittsburgh areas where the health of the economy depends appreciably on the prosperity of one industry, such as the transportation equipment and steel industries, respectively, the industrial composition of the St. Louis metropolitan area is relatively well diversified. Table 7 lists the most important industries in the local economy in terms of percentages of manufacturing employment in 1954. There were 3,128 manufacturing establishments, employing 251,766 persons, which produced 347 classes of products, or 74 per cent of the possible 468 classes of the Census Bureau. In terms of employment, salaries of employees, and value added by manufacture, the St. Louis metropolitan area ranked ninth nationally.

TABLE 7

EMPLOYMENT IN MAJOR INDUSTRIES, 1954

Industry	Per cent of total manufacturing employment
Food products	13.6
Transportation equipment	11.2
Primary metals	8.2
Fabricated metal products	8.0
Machinery, excluding electrical	7.5
Chemicals	7.5
Electrical machinery	6.3
Apparel	6.0
Printing and publishing	5.0
Leather products	4.4
Stone, clay, and glass products	3.6
Paper products	3.3
Petroleum and coal products	3.2
Furniture	2.0
Miscellaneous	10.2

SOURCE: *United States Census of Manufactures*, U.S. Bureau of the Census, Bulletin MC-124 (Washington: 1954), pp. 13–14.

A high degree of economic diversification has been typical of the economy of the St. Louis metropolitan area since about 1900. Some changes have occurred during the current century in both relative importance of the industries and degree of concentration. For instance, employment in apparel and leather goods has been declining, reflecting the movement to small outlying towns where the wage rates are lower. During this time the significance of the transportation equipment industry has been increasing as St. Louis has become the second largest automobile assembly center in the country and a major producer of military aircraft. In mid-1957 the transportation equipment industry accounted for about 16 per cent of the manufacturing employment in the area, a considerable increase from the 11 per cent in 1954. The expansion of the manufacture of durable goods such as steel, appliances, and machinery, as well as transportation equipment, has made the St. Louis metropolitan area more responsive to the fluctuations of the business cycle than in the past. Also, the demand for defense goods, such as aircraft and ordnance, is subject to sharp and often unpredictable changes. Thus, the St. Louis metropolitan area has become potentially less stable than in the past.[4]

Approximately 60 per cent of the employment in manufacturing in the metropolitan area is located in St. Louis City and 13 per cent is in the County. For many years the City has had a concentration of light and semiheavy industries. St. Louis County was almost entirely residential and agricultural until the 1940's when defense plants were constructed on its farmland. Subse-

---

[4] The impact of the 1957–58 recession on the St. Louis metropolitan area reflects this trend. In March, 1958, unemployment in the area reached 74,400 persons or almost 9 per cent of the total civilian labor force, compared with only 38,700 or less than 5 per cent in March of the previous year. Over half this decline was in manufacturing; the most severe employment reductions occurred in transportation equipment, ordnance, and primary metals. Unemployment in nonelectrical machinery reflected curtailment of production of automobiles with layoffs in the manufacture of piston rings, carburetors, and other accessories. Electrical machinery followed the national pattern owing to high inventories and few orders. Increased unemployment in railroads, trucking, and wholesale and retail trade reflected the general economic trend. The Bureau of Labor Statistics classified St. Louis as a substantial labor surplus area, comparable to the rating of Chicago, Cleveland, and Kansas City, but not as serious as the surplus of Detroit and Pittsburgh.

The recession had its greatest impact on City residents. A higher percentage of the semiskilled and unskilled workers who were more seriously affected lived in the City. The St. Louis office of the Missouri Division of Employment Security estimated that there were 38,800 unemployed persons residing in the City and 12,500 in the County.

quently the industrial movement westward outside the City accelerated as private companies seeking large tracts of land developed industrial areas in the County. Today the County has some of the larger employers, especially in transportation equipment, electrical machinery, machinery other than electrical, fabricated metal products, and chemical products. Nevertheless, the City remains the industrial core of the City-County area. Its manufacturing industry in 1954 was about four times larger than that of the County. Many manufacturers apparently plan to retain and even expand their plants in St. Louis City. In 1954, 51 million dollars was spent for new plants and equipment there while only 11 million dollars was expended in the County. The largest capital expenditure in this year, however, took place in Madison and St. Clair counties where the expanding heavy industries require extensive investments (see table 8).

TABLE 8

MANUFACTURING, 1954

Area	Number of establishments	Number of employees	Salaries and wages (000 omitted)	Value added by manufacture (000 omitted)	Capital expenditures (000 omitted)
St. Louis metropolitan area	3,128	251,766	$1,060,335	$2,053,083	$131,184
St. Louis City	2,230	158,092	644,120	1,207,787	50,642
St. Louis County	419	35,678	160,712	326,687	11,012
St. Charles County	29	2,309	9,348	16,472	357
Madison County	199	32,825	150,016	332,077	45,693
St. Clair County	251	22,861	96,138	170,059	23,478

SOURCE: *United States Census of Manufactures: 1954*, Vol. III, *Area Statistics*, U.S. Bureau of the Census (Washington: 1957), pp. 124–4, 124–5, 112–5.

RETAIL TRADE

The St. Louis metropolitan area is the eighth largest retail center in the United States with sales in excess of 2 billion dollars. Retail sales in the area increased 34 per cent from 1948 to 1954, which approximates the growth in competing metropolitan areas. Retail trade is heavily concentrated in St. Louis City. The importance of the central business district, however, has declined in recent years. This trend is typical of most metropolitan areas that have experienced an out-migration of population to the suburbs and a parallel movement of retail trade. The principal problem of the downtown business district is the inconvenient location for suburban residents. Furthermore, many buildings are old and still in need of extensive rehabilitation in spite of large expenditures for expansion and improvements such as air conditioning, modern interiors, and parking facilities. Consequently, despite a 10 per cent decline in retail sales in this recent period, the central business district still holds the dominant position in the metropolitan area.

Exclusive of the central business district, the City had a 31 per cent increase in sales in the 1948–1954 period; including the central business district, sales in the City rose 19 per cent. The rapid increase in sales has resulted from the development of a number of neighborhood shopping centers such as Hampton Village Plaza and Southtown.

Between 1948 and 1954 the importance of retail trade in St. Louis County increased 80 per cent; during this time some downtown stores opened suburban branches and numerous new enterprises sprang up in the suburban shopping centers. The greatest expansion in the County has been in Clayton, the county seat, which is conveniently located for residents of the densely settled suburban municipalities. Northland, Westroads, and Crestwood are new shopping centers serving the northern, western, and southern parts of the County since 1955. The core of each one is a branch of a major downtown department store.

WHOLESALE TRADE

Because of its strategic location, the St. Louis metropolitan area has long been one of the nation's great merchandising centers, acting as a distribution hub for products locally produced or shipped in by rail, truck, and barge. Today, the area ranks eighth in wholesale sales and seventh in wholesale employment. Locally there are 3,278 wholesale establishments, and their total sales exceed 4.5 billion dollars. Over 50,000 metropolitan residents, who constitute approximately 6 per cent of the total labor force, are employed in the wholesale industry.

The growth of the area's wholesale activity has not kept pace with that of many other metropolitan areas. Older wholesale locations, such as the St. Louis and Chicago metropolitan areas, are apparently losing ground to such newcomers as the Los Angeles and Dallas–Fort Worth areas. Employment in wholesale trade in the St. Louis metropolitan area increased 4 per cent between 1948 and 1954, but that of the United States as a whole increased 13 per cent. During this period six wholesale establishments left the area, a trend that has continued subsequently.

The decline of the area as a wholesale center cannot be attributed to any single factor. The slow economic growth of the mid-America region has contributed to the problems of wholesale trade in St. Louis. Moreover, the channels through which products are distributed from the producer to the consumer have undergone changes. Producers have been integrating their operations forward, thus adding commercial activities; retailers have been integrating backward, assuming wholesaling and sometimes even manufacturing functions.

Over four-fifths of the wholesaling activity of the metropolitan area is conducted in the city of St. Louis. In recent years when more wholesalers have moved to St. Louis County, County employment in this field has increased 150 per cent. The County, however, accounts for only 6 per cent of the total wholesaling in the metropolitan area. Over half the wholesale trade in the County is concentrated in five municipalities: Clayton, University City, Brentwood, Wellston, and Maplewood.

SELECTED SERVICE TRADES

With the general rise in the standard of living, the service trades, both personal and business services, have experienced great increases. In the St. Louis metropolitan area there are 9,351 selected service establishments whose gross receipts are over 341 million dollars. Between 1948 and 1954 service receipts expanded 182 per cent in the City and 261 per cent in the County. Despite the great increase in the County, the City remains the center for both business and personal services. Almost 90 per cent of the area's business services and 62 per cent of its personal services take place in the City.

INCOME

Total income payments to residents—wages and salaries, rent, interest, and profit—represent the most comprehensive single measure of economic activity. In 1955 the total income of the metropolitan area was $3,868,595,000. After the payment of taxes to national, state, and local governments, the effective purchasing power exceeded $3,300,000,000. Almost half this income was paid to residents of the City and approximately one-third to people living in the County. Municipalities in the County with the greatest buying power were University City, Clayton, Webster Groves, Kirkwood, and Richmond Heights. The average purchasing power for each household was approximately $4,800 in the City and $6,000 in the County. Per capita income in the metropolitan area was $2,032 in 1955. In St. Louis County the per capita income was $2,283 as compared with $2,230 in the City.

Per capita income in the local metropolitan area in 1955 was considerably above that of 1950, due partly to the higher wage rates that accompanied the increased activity in durable goods manufacture and to the general rise in the economy's wage structure.[5] In 1950 per capita income in the St. Louis metropolitan area was $1,686 or 117 per cent of the United States average. This is a low figure in comparison with competing metropolitan areas. The Kansas City metropolitan area, for example, had a per capita income of $1,746 and the Chicago area had $1,994. Although per capita income in the St. Louis metropolitan area has risen through the years, it has not increased so rapidly as in other parts of the country. Consequently, local per capita income in comparison with the national average declined 10 per cent from 1929 to 1954.

A summary of economic activity in 1954 and buying power in 1955 for the St. Louis metropolitan area is presented in table 9.

TABLE 9

INDUSTRIAL AND COMMERCIAL ACTIVITY, 1954, AND EFFECTIVE BUYING POWER, 1955

Area	Retail sales (000 omitted)	Wholesale sales (000 omitted)	Selected services receipts (000 omitted)	Value added by manufacture (000 omitted)	Effective buying income (000 omitted)
St. Louis metropolitan area	$2,062,538	$4,553,896	$341,286	$2,053,083	$3,353,779
St. Louis City	1,161,257	3,700,524	257,785	1,207,787	1,605,587
St. Louis County	456,376	225,785	46,216	326,687	1,022,602
St. Charles County	35,593	9,250	1,659	16,472	45,809
Madison County	196,413	103,840	16,771	332,077	337,403
St. Clair County	212,899	514,497	19,055	170,059	342,378

SOURCE: *United States Census of Business: 1954*, Vol. II, pp. 13–12, 13–14, 25–12, 25–20; Vol. IV, pp. 13–9, 13–10, 25–9, 25–12; Vol. VI, pp. 13–10, 13–11, 25–10, 25–14, U.S. Bureau of the Census (Washington: 1956); *United States Census of Manufactures: 1954*, Vol. III, *Area Statistics*, pp. 112–15, 124–4, 124–5, U.S. Bureau of the Census (Washington: 1957); and "Survey of Buying Power," *Sales Management*, 76 (May 10, 1956), 279, 280, 572.

[5] Income data for 1955 are not strictly comparable with those of earlier years inasmuch as different sources and methods were used in assembling this information.

It shows that the City leads the area in all phases of industrial and commercial activity, despite the recent rapid growth of the County.

ECONOMIC ADVANTAGES

TRANSPORTATION FACILITIES

Situated in the midst of a vast economy, the St. Louis metropolitan area is close to raw materials and markets throughout the United States. Its location has stimulated new markets and has made possible the economical production and distribution of numerous goods and services. Because the St. Louis metropolitan area is at the center of the Mississippi River inland waterway system, it benefits from low freight rates of barge traffic for the north and south transportation of products. In addition, St. Louis is the second largest railroad center in the United States and an important junction for the nation's great eastern and western railroad systems. Eighteen major trunk lines and six short-line and switching railroads serve St. Louis.

St. Louis also ranks as the second largest trucking center in the United States. About 3,000 tractor-trailer units daily enter and leave the metropolitan area. About 350 motor freight companies offer direct trucking service to more than 25,000 cities in the United States, Canada, and Mexico. Several hundred independent trucking companies and transfer companies operate in the metropolitan area and nearby markets.

The St. Louis area is served by eight major commercial airlines, which together offer direct and rapid transportation to all major cities. The new, attractive Lambert–St. Louis Municipal Airport can accommodate the largest transport planes now in service.

NATURAL RESOURCES

Some metropolitan areas, such as Los Angeles, have to go hundreds of miles for their water supply—a supply that in some instances will soon be insufficient. In the St. Louis metropolitan area, abundant water resources, together with excellent purification and distribution facilities, provide reliable water supplies for all uses. The City is served by a municipally owned waterworks; most water in the County is supplied by a private company. Few competing areas have lower water rates for industrial use than St. Louis City. In the local metropolitan area water is pumped from the Mississippi, Missouri, and Meramec rivers and from wells throughout an extensive subsurface water-bearing region. Treatment plants presently have a 400-million-gallon daily capacity, which is being increased. These sources are considered adequate for all present and foreseeable future requirements.

Natural gas is brought into the St. Louis area from fields in Louisiana, Oklahoma, and Texas. Eleven gas and oil pipelines enter the area and fuel oil and petroleum are refined at four locations in Wood River and East St. Louis, Illinois. Although local gas and petroleum prices are relatively low, other metropolitan areas closer to major oil fields benefit from still lower rates.

The St. Louis metropolitan area is near the western border of the extensive coal fields of Illinois, Indiana, and western Kentucky. Approximately 80 per cent of the coal used in the St. Louis area is supplied by nearby mines. Local coal prices compare favorably with those in competing areas. The price of coal will probably increase relatively little in the next ten to twenty years; technological improvements should offset expected wage and freight rate increases. Proximity to coal will tend to enhance the competitive position of St. Louis in relation to areas that are close to oil fields. Because most electricity is generated locally from coal, rates are likely to be more stable than those in areas using gas and oil to generate electricity.

Electric rates in the St. Louis metropolitan area compare favorably, also. Power is furnished by two electric companies with a total capacity of more than two million kilowatts. A combination of hydroelectric and steam power plants together with interconnections with a power pool permit the efficient production of power at low cost.

Waste disposal in the St. Louis area is no problem because the Mississippi, Missouri, and Meramec rivers can be used for treatment and dilution of plant effluence. State laws concerning the treatment and disposal of effluence have been tightened, but waste disposal should remain easy and relatively inexpensive.

SKILLED LABOR FORCE

The St. Louis metropolitan area also has an ample supply of available skilled manpower. In 1950, the last year for which detailed data are available, 9 per cent of the employed belonged to the professional and technical group, another 9 per cent were managers and officials, 17 per cent were clerical, 8 per cent were sales workers, and 15 per cent were craftsmen and foremen. The rest, 42 per cent, were semiskilled and unskilled.

The diversity of industry in the St. Louis metropolitan area results in a wide variety of skills. The depth, variety, and quality of the manpower reservoir of this area compares favorably with that of other metropolitan areas.

DIVERSIFIED ECONOMY

As previously mentioned, the St. Louis metropolitan area has a well-diversified economy. It is a manufacturing center, producing an extensive variety of goods. Trade and services, transportation and public utilities, finance and government, add to the stability of the local economy.

These are some of the locational advantages of the St. Louis metropolitan area. They must be considered, however, in the perspective of some of the major problems that exist in the area.

ECONOMIC DISADVANTAGES

Despite its locational advantages, the economic development of the St. Louis metropolitan area has been less impressive than that of its competitors. This is demonstrated by its slower growth in population, labor force, manufacturing activity, and per capita income.

SLOW GROWTH OF HINTERLAND

The relatively slow development of the local economy reflects somewhat the sluggish industrial growth of the mid-America region, particularly the 109-county belt around St. Louis. The lagging industrialization and urbanization of the immediate hinterland where the St. Louis area does much of its business has retarded the growth of local industry and commerce. Unlike other metropolitan complexes, the local area has not benefited from greatly increased demand and purchasing power generated by a vigorously growing adjacent territory.

Although the progress of a metropolitan area is reflected in the expansion of its population and economic activity, growth is not the only indicator of an area's well-being. The process of metropolitanization creates many social and economic problems that increase the cost of living and of doing business. Furthermore, the seriousness and costliness of these problems are related to the rate of growth. Through the years, the St. Louis area has adapted its economic structure to the changing national economy and thus has retained many of its comparative advantages over other economic centers. The great danger is that the St. Louis area might lose its comparative economic advantages as the rising cost of metropolitanization is multiplied by the disadvantages.

SHORTAGE OF INDUSTRIAL SITES

One of the greatest local disadvantages is a shortage of suitable, readily available industrial sites, particularly in St. Louis City and County. The shortage of industrial sites in the City makes it impossible to attract much more new industry or to provide for expansion of firms already located there. Only about 700 acres of open land that is free of flooding remain for industrial or commercial development in tracts of at least three acres. Of this small amount of land, 379 acres are zoned industrial, 30 acres commercial, and the remainder residential.

Plans for the redevelopment of some of the obsolete and substandard industrial, commercial, and residential areas of the City are currently progressing. The Land Clearance for Redevelopment Authority of St. Louis is preparing to redevelop about 458 acres in the Mill Creek area, a substantial part of which will be used for industrial and commercial purposes. The redevelopment of about 236 acres in the Kosciusko area has been outlined; almost all this land will be used for the expansion of present firms. If more industry is to come into the St. Louis metropolitan area, most of it must locate beyond the City's limits.

A large portion of St. Louis County is still undeveloped and much land could be assigned to industrial purposes. At present, however, only about 3,800 acres are zoned and immediately available to light industry and only 1,800 acres are zoned for heavy industry. About 17 per cent of these 5,600 acres that are zoned for industry but not yet in such use is considered uneconomical for construction. Another striking inadequacy is the scarcity of large tracts of industrial land. The fact that industrially zoned land is scarce has raised land prices until they are substantially above those prevailing in other metropolitan areas competing for the location of industry.

Industrialists who seek a new plant location prefer land that is already zoned for their purpose. They know that rezoning proceedings usually extend over a long period of time, can be most aggravating, and may antagonize people who later will be their neighbors.

The absence of an up-to-date land-use plan and appropriate zoning legislation in St. Louis County has prohibited interested industries from finding suitable sites. However, County officials are now taking steps to remedy this situation; the County council has appropriated sufficient funds to inaugurate a comprehensive land-use study and has also taken a more realistic attitude toward rezoning suitable land for industrial purposes.

There is ample industrial space in Madison and St. Clair counties. Industry, nevertheless, has shied away from locating there because of the undesirable social, economic, and political climate the East Side is reputed to have.

St. Charles County has remained relatively dormant, although some industrial growth has occurred in recent years. The county will soon be connected by expressways with the central parts of St. Louis City and St. Louis County; its extensive farmland thus may become industrial sites of the future.

The economic assets and liabilities are shared by all parts of the St. Louis metropolitan area, particularly by St. Louis City and St. Louis County. Today the City, with its mature economy, is working to retain its economic base and redevelop and rehabilitate its declining sections. St. Louis County has been growing in a rapid but unplanned manner, thereby creating problems. Because of the high degree of interdependence of the economies of the City and County, their future progress depends on their overcoming this lack of cohesiveness and coöperating to capitalize on their advantages and lessen their disadvantages.

3

Government and Politics

THE ST. LOUIS City-County area is large in territory, population, and number of local governments. It has more than 550 square miles and almost one and one-half million residents. Its local public activities are scattered among 149 operating governmental units which are numerous both in total and in types and kinds. Some of them are small in area and contain few people; others encompass much land and many people. Some are legally able to exercise only one function; others are empowered to carry out a broad variety of services. The 149 local governmental units consist of ninety-seven municipalities, thirty school districts, eighteen fire districts, one county government, one public water district, the Metropolitan St. Louis Sewer District, and the Bi-State Development Agency.[1] Each of them, irrespective of territorial size and responsibilities, has its own set of officials, its own sphere of public authority, and its own means of raising public funds.

CITY OF ST. LOUIS

The most populous and most important general unit of government is the city of St. Louis, which is the main commercial, in-

---

[1] Two municipalities (one of which has a population of fourteen), two fire districts, and one school district for handicapped children (all in St. Louis County) have been created since completion of the Survey's research on which its recommendations were based. They swell the total of local governments to 154. In addition, twenty-three nonoperating sewer districts will levy taxes until their bonded debt is paid.

dustrial, and cultural center. The City contains a resident population of approximately 850,000, more than the total population of St. Louis County, and it provides a range of public services that is unmatched by any other local government in the area. A number of services are available both to its own residents and to numerous nonresidents who work in the City or use its recreational, cultural, and other facilities. Examples indicate the extensive nature of the governmental activities of the central city —a library system of a million books, twenty-two hundred police officers and employees, a thousand uniformed fireman, a thousand miles of improved streets, more than seven thousand low-rent public housing units, seventy parks and forty-two playgrounds, an art museum, a teachers' college, two general hospitals, a tuberculosis hospital, a chronic hospital, a water system, and an airport.

UNUSUAL FEATURES

The city of St. Louis is unusual in a number of other respects, the most prominent of which is that it is not a territorial part of any county. From 1808, when this urban settlement incorporated, until 1876, the City lay within St. Louis County. Dissatisfaction over City-County governmental relationships was mounting before the latter date for well over two decades, a period of rapid population growth in the City. The controversy centered largely on criticism by the City of the relative representation of urban and rural areas on the governing body of the County and the County's taxation and expenditure policy. It led to the inclusion in the new state constitution of 1875 of a procedure to permit the City to withdraw from the County and to draft a home rule charter.

Several months after the adoption of the new constitution, the voters of St. Louis County (including those in the city of St. Louis) elected a board of thirteen freeholders to draft a scheme of separation for the County and City and a home rule charter for the latter. After securing the necessary local popular approval, both the separation scheme and the home rule charter became effective in October, 1876. Under the scheme of separation, the City increased from eighteen to sixty-one square miles, extending its boundaries to include large undeveloped areas in what was then the County, but no provision had been made for subsequent boundary adjustments between the City and the County.

Although since the time of separation a home rule charter (the first constitutional one to be adopted by any municipality in the United States) has been in operation in the City, home rule in St. Louis has been severely limited by court interpretation and state legislation. Court rulings about county offices in the City are illustrative: the courts have held that since the City is legally required to perform the functions of a county, it must maintain a complete set of county offices as prescribed by general state law. This means that the method of selection, terms of office, and salaries of personnel in these county offices are determined by state law and not by City charter or ordinance. These decisions have had three principal effects. Various county officials must be elected and they thus cannot be integrated into the organizational structure of the City through charter provisions. Employees of the county offices are excluded from the City merit system. A part of the expenditures of the City is removed from regular budgetary controls.

The City does not operate the local election machinery. A long-standing state law provides for the appointment of a board of election commissioners by the Governor; similar boards function in several other places, including St. Louis County. Home rule in St. Louis is weakened not only by certain restrictive laws passed by the state legislature, but also by its refusal or reluctance to grant certain authorizations. In recent years, for example, the legislature has refused to grant the City the right to condemn residential property for off-street parking or to permit earmarking of parking meter funds for retirement of bonds issued for acquisition of off-street parking facilities. In addition, recent legislative sessions have witnessed constant struggles by the City to get enabling legislation to continue or increase the local earnings tax, which is a very important revenue source.

Another unusual feature of St. Louis City government (found elsewhere in the state only in Kansas City) is the state-controlled police department, an operation that dates back to Civil War days. Police matters are administered by a five-member board, consisting of four appointees of the Governor, one of whom is designated as chairman, and the mayor serving ex officio. Although this administrative arrangement is an obvious infringement on local home rule, the City has not been seriously interested in gaining jurisdiction over the administration of police affairs other than to establish general budgetary controls.

MAYOR-COUNCIL GOVERNMENT

The city of St. Louis operates under a mayor-council form of government, which is the central feature of its charter adopted in 1914. The governing body consists of twenty-eight aldermen elected by wards and a president elected at large; it is by far the largest legislative body in the City-County area. The independently elected mayor possesses strong formal powers, except over financial administration, and Raymond R. Tucker, the present incumbent, has demonstrated considerable leadership and has gained a national reputation. An engineering professor at Washington University who became well recognized for his service as smoke abatement commissioner of the City, Tucker in 1953 overcame the local Democratic party organization to gain the nomination and subsequently won in the general election. In 1957 he easily defeated his opponent, who filed late, in the party primary and decisively trounced his Republican adversary in the general election. Mayor Tucker has been highly successful in getting most of his programs, such as large-scale capital improvements, slum clearance, and urban redevelopment, accepted by the voters and civic leaders and in obtaining limited state legislative support for retention of an earnings tax. His first major civic setback was the voters' resounding rejection in 1957 of the proposed new city charter whose formulation he had followed carefully and for whose adoption he had campaigned vigorously.

PARTISAN ELECTIONS

The City is the only municipality in the City-County area which has partisan elections. It is overwhelmingly Democratic, and Democrats hold all elective offices except three aldermanic seats. These are fairly recent developments. Although the City went Democratic in 1932, a Republican subsequently served two terms as mayor of St. Louis. All nonelective City offices—that is, all positions in the City government except the previously discussed county offices—operate under a full merit system.

ST. LOUIS COUNTY

St. Louis County is the largest territorially and the second most populous of the general governmental units. Containing approximately 500 square miles and an estimated 571,000 people, it has almost nine times the area and about two-thirds the population of St. Louis City. Predominantly rural at the time the separation went into effect (when nevertheless it was the third most populous county in the state), it remained so well into the present century. Now after recent years of rapid population growth, about 30 per cent of the territory of the County is classified as urban.

OLD AND NEW SERVICES

The County is a supplier of many services, which are a mixture of old and new activities. The County furnishes some because of its traditional role of facilitating the performance of state functions—collecting state and district taxes, recording deeds, conducting national, state, and county elections, and serving process for the courts, for example. Some others of a less traditional nature, such as certain health and sanitation services and park and recreational facilities, are also available to all County residents. Others, including building, electrical, and plumbing inspection, restaurant inspection, rabies, rodent, and mosquito control, and law enforcement are available to all residents of unincorporated areas and to inhabitants of incorporated places under contractual arrangements with municipalities.

Other actions of the County government, including establishment of an official planning and zoning commission, enforcement of a comprehensive traffic code, and enactment of subdivision regulations, are applicable only to unincorporated areas. Such areas in total contain more than one-fifth of the people and many of them are highly urbanized, largely as the result of rapid population gains in the last five years. Many tens of thousands of people who live in the densely settled unincorporated areas are urbanites without a municipality, city dwellers without a city.

The functional roles of the County government have changed over the years. It has become the provider of more services, particularly more urban services. It has become a bigger and a more important government.

MODERATE STRUCTURAL REFORM

St. Louis County is the only county in Missouri (and one of the few in the nation) that operates under a home rule charter. The charter, which was adopted in 1950, five years after the constitutional permissive grant was authorized for use in the more populous counties of the state, reflects the growing importance

of the County government. It brought some integration to a
highly diffused organizational structure that typified the usual
baronies of many independently elected county officials. It
broadened county powers and freed the county government from
certain unduly restrictive state laws.

The most important officials are the supervisor, who is the
elected-at-large chief executive, and the County council, which
is the legislative body whose seven members are elected by districts. The supervisor prepares the annual budget and appoints
and removes certain department heads, but he is the chief executive only in a limited sense. Many heads of administrative departments, including the clerk, highway engineer, recorder of deeds,
sheriff, coroner, collector, treasurer, and assessor, are independently elected. Moreover, control over fiscal affairs is scattered
among several autonomous officials.

PARTISAN ELECTIONS

Elections are partisan, and Republicans have occupied most
County elective offices for many years. The supervisor, a majority
of the County council, and most other elected officials are Republicans. The Democrats, however, made noticeable gains in 1956
at the general election, taking over several elective administrative
posts that had long been held by members of the opposition party.[2]
Elected officials possess broad discretion in selecting and retaining their employees, for they can use their own particular tests
of fitness. The formal merit system of appointment and removal
applies only to employees in the departments of public health,
hospitals, public welfare, and parks and recreation. In addition,
the County police department, which was created in 1954 by a
charter amendment that stripped the sheriff of practically all his
police and law enforcement functions, operates its own personnel
system on a merit basis.

COUNTY MUNICIPALITIES

The suburban municipalities, the incorporated places in the
County, are the most numerous group of governmental units in
the City-County area. There are ninety-six of them, more than
three-fourths of which have come into legal existence since 1935.

---

[2] In the fall, 1958, election the Democrats unseated a Republican on the
County council, thus gaining a four-to-three majority, and won all County-
wide offices at stake, including those of supervisor, prosecuting attorney,
County clerk, and several others that had been held by Republicans.

These municipalities vary greatly in population, area, and tax resources. One incorporated place has 60 people, another has 53,000; one covers 32 acres, another, almost 9 square miles; one has a density of 80 per square mile, another has 14,000. The assessed value of real and personal property, which is the main municipal tax base, ranges from $105,000 in one locality to one thousand times that amount in another.

VARIATIONS IN SERVICES

The most crucial variances among suburban municipalities, which have experienced most of the population growth of the County in recent decades, are found in the services they provide. This is an extremely important matter because more than 75 per cent of the people of the County are residents of these communities and must rely heavily upon them for services necessary to satisfactory urban living. Furthermore, most of these incorporated areas, which collectively occupy approximately one-fourth the total territory of the County, are located in tiers contiguous to one another, with the easternmost tier bordering on the city of St. Louis. Consequently, the existence and quality of basic services are significant to both residents of individual municipalities and inhabitants of other parts of the City-County area.

Most County municipalities perform only a limited number of ten basic municipal services—police, fire, garbage and rubbish collection, health and sanitation, street repair, street lighting, street cleaning, library, park or playground facilities, and zoning control. Fifty-four of eighty-six of them, which is more than three-fifths of the total, provide fewer than six such services.[3]

Many of these suburban municipalities are staffed by part-time (and frequently nonsalaried) employees. Many are night-time governments, possessing only employees who hold private full-time jobs in the daylight hours and carry out municipal business in their homes later in the day. Even now when the demands on municipal governments in the City-County area are increasing rapidly, forty-six County municipalities function without a single full-time employee, and forty-seven have no city hall or office but operate from the residences of local officials and employees.

---

[3] Information from the ten remaining municipalities was unobtainable by the Survey because of either the lack or incompleteness of records or the refusal of local officials to coöperate. All ten are small in population and most of them supply few or no services.

Number of Services Performed by Eighty-Six
Municipalities in St. Louis County

Number of municipalities   Number of services performed

Number of municipalities	Number of services performed
1	0
2	1
4	2
10	3
20	4
17	5
11	6
9	7
3	8
5	9
4	10

The sketchy service pattern of a number of these incorporated communities is supplemented in one or more piecemeal and limited ways. A municipality becomes part of a fire protection district. Service contracts are arranged between individual municipalities and either private contractors or the County government, or individual householders make their own agreements with private firms.

The small number of basic services and employees of many municipalities in St. Louis County indicates that they in fact approach being ghost governments—corporate entities empowered to undertake numerous functions, but actually exercising very few of them. Two of the most prevalent reasons for incor-

TABLE 10

Number of Municipalities Using Paid and Unpaid Personnel for
Major Services, 86 Municipalities in St. Louis County

Municipal service	Municipalities with one or more full-time paid employees	Municipalities with part-time paid employees only	Municipalities with no paid employees
General government (such as city clerk's functions)	30	42	14
Police protection	40	20	11
Fire protection	17	0	0
Street maintenance	25	6	0
Parks and playgrounds	9	1	6
Library	11	0	0

porating have been to prevent annexation by neighboring municipal governments and to become immune from the provisions of the building and zoning codes of the County government. Incorporation is extremely easy under the state law that stipulates no minimum number of inhabitants and grants practically no discretionary power in incorporation proceedings to an agency of any government.

NONPARTISAN ELECTIONS

All municipal officials in St. Louis County are elected on a nonpartisan basis, and political parties play no detectable behind-the-scenes role in these elections. Most municipal governments operate under either the board of trustees form, which in reality is the commission system, or the mayor-council form. The council-manager plan is functioning in all home rule cities, of which there are only five, and in one general law municipality. A formalized merit system does not exist in most County communities. There are few significant differences in the powers of the various classes of general law and special charter municipalities—towns and villages, and third class, fourth class, and special charter cities. Home rule cities, which must contain more than 10,000 people at the time a local charter commission is elected, have more extensive powers relating to functions, finances, and organizational arrangements.

SCHOOL DISTRICTS

All the remaining many local governments that operate in the St. Louis City-County area may be termed "special districts," for unlike the previously described general units they each perform only one or a few functions. The most numerous and financially important are the thirty school districts, all but one of which are located in St. Louis County. Governing body members, an even number in each district, are elected on a nonpartisan ballot. Twenty-seven districts provide education through high school; three maintain elementary grades only.

The function of school districts, the provision of public education, is the most expensive of all local governmental services, and both its quality and its cost have a direct bearing on virtually everyone. School districts absorb a large proportion of the total general property tax. Within the areas of the fifteen most populous municipalities in St. Louis County, for example, 62 per cent of this tax goes to school use. In St. Louis City, the school district obtains 39 per cent.

PROGRAM DIFFERENCES

Wide disparities are present in the quality of the educational programs offered by school districts. They depend heavily on local property taxes, and broad differences exist in the amount of assessable property within their respective boundaries. One district has seventeen times more assessed valuation per pupil in average daily attendance than another. One district spends over five times more per pupil than another. Moreover, the school districts that spend the most per pupil usually have the lowest tax rates. Low expenditures by districts, a number of which have high tax rates, are usually symptomatic of their lack of financial ability rather than their unwillingness to support an adequate educational offering. As a result of insufficient financing, several districts are classified by the state department of education as providing programs that are the very minimum for accreditation.

AREA AND NUMBER

School districts overlap but frequently are not coterminous with municipalities. Thirty-five incorporated cities and villages lie in more than one school district. Each of five municipalities is located in four different school districts; each of five others is in three different school districts. This pattern of overlap results in variations in educational opportunities for children, even though they live in the same municipality. In one city, for example, some children are eligible to receive education in a district that spends $308 per pupil in average daily attendance, others attend school in a district where the comparable expenditure is $337, and still others go to school in a district that spends $615 per pupil.

The number of school districts in St. Louis County has declined appreciably in recent years during a period when municipalities have been increasing rapidly. The recent extensive reduction in separate school districts represents a sharp break with the past. At the time of the City-County separation, more than eighty years ago, there were eighty-five school districts in the County. In 1910, there were eighty-eight, and the number fluctuated very little between that year and 1948 when the total was eighty-six. The reduction to twenty-nine districts took place in the six-year period from 1949 through 1954 and began soon after passage of the state school reorganization law.

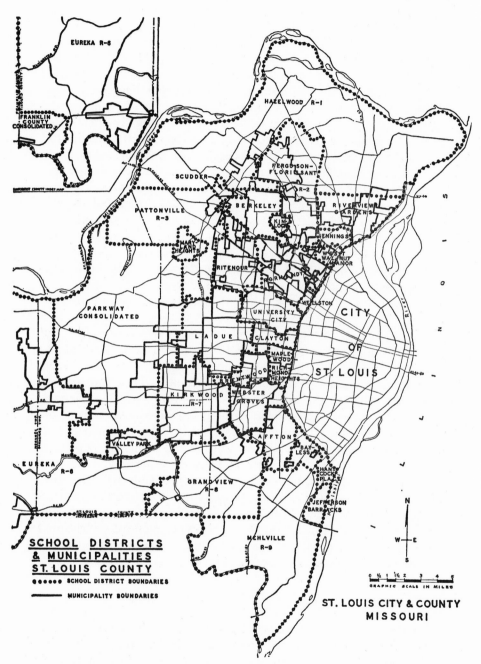

Fig. 3. School districts and municipalities, St. Louis County.

The state school reorganization law was enacted in response to growing concern about mounting school costs and the state's substantial contribution to them, the uneconomic size of many small districts, and equalization of educational opportunities. The law deviated in two important respects from the little-used school consolidation and annexation legal provisions, which continued to be available. It called for presentation of plans for enlarged districts by a county-wide agency, the newly constituted permanent county board of education, rather than local district initiation of changes in district boundaries. It stipulated an over-all majority vote in the districts concerned for acceptance of a proposal rather than separate approval in each district.

The reorganization act has had substantial direct and indirect effects. Successful elections on some, but not all, reorganization proposals have noticeably reduced the number of school districts. Moreover, the old and generally dormant consolidation and annexation laws have been used deliberately to avoid more comprehensive reorganization proposals. Further numerical decrease thus has resulted from one consolidation and a series of annexations.

The reduction in number of school districts is impressive, but the actual effects pertain mainly to the more rural parts of the County. In general, the nine enlarged districts lie outside the most highly urbanized sections of the County. They contain less than one-third of the total assessed valuation, pupils, teachers, and school costs—factors that directly affect educational opportunities. The other twenty districts in the County, which predominantly are long established and located in highly populated areas, have not been involved in recently completed boundary changes. No important degree of equalization of education throughout the County has been attained. Very recent urgings in support of further decreases in school districts, even to the point of establishing a single County-wide general educational district, have not reached the action stage. No successful effort to reduce the number has occurred since 1954.

FIRE PROTECTION DISTRICTS

Fire protection districts are important to large parts, both incorporated and unincorporated, of the County. The eighteen districts provide service to more than two-fifths of the County residents. They contain approximately one-third of the assessed

Fig. 4. Fire protection districts of St. Louis County.

property value and cover two-fifths of the area of the County, including part of or all the territory of fifty-one municipalities. Most fire districts serve incorporated areas, but in only one instance are fire district boundaries coterminous with municipal limits. One fire district includes portions or all of fifteen cities and villages, another includes fourteen, and still another has nine. Four cities are divided by the boundaries of fire districts. One of them has its own municipal fire department, but a part of the city is in a fire district.

Fire districts vary considerably in area, population, assessed valuation, and fire-risk class. One-half of them have no full-time, paid fire fighters, and all except one of the others use volunteers along with a small number of full-time employees. Each district is governed by three elected directors.

The fire district law is of recent origin and is receiving widespread local use. The organization of twelve districts between 1948 and 1957 indicates a general realization by parts of the County of the need for a municipal service that was not being adequately furnished by other governmental units. Although most fire districts are relatively new, they are strongly entrenched in their local areas. None has been dissolved or absorbed by a general local government since its establishment. Part-time and volunteer fire personnel in particular exhibit considerable fervor for district affairs, and a number of districts serve as centers for various kinds of social activities. Fire districts are social clubs as well as public agencies for fire fighting.

WATER DISTRICT

A water district operates in an area of twenty-five square miles in southeastern St. Louis County. It is a relatively small operation, employing three full-time and ten to fifteen part-time workers. Like school and fire districts, its governing body consists of elected directors; they are three in number. Established in 1941, this district purchases its water supply from a private water company, which serves most of the urban parts of the County, and distributes it through its own system.

BI-STATE DEVELOPMENT AGENCY

The most unusual special district is the Bi-State Development Agency. It is territorially the largest governmental unit, covering not only all the City-County area (which is not included in its entirety in any other local government), but also two other counties in Missouri and three in Illinois. It came into legal existence in 1949 through the Missouri and Illinois legislatures entering into an interstate compact that had been previously ratified by Congress and approved by the President. It is governed by ten appointees of the two governors. It is a local government mainly in the sense that it is territorially restricted to the St. Louis City-County area and surrounding counties.

Although in organization and powers the bi-state agency was modeled after the Port of New York Authority, the resemblance stops there. When established, the local agency was endowed with a broad grant of authority, including constructing and operating bridges, tunnels, airports, and terminal facilities, and making plans for the coördination of highways, parking areas, and sewage disposal. It has done little, however, in part because of financial restrictions and legal disputes concerning its powers. Its revenue bonds, for example, have not been made legal for investment by trusts, estates, and similar funds. The necessary legislation to accomplish this purpose has passed in the Illinois legislature, but has not been approved by the state legislature in Missouri. (This deficiency was finally corrected in 1959.) Furthermore, the agency is authorized in the compact to "plan, construct, maintain, own and operate bridges." Nevertheless, the proposed purchase of a bridge was legally contested on the ground that the compact did not grant the power to buy a bridge. The question still is pending in the Illinois courts.

The activities of this government, whose potentialities were much heralded at the time of its establishment, have been few. It constructed a wharf on the Illinois side of the Mississippi River from funds lent by a private steel company, which was subsequently repaid from the proceeds of the sale of revenue bonds. Two-thirds of the wharf is leased by this steel company and the remainder is operated as a public facility. The rental of these wharf facilities is the bi-state agency's only current source of revenue.

The agency's authority in the field of planning has been largely unused. In 1950 it hired a consulting firm that urged the preparation of a comprehensive master plan; nothing has been done about the matter. The Bi-State Development Agency is like a sleeping giant who lacks the means to arise from the lethargy that has enveloped him since birth.

METROPOLITAN ST. LOUIS SEWER DISTRICT

The final special district and governmental unit that functions
in the St. Louis City-County area is the Metropolitan St. Louis
Sewer District. Its creation in 1954 marked the first successful
attempt since the separation to adjust the governmental relations
between St. Louis City and St. Louis County.

Under its locally drafted charter, which was approved by decisive separate majorities in the City and the County, the district
was given complete responsibility for all existing and future public sewer systems and facilities within its territory. Its original
boundaries, which can be extended to any area in St. Louis
County that can be served efficiently by the district's sewer or
drainage facilities, included St. Louis City and the more urban
territory of St. Louis County; the district serves approximately
90 per cent of the City-County residents. The governing board
members are appointed and, once selected, they possess considerable formal independence from the appointing authorities. Three
trustees are selected by the mayor of St. Louis, with the approval
of the circuit judges in the City; a comparable number is chosen
by the supervisor, the chief executive of the County, with a
similar type of judicial consent.

The establishment of the metropolitan sewer district represented the transfer to a new government of a function that had
formerly been handled separately by twenty-eight sewer districts,
which ceased operations, and a number of the more populous
municipalities, including St. Louis City. The district took title to
2,200 miles of public sewers several months after its legal creation. Numerous subdistricts, which are the equivalent of special
benefit districts, have been established for the purpose of constructing and financing new sewers.

Faced with a major task of catching up with long-overdue
improvements in service and facilities, the district in the first
several years was the target of justifiably severe criticism. The
board proceeded hesitantly and with undue caution; in some instances when the board did act, its actions were judged to be
arbitrary. There also was failure by the board to communicate
sufficiently with the public in explaining its program and problems. Recently the censure has dwindled, partly because of the
board's more positive action and better public relations.

LOCAL GOVERNMENTAL FINANCE

The growth of metropolitan areas has created demands for new governmental services and intensified the need for raising the levels of the old. Expansion and betterment of services together with the rising costs of personnel and goods have seriously aggravated metropolitan financial problems. In the City-County area the total cost of local government rose by approximately 31 per cent between 1951 and 1955. This increase has placed severe demands on the tax structure and fiscal resources of the area. Existing taxes have been raised, new sources of revenue have been tapped, and additional taxing units have been created in attempts to meet the financial needs of local government. The local experience is not unique; it is closely paralleled in other urban centers.

All the 149 local government units in the City-County area, except the Bi-State Development Agency, have the power to tax. In addition to the operating units of government, there are twenty-three individual sewer districts in St. Louis County that are levying taxes. Construction and maintenance of public sewers in the urbanized portions of the City-County area were taken over by the Metropolitan St. Louis Sewer District in 1954, but the existing sewer districts were retained for the sole purpose of paying off their bonded indebtedness through local tax levies. These districts will cease to exist when their debts are paid.

Four units of local government are operating within the territorial limits of St. Louis City: municipal (which includes county offices), school district, metropolitan sewer district, and Bi-State Development Agency.

In St. Louis County, the number of overlapping local governments varies from three in some sections to six in others. The minimum number (County government, school district, and bi-state agency) is found in the unincorporated parts of the County that are still primarily rural in character; the largest (municipal, County government, school district, fire district, metropolitan sewer district, bi-state agency) is in the urbanized areas.

The local governmental units receive a total annual revenue of $144.5 million or $103 for every man, woman, and child living in the area.[4] Of this amount, local governments functioning in

---

[4] The data in this section relate almost entirely to 1955, the last complete fiscal year at the time the Survey was in progress. Spot checks since that time reveal that the financial pattern remains substantially the same with proportionate increases occurring in the various types of local governments.

the City receive $91.3 million or $107 per capita, and those operating in the County, $53.2 million or $96 for each person. Thus, although the aggregate local revenues in St. Louis City are approximately 60 per cent greater than those in the County, its per capita revenues are only 11 per cent more.

GENERAL PROPERTY TAX

The mainstay of local finance in the City-County area, as with most local governments throughout the United States, is the general property tax; it provides 57 per cent of all local revenue and about 86 per cent of all local tax monies. Dependence by local units on this source varies from zero to 96 per cent (see figure 5). The metropolitan sewer district, although having the power of taxation, relies wholly on a service charge to finance its operations; the fire districts are completely dependent, apart from voluntary contributions, on the general property tax. There is less variation in revenue dependency among governments of the same type than among those of different types. The average dependence of municipalities on the general property tax ranges only from 35 per cent to 48 per cent despite the wide differences in their population. Similarly, the lowest school district in the area receives 65 per cent and the highest 77 per cent of its revenue from the general property tax.

The percentages of revenue derived from property taxes by types of government are:

Fire districts	96%
Municipalities (including St. Louis City)	46
St. Louis County government	73
School districts	68
Water district	23

The Bi-State Development Agency has no taxing powers; it must derive its income from state appropriations and the revenue-producing facilities that it operates.

The general property tax rate varies widely even among local units of the same type. In 1955, municipal tax rates ranged from no levy in eight small towns to $1.30 per $100 assessed valuation, school district rates from $1.68 to $3.58, and fire district rates from 11 to 32 cents. The tax rate in the city of St. Louis for municipal (including county) purposes was $1.88; the St. Louis County tax was 78 cents.

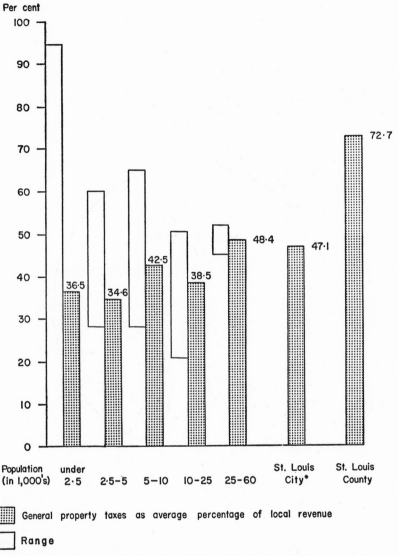

Fig. 5. Property taxes as percentage of revenue for municipalities and St. Louis County, St. Louis City-County area, 1955.

OTHER REVENUE SOURCES

Apart from the general property tax, the other revenue sources relied upon by the local governments differ considerably in type and extent of use (see figure 6). The sources most commonly tapped by municipalities are gasoline taxes (ranging from one-half cent to one and one-half cents per gallon), licenses (including merchants and motor vehicles), taxes on the gross receipts of utilities, and parking meter fees. Fifty-three of the ninety-seven municipalities in the area have a merchants tax, thirty-nine a city gasoline tax, thirty-six an auto license fee, thirty-six a utilities tax, and twelve have parking meters. The combined receipts from these sources constitute approximately 11 per cent of total municipal revenues.

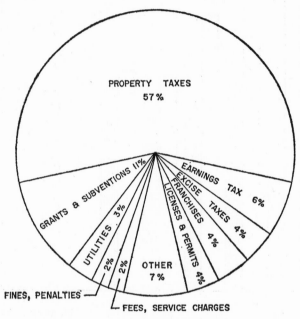

Fig. 6. Total revenues of all local governments, St. Louis City-County area, 1955.

Service charges are not employed extensively by the local units. The Metropolitan St. Louis Sewer District finances its operations with such a charge and thirteen County municipalities use this means to meet the cost of garbage and rubbish collection. The Bi-State Development Agency finances its operations at the present time by fees received from its terminal operations. Building and related inspection fees have provided a lucrative source of income for some rapidly developing County communities.

State aids to local governments in Missouri are significant only in the field of education. School districts in the St. Louis area receive approximately one-fifth of their total revenue from the state government, but municipalities and other local governments are given no direct financial aid. The major welfare programs, such as old-age assistance, aid to dependent children, and assistance to the blind, are administered by state agencies. Indirect fiscal aid to local government is contained in the highway program. The state maintains several designated state highways that run through municipalities, and currently with the aid of federal funds it is constructing three major expressways from outlying sections of the County into downtown St. Louis. The municipal government of the City and the St. Louis County government are paying only a relatively small part of the costs involved in acquiring the necessary right-of-way. All other costs and the responsibility for maintenance have been assumed by the state.

The County government renders some financial assistance to the municipalities located within its boundaries. It levies a special tax on property for road purposes and returns 50 per cent of the amount collected to the municipality of origin. This rebate may be used by the local community only for road construction and maintenance. In addition, residents in municipalities that operate their own libraries are exempt from the County library tax of 12 cents on each $100 assessed valuation.

The city of St. Louis is the only local unit permitted by law to utilize the earnings tax as a revenue source. The City presently levies a tax of one-half of 1 per cent on the gross salaries of all persons employed within its limits, whether residents or not, and on the net receipts of business and industrial establishments. The earnings tax has become an important part of the City's tax structure. Approximately 15 per cent of its total income is derived from this source.

TAX BASE

As a result of the distribution of tax sources and the heavy dependence on general property taxes, the ability to provide services (tax capacity) is largely determined by the amount and type of taxable real and personal property within the various governmental boundaries. The total assessed valuation of property in St. Louis City is $1.7 billion or $2,000 per capita and in St. Louis County $1.0 billion or $1,750 per capita. The total assessed valuations among the County municipalities range from $106,000 in one community to $107 million in another.

1955
Assessed valuation   *Number of*
(000,000 omitted)   *municipalities*

Under 5.0	66
5.0 to 9.9	12
10.0 to 24.9	12
25.0 to 49.9	4
50.0 to 99.0	1
Over 100.0	1

In St. Louis City only 50.3 per cent of the total assessed valuation is derived from residential properties and 48.1 per cent from commercial and industrial uses. This means that a substantial part of the property in the central city is devoted to high tax yield uses. The reverse situation exists in St. Louis County where only 17.4 per cent of its assessed valuation is industrial and commercial and 76.4 per cent residential.

TABLE 11

ASSESSED VALUATION BY TYPE OF PROPERTY
ST. LOUIS CITY AND ST. LOUIS COUNTY, 1956

	St. Louis City		St. Louis County	
Land use	No. of properties (000 omitted)	Per cent of assessed valuation	No. of properties (000 omitted)	Per cent of assessed valuation
Residential, single-family	121.9	42.0	133.6	73.8
Residential, multiple-family	3.9	8.3	.2	2.6
Commercial	7.4	27.0	14.0	12.3
Industrial	3.2	21.1	0.2	5.1
Farm	0.0	0.0	1.8	1.1
Vacant	7.9	0.7	92.5	4.7
Other	0.8	0.9	0.2	0.4
Total	145.1	100.0	242.5	100.0

SOURCE: U.S. Bureau of Census, *Real Estate Assessments in the United States*, 1957 Census of Governments, Advance Release No. 3 (G-CGA-No. 3), May 31, 1957, Tables 3–4, pp. 11–12.

The assessed value–sales price ratios for St. Louis County and St. Louis City are 28 per cent and 35 per cent, respectively. The failure to maintain a continuing program of reëvaluation, particularly in St. Louis County, has resulted in wide discrepancies in assessment ratios between individual parcels of property. To correct such inequities, comprehensive reassessments of real property are presently being conducted in both the City and the County.

TAX LIMITATIONS

In accordance with a practice in many states, property tax limitations are applied to all local governments in Missouri by legislative and constitutional provisions. The limit varies with the type and class of unit. Permissible tax rates for general operating purposes are as follows:

Governmental unit	*Rate per $100 assessed valuation*
Municipalities	
St. Louis City	$1.00
Cities (other than fourth class)	1.00
Fourth class cities	.75
Towns and villages	.50
Counties	
With more than $300 million assessed value (includes St. Louis County; St. Louis City, which performs the functions of a county within its boundaries, is also authorized to levy this amount)	.35
With less than $300 million assessed value	.50
School districts	
Urban districts	1.00
St. Louis City district	.89
Other school districts	.65
Fire districts	.30
Metropolitan sewer districts	.10

These limitations may be exceeded for certain purposes and under certain conditions. Municipalities, for example, may tax up to an additional 30 cents per $100 assessed valuation for general purposes, provided two-thirds of the voters consent. Cities, but not towns, may also exceed the limitations up to a total of 60 cents by levying taxes earmarked for certain specified functions such as health, library, and recreation. A majority popular vote is usually required in such cases. School districts may increase their rates to three times the specified limit by majority vote. Any such increase, however, must be submitted to popular vote each year. The limitations on tax rates for any of the local units do not apply to taxes levied for the purpose of paying bonded indebtedness. Separate limitations in terms of percentage of assessed valuation apply to such debts.

EXPENDITURES BY GOVERNMENTS AND FUNCTIONS

In common with other metropolitan centers, the City-County area has been experiencing a rapid increase in governmental expenditures. The local units spent (including capital outlays) a total of approximately $111 million in 1951; by 1955, this amount had increased to over $157 million. Of these amounts, local gov-

TABLE 12

PER CAPITA AND PERCENTAGE DISTRIBUTION OF EXPENDITURES BY FUNCTION,[a]
ST. LOUIS CITY–ST. LOUIS COUNTY AREA, 1955

Service	Per capita		Percentage distribution
General government		$ 7.19	7.9%
Administration	5.29		5.8
Building inspection	.54		.6
Other	1.36		1.5
Protection of persons and property		14.88	16.4
Police	9.27		10.2
Fire protection	5.53		6.1
Civil defense	.08		.1
Judicial administration		2.68	2.9
Judiciary	1.55		1.7
Sheriff	.46		.5
Detention	.40		.4
Coroner	.09		.1
Constables	.18		.2
Health and sanitation		15.99	17.5
Health and hospitals	9.95		10.9
Sanitation[b]	2.04		2.2
Refuse collection	3.08		3.4
Sewers	.92		1.0
Education and cultural activities		39.41	43.3
Education[b]	34.89		38.3
Parks and recreation	3.27		3.6
Libraries	1.25		1.4
Welfare		1.17	1.3
Roads and streets		5.52	6.0
Debt service, general		4.30	4.7
Total		$91.14	100.0%

[a] Certain services that yield a profit and are not common throughout the area, such as wharfage, airports, and water utilities, are excluded from this tabulation.
[b] These per capita figures include debt service costs.

ernmental units operating in the City in 1951 spent $78,467,000 or about $91 per capita and in 1955 $96.5 million or $112 for each person. Total expenditures for the local governments in the County were approximately $32 million or $73 per capita in 1951 and $60.5 million or $109 per person in 1955. The greater rate of increase in the County reflects the rapid growth and expansion of the suburban areas and their consequent need for new services and facilities.

Public education is by far the most expensive local govern-

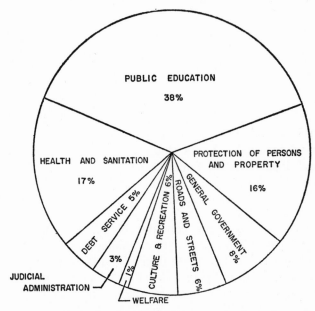

Fig. 7. Total local expenditures exclusive of capital outlays, St. Louis City-County area, 1955.

mental service (see figure 7). Moreover, there are indications that a larger part of total costs, both in terms of absolute dollars and percentages of total dollars, will be used for education in the near future. During the 1951–1955 period, the school districts' share of total expenditures (including capital outlay) by local governments increased from 37 per cent to 41 per cent while municipal expenditures dropped from 56 per cent to 51 per cent of all local government costs. When St. Louis County is considered alone, school districts spent 66 per cent of the total by local units in the County in comparison to 17 per cent expended by the ninety-six municipalities and 15 per cent by the County government.

Hospitals and public health and sanitation constitute the next largest category of expenditures. Almost 21 per cent of the operating budget of the city of St. Louis (or 9 per cent of the expenditures by all local governments in the City) is allocated to these needs. Units in the County spend a smaller proportion of their revenue for similar purposes: 11 per cent of the operating costs of the county and municipal governments or about 4 per cent of the total expended by all local governments in the County. Expenditures for police and fire protection, street maintenance, and parks and recreation follow in that order.

DEBT

The total bonded indebtedness of all local units in the City-County area in 1955 was $105,849,300. It was apportioned as follows:

City of St. Louis	$31,348,000
Local governments (other than school districts) in St. Louis County	13,511,200
School district in St. Louis City	15,776,000
School districts in St. Louis County	43,761,100
Bi-State Development Agency	1,453,000

These figures will increase considerably as the proceeds from presently approved bond issues are expended. The largest increase will take place in school districts in the County where the pressure of population growth is being felt acutely. Large capital expenditures for road construction, sewers, parks, and public institutions are also being planned by other local governments.

The Missouri Constitution places limitations upon the amount of capital indebtedness that may be incurred by a local government. All bond issues must be submitted to popular vote and must be passed by a two-thirds majority. The total amount of the indebtedness represented by general obligation bonds cannot exceed a certain percentage of the assessed value of taxable tangible property within the governmental units involved. For school districts this limitation is 10 per cent and for other units it is generally 5 per cent. Revenue bonds may also be issued by a municipality for the acquisition or construction of utilities provided four-sevenths of the voters approve. The limitations, particularly those on school districts, are beginning to constitute a hindrance to the development of the area. Approximately one-half of the school districts in the County have already reached or are rapidly approaching their debt ceilings.

The pattern of local government finance in St. Louis City–St. Louis County resembles that of other metropolitan areas. Expenditures have been rising rapidly as expansion and growth have created new needs and new service demands. The per capita costs in the suburbs have risen more rapidly than in the central city until there is no longer an appreciable difference between the two. The majority of cities and towns in the County are spending substantially less per capita on municipal services than the city of St. Louis, but the higher school district taxes that suburbanites pay largely offset this difference. The problem of adequately financing local government on a basis that is equitable for all residents of the metropolitan community continues to grow more serious.

ATTEMPTS TO ADJUST CITY-COUNTY RELATIONS

The scheme of separation popularly approved in August, 1876, made no provision for subsequent boundary adjustments between the City and County. At that time there seemed to be no reason to include such a procedure. Under the terms of the separation, the detached city was increased from approximately eighteen to sixty-one square miles. Less than one-half of the enlarged city was then urbanized, and St. Louis seemed to be in the enviable position of having ample room for future growth.

For a quarter-century the judgment of the board of freeholders who had formulated the scheme of separation seemed sound. There was moderate growth of some localities in the County, but most of the population increase in the City-County area occurred in sections that had been added to the City when it separated. No cause for renewal of the earlier controversies between the City and County existed.[5]

Soon after the beginning of the twentieth century, population growth accelerated in the County, particularly in several areas adjacent to the City. There was a noticeable residential movement

[5] An exhaustive analysis of City-County relations from the time of separation is contained in William N. Cassella, Jr., "Governing the Saint Louis Metropolitan Area" (unpublished Ph.D. dissertation, Harvard University, Cambridge, 1952). This study, which has been a helpful source of information in preparing this section on adjustments in City-County relations, is being revised for publication by the University of Missouri.

of people directly west from the center of the City and across the corporate boundary into the County. Most of the population gain took place, as in earlier years, within the City, but the population increase in the County was becoming increasingly noticeable. From 1900 to 1910, for example, the County registered a larger increase, more than 32,000 inhabitants, than in any previous decennial period.

Only a handful of incorporated suburban municipalities existed during the first decade of the present century, and the rural government of the County could not adequately handle numerous problems that were resulting from greater urbanization. An illegally operated race track, various gambling operations, and other fraudulent schemes flourished in the County just beyond the corporate limits of the City. The state supreme court decided in 1905 that St. Louis police lacked authority to make arrests in St. Louis County for offenses committed beyond the City's territorial limits. Territorial enlargement of the City was impossible under existing law.

ANNEXATION

As the number of incorporations of nearby areas in the County began to increase perceptibly, the City seriously tried to obtain legislative authorization to annex adjacent territory. In the legislative session of 1915 a very general annexation proposal was introduced, but never reached the voting stage. Numerous bills, similar in most details to one another, were presented in the following three sessions. All were worded in general language to avoid the constitutional prohibition against special legislation, but each was in fact applicable only to St. Louis. In 1917 one bill passed the Senate, but an identical bill was not acted upon in the House. This 1917 bill required majority approval by the voters in the County of any proposal for the City to annex unincorporated County territory and a four-sevenths majority of the voters in any incorporated municipality included in the County area to be annexed.

The 1917 bill was reintroduced in the Senate in 1919, but this time did not pass. The same bill was given a "do not pass" committee report in the House. A similar measure subsequently introduced also got a "do not pass" report from the same committee. A comparable bill, introduced under a different title to avert being referred to the committee that had twice reported unfavorably on annexation proposals, was buried. In 1921, still another bill attempted to gain legislative authorization for annexation by St. Louis, but was defeated by a vote of the lower house.

All these many attempts to acquire legislative permission for St. Louis to annex were vigorously opposed by legislators from St. Louis County. Efforts extending over four successive legislative sessions indicated the hopelessness of seeking to alter the relations of the City and the County through legislative means. The City channeled its energies into another legal direction.

CONSTITUTIONAL CONVENTION AMENDMENT

The opportunity for the City to try to acquire another legal method for adjusting City-County relations was made possible by the passage of a constitutional amendment in 1920. It required submission of the question of calling a state constitutional convention to the voters each twenty years. The calling of such a convention was approved in August, 1921, and the convention began its work in mid-1922.

The convention delegates were presented with a considerable number of proposals regarding changes in City-County relations. Numerous approaches were suggested, including expansion of the limits of the City to include the entire County, reëntry of the City into the County, complete consolidation of the City and the County, establishment of incorporated districts whose territory would extend over more than one municipality or county and whose powers would be limited to highways, sewers, and public works, and annexation by the City of some territory in the County. Some of the proposals called for effectuation by direct constitutional provision. Others were permissive and stipulated local consent. The most frequent arguments in support of some kind of City-County integration centered on inadequacies in sewerage and fire and police protection in the County. Fears of possible domination of the County by the City and the need to protect rural County residents were expressed.

The convention delegates after almost a year and a half of activity adopted twenty-one amendments. One of them included a lengthy and complicated series of sections providing for adjustments in City-County relations. One section, which declared St. Louis to be a county for the purposes stated therein, permitted changes in county boundary lines and the consolidation of adjoining counties through separate popular majorities in each affected county. Another section provided that any city, including St. Louis, may extend its boundaries and contiguous cities may be consolidated or merged, without regard to county boundaries, in the manner prescribed by law, provided that any such extension or consolidation obtains the approval of a majority of the voters in the affected incorporated territory. A third section authorized the election of a board of freeholders, six from the City and a similar number from the County, to prepare a scheme for the reëntry of the City into the County and partial or complete consolidation of the City and County. It stipulated that the scheme was to be submitted within one year and would go into effect only if approved by popular majorities in each of the two governmental jurisdictions.

The amendment, which also contained sections on the alteration of the local governmental system in rural areas, passed in St. Louis, St. Louis County, and the Kansas City area in an election of February, 1924. Outstate opposition, however, resulted in its defeat by approximately 20,000 votes. Consequently, the City-County area was still without legal means of adjusting its relations.

THREE ALTERNATIVES

Even before the constitutional convention had completed its work, new activity on behalf of some type of adjustment started. Soon after the defeat of the amendment in early 1924, leaders of both the City and County met to work out a compromise that could be submitted as an initiated constitutional amendment. This new proposed amendment utilized the board-of-freeholders device. It specified the appointment, upon petition of a stated number of voters in the City and County, of a freeholder board of eighteen members, nine by the mayor and circuit court judges of the City, and nine by the governing body and circuit and probate judges of the County, to prepare a scheme of adjustment that featured one of three alternatives. The alternatives made available to the freeholders were City-County consolidation under the municipal government of the city of St. Louis, reëntry of the City into the County and granting the City the right of annexation afforded under general law to other municipalities, and annexation of part of the County by the City. The scheme would have to be submitted within one year after the board's appointment and obtain dual majorities in the City and County to become effective.

The amendment qualified for the state-wide ballot at the general election of November, 1924. It passed decisively in both the City and County and carried by a margin of 90,000 in the state.

Finally, almost fifty years after the separation, a legal procedure for City-County adjustment became available.

City-County Consolidation

Prompt use was made of the new constitutional section; seven months after the amendment passed, a board of freeholders was appointed. From the organizational meeting through the completion of the work, the board split into City and County blocs. Thus fraught with disharmony, the board frequently acted in short-sighted and spiteful ways. At the first two meetings, when the County members possessed a numerical majority because of the absence of a City freeholder, they determined the types of committees and constituted the membership of them to their advantage. The minority, the City members, of the committee on permanent organization early suggested the creation of ten subcommittees to study various substantive problems. The suggestion was rejected, the board thereby denying itself the opportunity to undertake an inquiry of some intensity into City-County difficulties.

Informal discussion of problems by the board was made virtually impossible by the adoption of an elaborate set of fifty rules. Excessive formality and legalism prevailed, with each of the two groups apparently operating from predetermined positions. Delaying tactics were utilized by the County bloc during the first several months. A suggestion that the board meet more than once a month got a cool reception. Only two outsiders were invited to address the board. Some freeholders in each bloc took extremely dogmatic positions. When the committee on scope and plan reported, it rejected without explanation all six plans that had been introduced by various freeholders.

With about two months of the twelve months of the board's legal existence remaining, the City group decided to meet separately to draw up a scheme upon which all the City freeholders could agree. Complete City-County consolidation—the absorption by the City of the County and all its municipalities—was accepted by the nine City freeholders as a result of the aggressive advocacy of the proposal by one of them. A few days before the constitutional life of the board expired, the City group persuaded one County member to sign the City's plan. This satisfied the legal requirement that a plan have signatures of at least ten of the eighteen members before it could be submitted to the voters.

The special election on the City-County consolidation proposal

was set for late October, 1926, approximately five months after
the finish of the freeholder board's work. The opposition organized more rapidly and obtained more extensive financial support.
The County chamber of commerce, officeholders in the County
government, and municipal governments in the County became
active members of the opposition. Partisan politics had no bearing
on the campaign; the Republican party was in power in both the
City and County and the supporters and opponents of the proposal
were principally Republicans. The advocates of consolidation
were slow to mobilize, operated with insufficient funds, and relied
greatly upon newspaper statements. No concerted appeal was
made to the voters of the City; their support was thought to be
automatic.

The election results were as expected. The only surprise was the
very small turnout in the City, where only 22 per cent of the
electorate cast ballots. Sixty-seven per cent of the County voters
balloted. The City returns were almost seven to one in favor; the
County results were more than two to one in opposition. The
failure of the consolidation proposal to receive affirmative majorities in both jurisdictions meant that no change in the existing
City-County governmental arrangements was accomplished; the
legal separateness of the City and County continued to prevail.

FEDERATION

A major revival of interest in adjusting City-County relations
developed about a year after the consolidation election and culminated in 1930 with the presentation of a constitutional amendment that authorized the utilization of another approach. The
renewal of interest started in the County late in 1927. Soon the
City and County chambers of commerce began to hold joint meetings whose objective was to decide upon some type of governmental arrangement that the City and County might utilize to
deal with their common problems. They ultimately agreed that a
recognized expert should be employed to study the local situation.

The chamber committees were supplanted by a newly organized
City and County metropolitan development committee of twenty-
six members—the two chamber presidents, serving ex officio, and
twenty-four other individuals chosen by the City and County
chambers and the mayor of St. Louis. Thomas H. Reed, a well-
known authority in urban affairs, was hired to direct the study,
and the professional research work was financially underwritten
by funds collected from industrial sources in the city of St. Louis.

A broad-based council on metropolitan government, which consisted of more than 300 members, was also created. It was divided into thirteen committees, each of which had responsibility for investigating a specific functional problem; they held numerous meetings where the various problems received thorough consideration.

The goal of the metropolitan development committee was the preparation of a constitutional enabling amendment that would permit an adjustment in City-County relations different from the three alternatives provided in the constitutional amendment of 1924. A tentative plan, which provided for governmental federation of the City and County, was publicly released for the purpose of getting comments that would be helpful to the committee before completion of the proposed amendment. Various County factions criticized its substance as well as the activities of the metropolitan development committee. In May, 1930, the final draft of the proposed federation amendment was issued, and activity got under way to obtain sufficient signatures on initiative petitions to place the amendment on the November ballot.

The amendment contained more than 3,000 words; it was excessively lengthy and complex, containing much detail about specific provisions. It was, in fact, an attempt to legislate in the constitution. The amendment was designed to provide a legal means whereby a new governmental unit, encompassing the City and County, would exercise specific functions of area-wide importance; the twenty municipalities would continue in existence as municipal districts that would perform certain functions, and the county government would be retained for limited purposes. Under the amendment's provisions, a charter would be drafted by a private group and submitted by initiative petition. Dual popular majorities in the City and County would then have to be obtained to put the charter into effect.

The campaign over the amendment became very heated. An important event was the announcement by the board of estimate and apportionment of the City of its opposition to the constitutional proposition. The board, which consisted of the mayor, the comptroller, and president of the board of aldermen, contended that excessive obligations would be imposed on the taxpayers of St. Louis.

The federation amendment, as well as five others, was decisively defeated at the November, 1930, election. It passed in the City by the narrow total of 4,500 votes and lost in the County by a three-to-two margin. Its state-wide rejection was by more than 150,000 votes.

A New Constitutional Option

It was many years before another proposition to adjust the relations of the City and County was presented to the voters. Meanwhile, the number of municipalities in St. Louis County increased rapidly, spurting from twenty in 1930 to forty-one in 1940 to ninety-two in 1950. The population of the County almost doubled between 1930 and 1950, increasing by approximately 195,000 people. In the same period, the City gained only a total of 35,000; however, in 1950 it was still more than twice as populous as the County.

The type of effort finally advanced derived its legal authorization from a provision in the new constitution prepared by the 1943–44 state constitutional convention and adopted in 1945. The provision retained the board-of-freeholders procedure (adding a nineteenth member appointed by the governor) and the three alternatives approved in 1924, and it added a fourth option—the establishment of one or more metropolitan districts for the functional administration of services common to the area.

This fourth option was successfully utilized. In 1954 the people of St. Louis and St. Louis County separately approved by three-to-one margins the creation of the Metropolitan St. Louis Sewer District. The plan adopted was formulated by a board of freeholders which was organized after extensive studies of the sewer problems of the City and County. The district provides an integrated sewerage system for all the City and the heavily urbanized portion of the County (including approximately nine-tenths of the County residents); it can be empowered with additional functions upon the separate consent of the electorate of the City and County. Its establishment represents the first adjustment in City-County relations since the separation of the City and County almost eighty years before.

A subsequent effort at adjustment was aimed at creating a metropolitan transit district, a single-purpose metropolitan government independent of the recently established sewer district. No comprehensive study, such as had been undertaken on sewer problems, preceded the organization of the board of freeholders that constructed the transit plan. When submitted to the voters in 1955, the plan failed to receive a majority in either the City or County.

During much of the current century, efforts have been made to bring about various types of metropolitan governmental reorganization in the St. Louis City-County area. The approaches most frequently suggested or attempted in other metropolitan areas— annexation, consolidation, federation, metropolitan district—have all been included in proposed or adopted legal enabling provisions applicable to the City-County area, and some of them have been voted upon locally.

It has been difficult to gain legal authorization to present proposals to the voters of the local area. Bills failed in four successive legislative sessions and two state constitutional amendments were rejected. Moreover, it has been almost impossible to obtain the consent of the local voters on specific plans of reorganization, in part because each of them has had to acquire two majorities, one in the City and one in the County. Two such plans were defeated; one of them received a decisive over-all margin of the votes but failed because of the necessity of receiving dual majorities.

Limited success has been experienced in seeking constitutional permission and in attaining local consent for a particular proposal. The constitutional provisions that have been adopted provide in total only two alternatives—City-County consolidation and metropolitan district—that have any possibility of being applicable to the entire area. A proposal formulated within the terms of one of these alternatives received the two necessary local majorities in recent years. After failure to gain either state legal authorization or acceptance by the local electorate of numerous comprehensive methods to adjust governmental relations between the City and County, an approach limited to one function was finally adopted. Thus, the acceptance of a mild reform in 1954, the establishment of a metropolitan sewer district, was the main result of the tremendous amount of energy that was expended over almost forty years from the first concerted effort at adjustment.

4

Governing a Metropolitan Area

DESPITE various predictions, the failure of most metropolitan areas to adopt comprehensive governmental reorganization has not resulted in catastrophe. The existing governmental structure operates well enough to prevent a general breakdown in the functioning of urban areas. Essential public services are being provided in some fashion by some agency of government.

Experienced observers of the metropolitan scene may be acutely aware of the defects and potential dangers that lie in the present system, but the average citizen has little such consciousness. He may be dissatisfied with the performance of certain functions, he may desire better or additional services, he may wonder at times where all this explosive growth is leading and what it means to him in terms of his daily living, but he is not deeply troubled. He feels no impelling need, no urgency, for any major restructuring of the governmental pattern of the area. Oriented mainly to his neighborhood or local municipality, he is not accustomed to think of the metropolitan area as a "community." He is not fully aware of the interrelatedness of its parts nor is he as yet conscious of his role as a "metropolitan citizen."

How does a rapidly growing metropolitan area manage to survive without major surgery? How, with its fragmented pattern of government, is it able to adapt itself to area-wide needs? And what price does it pay for its persistent refusal to establish a government with at least limited jurisdiction over the entire urban complex? These questions and others of a similar nature might be asked about most metropolitan areas in the United States. Moreover, careful analysis of the answers might lead to a better understanding of both how a metropolitan area is actually governed and factors that might be utilized to secure reorganization.

The St. Louis City-County area provides an interesting example, and to a large extent a typical one, of the manner in which government operates in a large urban center composed of many autonomous local units. It illustrates the various means and factors that make it possible for a community with dispersed governmental powers to ward off metropolitan catastrophe. Some of them are easily recognized; others are more intangible. In the first category are the widely used formal institutional devices for meeting common needs without substantially disturbing local autonomy. In the second category are the informal coördinating devices and the various factors and influences that tend to encourage areawide coöperation.

FORMAL COÖRDINATING DEVICES

The metropolitan area is an extremely complex social and economic mechanism. To satisfy their multifarious needs, the people of such an area organize themselves into a large number of private and public associations, including governmental units of various kinds. It is the purpose of these latter agencies to furnish the services that the citizens need and want from their local government. Because of the dispersal of governmental power which characterizes the St. Louis metropolitan community, responsibility for supplying the public needs of the people is divided among many local units. The heterogeneity of the governmental pattern is particularly noticeable with respect to those requirements that transcend municipal and even county boundaries. Some of these needs, such as sewage disposal, may be common to the entire area; others, such as intensified fire protection, may pertain only to a group of urban centers.

As the many governmental units now existing in St. Louis City–St. Louis County are each limited to a small segment of the total powers and functions that are necessary to operate a metropolitan community, various formal coördinating devices and arrangements have been utilized. They consist of

1) creation of special districts
2) intergovernmental contracts

3) enlargement of the County government's role
4) establishment of a bi-state agency through interstate compact.

SPECIAL DISTRICTS

Special districts constitute an important part of the governmental pattern of the City-County area. Of the fifty-one such districts now in existence, two are of metropolitan character (Metropolitan St. Louis Sewer District and Bi-State Development Agency), nineteen are less than area-wide (eighteen fire protection districts and one water supply district), and thirty are school districts.[1]

As St. Louis County increased in population after 1935, twenty-eight special sewer districts were created in attempts to meet the need for sanitary and storm water sewers. Only the larger municipalities had the fiscal capacity to finance sewer construction; smaller areas had to combine their resources to try to obtain the necessary financing. The efforts to provide sewers through the creation of special districts failed because not only did the districts separately cover less than a whole watershed, but also individually many of them still lacked adequate financial resources to do the job properly. The increasing health hazard to the entire City-County area alerted public officials and citizens to the need for coördinated action. An epidemic of encephalitis, which some people attributed to the sewage condition, further stirred up public attention. It was in this general atmosphere of crisis that a single sewer district was created. The history of the sewer problem in St. Louis County is illustrative of the manner in which metropolitan areas resort to *ad hoc* remedies to meet immediate and pressing needs. When individual municipalities proved unable to cope with the problem, sewer districts encompassing a number of them as well as unincorporated territory were established. When these districts could no longer meet the needs, the people turned to an area-wide agency with control over sewers.

Geographically, the Bi-State Development Agency extends beyond the Census-defined metropolitan area to include two additional counties, Monroe in Illinois and Jefferson in Missouri. The motivating force behind the establishment of the agency was the Metropolitan Plan Association, a nonprofit organization inter-

---

[1] Since the Survey's recommendations were made, three additional special districts, a County-wide school district for handicapped children and two fire protection districts, have been established.

ested primarily in regional planning. Established by interstate compact between Missouri and Illinois, the Bi-State Development Agency was given authority to construct and operate bridges, tunnels, airports, and terminal facilities, and to prepare a comprehensive master plan for the development of the area. Modeled after the Port of New York Authority, the agency was designed to cope with those problems of the metropolitan community that were interstate in character.

Fire protection, like sewage disposal, became a major problem in St. Louis County as expansion took place. The County government had no authority to provide fire-fighting facilities; the responsibility rested with the local communities. Only the larger municipalities had the fiscal capacity to maintain and operate fire departments. When population clusters began to spring up outside these municipalities, volunteer fire departments serviced the newly developed areas. Financed by contributions, carnivals, turkey shoots, and fees on households, the inadequacy of these units became more and more evident as population density increased. Without power of taxation, the volunteer departments had difficulty in financing the new and expensive equipment necessary for protection of an urbanized area.

Those who were active in the volunteers had by this time acquired a proprietary feeling toward the departments. Their interest was not financial but psychological. The volunteers looked upon the departments as their creation and their personal responsibility. Although they realized the need for making the departments public agencies in order to secure a tax base for effective operation, they were reluctant to give up their control over them. Common interest in fire fighting with its natural fascination for many had created closely knit and well-organized bands of volunteers. Principally through their efforts, eighteen fire protection districts were organized in St. Louis County. These districts cover over 202 square miles of territory and provide fire protection for an estimated 250,000 residents of the County. Volunteers continue to predominate in the manning of the departments, although the use of full-time personnel is steadily growing. At the present time, nine districts have no full-time fighters and all but one of the remainder use volunteer personnel along with a small number of full-time employees.

The use of the special-district device has provided large sections of St. Louis County with fire protection of reasonable adequacy. Fifty-one municipalities, in addition to most of the urbanized unincorporated areas, are included within fire protection districts. Their operation has met with general public approval; little criticism has been directed against them by either the press or individual citizens. Disputes have occasionally arisen between fire districts and municipalities within their boundaries over matters such as building code regulations or safety measures, but most of them have not been significant.

The school district, which is the third type of special district in the St. Louis City–St. Louis County area, has evidenced in recent years a strong tendency toward consolidation rather than proliferation. The reduction in the number of school districts in the County from eighty-six to twenty-nine since 1948 has occurred in response to felt needs. Substantial inequalities in educational opportunities among the many districts, which were caused by wide variances in fiscal resources, prompted the consolidation movement. Organized support led by parent-teacher associations resulted in action. Inequalities among the remaining districts still exist and a movement for further consolidation or some other form of equalization is now under way. Although school district reorganization has been relatively successful, the tendency to create additional governmental units to meet particular needs has not been entirely eradicated even from this field. This tendency was apparent in the recent establishment of a separate, County-wide school district to serve the needs of handicapped children. Educators pointed out that none of the existing districts in the County could afford to offer the specialized training necessary for mentally retarded, blind, deaf, or orthopedically handicapped children.

INTERGOVERNMENTAL CONTRACTS

Contractual agreements among local governments are receiving an increasing amount of use in metropolitan areas. Their utilization has encouraged a degree of coördination in certain fields without in any way changing the fragmented character of the governmental pattern. Units too small to perform particular public services economically and efficiently have been able to meet their needs by contracting with larger units.

The most extreme example of intergovernmental contracting is embodied in the "Lakewood Plan," named after the city of Lakewood, California. Under this scheme a municipality relies extensively, at least in its early years, on another government's functional organization. The city retains its legislative and policy-formulating powers together with certain staff administrative functions, such as budgeting, but contracts with the county government for all or many of its services.

Less inclusive contractual arrangements are employed in many other metropolitan centers. These include both contracts between municipalities and the county and agreements between practically every type and level of government. The contract device has proved to be quite popular because it has permitted the smaller units to provide for the administration of a service without relinquishing ultimate jurisdiction over the function itself.

The Missouri Constitution contains two broad grants of contracting powers to local units. One (Article VI, Section 16) authorizes any municipality or political subdivision to contract with other municipalities or units, or with other states or their political subdivisions, or with the national government for the "planning, development, construction, acquisition or operation of any public improvement or facility, or for a common service." The other provision (Article VI, Section 18c) permits a home rule county to perform any of the services and functions of any municipality or political subdivision in the county, except school districts, when accepted by majority vote of the people in the municipality or other unit. Although St. Louis County has a home rule charter, the latter authorization has not been used because of the popular ratification requirement. The former, however, has been extensively employed as the legal basis for contracts between the County government and other local units.

At the present time, the St. Louis County government under contractual arrangements provides three types of services to municipalities within its borders: health, police protection, and building inspection. The health department has 110 contracts with local governments. These agreements include various kinds of public health services to fifty-one municipalities and sixteen school districts. Since the inauguration of the program in 1954, the number of health contracts has increased each year. There are indications that this coverage will be more widely extended in the near future.

The County police department has comprehensive law enforcement contracts with eight municipalities, the largest of which has a population of approximately 2,500. Under the terms of the agreement, County police enforce not only state laws but local ordinances as well. By means of these contractual arrangements, the communities involved are able to furnish full and professional police coverage to their residents. The tax capacity of these communities would not, on the other hand, permit the maintenance of a full-time local force. The County police department also has contracts with thirty-nine other municipalities to provide them with radio dispatching service.

In the field of building inspection, the County department of public works performs the electrical inspections for fifty municipalities and the plumbing inspections for thirty. A large degree of uniformity is secured in this way because the contracting municipalities are obliged to adopt the County electrical and plumbing codes. No such coördination, however, has been secured in building construction supervision. Only one municipality has contracted with the County for this service. The local units apparently find it more profitable financially to do their own building inspection.

There are many other instances of contractual agreements among local governments in St. Louis County. Nine of the smaller towns contract with other communities for fire protection and four for police protection. Thirteen municipalities have a mutual fire-fighting agreement that establishes a system of mobilization in case of emergency. Twelve communities in the north part of the County have set up a radio dispatch center for their police departments. The County council has recently passed an ordinance authorizing the County collector to collect the general property tax for municipalities under contract. Under existing laws the County has been performing this service for school and fire districts but not for municipalities. Six communities that had been employing a private firm (about forty small towns employ this private collector) have now contracted with the County. One town estimates that the annual fees of approximately $750 that it has been paying to the private collector will be reduced to $40 under the terms of its contract with the County.

There are relatively few City-County or intercounty contracts in the St. Louis area. The city of St. Louis has an agreement with the County police department for the services of three police officers at the City-owned airport located in unincorporated County territory. The City and County offices of civil defense have an agreement to collaborate in the development of a civil defense plan, and a joint control center to be operated by the two agencies is presently under construction. The City and County also have a mutual aid agreement with Madison, St. Clair, and Monroe counties in Illinois covering civil defense emergencies. The health departments of the City and County have contracted to accept the milk inspections of each other. The two jurisdictions also have an agreement covering the hospitalization of indigent residents of the City who are stricken in the County and residents of the County who require emergency treatment in the City. The only formal contract between the City and a County municipality is an agreement for the sale of water by St. Louis to Webster Groves. The latter, however, purchases its main supply from a privately owned water company in the County and seldom utilizes the City's facilities.

EXPANDING ROLE OF THE COUNTY GOVERNMENT

A prominent characteristic of twentieth-century government in the United States has been the shifting of functions from smaller to larger political units. Although this process has been less noticeable at the local than at the state level, it has brought significant changes in the metropolitan pattern. Special districts, as noted earlier, and counties have been the chief recipients of this trend. The county has assumed an increasingly important role in the government of metropolitan areas. Because of growing urbanization, it has been assigned new duties that previously had been considered municipal in character. Libraries, parks and recreation, public housing, planning and zoning, and subdivision regulation are among the newer fields of county activity. In some instances the county has been given responsibility for administering functions of this type in both incorporated and unincorporated areas. Generally, however, its exclusive jurisdiction over these activities has been confined to unincorporated territory.

Early in the present century an astute observer of the American scene referred to county government as the "dark continent of American politics." Weaknesses in structure and organization, lack of administrative competency, and gross inefficiency were common characteristics of county units. Although the situation has not changed in many counties, improvement has been effected in some of them in recent years. This betterment is most noticeable in urban areas where the increasing demands upon county government have precipitated reorganization. In a majority of instances, the reforms have been minor and partial; in a few, however, major restructuring has been accomplished. The urbanized county is gradually being forced to adapt itself to new conditions and to satisfy public needs that are unfulfilled by other governments.

The St. Louis County government has followed the general
pattern of change. For many years the County was governed by
an elected board of three members and twelve other elected officials who performed administrative duties. In 1950 the adoption
of a home rule charter brought about certain revisions in administrative organization and broadened the powers of the County
government. The charter vested legislative power in a council of
seven members, provided for an elected chief executive, and
reduced to eight the number of elected administrative officials.
The reform was only partial, but it resulted in some improvement
and enabled the County to operate at a higher degree of efficiency.
At the present time, a strong movement exists to strengthen further its administrative machinery.

The changing role of the St. Louis County government is reflected in both the increasing use made of its functional organization by local units and its extension of municipal-type services to
the growing unincorporated areas. The first has already been
noted in the discussion of contractual arrangements between the
County and the municipalities. The second is typical of the trend
that has been taking place in many metropolitan centers. The
home rule charter gave the County government power to provide
certain municipal services to the unincorporated areas. As these
activities are extended, residents of the urbanized unincorporated
areas find that many of their local public needs are being satisfied.
A new County police department provides them with protection
at a level higher than that performed by many municipalities, the
County health department takes care of their health and sanitation problems, the County department of parks furnishes them
with recreational facilities and the County libraries with books,
the County highway department maintains their streets, and
County zoning and building and subdivision regulations help to
preserve their property values. Since fire protection is furnished
by a fire district and a metropolitan sewer district is now responsible for sewage disposal, residents of these areas have shown a
decreasing interest in incorporation. They see no need to pay
a municipal tax when they are already getting what they consider the basic services.

At the present time an estimated 125,000 people or 25 per cent
of the total population of the County live in unincorporated sections. In many ways, these areas actually constitute a single
municipality with the County serving as their city government.
This point was made in a recent opinion handed down by the

Circuit Court of St. Louis County. In denying a city in the County the right to annex adjacent territory, the Court held that by virtue of the County government's authority to exercise municipal-type powers in the unincorporated portion of the County, such areas had become in effect a municipality. If this decision is upheld on appeal, further annexation and incorporation will be virtually impossible in St. Louis County without amending the state constitution. Presumably the laws relating to the annexation of incorporated territory would apply to any attempt by a municipality to extend its boundaries. This means that the residents of the entire unincorporated portion of St. Louis County would have to approve any annexation of unincorporated territory.

INTERSTATE COÖRDINATION

The St. Louis metropolitan area is one of twenty-four complexes that lie in more than one state. Twenty-three per cent of the total population of the local metropolitan area resides on the Illinois side of the Mississippi River. Problems of mutual concern to the territorial segments of the metropolitan community in both states prompted the establishment of a public agency with interstate jurisdiction in certain fields. The Bi-State Development Agency of the Missouri-Illinois Metropolitan District came into existence with high hopes. It represented an attempt to provide a governmental mechanism for handling certain metropolitan matters that transcended state lines. Its sponsors envisioned it as an instrumentality for guiding and integrating the development of the area. For various reasons outlined earlier, these hopes have not materialized (see pp. 48–49). The agency has continued in existence as no more than a promising device for securing integrated community action on an interstate basis. Thus far it has played a negligible role in the governance of the area.

INFORMAL COÖRDINATING DEVICES

Many informal or extralegal forces of a coördinating nature are present in a metropolitan community. These forces may arise from or be shaped by the policies and activities of higher levels of government. They may develop out of personal relationships among public officials, the activities of political parties and other groups, the influence of the newspapers, or the sheer need to coöperate in order to survive. Because of their wide diversity, no precise classification or even enumeration is possible. They may be grouped into six broad categories:

1) state and federal programs
2) informal coöperation
3) personal relationships
4) political party activities
5) the activities of nonpublic groups organized on an area-wide basis
6) the influence of the press.

STATE AND FEDERAL PROGRAMS

A degree of metropolitan coördination in the St. Louis area has been brought about by the activities of the state and national governments. This is particularly evident in road construction and public welfare. Presently, three expressways, financed largely by state and federal funds, are being built from outlying sections of the County to downtown St. Louis. Agreement on the routing and financing of these roadways among the numerous local governments would have been a virtual impossibility. Even so, local bickering over the routes caused the state to delay the projects for several years. The expressway system, which is the first step in the establishment of a comprehensive traffic pattern for the area, was made possible largely because final control was vested in governments that transcended the local units.

Federal grants-in-aid influence the governmental process at the metropolitan level. Direct federal grants to local units for slum clearance and urban renewal enable a segment of the total community to cope with blight and decay that might eventually affect the entire area. Federal aid for airport construction frequently permits a single local government to maintain air facilities for the whole community. Without assistance of this kind, these functions in many instances could not be undertaken except by an area-wide government. Many of the federal grants-in-aid to the states are also channeled to the urbanized centers. The usual requirement of state and local compliance with certain standards assures a degree of uniformity in administration throughout the area involved. In Missouri the federal grants for public assistance and welfare are state-administered. This centralized control of a significant and traditional local function further contributes to the coördination of government in the St. Louis metropolitan community.

INFORMAL COÖPERATION

A large network of informal coöperative agreements and understandings exists among governmental units in the City-County area. Many of them arise out of mutual needs; others are simply motivated by the desire to help one's neighbors. Informal agreements to assist each other in emergencies are common among the police departments of small municipalities; the County police department similarly stands ready at all times to answer the calls of any local department. Upon request, it furnishes criminal investigation services to any municipality and even patrols those that have no force of their own. The St. Louis City police department and the state highway patrol provide crime laboratory work to the County police department and to the various municipalities without charge. Mutual-aid understandings also exist among many fire departments. In a recent gas station fire in one of the small County municipalities, equipment from thirteen other cities assisted the local department.

A surprisingly high degree of coördinated zoning along municipal boundary lines has been attained. The Survey made a careful check of zoning along the twenty-three-mile line dividing the City and County. Ten municipalities as well as unincorporated territory lie immediately adjacent to the City. Only one instance of incompatible zoning was found along this entire strip. Spot checks in other sections of the County also failed to disclose any serious incompatibilities. This fortuitous situation cannot be attributed wholly to accident or fear of reprisal. A large share of the credit is owing to the willingness of municipalities to coöperate with their neighbors so long as their autonomy is not jeopardized.

PERSONAL RELATIONSHIPS

Personal relationships among public officials and private influentials are important factors in the governmental process of a metropolitan area. Close personal contact between officials of different political units frequently lays the basis for formal coöperative action. Moreover, the relations between public officials and important private citizens may actually result in the establishment of extralegal control systems. There is no way of measuring the force of these interpersonal relationships; that they play some active role has been demonstrated by the power structure studies made in recent years.

In the St. Louis area, business and industrial interests are centered chiefly in the City, but many of the executives and major stockholders live in the County. These influentials are thus concerned with both the central city where their economic interests lie and the suburban community where their residence is located. Their dual interests make them conscious of the interdependence of City and County and the need for coöperation between the two. Those who have lived in the area for a long period of time generally desire to retain the autonomy of their local community, although they are willing to support measures for coördinating area-wide functions. Newcomers to the area, particularly those in the managerial class, are less committed to the retention of their local community as a separate entity and are usually sympathetic to a more drastic reorganization of the governmental pattern.

The background and mode of life of municipal officials in St. Louis County are also conducive to their enlightened view of area relationships. Seventy-four per cent of those who hold public office in the County municipalities work in a community other than their place of residence; most of them have jobs within the city of St. Louis. Many are well educated and hold responsible positions in private industry. Fifty-five per cent of the elective officials and seventy-six per cent of those appointed to public boards and commissions are in the professional and managerial categories. Presumably, officials of this character are more aware of the interrelationship of the metropolitan area and are more willing than the full-time officeholders to work out coöperative accommodations. The greatest opposition to metropolitan reform by municipal officials in St. Louis County comes from those whose place of business or work is in the community where they hold office and from those who rank low on the occupation-education scale.

POLITICAL PARTY ACTIVITIES

Political parties commonly have as part of their organizational machinery a county-wide structure, including the county committee and county chairmanship. It thus would be reasonable to expect such county-wide party machinery to bring about a greater degree of unity in policy-making throughout the entire area involved than would be the situation without it. Nevertheless, such an expectation is not realized in either the St. Louis City–St. Louis County area as a whole or even within St. Louis County.

In the City-County area as a whole, the primary factor that militates against such party effectiveness is the legal separation of City and County. Each party has two separate organizations, one in each jurisdiction. There is little formal intercommunication on matters of local or area-wide concern; there is also little evidence to suggest any significant informal efforts toward the development of a unified point of view on local or area policy questions. On the contrary, often disagreement rather than agreement appears between the City and County organs of the same party. For example, even though a metropolitan government organized on a partisan basis would give the Democrats a clear majority of the registered voters, Democratic politicians in the County have viewed such an arrangement with something less than enthusiasm. Apparently quite a few County Democrats would prefer to limit their battleground to the County, where their party is definitely weaker than in the City, rather than cast their lot with the stronger City Democrats in a metropolitan government.[2]

Some City Democrats, on the other hand, have unofficially said that they would support some form of metropolitan government if it were established on a partisan basis. The Republican party organization in the City, admittedly very weak at this time, has not spoken with any authority on either local or metropolitan matters. The County Republicans, as might be expected, are vigorously opposed to any governmental reorganization that would involve area-wide partisan elections.

Within St. Louis County there is also a factor—nonpartisan municipal elections—that prevents County party organizations from effectively promoting any uniformity of policy in matters requiring action at the municipal level. All municipalities except first class and home rule charter cities are legally required to have nonpartisan elections for municipal offices. First class cities (there is none presently) must have partisan elections; the city of St. Louis and the several home rule charter cities in the County are permitted to prescribe the type of election.

Nonpartisan elections are in effect in every one of the County municipalities. Even behind-the-scenes partisan activity is seldom discoverable. On the contrary, frequently a slate of candidates in a municipal election will include both Democrats and

---

[2] The sizable victory of the Democrats in the November, 1958, contests for County offices in St. Louis County did not substantially alter the relative strength of the Democrats in the City and the County.

Republicans. A possible explanation of why these elections remain nonpartisan in fact is that the rewards of victory in the local elections are, by comparison with those involving offices in the County government, not attractive enough to warrant the expense and effort that would be required by the political parties. Only one County municipality exceeds 30,000 in population and only three have more than 20,000 residents. Moreover, the organization of political parties in St. Louis County, which is based upon townships, bears no relationship to municipal boundaries, and this works against the development of partisan organization on any basis corresponding to such boundaries.

As the St. Louis County government is partisan in character, both the Democratic and Republican party organizations look favorably upon any extension of its powers. (They are both, however, generally lukewarm to County government structural reform because they fear that it will result in a diminution of patronage opportunities.) Their support has been an important element in enlarging the role of the County government. Unfortunately, neither party in the County has really strong leadership, and the caliber of the candidates who receive organization support is generally mediocre. As a result, the County government has been unable to generate a high degree of public respect or to win the full trust and confidence of the people. Its failure to do so has impeded the movement toward further centralization.

NONPUBLIC GROUP ACTIVITY

Coördination in a metropolitan complex is not wholly dependent on governmental action. Private organizations that function on an area-wide basis contribute to the cohesiveness of the community. They include interest groups such as the chambers of commerce and the unions, welfare agencies such as the Social Planning Council and the Red Cross, and civic associations such as the League of Women Voters. The interests of most of these groups transcend the individual political boundaries and, whether economic or social, are closely related to government. Rezoning for the establishment of a large industrial park may be of considerable concern to both the labor unions and the chamber of commerce. An urban renewal project may involve a number of social welfare agencies as well as the local government.

The fact that these organizations are constituted on an area-wide basis permits them to review problems in broader perspective and to consider their relationship to the metropolitan community as a whole. Moreover, as their membership is drawn from the entire area, they are not impeded in their policy formulations by narrow territorial restrictions. Thus, the Chamber of Commerce of Metropolitan St. Louis was able to sponsor and secure the adoption of a comprehensive traffic plan by many of the municipalities in the area.

Several organizations of public officials provide a medium for the exchange of ideas and opportunities for the development of closer interpersonal relations. The most important of these groups is the St. Louis County League of Municipalities, which has a membership of sixty-three cities and towns. The league has been little more than a forum for the discussion of common problems; its accomplishments in the field of intergovernmental coördination have been meager. Agreement on major issues, such as the establishment of a uniform speed law or the adoption of a common building code, has been virtually impossible. The chief value of the league of municipalities has been educational—it has brought major problems to the attention of the members and it has unwittingly demonstrated the impossibility of solving many of them by voluntary coöperative action. Its more perceptive members have become convinced that basic changes are needed in the governmental pattern of the area. Some of these members have now emerged as leaders in the movement for metropolitan reform.

In addition to the league of municipalities, there are in St. Louis County organizations of city clerks, police court judges, fire district officials, fire fighters, a north county police association, and several other similar groups. They are largely interested in preserving the status quo. Their outlook tends to be narrow and provincial; they are suspicious of and hostile to all movements for metropolitan government. These various organizations, nevertheless, play more than a negative role. They stimulate a certain amount of coöperation among local political subdivisions, encourage the adoption of common techniques, and provide some training for their members.

NEWSPAPERS

Two major metropolitan newspapers, the *St. Louis Post-Dispatch* and the *St. Louis Globe-Democrat,* serve the St. Louis area. Both have been strong proponents of City-County governmental coördination. In editorials and news columns they have repeatedly emphasized the interdependency of the area and the need for metropolitan reform. They have also publicly called upon the political and civic leaders to take action in this field. In a sense, these papers have served as the civic conscience of the metropolitan community. They have helped to promote an attitude of concern toward area-wide needs among many influentials and other perceptive citizens. Some coöperative efforts that have been made by local government have undoubtedly been stimulated by press activity.

In addition to the two major papers, approximately twenty-five community or neighborhood weeklies circulate in the City and County. Unlike their metropolitan counterparts, the community papers (particularly those in the suburbs) are staunch defenders of the status quo in local government. They look with suspicion upon any movement to change the existing pattern, apparently feeling that the continued existence of many small governmental units is essential to their business interests. To some extent their attitude is a reaction against the strong position taken by the two dailies. The community press has consistently demonstrated a noticeable tendency to take stands on public issues contrary to those of the *Post-Dispatch* and the *Globe-Democrat*.

The influence of the suburban press on local issues and matters of local concern cannot be overlooked. The Survey's sample survey of citizen attitudes, for example, revealed that over 40 per cent of the County respondents felt their community paper helped them most in making decisions about local elections. Only 17 per cent stated that the two dailies were most helpful. Part of this disproportion can be accounted for by the fact that the large papers devote considerably less attention to local elections in the County than the suburban press. The figures nonetheless indicate that the community papers are widely read and that they constitute a persuasive medium in local matters. The position they take may well be crucial in determining the outcome of metropolitan reorganization efforts, since such reform inevitably impinges on the local community.

GRASS-ROOTS GOVERNMENT IN
A METROPOLITAN COMMUNITY

Attempts at structural reorganization in a metropolitan community are frequently met with the argument that government must be kept close to the people. Those who advance this position maintain that small units of government stimulate the interest of the people and provide them with the opportunity to participate actively in the affairs of their local community.

If it is true that small governments foster a high degree of political action, widespread grass-roots opposition might be expected to any movement designed to lessen local autonomy. The viability of this principle, in other words, would act as a severe check on governmental coördination and make more difficult the functioning of a metropolitan area. Several studies made by the Survey, however, raise serious doubts about the validity of the belief that small political units constitute the best means of keeping government in the control of the people. In fact, these studies indicate that the "small government" argument is in many respects a myth.

Three indexes were used by the Survey to measure political activity in municipalities: voting participation, competition for public office, and informal participation. These criteria were applied to a wide range of incorporated communities in the County and to the city of St. Louis in order to determine any relationship between size and political activity. In each instance the results failed to substantiate the assumption that the small unit of government promotes greater citizen participation.

FORMAL PARTICIPATION

Voting records of local elections for the years 1950 through 1956 were tabulated for eighty County municipalities that ranged in population from less than 500 to 56,000. The mean voting participation during this period was 29 per cent, with no significant differences appearing according to size. A more detailed analysis was made of the 1953 municipal elections in seventy municipalities because a comparable local election took place in the city of St. Louis in that year. The results showed that the size of the municipality did not consistently affect the extent of voter participation. Actually, the city of St. Louis had a higher rate than that found in 57 per cent of the County municipalities.

The attitude survey offered further substantiation that the residents of smaller communities do not vote in local elections with any greater frequency than those in the larger cities. In answer to "Have you ever voted for any local official since you've been living here?" respondents replied as follows:

Size of city	Yes	No	Ineligible
City of St. Louis (about 850,000)	66%	30%	4%
20,000–56,000	71	26	4
10,000–19,999	66	23	10
3,000–9,999	71	22	7
Less than 3,000	70	22	8

The municipalities in the central part of the County which possess a high social ranking showed a higher rate of participation than those in the lower-ranked northern part of the County where the rate closely coincided with that of the City. This indi-

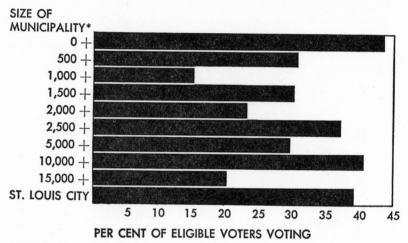

SIZE OF MUNICIPALITY*

PER CENT OF ELIGIBLE VOTERS VOTING

* 1955 estimated population.

Fig. 8. Average percentage of estimated eligible voters voting in the 1953 municipal elections, St. Louis City and 69 County municipalities by size.

cates that social rank is a more important determinant in local elections than size of city. It is also significant that the statement "a good many local elections aren't important enough to bother with" elicited the highest percentage of agreement (26 per cent) from residents of municipalities of less than 3,000 population.

Although size is of little or no importance in determining the extent of voting, it does appear to bear some relationship to competition for public office. However, the relationship is the inverse of that implied in the grass-roots theory. If competition is a measure of healthy political activity, greater contention for public office in the smaller communities would be expected, according to the popular belief. Analysis of elections in sixty-nine County municipalities and the city of St. Louis from 1950 to 1956 does not support this conclusion. On the contrary, the findings show that there is a distinct tendency for the proportion of contests to increase with the size of the municipality. In the smaller municipalities (those with less than 2,000 people) the average proportion of offices contested was under 50 per cent. In the city of St. Louis, on the other hand, competition for office approximated 100 per cent.

INFORMAL PARTICIPATION

Aside from formal participation, an argument advanced in favor of small governments is the greater opportunity afforded by the small community for informal participation in local public affairs. Mentioned among these informal means are attendance at town meetings, greater interest in local matters, more opportunity to persuade others on local issues, and more effective access to local government officials.

With one exception, the sample survey produced little evidence that the residents of the smaller communities informally participated more than those in the larger cities. A large majority of local residents who live in municipalities of various sizes have never attended a council or other public meeting on local government issues. Similarly, no significant variances according to size of municipality were produced in answer to the question "How interested would you say you are in local government affairs?" The same result was obtained to the query concerning whether the respondent ever discussed local affairs and politics with anyone outside his family.

Only in the matter of access to local officials was there any evidence that the small unit of government encourages citizen activity. Respondents were asked a series of questions to determine whether they had felt like complaining about their local governmental services, whether they had in fact complained, and if so to whom. Although the same percentage in the City and County (38 per cent) had felt like complaining, 54 per cent of the County residents who felt this way had actually complained as compared to only 32 per cent in the City.

There was also an important difference in the manner of making the complaints. Forty-one per cent of those in the County and 25 per cent in the City complained to specific people such as the mayor, councilman, city manager, or department head; the remainder simply called the city hall or a particular department. Twenty per cent of the complainants in the County as against only 5 per cent in the City had spoken directly with elected officials.

These findings indicate that suburbanites at least feel they have greater access to their local government. The many governments in St. Louis County provide a large body of over 800 elected officials; they are apparently accessible to the people and ready to listen to their grievances. In many ways they seem more comparable to union stewards than to executive and legislative officers.

Despite greater opportunity for access to local officials in small communities, only a minority of all respondents in all sizes of municipalities felt that informal participation was an effective means of influencing government. Seventy-five per cent agreed with the statement "voting is the only way that people like me can have any say about how the government runs things." Significantly, 80 per cent of those in communities under 3,000 answered in this manner. There was also little difference, according to size of municipality, among those who had "tried to persuade other people on local government issues." Only about 21 per cent of the municipal dwellers in the County had ever attempted to convince others on such a matter. In the city of St. Louis this figure was 17 per cent.

CONSEQUENCES OF METROPOLITAN FRAGMENTATION

The pattern of local government in a metropolitan area provides the institutional framework within which the area's social and economic development takes place. Because the metropolitan complex is a community, at least in the sense that the population is interrelated and integrated in its daily requirements, it must possess some means of acting as a unit in matters that are of area-wide concern. In the absence of a local government with general jurisdiction over the entire community, integrated action can be taken only through voluntary coöperation among a large number of independent units. Lacking an institutionalized center of public policy formulation, the metropolitan community must depend for its governance and direction upon many coördinating arrangements and forces. Some of the consequences of this dependency are manifest in the St. Louis City–St. Louis County complex.

Formal coördinating devices have enabled the City-County area to meet certain pressing needs. With the exception of the metropolitan sewer district and the ineffectual bi-state agency, however, these devices have been confined almost entirely to the County.

The city of St. Louis, unlike many core cities, provides practically no services to governments outside its boundaries. The few formal contracts, as well as the informal arrangements, that it has with County units are of minor significance. The local governments in the County have consistently sought to develop their own functional organizations to supply the public needs of their residents. This independence from the core city government has given them a feeling of confidence in their ability to handle their own matters. Consequently, a number of public officials in the County believe that most of its problems can be solved by reorganization of the County's governmental pattern without involving the city of St. Louis.

A restructuring of local governments in St. Louis County could eliminate many present difficulties. Taken as a whole, the County has the fiscal capacity to provide adequately such services as police, fire, public health, and education. Reorganization on the scale necessary to achieve satisfactory results would require extensive consolidation and elimination of many existing governmental units. Such reform would also strengthen the general metropolitan community by bringing more effective government to one of its important segments. It would not, however, solve problems that surpass City-County lines such as traffic, mass transportation, and area-wide planning. The last is particularly important for the orderly development of a metropolitan community. In the St. Louis area there are numerous planning commissions, each concerned with only a portion of the total community. They have no formal or informal mechanism to coördinate their activities; each formulates its plans in virtual isolation from the others. By their very nature these agencies are limited in outlook, perspective, and purpose.

Although incompatible zoning along corporate boundary lines usually has been avoided, the results of uncoördinated planning are now becoming strikingly apparent. Excellent industrial sites have been used for residential building, provisions for park and recreational facilities have been overlooked in the phenomenal growth of the area, and land has been put to uneconomical use. An antiquated road system has been perpetuated, schools and other public institutions have been improperly located, and gross inequities in educational programs have been permitted. These examples underscore the elementary fact that the direction of growth in a metropolitan area cannot be left exclusively to chance or to the individual decisions of each of its parts.

Experience in the St. Louis City-County area indicates that a fragmented pattern of government tends to foster inequities, impede effective administration of certain important functions, and prevent democratic decision-making in area-wide matters. Inequities arise particularly from the uneven distribution of the tax base, the use of one community's facilities by residents of another, and the subsidization of the urbanized unincorporated areas. One section of the area may enjoy a highly favorable tax base because of the location of industries within it. The taxing units in this section benefit greatly from such a financial situation while adjacent local governments that help to carry the burden of servicing the industry are excluded from sharing in the tax receipts. Many employees of the industry may live beyond the community and school district in which their place of work is located. They generate traffic problems for the neighboring municipalities and they send their children to schools that receive no tax benefits from the industry. Because of this uneven distribution of tax resources, some municipalities and school districts do not have the fiscal capacity to support public services at even a minimum level. For example, the Kinloch School District in St. Louis County, which consists entirely of Negro students, was able to spend only $113 per pupil in 1956 in comparison to an average throughout the County of almost $300.

In many metropolitan areas, residents of one community often benefit gratuitously from the services offered by other cities or towns. This situation exists particularly with reference to the core city, but also on a lesser scale in other communities. The city of St. Louis maintains many cultural and recreational facilities, such as the art museum and zoo, that are used extensively by suburbanites. Also, the City's libraries, which contain over 1,200,000 volumes, are indispensable to area residents. The total number of volumes in all the library facilities of the County (the County library and eleven municipal libraries) does not exceed 350,000, the large majority of which are primarily for children. The City's many private hospitals and medical institutions, all of which must be serviced by the City without any tax return to it, are relied on heavily by residents throughout the metropolitan community. Some of the expense to the city of St. Louis that is occasioned by nonresidents is recouped through the earnings tax, but this tax affects only those who work within its boundaries.

As unincorporated areas become urbanized, they must either incorporate, be annexed, or turn to the County government for municipal-type services. In St. Louis County the last device has become increasingly popular in recent years. There is little support for incorporation and strong resistance to annexation among residents of the unincorporated urban fringes. The County government furnishes these areas with such urban services as zoning and subdivision regulation, police protection, street maintenance, and public health and sanitation. These services are financed out of taxes paid by all County residents including those who live in municipalities. The latter support these same functions in their own community by city or town taxes. Since the bulk of the municipal-type services furnished by the County government primarily and largely benefits the residents in the unincorporated areas, municipal dwellers are placed in the position of partially subsidizing these activities. In some metropolitan areas special service districts have been created to eliminate this inequity. Such a solution, however, merely aggravates an already complex governmental pattern.

There are certain functions, such as water supply and sewage disposal, that cannot be efficiently administered by small units of government. Others, such as mass transit and civil defense, must be coördinated over the whole urban sector in order to achieve adequate operation or control in any part of the community. Because the areal extent necessary for efficient administration differs from function to function, it is possible to establish two or three units of government with varying territorial jurisdiction. This pattern has much to offer so long as it avoids undue complexity and provides some device for coördination among the various units.

METROPOLITAN CONSENSUS

The important question for a metropolitan area is not the number of governmental units, but the existence of adequate machinery for reaching consensus in a democratic fashion on issues of area-wide concern. This consensus involves two aspects:

agreement on what matters are of area concern and agreement on how each is to be handled. In addition, legal and institutional means must exist for making and executing such decisions. The sheer proliferation of governments in a metropolitan area that does not have an area-wide policy-making agency raises a serious question about the possibility of democratic and responsible citizen control on these matters. Such fragmentation creates a host of public decision-making units without any over-all or central focus. Policy that affects the entire area may be made by one local government, yet only a small segment of the total metropolitan community may be eligible to participate in its formulation.

Consensus on matters of area-wide concern must be reached within the framework of the total community welfare. Lacking an area-wide government, voluntary coöperation together with informal and private means must be used to reach any decision. Such methods are generally insufficient; they frequently lead to no agreement or to agreements that cannot possibly be carried out within the existing governmental framework. They are, moreover, partial and particular rather than complete and general devices. Without a formal mechanism for central decision-making in a metropolitan area, there can be no way of evaluating the segmented forces of interest and pressure groups in the light of the functional aims and well-being of the whole community. Nor can there be any effective way for the citizen to participate in the decision-making process at the metropolitan level.

The present practice of resorting to *ad hoc* remedies in metropolitan areas may avoid immediate catastrophe, but implicit in such practice is the danger that it may serve as a temporary palliative to a condition that calls for major change if local residents are to avoid future disaster.

Part Two
FORMULATING A
PLAN OF GOVERNMENT

5

Major Determinants

THE MAJOR objective of the Metropolitan St. Louis Survey was the formulation of recommendations that would constitute a plan of governmental improvement for St. Louis City and St. Louis County. The decision to concentrate the governmental studies on this section of the total metropolitan area was made by the Survey during the planning of the work.

Several factors prompted this decision. First, it was judged that a careful analysis of important social and economic factors would result in more intelligent recommendations about governments and public problems. This judgment meant that the financial resources available to the Survey were not sufficient to examine thoroughly the governmental pattern and difficulties of the entire area. Second, time was essential. Before the Survey actually began its activities, a citizens' committee was already circulating petitions for the appointment of a board of freeholders to draft a plan of government for the City and County. Although this committee agreed to withhold the filing of its petitions until the Survey was completed, or in its final stages, it would not postpone this action for more than twelve to fifteen months.

An additional factor also entered into the Survey's decision to center its governmental research on the City and County. The interstate character of the metropolitan area meant that any governmental reform involving both the Missouri and Illinois sections could be accomplished only by compact between the two states or by enlargement of the powers of the already existing

Bi-State Development Agency. The experiences of this agency demonstrated the difficulty of securing any action on an inter-state basis under existing legal and political circumstances. Created in 1949 by interstate compact between Illinois and Missouri to handle certain common functions in the St. Louis metropolitan area, the Bi-State Development Agency has been virtually in-active since its inception. The Illinois legislature has been rather favorably disposed, but the Missouri General Assembly has con-sistently refused to appropriate any funds for the operation of the agency or even to grant sufficient powers to make its bonds more marketable.

The Survey believed that if effective reorganization of the governmental pattern could be accomplished in the major seg-ment of the metropolitan community, the groundwork would be

Courtesy: St. Louis Post-Dispatch

Fig. 9. Gulliver among the 149 Lilliputians.

laid for action on a broader basis in the future. St. Louis City and St. Louis County include approximately three-fourths of the metropolitan population. They are closely related by social, economic, and governmental ties, with St. Louis City serving as the economic core of the metropolitan community. Moreover, the complications accompanying rapid suburban growth have been greater in St. Louis County than elsewhere in the area.

Considerations of a somewhat different nature also influenced the Survey's decision; both the Ford Foundation and the Mc-Donnell grants were made on the assumption that an action program would follow the completion of the work. In their initial investigation of the grant application, representatives of the Ford Foundation questioned City and County leaders on the desirability and possibility of accomplishing governmental reforms, and whether the time was appropriate. From the beginning, therefore, the focus of the Survey's research was the governmental pattern of the City and County.

IMPLEMENTING THE RESEARCH DESIGN

The Survey staff first prepared a working outline to serve as a guide for the necessary research. This outline set forth (1) certain basic assumptions concerning the governments of the area, (2) a research design that included both the hypotheses to be tested and the categories of data to be collected in relation to each hypothesis, and (3) a general chronology of procedure (see Appendix A). The research design was structured to provide an empirical basis for drafting the plan of government.

The contents of this document emanated from the social science backgrounds of individual staff members, their experience with metropolitan problems generally, and their specific knowledge of the St. Louis area. Copies of the outline were then sent to five social scientists who had agreed to discuss the proposed procedure with the staff. These consultants were selected primarily because of their experience in urban and metropolitan studies. The group included an economist, a sociologist, an urban planner, and two political scientists. During a three-day session the conferees carefully evaluated the design, scope, and proposed methodology of the entire program of proposed governmental, economic, and social research. As a result of the conference, refinements and minor changes were made in the outline, but its general character and orientation were not disturbed.

While collecting and analyzing data, the Survey members discussed the general objectives that a plan of government should seek to attain in a metropolitan area. As finally agreed upon, these objectives were to:

1) Establish a framework of local government within which the area will be better able to foster its social and economic development.

2) Provide the machinery necessary to handle those governmental problems affecting the well-being of the area.

3) Assure the efficient, economical, and adequate execution of vital public services.

4) Remove inequities in municipal-type services by assuring a reasonable level of such services to all residents of the area.

5) Provide a governmental structure that will be responsive to the people and that can be held responsible by them.

6) Preserve the values of local government while strengthening its ability to cope with the needs of an expanding urban society.

After the general objectives were established, the staff formulated a list of guidelines to be observed in drafting governmental recommendations. These guidelines embodied principles that in the consensus of the Survey members were sound, realistic, and applicable to the local situation. They consisted of the following:

1) There is no model plan that can be applied to all metropolitan communities; each area must be considered on the basis of its own characteristics and its own problems.

2) The plan should take into consideration the needs of the area, its tradition, and the attitudes and desires of the people and their community leaders.

3) The plan need not require the attainment of the desired objectives by a single solution; several approaches or steps, each dealing with a particular phase of needed reorganization, might be proposed.

4) The fact that a problem might be affecting the well-being of the metropolitan area does not necessarily imply the need for a solution by an area-wide government.

5) Emphasis should be given to the solution of the most immediate and pressing local and metropolitan problems.

6) Existing governmental units should be utilized to the fullest extent of their capabilities. New units of government should be created only when the need can be clearly demonstrated.

7) The plan should be adjustable to future needs.

8) The plan should be politically attainable; its major elements should attract substantial public support.

MAJOR FEATURES OF THE AREA

Various Survey findings about the characteristics of the St. Louis area and the attitude of its people were persuasive influences in drafting the governmental recommendations. These findings are summarized here in order to indicate some major aspects of the factual environment in which the Survey worked. The environment in turn helps to explain the general approach to the plan of government and its basic philosophy.

SEPARATION OF CITY AND COUNTY

Since 1876 the city of St. Louis has been legally separated from St. Louis County. The separation took place at the insistence of residents of the City who wanted to free themselves from control and taxation by the County. Early in the present century, the City's growth extended to the boundaries set by the Act of Separation. Because of its dual status as city and county, St. Louis has been unable to extend its corporate limits by annexation; consequently, growth in the last two decades has taken place largely in the County.

The prolonged governmental separation of the City and the County is reflected in the attitude of the residents in each jurisdiction. There is, for example, decided opposition by County residents to the reëntry of the City into the County; 53 per cent of the County residents interviewed in the attitude survey expressed opposition to such a solution. More City residents reacted favorably, but still only 47 per cent of those who expressed an opinion indicated support of the proposal. Similar reactions were received from political and civic leaders.

The two metropolitan newspapers, the *St. Louis Post-Dispatch* and the *St. Louis Globe-Democrat*, are strong supporters of some form of metropolitan government. On the other hand, the major community papers in the suburbs are distinctly cool if not hostile toward any kind of governmental arrangement that would involve the City and the County.

ABSENCE OF CERTAIN METROPOLITAN PROBLEMS

The St. Louis City-County area is not faced with certain major problems, such as water supply, sewage disposal, sanitation, and air pollution, which confront a number of other metropolitan concentrations. Water is furnished to City users by a municipally owned plant, and County residents are adequately supplied by a privately owned utility. Sewer construction and maintenance in the City and the urban sections of the County are the responsibility of a single-purpose metropolitan district that was created in 1954. Public health and sanitation activities are concentrated in two agencies, the City and the County health departments. The latter is actually a County-wide agency serving the needs of both incorporated and unincorporated sections. Only two County municipalities maintain their own full-time health departments; most of them contract with the County for this service. There are only two public hospital systems, the City and the County; no County municipality operates a hospital. The city of St. Louis exercises strict control over air pollution, and although the County has no integrated program in this field, the general lack of industrialization there has given rise to no air pollution problem.

The increase of population in St. Louis County has expanded public service needs, raised taxes, and created a proliferation of governmental units. Although many of the accompanying problems have been met on an improvised basis, most of the immediate public needs of the people have been satisfied. No municipality in the County depends on the city of St. Louis for any of its services. Any subsidy to County residents which results from the use of City streets and cultural facilities is at least partially compensated for by an earnings tax paid by County residents employed within the City. A number of the local governmental units in the County are long established, are operating efficiently, and are highly regarded by their residents.

POLITICAL CHARACTERISTICS

The City is predominantly Democratic. Twenty-six of the twenty-nine members of the board of aldermen, the mayor, the comptroller, all elected officials holding so-called county offices (such as treasurer, collector, sheriff), and the two congressmen are Democrats. In contrast, the County has a Republican majority, but it has been dwindling in recent years as more blue-collar workers settle there. At the present time the County supervisor, who is elected at large, and four of the seven County council members, who are elected by districts, are Republicans.

POPULATION CHARACTERISTICS

The City's Negro population has been increasing steadily. In 1950 it was 18 per cent; at present it is estimated to be 25 per cent. The Negro population in the County is small, less than 5 per cent, and there has been relatively little increase in total number in recent years.

A distinct belief held by some City and County residents is that the City will become increasingly Negro and low-income white, and that as this change occurs the problems of fiscal crisis and irresponsible political leadership will become more acute. This subject came up repeatedly in interviews with various civic and political leaders during the course of the research. The attitude survey indicated, however, that the general public's image of the City and its government is not as negative as the leadership interviews indicated.

OTHER CHARACTERISTICS

St. Louis City and St. Louis County have certain common problems, but they also have individual difficulties that arise from their different characteristics. The City is a densely settled community with very little usable land that is still available. It is an integrated political unit (except for its county offices) with only three additional local governmental units operating within its limits: school district, metropolitan sewer district, and bi-state development agency. During the past several decades its population has remained relatively stable and school attendance has shown no notable increase. As an old community with many old buildings and residences, its most urgent task is to curb blight and decay through slum clearance and neighborhood rehabilitation.

In contrast to the City, the County is an expansive area with substantial room for development. Its local governmental activities are scattered among 147 independent units that function within its boundaries. Its population has been growing rapidly since 1940, and the number of school children has been steadily mounting. As yet it is not faced with serious problems of blight. Its most pressing needs are new and enlarged public services and facilities, new schools, and new industry and commerce to balance its tax base.

POPULAR ATTITUDE TOWARD CHANGE

Although some community leaders and private citizens express concern about the governmental problems of the area, there seemingly is no general feeling of urgency. Apparently conditions have not yet reached the point where they are seriously inconveniencing the average citizen. Although 81 per cent of those interviewed in the attitude survey, for example, thought the City and the County share major problems, one-fourth of this number was unable to name a specific problem and another one-fourth could list only one. Despite the lack of any strongly felt need for change there nevertheless are indications that a majority of the people are dissatisfied with the present governmental pattern. Sixty per cent in the City and 57 per cent in the County expressed dislike for the status quo. A substantial majority, moreover, thought that a plan for governmental reorganization should be submitted to the people in the near future. Yet when asked the question, "Putting your own preferences to one side, do you think any changes are likely to take place in the future?" only 46 per cent in the City and 40 per cent in the County who responded answered affirmatively.

LEGAL MEANS FOR CHANGE

The people of St. Louis City and St. Louis County can attack their metropolitan problems through existing legal means; unlike their counterparts in many other metropolitan areas, they do not first have to seek statutory or constitutional change. Article VI, Section 30a, of the Missouri Constitution provides four ways of adjusting governmental relations between the City and the County to meet common problems. They are:

1) merger of the governments of the City and the County into one municipal government,
2) reëntry of the City into the County,
3) enlargement of the limits of the City, and
4) establishment of a metropolitan district or districts for the functional administration of services common to the area.

Steps to take advantage of this enabling grant are initiated by popular petition. A board of freeholders consisting of nineteen members is then appointed to draft a plan embodying one of these alternatives. Nine members are named by designated officials of the City, nine by County officials, and the nineteenth member is appointed by the Governor from outside either jurisdiction. The board must submit a plan to the voters of the City and the County within one year after its appointment. Separate majority votes in each of the two areas must be obtained for adoption.

Legal provisions for governmental reform on less than an area-wide basis are not so favorable. St. Louis County operates under a home rule charter that may be amended by vote of the residents; its urban-type powers, such as planning and zoning, however, are constitutionally restricted to the unincorporated areas. Its ability to finance County-wide services is also restricted by unrealistic constitutional limitation on its taxing powers.

Legal impediments of equal difficulty lie in the path of municipal consolidation. Present state laws require that any proposed merger be approved by a two-thirds vote in each municipality involved and that the petitioners post a bond to reimburse the communities for the cost of the election in the event the proposal fails to pass. In contrast to the rigid consolidation requirements, the laws pertaining to municipal incorporation are extremely liberal. Whenever the required number of residents in an area present a petition to the County council for incorporation as a town or a city, the council must grant the request. Under this procedure forty-four new cities and towns, some with a population of less than 100, came into existence within a five-year period (1945–1950). In most instances, incorporation was sought to prevent annexation by neighboring municipalities or to avoid the zoning and building codes of the County.

School district consolidation in St. Louis County has met a better fate and the prospects for further accomplishment in this field are encouraging. In the last ten years the number of districts has declined from eighty-six to twenty-nine. This reduction has been made possible by a state school reorganization act passed in 1948 which authorizes the county board of education to prepare and submit consolidation proposals to the voters. Unlike previous consolidation laws, which required a favorable majority vote in each district involved, the 1948 law requires only an overall majority in the districts included in the proposal.

GOVERNMENTAL PROBLEMS

Consistent with its guidelines, the Survey sought to separate the governmental problems of the City and County into two meaningful categories: those that could be handled adequately by existing units, provided certain reorganizational changes could be brought about, and those that lay outside the capabilities of the existing governmental pattern. Up to this point the many governments of the City and County had been examined as individually functioning units and as interrelated units, and a number of common problems had become apparent. The staff now realized that this orientation had not altogether produced the kind of data essential to an intelligent documentation of area-wide problems.

Field investigators had thoroughly examined and documented municipal personnel and fiscal systems as well as services and problems. The sheer bulk of the data hindered distinction between the trivial and the significant in relation to metropolitan reform. It became necessary at a later stage of the Survey to turn the research emphasis from governments as such to over-all problems. The data already compiled had to be supplemented by additional investigation of each major problem or service. Conceivably, greater emphasis should have been placed on problems or functions at the outset of the study. By hypothesizing each indicated problem as area-wide or less than area-wide in character and by devoting more of the research activities to establishing or disproving these hypotheses, the end product of the study could probably have been attained more quickly.

Analysis of the data collected in the field clearly revealed that the governmental problems in the St. Louis area could be grouped geographically as well as functionally. Some of the problems were common to the entire City-County area, others involved only the City or County, and still others were peculiar to certain sections or to the municipalities of the County. A number of these problems were basically metropolitan in nature and required area-wide treatment under all circumstances. It was equally apparent that some problems had assumed a more than local character primarily because the existing units of local government were improperly organized or too small in size to handle them. The Survey concluded that a system of strong local governments could assure the retention of many functions at the municipal or county level that otherwise should be turned over to an area-wide authority. It felt, for example, that a single fire department would not be necessary if the local units maintained adequate fire-fighting facilities and if measures for coöperation and central control in emergencies were established.

Proceeding on this basis, the Survey made the following division of governmental problems:

Area-wide solution required	*Less than area-wide solution required*
Assessment	Fire
Civil defense	Garbage collection and
Over-all planning	disposal
Sewerage and drainage	Health and sanitation
Traffic	Parks
Transportation	Police
	Public hospitals
	Schools

AREA-WIDE PROBLEMS

There was little question but that the traffic and transportation problem in St. Louis City–St. Louis County should be attacked on an area-wide basis by correlating expressways, major arteries, feeders, bridges, and parking facilities with an efficient mass transportation system. Mass transit and private vehicular traffic are parts of the same problem and they cannot be singled out for separate treatment and control nor solved by piecemeal efforts. Under the governmental pattern of the area, the city of St. Louis, the 96 municipalities of St. Louis County, and the County government itself were each limited to a segment of the traffic and transportation job. Recent efforts by a committee of the St. Louis Metropolitan Chamber of Commerce to secure voluntary acceptance of a master traffic plan by the municipalities had proved generally futile. The growing seriousness of the problem calls for vigorous action. Passenger car registration in the City-County area during the 1945–55 period had increased from 206,341 to 388,016, while the number of passengers using mass transit facilities had declined from 207,241,000 in 1951 to 144,-483,000 in 1955. Traffic congestion, lack of off-street parking facilities, an inadequate street system, and increased costs of transporting people and goods locally were becoming serious impediments to the livability and development of the area. These deficiencies were reflected in the survey of citizen opinion; residents of the City and County viewed traffic congestion as the most important governmental problem facing the area. No other service evoked so much criticism.

The Survey agreed that planning should be included as an

area-wide function. The lack of metropolitan planning had brought about widely apparent, undesirable results. Prime industrial and commercial land had been used for residential development, desirable park and recreational sites had been converted to other uses, and a fantastically uncoördinated road system had developed. Both the City and County planning directors in discussions with the Survey staff emphasized the critical need for a single agency to do over-all planning for the area.

The Survey was similarly convinced that civil defense should be a metropolitan function. The city of St. Louis, the government of St. Louis County, and only nine County municipalities had organized civil defense programs. Much had been accomplished on the basis of voluntary coöperation between City and County authorities, but the complete coördination necessary for a satisfactory civil defense program had not been attained because of the lack of sufficient coöperation or the absence of a civil defense program in many communities.

The need for integrated control of sewer construction and maintenance in the City and County had been demonstrated several years prior to the Survey's research. The Metropolitan St. Louis Sewer District had been created in 1954 in response to this need. Its boundaries had been fixed to include the city of St. Louis and the portion of the County then largely urbanized. Since that time, at least five large private sewer systems had been constructed outside the district's limits and more were being planned. The Survey concluded that in view of present and expected population increases in the outlying sections, unified control over sewer development should be extended to the entire City-County area. It felt that if this action were not taken, the same conditions that led to the creation of the metropolitan sewer district would soon plague County territory beyond the district.

Property assessment presented a different type of problem. Although only two assessment agencies—the City and the County governments—exist, the staff felt that a metropolitan government should assume the responsibility because some of the area-wide functions would undoubtedly be financed by general property taxes. Even with only two independent assessment agencies, the problem of securing uniformity in property valuations for an area-wide tax would remain. The difficulty of working under two assessment ratios had previously been experienced by the metropolitan sewer district. In an attempt to compensate for the variation, the sewer district had initially levied a different tax rate on the two jurisdictions. This effort was nullified by the Missouri Supreme Court on the ground that taxes shall be uniform upon the same class of subjects within the territorial limits of the government levying the tax.

LESS THAN AREA-WIDE PROBLEMS

Neither police nor fire protection functions in St. Louis City and St. Louis County appeared to call for area-wide action. No serious breakdown was evident in either service. Most of the more populous municipalities in the County maintain their own police department at a reasonably high standard, while the unincorporated areas and many smaller municipalities are patrolled by the County police department. Obvious inadequacies exist, particularly in the small communities, but it seemed apparent that these could be corrected without metropolitan action. The same situation prevailed in fire protection. Practically all the County communities either maintain their own fire departments or are situated within fire districts. Certain features of these arrangements should be remedied, but again the Survey did not consider the deficiencies of such a nature as to require complete area-wide control.

Public health and sanitation, as previously noted, are handled principally by two agencies, the health departments of the City and the County. The latter, in addition to maintaining the regular disease-controlling functions on a County-wide basis, furnishes through contract a broad range of sanitation services to forty cities and towns. Only two County municipalities have their own organized health departments. The maintenance of public hospitals follows a similar pattern. St. Louis City operates its own system and the County government is responsible for all public hospital facilities in St. Louis County. No suburban municipality maintains a hospital.

A study of public health and hospital facilities in the City and County was conducted by the American Public Health Association while the Survey work was in progress. The Survey staff kept in close communication with those who were making the health study, and its recommendations were made available to the Survey before their publication. These proposals called for greater coöperation between the City and County departments in certain programs, but they specifically recommended against merger of the two units. On the basis of these judgments, the Survey decided that it would be ill-advised to place public health and hospitals in the category of metropolitan problems at this time.

Garbage and refuse collection is provided in several ways. Some suburban municipalities have their own service, some contract with private haulers, and others leave it to their citizens to hire private collectors. These arrangements are not altogether satisfactory; they result in wide differences in cost and service to suburban residents. The Survey staff felt, however, that the problem could be handled locally by the municipalities and the County government. It also felt that disposal by either the use of land fills or incineration should be the responsibility of the County government.

Public education, it was decided, should not be considered an area-wide function. First, the staff had serious doubts that the creation of one huge school district for the area would be wise or advantageous. Second, the statistical study of factors affecting local governmental costs did not show that substantial economies would result from area-wide or large-scale consolidation of schools. Third, there was strong feeling among residents of many suburban school districts that their schools were superior to those in the City and that consolidation would result in lowering educational standards. Fourth, prevailing legal opinion strongly indicated that a City-County board of freeholders would have no power to include schools in a governmental plan it might propose. Fifth, the state laws relating to school district consolidation made no provision for intercounty reorganization; hence a single school district for the City and County could not be achieved under existing statutory provisions.

The Survey distinguished between local and regional parks. In the first category are the small playfields that are used primarily for supervised recreational activities; in the second are the large park areas for picnicking, golfing, hiking, boating, and zoos. Local parks mainly serve residents of the surrounding neighborhood whereas regional parks attract patrons from a wide area. The designation of local parks as a metropolitan responsibility was quickly rejected, for they could be adequately operated at the municipal level. The inclusion of regional parks as such a function was seriously deliberated, but rejected. The City has a number of well-maintained parks of substantial size. The County also has several large parks in operation and had recently begun to use bond issue funds to acquire additional sites. The Survey felt it would be unwarranted to interfere with the emerging pattern.

The question of airports was also considered. The city of St. Louis operates the only major airport in the area and, according to traffic projections, it will not reach the saturation point for ten to fifteen years. Since the airport is a revenue-producing facility for the City, any attempt to transfer it to a metropolitan agency would be vigorously resisted by City officials. The Survey realized that the question of future airport facilities for the metropolitan area could not be postponed indefinitely. At the same time, it considered inadvisable the inclusion of this item in the list of functions that should be immediately transferred to a metropolitan agency.

6

A New Metropolitan Government

THE ALTERNATIVES

IN DECIDING upon the method of handling functions that called for area-wide administration, the Survey gave extended consideration to four possible alternatives: (1) merger of all the local governments (exclusive of school districts) of the City and County into one municipal government, (2) the establishment of an urban county through the reëntry of the City into the County and the extension of the County government's jurisdiction over matters of metropolitan concern, (3) enlargement of the powers of the County government and the establishment of a coördinating agency between the City and County, and (4) the creation of a multipurpose metropolitan district. Only the first and last of these possibilities could be attained through using the constitutional section (Article VI, Section 30a) permitting adjustment of City-County governmental relations. The two other solutions permitted by this act, the reëntry of the City into the County (but not the conversion of the County government into a metropolitan unit) and the enlargement of the City limits, were from the outset rejected as unsatisfactory. Because the former alternative makes no provision for increasing the powers of the County government, reëntry of the City would not solve any metropolitan problems. And the other alternative, essentially an annexation plan and a piecemeal approach, has little to offer at this late date toward the solution of area-wide governmental difficulties.

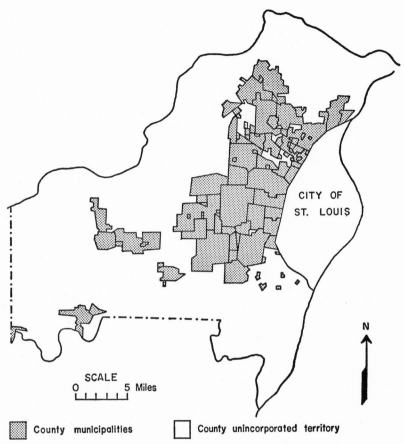

CITY OF
ST. LOUIS

N

SCALE
0   5 Miles

County municipalities   County unincorporated territory

Fig. 10. St. Louis City-County area: 96 County municipalities, unincorporated County territory, and the city of St. Louis.

MERGER

Theoretical and practical objections militated against the creation of a single government for the area. Although the substitution of one municipal government for the numerous local units now in existence would integrate authority and eliminate jurisdictional division, the drawbacks are serious. Research has not been sufficient to assess the comparative effect of the large and small municipality on civic interest and participation. The Survey's studies in the St. Louis area indicate that there is much less difference in the extent of participation according to size of community than commonly believed. Much more work, however, remains to be done in this field before it will be possible to speak

with substantial assurance about the effects that political integration has on citizen interest and participation.

The staff was by no means convinced that it would be wise to
recommend the abolition of the more populous, well-established
municipalities in the County, a number of which are more than
fifty years old. They are well regarded by their residents and
provide a relatively high level of services. The Survey's study of
factors affecting local governmental expenditure levels indicated,
moreover, that no significant economies of scale could be expected
from a merger of these units.

From the standpoint of popular acceptance, proposing amal-
gamation appeared wholly unrealistic. Fifty-seven per cent of the
County residents (66 per cent in its highly influential central
section) expressed disapproval when asked if they would favor
the merger of the City and County into one municipality. City
residents viewed this proposal more favorably, with 56 per cent
voicing their approval. The great majority of County civic and
educational leaders who were interviewed expressed opposition
to any merger plan. Republican party officials and most County
municipal officials who were interviewed were unequivocally
hostile to the idea.

URBAN COUNTY

Two-pronged action—reëntry of the City into the County and
enlargement of County powers—offered certain distinct advantages. No additional level of government would be required because the County would actually become the metropolitan unit.
All services requiring administration on a City-County basis could
thus be assigned to it. The county offices in St. Louis City would
be abolished and the functions presently performed by the Metropolitan St. Louis Sewer District would be absorbed. This alternative would simplify the governmental structure and eliminate
many deficiencies in the existing service pattern of the area.

Despite the impressive merits of an urban-county arrangement, the Survey decided that it would be inadvisable to recommend its adoption. Three major factors prompted this decision:
the absence of an existing legal means of putting such a plan
into effect, the need for major reorganization of the County
government, and the political unpalatability of the plan. A board
of freeholders appointed under Article VI, Section 30, could draft
a proposal providing for only the first step in the creation of an
urban county—the reëntry of the City into St. Louis County. It

could not include the second essential step—the extension of the County government's jurisdiction over matters of metropolitan concern in incorporated as well as unincorporated areas. This enlargement of powers could not be accomplished currently by local action; it would require state constitutional as well as possibly state legislative changes.

Considerable reorganization of the County government, particularly of its administrative machinery, would also have to be made before it could function effectively as a metropolitan agency. The necessary changes include a reduction in the number of elective officials performing administrative duties and an extension of the merit system. Of even more importance, these organizational reforms would have to be accompanied by a change in attitude toward the County government. Both citizens and public officials alike have generally been reluctant to recognize the new role that the County must assume in a highly urbanized area. Many of them apparently cling to the belief that the municipal governments rather than the County should perform all urban services. They are as yet unwilling to accept the fact that many of these functions now go beyond municipal boundaries and therefore call for administration on a broader geographical base.

The political drawbacks to the adoption of an urban county include the opposition of Republican leaders in the County and the fear of many suburbanites that County affairs would be dominated by City residents under such an arrangement. There is also the potential opposition of City Democratic organizations, as the county offices in the City would be abolished and these patronage sources would disappear.

ENLARGEMENT OF COUNTY POWERS

Some County political and civic leaders who were interviewed said the need for a metropolitan agency would be eliminated if the County government assumed control over functions that the suburban municipalities are individually unable to handle adequately; one government in St. Louis County possessing such responsibilities could easily coördinate its activities with those of the City. There seemed little doubt that an arrangement of this kind would be palatable to the political leaders in the County. There was also the possibility that this proposal might stimulate the County government to reshape its organization and structure in order to avoid a more far-reaching solution. The mayor of the

city of St. Louis also felt that coördinated action could be successfully achieved if the City could deal with a single government in
the County.

This approach contemplates in essence the creation of an urban
county that does not territorially include the city of St. Louis.
The Survey staff carefully examined the feasibility of such a
proposal, but concluded that it offered no solution to the problems
of the metropolitan area. The staff considered the establishment
of a City-County commission composed of representatives of the
two governments who would serve in advisory and coördinating
capacities. This kind of arrangement might be helpful in foster-
ing coöperation in certain fields, such as public health and police
protection, but it would provide no remedy for those area-wide
functions requiring unified administration and unified financing.
Sewage disposal, the control of mass transit and traffic, and
similar services cannot be handled satisfactorily on a coöperative
basis by different governmental units. Special metropolitan districts would still be required.

METROPOLITAN DISTRICT GOVERNMENT

As the work of the Survey proceeded, the desirability of creating a metropolitan level of government to handle area-wide
functions became more apparent, and such a solution closely
conformed to the Survey guidelines. The staff members felt that
the proposal for such an agency, together with the other recommendations pertaining to the local units, would create a governmental pattern capable of meeting the needs of the community.
They also felt that the establishment of a metropolitan level of
government might spur the local units to solve or alleviate less
than area-wide problems for fear that if they did not do so, additional power would gravitate to the metropolitan agency.

The staff members recognized the shortcomings of the metropolitan district approach. They were aware that it adds another
unit of government to the metropolitan community (the layer of
which this unit would be a part, however, already existed in the
form of the Metropolitan St. Louis Sewer District) and that it
creates jurisdictional questions as any system of divided powers
does.

On the other hand, they were impressed by its decided advantages. The metropolitan district approach offers an effective
means of satisfying unmet area-wide needs of important public
concern while least disturbing the existing governmental pattern.

It is a device that is readily adaptable to local circumstances and requirements and it permits the preservation of local self-rule. Discussions with influential individuals and groups and the sample survey of citizen opinion suggested that such a solution was the only one that would have a reasonable chance of popular acceptance.

When the question was asked in the sample survey whether the persons being interviewed liked or disliked each of five governmental alternatives—City-County merger, the federal system, reëntry of the City into the County, consolidation of County municipalities into a smaller number, and retention of the status quo—the federal system, or the multipurpose metropolitan district plan, received the highest favorable response—54 per cent (61 per cent of those who had opinions). When the question of which proposal the respondents most liked was asked, merger (34 per cent) and status quo (21 per cent) received the highest response. However, these alternatives also received the highest number of "most disliked" responses (27 per cent and 29 per cent, respectively). The federal system was third on the list of best liked proposals with 15 per cent, but it was also the least disliked of all the proposals (10 per cent). Both those who favored merger and those who favored the status quo disliked the federal system least.

It was evident that there was a substantial core of individuals who were strong supporters of merger and another substantial core who firmly supported the status quo. Neither group, however, expressed strong dislike of the federal system.

In proposing a remedy believed adequate to meet the needs of the City-County area, the Survey had two constitutional choices —merger or a metropolitan district. Although merger had substantial support, only 38 per cent in the City and 26 per cent in the County most liked it, whereas 19 per cent in the City and 40 per cent in the County most disliked it. On the basis of this evidence, the staff concluded that merger could not possibly carry in both the City and the County. It also concluded that the federal system or multipurpose metropolitan district was the most feasible. (It should be remembered, however, that the Survey's choice of the metropolitan district was based on more than its mere feasibility.) The federal system was liked by a large percentage of the people, although it was not the first choice of a majority, and it was least disliked of all the various alternatives. The Survey felt that those favoring the other two moderate proposals—reëntry of the City into the County and consolidation of County municipalities into a smaller number—would not be adverse to the federal system. Also, the federal system would be acceptable to many mergerites who would be willing to support less than their full demands. On the basis of the sample survey findings, the conclusion that the district approach seemed to be the alternative most acceptable to the voters was justified.[1]

ORGANIZATION OF THE METROPOLITAN GOVERNMENT

After having made the decision to recommend the creation of a metropolitan district with jurisdiction over certain functions, the Survey faced the next important question: How should such a government be organized? In the lively discussions that followed, the lack of any well-established guidelines for the organization of a metropolitan agency became clearly evident. The relatively little experience thus far accumulated in this field and the complete absence of empirical studies on representation, size of policy-making bodies, and executive leadership in a metropolitan context left the door wide open to diverse views.

The staff readily agreed that any proposed governmental structure should be democratic in concept and administratively flexible. It recognized that these objectives could be attained only if the metropolitan agency were organized in such a way as to (1) assure adequate and fair representation, (2) be responsive to citizen control, (3) provide an efficient administrative system with clear lines of authority and accountability, (4) secure professional competency in administration, and (5) be adaptable to changing conditions. Although there was consensus among the staff concerning broad principles, there was considerable disagreement as to how they could be translated into a workable metropolitan government. Only after prolonged discussion did the Survey reach general agreement on the basic organizational elements of the proposed government. Several decisions were the result of compromise; others were accepted with reservations by individual staff members. As the Survey's second public report, *Path of Progress*, frankly admits, some organizational features recommended for the metropolitan agency are

---

[1] The Survey did not anticipate the opposition of large numbers of mergerites to the district plan, a development that became evident during the subsequent campaign. See chapter 8 for further comments about the campaign opposition.

"subject to differences of opinion"; they "may well evoke alternative solutions."

THE COUNCIL

The Survey proposed that the metropolitan government include a legislative body called the council, and a chief executive designated as the president, who would be both the head of administrative operations and the policy leader. The council would be composed of fourteen members: six elected by City residents, six by County residents, one appointed by the mayor of the City, and one appointed by the County supervisor. Three of the City representatives would be chosen at large and three in single-member districts. Similarly, three of the County members would be selected in County-wide elections and three by districts. The terms of office would be four years and elections would be on a nonpartisan basis with one-half the elected membership chosen every two years.

In determining the composition of the council, the Survey applied the principle of equal representation for the City and County. Precedent for this arrangement had been established in the metropolitan sewer district charter and the same principle had been followed in the defeated plan for an area-wide transit district. Another precedent was contained in the constitutional provision for the appointment of the City-County board of freeholders; under its terms there shall be an equal number of representatives chosen from each jurisdiction. Other important considerations pertained to the traditional and legal separation of the City and County and the general public feeling that neither area should be in a position to dominate the other. In the light of these practices and attitudes, equal representation seemed the only feasible solution. Although there is some inequity in allotting the same number of council seats to each area because of the larger number of City residents, the population differential between the two jurisdictions is rapidly narrowing. At the present rate of increase, the population of the County will equal that of the City by 1967.

The Survey members strongly supported the principle of popular election of council members. They felt that the policy-making function of any public agency exercising broad powers should be entrusted to an elective rather than an appointive board. Experience with the Metropolitan St. Louis Sewer District lent support to this position. Its governing board consists of six members, three appointed by the County supervisor with the approval of the circuit court judges in the County, and three appointed by the mayor of St. Louis with the approval of the circuit court judges in the City. A trustee may be removed by the respective appointing authorities only upon charges of malfeasance in office and only after a public hearing.

There has been considerable dissatisfaction with the sewer district among local officials and residents. A large part of the criticism is unmerited and arises out of impatience with the district's failure to do a ten-year job in two years. Some of the censure, however, seems warranted. The district's public relations and public reporting have been poor and the district has created the impression of detachment from citizen wishes. Moreover, it has acted highhandedly in several instances. Some of these deficiencies are gradually being corrected, but the general belief persists that the agency is not sufficiently amenable to citizen control. This view was emphatically presented to the staff by many community leaders, who clearly indicated that any proposal for an appointed board to govern a general metropolitan government would meet with considerable opposition.

Constituent unit representation, like that used in the Toronto metropolitan governmental system where at least one official of each municipality in the area is a member of the metropolitan governing council, was also considered. This possibility was rejected for two reasons that appeared compelling. First, it would not provide direct popular representation, a feature considered of major importance in view of the strong sentiment in the area against appointed policy-making bodies such as the metropolitan sewer district. Second, the unusually large number of municipalities and the disproportionate distribution of population among them would have made it difficult to arrive at an equitable and feasible system of representation. (An element of constituent representation was included in the plan of government for the City-County area: the mayor of St. Louis and the county supervisor of St. Louis County were each authorized to appoint one member of the metropolitan council.)

The size of the metropolitan council and the basis of its selection were difficult to determine. The staff first discussed the possibility of utilizing the seven existing County councilmanic districts and the seven wards proposed in a new charter soon to be voted upon in the City. By utilizing these areas, the problem of drawing up new ones would be eliminated and representation would be placed on the same geographical bases that the people had already accepted or might soon accept. This plan was rejected early in the discussions. The new metropolitan government might be too closely identified with the City and County governments if the same electoral districts were used. The ward area provision in the proposed City charter had, moreover, aroused intense opposition among numerous voters and there appeared to be a strong possibility (which later materialized) that the charter would be defeated. Some of this hostility would undoubtedly carry over to a metropolitan government plan that utilized the same district arrangement.

Although the suggestion to use these electoral districts was not adopted, the size of the council appealed to the staff. A fourteen-member council seemed to be reasonable in size, and such a body would be sufficiently large to be representative of the total metropolitan community and sufficiently small to be an effective working group.

The decision to elect one-half of the representatives at large and one-half by wards was based upon the unproved but generally accepted assumption that such a system helps to balance localism with area-wide views. Several staff members were dubious; they suggested that all council members (except the two appointees) be elected by district. This arrangement, they argued, would be more acceptable to the people and would meet with less opposition than the combined district and election-at-large proposal. In support of their position, they pointed to the formidable opposition that was being directed against the provision in the proposed City charter to elect one-half of the board of aldermen at large. The Survey finally decided that, in the absence of reliable evidence, it would be wise to recommend the theoretically desirable solution and leave the decision of practicability to a board of freeholders.

The Survey also discussed but rejected the possibility of using representation on the metropolitan council as an incentive for municipal consolidation in St. Louis County. In this connection it considered giving an additional representative to each city reaching a population of 100,000, in the expectation that some of the communities might consolidate in order to strengthen their metropolitan representation. There was considerable doubt, however, that the inducement would have much effect. Such a proposal, moreover, would complicate the problem of representation. In order to maintain equality between the City and County, assuming that no other basis would be politically acceptable, it would be necessary to add to the representation of the former each time a County municipality became entitled to an additional representative.

From the outset of its deliberations on the plan of government, the Survey accepted the principle of nonpartisan elections for the council and chief executive. In the first place, the difference in political composition between the City and County would plunge any plan involving party elections into a bitter partisan fight. Second, the tradition of nonpartisan elections for all local governments (except the city of St. Louis and the County government) was well established in the area. Third, it was essential to keep metropolitan government as free as possible from the charge that it would be dominated by one or the other party. Already some County Republicans viewed the metropolitan government movement as an attempt by City Democrats to gain political control of the County.

THE CHIEF EXECUTIVE

No part of the plan of government evoked more argument among the staff than the manner of selecting the chief executive of the metropolitan government. On the one side were those who maintained that he should be popularly elected on an area-wide basis: the success of the new government would be largely dependent on strong leadership, and a popularly elected chief executive would be better able than an appointed official to provide areawide policy leadership. He would also be in a more advantageous position to bring the people of the area closer together in spirit and objective, to spark their imagination, and to unite their energy in a coördinated program of over-all development. A chief executive elected at large would enjoy great prestige and would be able through bold and imaginative leadership to awaken or shape a metropolitan point of view among the people of the whole area. Since he would be the only elected official who had the entire City-County area as his constituency, he would symbolize or represent the evolution of a genuine metropolitan institution.

The staff members who favored the elected chief executive proposed the establishment of the position of director of administration or chief administrative officer whose occupant would be appointed by and would be responsible to the metropolitan president. In this way executive leadership could be coupled with professional competency.

On the other side of the argument were those Survey members who supported a manager type of government with the administrative head appointed by the council. They contended that this was the more feasible way of insuring good administration and pointed to the trend toward council-manager government in the larger County municipalities. Expressing doubts that a competent individual could be induced to run for election to the metropolitan presidency, they feared that the office would degenerate into a second-rate political post. They also thought that any proposal for an area-wide election would meet with formidable opposition.

During the course of this debate within the staff, which occurred near the close of the deliberations over governmental recommendations, the Survey held an all-day conference with sixteen outside consultants in the fields of government, economics, planning, and urban sociology.[2] The meeting was financed by the Ford Foundation as one of its series of conferences on urban problems. An outline of the tentative recommendations and plan of government had been sent to each of the participants. The consultants were divided into two groups with Survey members assigned to each. Later in the day, the two sections met jointly to discuss their findings and conclusions. During the course of these intensive sessions, the consultants expressed their views on the major aspects of the plan. The manner of selecting the chief executive proved to be one of the prominent points of discussion. A majority of the outside participants were favorably disposed toward popular election. Their reasons corresponded closely to those previously expressed by the staff members who were supporting the elective principle.

The affirmative position taken by many consultants was undoubtedly a persuasive factor in the Survey's decision to recommend popular election of the metropolitan chief executive. Because of the lack of consensus, however, the Survey decided to include in its recommendations report, *Path of Progress*, the statement that as an alternative to popular election "consideration could be given to the proposal that the metropolitan council appoint the chief executive." In this way, both proposals would

---

[2] The consultants were Ethan Allen, W. D. Bryant, Harvey Brazer, William Cassella, Jr., Edward Connor, Robert Daland, Henry Fagin, Lyle Fitch, Lee Greene, Luther Gulick, James Norton, Walter Phillips, Wallace Sayre, Harry Sharp, Frank Sherwood, and Robert Wood.

be before the public and the board of freeholders, with popular election indicated as the preferred method.

POWERS OF METROPOLITAN GOVERNMENT

At the beginning of their discussions about the kind and range of powers to be assigned to the metropolitan government, the Survey staff members agreed to (1) include only those powers that were essential to handle area-wide needs of immediate and vital concern, (2) outline these powers in broad terms so the public report would not become mired in details, and (3) recommend a realistic method of amending the metropolitan charter to permit the assumption of additional functions whenever warranted.

The Survey designed its recommendations for metropolitan powers on the basis of those problems that had previously been designated area-wide in character (see pp. 105-109). One additional function, the promotion of economic development, was added at a relatively late stage in the deliberations over recommendations. The Survey's findings definitely indicated that the local metropolitan area had failed to capitalize fully on its strategic location and its vast potentialities. They also demonstrated that in recent years the City, and more particularly the County, had been unable to foster industrial and commercial expansion on a scale adequate to maintain and strengthen the area's competitive position. As these findings emerged, the staff became convinced of the need for a metropolitan agency with power to assemble and develop large tracts of land for industrial parks. The proposal was presented to representatives of the chambers of commerce, to union officials, and to civic leaders; in each instance, the response was favorable.

The Survey members felt that the metropolitan powers over traffic and transportation must be broad and comprehensive if any substantial progress was to be made in moving people and goods. The powers as finally recommended were decided upon after a comprehensive study of existing transit authorities. Members of the staff visited Toronto to examine the operations of its metropolitan government and its transit commission. They also consulted with traffic and transportation experts in the St. Louis area and elsewhere. The recommendations made no attempt to outline the kind of transportation system that should be established or the manner in which it should be financed. At this time these matters were being intensively examined by another organization.

The Citizens' Metropolitan Transit Committee of St. Louis and St. Louis County, consisting of six members, three appointed by the mayor of St. Louis and three by the County supervisor, had been established in 1955 to make a traffic and transit study of the local area. Its report was due in September, 1958, about a year after the release of the Survey's recommendations. The Survey staff consulted frequently with the members of the transit committee and its engineers. Both groups were aware of the importance of close coöperation. The Survey felt that not only were traffic and transportation the most compelling reasons for the creation of a metropolitan government, but also the winning of public support for its recommendations at the area-wide level would depend largely upon the inclusion of these two functions. The transit committee similarly recognized that the Survey recommendations would pave the way for remedial action on the transportation problem. Both organizations realized that basic differences in their respective approaches to traffic and transit would be disastrous from the standpoint of public acceptance.

The traffic and transportation situation in the area, the two groups agreed, called for the establishment of a single governmental authority with power to plan, construct, and maintain expressways, principal arteries, and major off-street parking facilities, and to control mass transit. This agreement was evident in a memorandum, prepared by the transit committee's engineers for the Survey, which set forth the powers necessary for a governmental agency in the St. Louis area to do an effective job in transportation. The views contained in this memorandum coincided in general with those of the Survey.

As the discussions proceeded, however, it became evident that several members of the transit committee favored a single-purpose authority limited to control over transit and traffic. They indicated their skepticism about including these functions with others in a multipurpose metropolitan district, apparently favoring a specialized agency that would be as free as possible from political interference and that would provide proper insulation for its working staff from any pressures affecting the authority's efficient operation of its service responsibilities. Some of the committee members went so far as to maintain that the professional administrators should have complete power to allocate funds for street construction free from legislative determination. At one point they even carried their case to the mayor of the city of St. Louis. The mayor conveyed their fears to the Survey's executive officer–research director and several other staff members at a meeting in his office. Although the mayor did not comment on the transit committee's views, he told the Survey staff that he had serious doubts about attempting to solve area problems through the creation of either single-purpose or multipurpose districts. He obviously preferred complete City-County merger as the solution, but felt this approach was politically unfeasible. This was not the first occasion on which the mayor had expressed to Survey members dissatisfaction with the metropolitan district method.

The Survey staff tried to convince the transit committee that it would be ill-advised to have individual authorities for each metropolitan service, and that it would be illogical to separate transportation from such other functions as over-all planning. The committee's engineers agreed with this point of view, but the majority of the committee appeared unconvinced. Yet in spite of their preference for a single-purpose agency limited to transportation, the majority of the transit committee members concurred with the Survey proposal for popular election of the governing board. They were aware of the criticism directed at the metropolitan sewer district and they seemed convinced of the need to follow the elective rather than the appointive principle. Matters remained at this stage when the Survey reported its recommendations to the public.

In formulating the recommendations for over-all planning, the Survey was confronted with three basic choices: (1) transfer the planning and zoning function from the local level to the metropolitan government, (2) authorize the metropolitan government to formulate an area-wide master plan that would serve as a guide for, but not be binding upon, the local units, or (3) permit the retention of local planning and zoning powers, but require all local zoning to conform substantially to the metropolitan master plan. The first alternative was rejected as wholly impractical because no local power appeared to be more jealously guarded than zoning. The second choice was considered the most politically feasible of the three; a master plan wholly dependent upon the voluntary coöperation of the local governments would undoubtedly have some persuasive force. The Survey, nevertheless, felt that something more than this bare minimum was absolutely necessary for metropolitan development. It therefore proposed the third alternative modeled in many respects after the Toronto plan.

The Survey did not have much hope that the third alternative would ultimately be adopted by a board of freeholders. Yet it felt that by asking for more than could be expected to materialize, but not so much as to destroy all possibility for establishing a common ground of discussion, the stage would be set for some acceptable compromise. Such a compromise, for example, might take the form of an arrangement under which the metropolitan government would prepare the area master plan while the local units would be required to submit their zoning changes to the central agency for determination as to their conformance to the over-all plan. The decisions of the metropolitan government would be of an advisory nature only.

In deliberations about vesting certain planning and zoning powers in the proposed metropolitan district government, the Survey gave serious thought to a legal question that also was of concern in its decisions about assigning assessment and economic development functions to this new government. Are planning and zoning "services" that come within the scope of the constitutional provision that permits the establishment of one or more metropolitan districts for the functional administration of services common to the City-County area? The Survey decided that planning and zoning (as well as property assessment and economic development) probably did come within the meaning of the term in the constitutional grant, but it recognized that in the absence of judicial determination there was some doubt.

Deciding upon the nature of the other powers proposed for the metropolitan government occasioned little difficulty. The Metropolitan St. Louis Sewer District would cease to exist as a separate agency and its functions would be absorbed by the new metropolitan government, which would have jurisdiction over a territorially larger area embracing all of St. Louis City and St. Louis County. The civil defense responsibilities and powers of the local units were also defined under existing laws. It would be necessary merely to transfer these responsibilities to the new government.

Property assessment presented several possible solutions. An agency could be established to assess for metropolitan tax purposes; the metropolitan government could be authorized to equalize assessments between the City and County for metropolitan purposes only; or all assessment functions of the area could be consolidated in the metropolitan agency. The first alternative would result in considerable duplication. The second was attractive because it would not disturb existing assessment practices; it would involve, however, the difficulty of determining the actual differences in ratios between City and County assessments, a potential source of much dispute. The Survey selected the last alternative as the most workable and economical, even though it might generate the most opposition. By making one agency responsible for the assessment of tangible property throughout the entire area, uniformity in assessment would be assured and the assessment offices of the City and County would be abolished. City and County officials may not look upon this proposal with much favor for they are presently able to determine their own assessment ratios subject to the minimum set by the state tax commission. At present the minimum ratio is 30 per cent of true value.

FINANCING THE METROPOLITAN GOVERNMENT

The Survey decided to avoid an extended treatment of metropolitan financing in its recommendations to the public for several reasons. First, the charter of a metropolitan government should contain broad fiscal powers and should have considerable latitude in determining how its services are to be financed. The Survey recommendations therefore simply provided that the metropolitan government must have power to levy and collect taxes and to issue both general obligation and revenue bonds. Second, the principal problems of financing the agency related to the transportation and traffic functions. Because the transit committee as a major aspect of its work was intensively examining the area's fiscal needs in these fields and the best means of meeting them, it appeared inadvisable for the Survey to make detailed recommendations before the completion of the transportation study. Third, a successful method of financing new capital improvements had already been worked out in the charter of the Metropolitan St. Louis Sewer District. The district had taken over all public sewers but had not assumed any bonded indebtedness previously incurred in the construction of the sewers. This indebtedness remained the obligation of the individual municipalities or the old sewer districts. New construction was to be financed by the creation of subdistricts or benefit districts, with the cost being assessed against the property owners in such districts.

Under its recommended powers, the metropolitan government would have authority to take over certain roads and streets in order to establish an integrated traffic system. Because both the City and the County governments were financing new road construction of an arterial nature with bond issue funds, the Survey thought it essential to deal with this question. It accordingly recommended that any bonded indebtedness of a municipality or the County government that is directly attributable to the construction of any street or road designated as part of the arterial system will be assumed by the metropolitan government. Along similar lines, it also recommended that the municipalities and the County should be compensated for any property or equipment that may be taken over by the metropolitan government in the exercise of any of its functions.

AMENDMENTS TO METROPOLITAN CHARTER

The importance of keeping the metropolitan charter elastic enough to meet future needs was clearly recognized. This flexibility, the Survey concluded, could be obtained if liberal provisions for amending the charter were accepted. Survey members agreed that the requirement for separate approval of amendments by City and County voters as provided in the sewer district plan was entirely too rigid. They felt that the most desirable mode of amendment was by over-all majority vote of the electorate of the metropolitan district. Creating a metropolitan government also creates a new electoral base, a metropolitan electorate. Hence it is logical that after establishment of the metropolitan government, charter amendment should be accomplished by a single majority rather than dual majorities.

To determine reactions, the proposal for an area-wide vote was presented to the executive committee of the County Chamber of Commerce and to several other civic leaders in both City and County. The majority sentiment seemed to favor such an arrangement. Several County leaders, however, believed that an open-end approach of this kind would arouse suspicion in many people. They pointed out that some County politicians were already claiming that a multipurpose metropolitan district would be the opening wedge, "the foot in the door," for complete consolidation of the two areas. During the course of these discussions, the suggestion was made that certain services of a less controversial nature, such as public health or regional parks, be enumerated with the proviso that the metropolitan government could assume these particular services by over-all majority vote. All other charter amendments, including the transfer of nonenumerated functions or services to the metropolitan government, would require separate majorities in the City and County. This suggestion was rejected after some consideration; the Survey felt such a provision would be too restrictive as well as confusing to the public.

The question of the legality of amendment by over-all vote was also raised. The constitutional enabling provision specifies a dual majority vote for the adoption of the original plan to adjust City-County relations; does the same requirement apply to amendments? There was no judicial interpretation on this point and the opinion of lawyers varied. The Survey decided to recommend the method it considered the more desirable, namely, amendment by area-wide vote. It took the position that because the constitutional grant makes no reference to the method of amending a metropolitan charter, a board of freeholders would have full discretion to specify the process of amendment. There was no indication that such a proposal would detract from the main objectives of the metropolitan plan even though it would arouse some opposition. A board of freeholders would later be in a position to weigh the possibility that a requirement of this kind might defeat the plan.

In addition to the need for a reasonable amending device, the Survey recognized that the charter must be kept flexible enough to permit the metropolitan government to operate effectively in the future as the area develops beyond the City-County boundaries. It felt that this element of flexibility could be at least partially attained if the charter would authorize the metropolitan government to contract with surrounding counties for the joint handling of common functions. There was also the possibility, as discussed in the next chapter, of utilizing the Bi-State Development Agency for functions that transcend the Missouri-Illinois state line.

7

The Existing Governments

THE BI-STATE DEVELOPMENT AGENCY

THE EXISTENCE of a governmental unit covering the City and the County and two other Missouri and three Illinois counties appeared at the time of its establishment to offer an excellent opportunity for handling metropolitan problems that crossed the state line. However, as previously noted, the activities of this bi-state agency have been most disappointing. Its inability to generate widespread support, its lack of initiative, and its meager accomplishments have virtually stripped this governmental unit of all public prestige. These facts militated against the possibility of revitalizing the agency and endowing it with sufficient power to serve as an effective instrumentality for metropolitan coördination and planning. The Survey was convinced that any recommendations closely linked to the reactivation of the bi-state agency would be doomed to failure. It also felt that if strong emphasis were placed on extending the functional powers of the agency, such emphasis might detract from the proposals for the creation of a metropolitan government in the City-County area. Logically, certain powers, such as over-all planning and control of mass transportation, should be vested in an agency with jurisdiction over the entire metropolitan area. From a practical standpoint, any recommendation for endowing the bi-state agency with such authority would be wholly unrealistic under existing circumstances.

In view of these various factors, the Survey decided to underplay the potential role of the bi-state agency in the plan for governmental reorganization. Recommendations pertaining to the agency were consequently limited in scope and objective. The Survey proposed the removal of certain legal impediments so the Bi-State Development Agency could acquire the Mississippi River bridges and coördinate traffic between the two sides of the river. The agency would then be in a position to develop a unified scheme of traffic control that could be integrated with the arterial and major street pattern of the recommended metropolitan government for St. Louis City–St. Louis County and with the federal and state highway system in the area. As such an arrangement would call for close coöperation between the bi-state agency and the new metropolitan unit, the Survey further recommended that at least two of the Missouri representatives on the agency be officials of the latter government.

The recommendations pertaining to the Bi-State Development Agency are not of major significance. They would, nevertheless, give the agency a limited but important role in solving one aspect of the traffic problem in the area. The Survey's policy toward the bi-state organization was adopted with considerable regret, but no realistic alternative was available. Ideally, the agency might be converted into a true metropolitan government with limited jurisdiction over the entire area. To accomplish this result, action by the legislatures of the two states would be required. When it is realized that the Missouri General Assembly has consistently refused to make even minor changes in the bi-state law, the inadvisability of basing a plan of governmental reform on the reconstitution of this agency becomes apparent.

COUNTY MUNICIPALITIES

The Survey's determination to make recommendations about most types of local governments came soon after deciding the kind of metropolitan government to propose.[1] The promptness of reaching this conclusion grew out of the conviction that improvement of existing local units was the only alternative to assigning more functions to the new metropolitan government. Advocacy of a metropolitan organization other than complete consolidation and concern about the adequacy of local governments that would

---

[1] The decision to strengthen school districts was made apart from that relating to nonschool governments; the analysis of how determinations were reached about school districts is contained in a subsequent section.

continue to function made the Survey's task of formulating a plan of government much more difficult. To have taken another and easier course on either matter, however, would have done violence to the Survey's conclusions, based on extensive research, about what governmental pattern was best suited to the needs and desires of the people of the City-County area.

Analysis of data collected about the governmental units in St. Louis County revealed extensive evidence of need for reform that would improve municipal services. A total of ninety-six municipalities (cities, villages, and towns) range in population from 60 to 53,000 and in area from 32 acres to nearly 9 square miles. One has a density of 80 persons per square mile whereas another has 14,000 per square mile.

More significant than their differences in size are the variations in municipal services in the eighty-six municipalities that could or would supply full information about their functional activities. Of ten basic urban services—police, fire, garbage and rubbish collection, health and sanitation, street repair, street lighting, street cleaning, library, park and playground facilities, and zoning control—only four cities perform all ten and one performs none. Fifty-four municipalities supply less than six.

The variations in the quality of services rendered are also great. Only 33 of the 71 municipalities with police departments have more than one full-time employee. Only 59 municipalities make any expenditures for police activities; many use unsalaried officers on a part-time volunteer basis. Only 17 maintain fire departments with full-time personnel. Other municipalities are in special fire protection districts, contract with public agencies, or depend on private volunteer companies for their protection.

The staff of the Survey became convinced that greater uniformity in number and quality of services was needed in County municipalities, particularly for services in which the entire area is affected by the failure of some municipalities to perform them at an adequate level.

Research on municipalities also revealed the existence of unincorporated areas in the County whose population density approximates that of many local incorporated communities. In these sections the County government is required to render basic municipal services. Their cost is a drain on the general revenues of the County as no special benefit tax is levied. This inequity is a source of complaint from a number of the larger cities. The cities, in effect, pay the costs of municipal services within their own boundaries and help to pay for them in unincorporated parts of the County through general County taxes. Unincorporated urban areas thus receive certain municipal-type services from general County tax funds.

Wide ranges are present in the tax levies of County municipalities. Tax rates vary from no levy at all in a few small villages to $1.30 on $100 assessed valuation in one city. The average levy in nine of the largest cities that provide numerous services is 87 cents.

DECIDING ON PROPOSALS FOR CHANGES

Consolidation of all urban areas in County. Three types of proposals concerning County municipalities were considered by the Survey in addition to the recommendations that were ultimately advanced. One was to consolidate all existing County municipalities and the highly urbanized unincorporated areas of the County into a single large city. This would have resulted in a city of approximately 475,000 population, certainly large enough to supply the full range of municipal services. When this proposal was discussed with community leaders, it evoked strong opposition. Private conversations by Survey staff members with officials of a number of municipalities, particularly the larger ones, community leaders, and some officers of the St. Louis County League of Municipalities about service problems brought forth admissions that there were far too many municipalities in the County and that many of them should be consolidated, disincorporated, or annexed. Few of these individuals would take a public stand on the matter while the Survey work was in progress, but they did indicate that at the appropriate time they would support such a move. Many of them impressed upon the Survey staff members the practical difficulties involved in securing support for change. The local officials in each affected municipality would constitute a group that might oppose change, and they were in a position to influence many voters in their own areas to follow their lead.

In some instances the local municipal officials and employees who expressed opposition to governmental change were undoubtedly motivated by fear of losing their jobs or their positions of influence. In other instances, officials who opposed the loss of local autonomy sincerely believed in the continued existence of their municipalities; this attitude was especially prevalent in the larger suburban communities. These individuals were not concerned with losing their governmental offices; many of them occupied positions of influence in other spheres of private and public life. They were firmly convinced that their municipalities were providing a high level of service and were giving the residents better treatment on matters of local concern than they would receive from a bigger governmental unit. A number of prominent citizens in these communities expressed similar views. They had no desire, they stated, to get lost in the labyrinth of big local government. They felt they had greater access to their local officials and that their complaints were acted on more promptly than they would be in a larger unit of government.

The general reaction of leaders in the County toward government in the city of St. Louis influenced their attitude toward the proposal for a single city in the County. They were outspoken in their criticism of what they referred to as big-city politics. Elections in the City are on a party basis while nonpartisan elections are held in all County municipalities. Criticisms by County civic leaders followed a similar pattern, and both metropolitan papers regularly carried articles attacking politicians in the City. The papers maintained that political control in many City wards had resulted in the election of aldermen who did not work for improvement of the entire city, but rather for their own local ward areas. The well-established custom of aldermanic courtesy had made it almost impossible to develop programs of City-wide traffic control or protect the City's land-use plan against spot-zoning proposals. In short, County leaders opposed any proposition that they thought might bring to the County the kind of local political control they observed in the City.

The Survey staff was convinced that sufficient positive evidence of advantages resulting from the creation of a single city in the County could not overcome the strong opposition such a proposal was sure to encounter. And it was by no means ready to agree that small, well-governed municipalities are inconsistent with the goals of an urban population.

Extension of County powers. A second possible method to achieve more uniform services in the numerous County municipalities was to give the County government responsibility for performing certain basic municipal services, such as police, health, and fire protection, on a County-wide basis. St. Louis County under this arrangement would become an urban county performing many municipal-type services within both incorporated and unincorporated areas. Two factors made this approach impractical.

First, the provision in the Missouri Constitution which permits the more populous counties to exercise the power of home rule specifies that such counties can perform municipal-type services in unincorporated territory at their discretion, but that they can perform such services in municipalities only when approved by a vote in each municipality affected. Furthermore, any municipality can by majority vote withdraw such approval at any time. The urban county approach could be successful only if the County performed services in all County municipalities, and this could not be achieved except by amending the constitution.

Second, constitutional tax limits on large counties in Missouri are so rigid as to make the financing of municipal-type services by them virtually impossible. St. Louis County is largely dependent on general property taxes for its revenues, and the maximum the County can levy for general purposes is 35 cents on $100 assessed valuation. This limitation would not be serious if the County were permitted to levy special taxes applicable only in the areas where it supplied municipal services, but the state constitution is generally interpreted to require uniformity of County tax rates throughout the entire County. The inability of the County to establish special taxing districts and its limited taxing power made recommendations assigning major municipal services to it impractical.

The six-city proposal. A third proposal—consolidate the ninety-six existing County municipalities and the densely settled unincorporated areas of the County into six cities of nearly equal size —was considered by the Survey. This would result in cities with populations ranging from 75,000 to 100,000. Such an approach had certain advantages over the two discarded by the staff. Cities of this size could effectively provide a full range of essential services because of the extent of their financial resources and they would be small enough that people would feel their officials were responsive to their needs. Although community leaders had never committed themselves on how large they thought cities in the County should be, they had indicated that they would not view this kind of recommendation unfavorably.

At the time this six-city possibility was initially formulated, the Survey felt that its statistical study of factors affecting local governmental cost would demonstrate that cities of this size (or of some other size larger than generally existed in the County) could supply basic services much more economically than the many existing small municipalities. The consolidation into six cities was adopted tentatively as a working proposal. It was constantly considered subject to possible change in view of the forthcoming findings of this statistical study, one of whose concerns was whether the expenditure per unit of service decreases as population size of a governmental unit increases, either up to a certain point or indefinitely. If the statistical findings subsequently showed that economies stopped short of the 75,000–100,000 population level, the number of cities specified in the proposal doubtlessly would be increased beyond six. It is very doubtful, however, that the number would be further reduced if the statistical evidence conclusively indicated that even greater economies per unit of service would result in cities of more than 75,000 to 100,000. Such a proposal would too closely resemble the idea of complete consolidation of all urban territory in the County, which had been discarded earlier by the Survey.

Two factors led to the abandonment of the six-city approach. The County supervisor in a widely publicized speech recommended the establishment of six local political subdivisions in the County to replace all the current municipalities. The Survey had not suggested that the speech be delivered, but the supervisor was aware that the staff had a somewhat similar proposal under consideration. (One major difference of the Survey's proposal was that it did not involve the rural portions of the County.) In fact, the supervisor had discussed the matter of municipal consolidation with the staff. Although the Survey did not urge him to advocate consolidation publicly, his decision to make the speech proved helpful. Public reaction to his remarks was prompt and almost unanimously negative. Leaders in the large voting centers of the County were outspoken in their opposition.

The staff might have stayed with this approach in the face of such evidence of strong opposition if its study of the factors affecting local governmental cost had demonstrated clear and substantial economies of scale in a number of services provided by the more populous County municipalities. Evidence of substantial saving could seemingly overcome some of the opposition that had appeared so quickly to the supervisor's proposal. When this study found little possibility of significant economies, the staff lost the major basis of support for the proposal.

Not all staff members were convinced that the factor analysis study produced conclusive evidence that economies would not result from the consolidation of numerous County municipalities;

the number of cities in various population ranges was too small to give a solid basis for analysis. Only one city in the population range from 30,000 to 850,000 was available for use in the study. Some doubt also existed about the soundness of certain elements used in constructing some of the service level indexes. Measuring the level of service in a municipal government is most elusive and necessarily includes only those elements that can be quantified. Many elements not susceptible to statistical analysis may be significant in determining service level. For example, the number of police officers, their level of formal education, and the quantity and quality of available equipment can be measured objectively, but factors not so readily susceptible of such measurement also affect police service—the morale of the force, the degree of coöperation between various police units, the feeling of public duty instilled into police officers by their supervisors, and the extent of public coöperation achieved are all essential to effectiveness. Even though some staff members doubted the validity of the conclusions of the study of factors affecting local governmental cost, it was clear that opposite conclusions could not be adequately substantiated by other Survey research to serve as positive support for extensive consolidation.

Two basic values were considered significant in finally arriving at proposals for changes in municipalities. (1) Certain essential services need to be performed at an adequate level throughout the City-County area, and (2) local units should not be abolished unless it is demonstratively necessary to insure a desired uniform minimum level of service.

Three services—police protection, public health, and fire protection—were considered sufficiently significant to require assurance that they would be maintained at an adequate level, but sufficient evidence did not exist to demonstrate that they could not be performed satisfactorily at the local level. There was no question that the city of St. Louis had facilities to deal with these problems within its boundaries. Therefore the immediate need was to provide a framework to insure adequate levels of certain services throughout the County.[2]

---

[2] It is impossible to state conclusively whether the Survey would have recommended the consolidation of County municipalities into a much smaller number if the statistical study had shown important relationships between per unit expenditure and population size of local governments. The Survey probably would have done so because of its concern about the large number of municipalities, many of which seemingly had no sound reason for existing in a metropolitan community. On the other hand, it eventually was very impressed with the merits of the minimum service levels approach and the

Establishing Minimum Service Levels

Police service. Insuring adequate police service throughout the County was appraised to be very important. A reasonably good case could have been made for a single police force for the St. Louis City-County area, but a number of factors weighed heavily against such a recommendation. Only three years before, a special citizens' committee had been created to propose a plan for improving police protection in the County. This committee considered the feasibility of a single police force for the City-County area and finally advised against it, primarily because of the opposition sufficient to defeat such a proposal if presented to the voters. Instead, this commission proposed a county police force to replace the local sheriff and his deputies. Such a force has since been created and is rendering improved service. Its prestige in the County has been constantly increasing. The police forces in the larger cities of the County are greatly respected by the public and maintain high professional standards. Any attempt to replace them with a City-County, or even a County-wide, force would face the strongest kind of opposition. Survey research, moreover, did not discover definite evidence that either greater efficiency or economy would result from such consolidation.

Opponents of a single police department acknowledged the need for greater coördination and coöperation among the local forces in the County, and the County police department seemed the most appropriate agency to be given this responsibility. Administrators of local police forces readily admitted their inability to support certain special services. The Survey staff consequently decided to recommend the assignment of special police functions to the County police department on a County-wide basis. These services were (1) uniform record-keeping, (2) central dispatching, (3) training programs, (4) central crime detection laboratory service, and (5) special criminal investigation service. It was also recommended that local police officers be deputized by the County department and be subject to call by the County police chief in emergencies. These centralized services were to be supported by a County-wide tax.

The next major questions to be decided were (1) how to assure an adequate standard of service in each municipality, and (2)

---

objectives that could be attained as it developed the specific details of this proposal, which it finally recommended.

which municipalities should be permitted to maintain their own police forces. No objective measure existed to determine how large a municipality should be in order to maintain adequate police service economically. Therefore, the Survey staff decided on the basis of conditions existing in St. Louis County. It was assumed that no police service could be considered adequate unless maintained by full-time paid police officers on a 24-hour basis. This would require a minimum of four full-time officers in any jurisdiction. When this standard was applied to the municipalities of the County, only one of the 70 of them under 4,000 population came up to the minimum. Furthermore, only three above 4,000 failed to meet this minimum standard, and in them a large number of police officers were employed on a part-time basis. Because the municipalities seemed to be divided so clearly at the 4,000 mark, the staff decided to recommend that any one of 4,000 or more should be permitted to maintain a local police force if it so desired. Service for all other incorporated and unincorporated areas would be supplied by the County police department.

An arrangement had to be devised to insure that each municipality of 4,000 or more which elected to maintain its own force would meet a minimum standard of adequacy. A system of tax rebates was judged the most effective means. Fortunately, such a proposition could be easily justified because municipalities were already paying County taxes to support the County police department, even though the department's activities were limited almost entirely to unincorporated areas. The proposals provide that the legislative body of the County would, with special technical assistance, prescribe a "minimum level of adequacy" that a municipality would be required to meet in order to qualify for the tax refund. The amount of refund available to each city would be based upon actual cost of maintaining service at the minimum level computed by a formula established by the County council. No rebates would be available to municipalities, regardless of size, not meeting the minimum standard. The County police, however, would render service to any incorporated community that did not receive a rebate.

An additional feature was designed to have particular appeal to a number of larger County municipalities. Any city desiring to offer its residents a level of police protection above the minimum level prescribed by the County authority would be free to do so. This additional service would have to be supported by a local municipal tax and would not be included in computing the rebate.

This feature was expected to receive support from cities opposed to the creation of a single County-wide police force on the grounds that the central authority would not supply as high a level of service as these cities desired.

A certain amount of tax equalization would also be accomplished by these proposals. Cost of centralized police services would be supported by a uniform County tax. This would spread the valuation of large commercial and industrial properties over the entire County.

Public health program. The study of governmental units operating in St. Louis County indicated a complete lack of uniformity in the nature and extent of health services. Certain health services are provided by the County government to both incorporated and unincorporated areas. These include a child guidance clinic, a child dental clinic, and child health conferences. Programs designed to control tuberculosis, venereal diseases, and chronic diseases, and the keeping of vital statistics records, are also on a County-wide basis, and the county hospital serves all areas of the County.

Such health services as restaurant inspection, rodent and mosquito control, and rabies prevention are rendered at County expense to unincorporated communities. These services are also supplied by the County health department to municipalities, but only on a contractual basis and at the expense of the municipality served.

Only two municipalities maintain full-time health departments. Forty-five contract with the County for one or more of the various health services, but twenty-four provide none whatever.

The Survey took a position on public health similar to that on police. A minimum level of public health service is essential throughout the County. Failure to have such service in one area endangers other areas.

Certainly services supplied by the County health department on a County-wide basis should be continued. Other health services included in a general environmental sanitation program should also be supplied by the County to all areas except those municipalities willing and able to maintain minimum or better standards within their boundaries. No measuring devices could state the size at which a city was or was not able to support a standard health program, but analysis of data available on each municipality showed that none under 15,000 in the County was maintaining such a program. On the other hand, two cities over 15,000 were maintaining high-level public health programs. The evidence thus clearly demonstrated that cities under 15,000 could not be expected to establish adequate programs on their own initiative.

The recommendation was made that the County furnish the full range of environmental sanitation to all unincorporated areas, to all municipalities of less than 15,000, and to any larger city that did not maintain its own program at a minimum level. Any city over 15,000 would be free to maintain its own health program at or above the minimum level, and if it did so, a tax rebate equal to the cost of maintaining such a program would be made.

Little opposition was expected to this move toward greater centralization of public health services, since many municipalities were already contracting with the County health department. For two large cities maintaining their own departments, complete centralization at the County level would unquestionably have meant a reduction in coverage if not in quality of service.

The American Public Health Association was conducting a study of hospital service in the City and County at the time the Survey was in progress. Close working relations were maintained between the two projects, and the Survey recommendations were influenced by the fact that the health association study did not recommend the consolidation of City-County hospital facilities.

Fire protection. The third service for which a minimum standard seemed essential was fire protection. The quality of this protection in any urban center directly affects surrounding areas. Certain factors, however, made it difficult to deal with this service in the same manner as with police and health. First, the County government was not rendering fire protection in any part of the County. Second, most County municipalities were already convinced they could not afford to maintain their own fire departments. The existence of eighteen special fire protection districts serving a large number of County municipalities was striking evidence of this belief. That a large part of the County was still rural also presented a serious problem were fire protection to be made a County responsibility. Certainly these rural areas would oppose a centralized County department supported by a uniform tax; the great need for fire protection is in the urbanized areas.

While the Survey was doing its work, a disastrous fire in a private nursing home less than 100 miles from St. Louis prompted the County council to establish an office of supervisor of the division of fire and accident prevention. The function of this office was fire prevention rather than fire fighting, but the council's action did set up an administrative unit at the County level which could centrally perform certain useful services. The Survey recommended that this agency be authorized to prescribe and enforce a uniform fire code for the entire County, set up a training program for all fire fighters in the County and issue certificates of competence to those who met its standards, establish a central alarm system to serve all fire departments in the area, and supply leadership in working out coöperative agreements among the various departments to increase fire-fighting potential. No tax rebates were necessary on fire protection as the County would not be rendering any service to unincorporated areas that it was not also offering to municipalities.

The Survey concluded that if seven major services were assigned to a metropolitan district government and the three functions just discussed were performed at a standard level of adequacy under supervision of the County government, the remaining governmental services could be adequately handled by existing local units.

MUNICIPAL AND DISTRICT BOUNDARY CHANGES

Substantial evidence that a majority of the municipalities in the County were not performing basic services and were not financially able to do so prompted the Survey to make recommendations about disincorporation, consolidation, and annexation. The confused condition of Missouri statutes on the latter two subjects indicated a need for general revision.

Because under Survey recommendations important services generally performed by cities would no longer be within the province of the 71 municipalities of less than 4,000 people, such incorporated places might be encouraged to disincorporate, annex to larger cities, or join in a consolidation plan. To insure that the people in these communities would have an opportunity to vote on the question of disincorporation, the Survey recommended that this type of election be required in each municipality under 4,000. The County government would then perform municipal-type services for all such areas having voted to disincorporate, unless they consolidated or were annexed to another municipality.

Two requirements seem essential if substantial municipal consolidation is to be achieved. First, some authority should be required to plan an over-all consolidation program. This is a significant feature of the school reorganization law of 1948 and has largely accounted for its success. The authority should be representative and politically responsible if it is to gain public confidence. The County council seemed to be the authority that most nearly met these stipulations and the Survey recommended that it be assigned this responsibility. Second, if substantial consolidation is to be accomplished, there must be assurance that specific proposals will be presented to the voters. Experience with school consolidation demonstrated that little can be expected if a consolidation election has to be originated by local school districts.

The most significant change in the consolidation law recommended by the Survey relates to the vote needed for approval. The existing statute requires a two-thirds majority in each municipality involved. None of the school district consolidations that have taken place under the reorganization law would have been successful if such a vote had been required. A simple majority within the entire area to be consolidated and a simple majority vote within each municipality involved appeared desirable. Such a scheme would, however, permit a single small municipality to block a large consolidation proposal. The Survey therefore recommended that if an over-all majority was recorded but one or more individual municipalities cast an unfavorable vote, the County council should have authority to (1) declare the consolidation in effect as proposed, (2) declare the consolidation in effect except for those municipalities where the vote was negative; or (3) declare the proposal defeated. This approach is based on the judgment that the County council as the most representative body in the County should be competent to determine when the general interest of an area in which a consolidation election has been held should be paramount to the more local interests of its parts.

State statutes setting forth annexation procedures are badly in need of clarification. Before 1953, cities were permitted to annex adjacent unincorporated territory without a favorable vote of the residents of the areas to be annexed. After there had been compliance with such annexation procedures, residents could file suit in the courts to have the annexation set aside as unreasonable. In 1953 the statute was changed to require the annexing city to seek a declaratory judgment from the courts before an annexation could be completed. The city making the petition is required to show the reasonableness of the annexation and its ability to render municipal services to the area to be annexed. Court rulings on the new law have held that special charter and home rule charter cities are not subject to its provisions, and there is still doubt as to whether incorporated towns and villages are included.

Many small municipalities in the County had been annexing large areas of undeveloped land. When an area was annexed to an existing municipality, it was no longer under the authority of the County planning and zoning commission; this situation made extremely difficult the preparation and execution by the County of comprehensive planning and zoning. The Survey felt that a single authority should be empowered to pass on all proposed annexations; and as a recent legislative act had given this power to the courts in relation to certain classes of municipalities, it was decided to recommend that the declaratory judgment procedure be made applicable to all municipalities in the County.

A difficulty over the operation of the declaratory judgment law arose relatively soon after its passage. Petitions were often presented by two or more cities for annexing the same unincorporated territory, and the courts had no specific instruction about the order in which competing petitions should be heard. The Survey recommended the correction of this defect through giving the court authority to serve notice when a certain city had filed a proposed annexation petition and fix a time limit within which competing petitions could be filed; the court could then, after expiration of the time limit, determine which of the proposed annexations would be in the general interest.

The eighteen special fire protection districts serving a large number of municipalities as well as unincorporated urban areas presented a serious problem. The Survey staff felt that fire protection should be administered as a regular service by incorporated communities, with the County government performing a coördinating function. Until major municipal consolidations are completed, however, most of the municipalities will not be financially able to assume this function. There thus seemed to be no practical alternative to continuing fire protection as a function of a special purpose district. The high insurance classification of property in a number of these districts coupled with their heavy dependence upon volunteers showed that the present district pattern was unsatisfactory. Consolidation of existing districts offered the best current means of improvement. Since problems relating to merger of fire protection districts were the same as those encountered in municipal consolidation, the Survey recommended endowing the County council with the same authority over consolidation of these districts as over municipalities.

The Survey's approach to improved services in the municipalities of St. Louis County seemingly offered, under prevailing conditions, the best chance for success. Consolidation of all County municipalities into one large city or a small number of cities could not be accomplished without more positive evidence of resulting advantages than the Survey could produce, and constitutional obstacles made the urban county idea improbable. Therefore, the establishment of minimum levels of certain municipal services, with the County supervising and supplying the services, constituted a meaningful and practical approach.

ST. LOUIS COUNTY GOVERNMENT

The Survey's recommendation to retain the territorial separateness of the City and the County meant that the County government would be the only authority able to perform and supervise functions on a County-wide basis. Consequently, this government was assigned greater responsibilities in police protection, fire protection, public health and sanitation, and tax collection.

The staff was convinced that the County unit, as presently organized, could not effectively administer these new responsibilities. But even more important, strong evidence existed that a highly influential segment of the public would be unwilling to see the authority of the County increased unless significant changes were made in its structure. An increase in the power of the County would necessarily be at the expense of the powers of the municipalities in the County. Some of the larger cities were operating under recently adopted home rule charters and had gained a public reputation for efficiency. In fact, their residents had good reason to feel that the present County government was not so efficient as their own.

Furthermore, many municipal officials felt that the County government was inept and too politically motivated, and that some functions currently being exercised by it were not being performed competently. Evidence in some fields—poor assessment practices, failure to mechanize collection records, and impotency in expediting the bond issue programs—supported such attitudes.

Like other county governments in Missouri, St. Louis County was created to facilitate the performance of state functions within its boundaries. In general, county governments are more concerned with problems in the unincorporated areas than with services in municipalities. The rapid urbanization of St. Louis County, however, had forced the government to undertake many services of a municipal type, largely confined to the urbanized sections outside the corporate limits of any municipality. The changing nature of governmental problems in St. Louis County had convinced many of its leading residents that the old form of government set up by state statute was inadequate to meet current needs.

In 1950 the County voters approved a home rule charter pursuant to provisions of the 1945 Missouri Constitution. This charter provided for a governmental structure not unlike that of a city with a mayor-council form of government. The County executive, however, corresponded more nearly to a weak rather than a strong mayor, because a number of important administrative officers were popularly elected.

Dissatisfaction with the County government was already evident when the Survey began. In 1954 the people approved a charter amendment proposed by a citizens' committee which created a County police department to take over the law enforcement functions of the popularly elected sheriff and constables. Although this force was designed primarily to police the unincorporated areas of the County, it was authorized to contract with municipalities for such service.

Other evidence of dissatisfaction with the County government was the preparation by the County council of a group of proposed charter amendments designed to reorganize the administrative structure. The council was conducting a series of public hearings on its proposals at the time the Survey was in progress. Impetus for council action had come from several sources. A series of editorials in the metropolitan press had criticized the administrative structure provided by the County charter and called for quick reform action. Another voice for charter reform was that of the League of Women Voters of St. Louis (consisting of various units in the City and the County), which had been studying the charter with a view toward making specific recommendations or endorsing proposals emanating from the County council. The league was prepared to push for immediate County council action, but decided not to do so after consulting with the Survey staff, which felt that the movement was ill-timed in view of the Survey's forthcoming broader recommendations about County government. Moreover, several council members publicly stated that the council should make no reform proposals until the Survey's recommendations were issued. Not all of them took this position because of high regard for the Survey, but because it offered a justification for delaying reform at least temporarily.

NEW RESPONSIBILITIES

Certain parts of the Survey recommendations relating to municipal services called for action by the County government which would directly affect the County municipalities. It seemed imperative to provide a County government in which the officials of incorporated communities would have confidence if their support was to be secured. This applied particularly to police protection, fire protection, and health and sanitation. Basically, the County government was to establish minimum standards of service which municipalities were to provide if they were to be eligible for rebates. In the event they did not provide this minimum standard, the County government would furnish the services in those localities, and would retain the tax money. This proposal extended County authority over municipalities much further than exists under present conditions, and stiff resistance could be expected if no substantial changes were made in the County charter.

The County would also be responsible for the collection of general property taxes for all municipalities within its territorial limits—a function now performed separately by all but a few of them. The County police department would also, under Survey proposals, provide general police service to all municipalities with populations of less than 4,000. Additional duties relating to the disposal of garbage and refuse, the development of parks and recreational programs, and the establishment of a system of central financial reports for all governmental units in the County were provided in Survey recommendations.

Even if no additional duties were placed upon the County government, rapid urbanization would increase its burden. Some large unincorporated areas are already as densely settled as certain municipalities, and they are increasing in size and new ones are developing. Such areas require municipal-type services similar to those needed in incorporated centers. Such services can be supplied by newly formed municipalities, by annexation of the area to an existing one, or by the County government. Because the County council has attempted to resist new incorporations, and proposed annexations have produced extended litigation, many areas have demanded services directly from the County.

Attention has previously been called to the inequity involved when the County government by means of a County-wide tax renders services only to unincorporated areas. This inequity would not result if the County could legally establish special service zones in the urbanized areas and levy a special tax there to pay for localized services supplied by the County. This is not now possible; the state constitution requires taxes to be uniform upon the same class of subjects within the territorial limits of the authority levying the tax. The Survey did not want to recommend the creation of special service zones in the face of this constitutional inhibition.

CHANGES TO STRENGTHEN THE COUNTY

Examination of the County government convinced the staff that the executive and administrative provisions of the charter were the focal points of most responsible attacks. It therefore decided to concentrate on these matters in an effort to increase public confidence in this government.

The chief executive of the County was popularly elected. The incumbent had held one of the most important positions in the County government before the new charter was adopted. His integrity and devotion to duty were not challenged, but he was not a trained public administrator. In the County, all five cities having home rule charters had adopted the council-manager form of government, and the level of administrative competence in them was higher than in the County under the elected executive. The Survey seriously considered the advisability of recommending the substitution of a county manager for the elected supervisor. The fear that an appointive county manager could not provide the political leadership needed to gain public acceptance and Council approval for Countywide programs led some staff members to support the principle of popular election of the chief executive. The staff did not feel that one type of chief executive was clearly superior to the other for St. Louis County; therefore it submitted the alternatives of appointed manager and elected executive. The recommendations specify that in the event the latter is preferred, a general administrative officer should be employed to assist the chief executive.

The Survey staff was in complete agreement about other administrative changes. The eight popularly elected administrative officials—county clerk, highway engineer, recorder of deeds, sheriff, treasurer, collector, coroner, and public administrator—

should be abolished and their duties transferred to officers appointed by the chief executive. A unified finance department with all financial functions except auditing was essential if the chief executive was to function effectively. A formal merit system for all County employees seemed the only way to assure residents that public jobs would not be used primarily for political patronage.

If Survey recommendations were followed, the County would assume additional governmental responsibilities, particularly in such important functions as police, fire protection, and public health and sanitation. Reorganization of governmental structure was needed in order to win popular support for assigning the County these new functions and to insure an administrative structure capable of handling them economically and efficiently.

SCHOOL DISTRICTS

The steps that eventually culminated in drafting proposed changes in the school districts in St. Louis County illustrate how emphasis in a research project can shift as the data are collected and analyzed. At the outset, the Survey had no intention of making major suggestions about public education. For example, the "Working Outline of Project," which contains the original research design of the contemplated Survey work, makes only brief reference to public schools. It states that the examination of school districts will be confined largely to their interrelationships with other governmental units, and to the factors prompting and the techniques employed in school district reorganization (see Appendix A).

The first project outline relating to the study of school districts restated the limited objectives set forth in the working outline and attempted further to justify this restricted approach. The reasons behind the limited nature of the school district study, it said, are largely practical. (1) The constitutional provisions setting forth the methods for changing the governmental relationships between the City and the County are not generally interpreted broadly enough to include school districts. (2) The existence of school districts as special taxing units operating separately from general governmental units is specifically recognized in the constitution. (3) The separation of school administration from the administration of other governmental functions is so well established in Missouri that any suggested change might result in such determined opposition that proposals for changes in other governmental units would be endangered.

Staff members were not then aware of the major inequities in educational opportunities that existed among the various school districts in St. Louis County. Moreover, the differences in abilities of the various districts to finance an educational program were not known to the staff. School district reorganization had been advocated in the press, but there had been no concerted attempt to place before the public facts indicating a need for changes in school districts, such as had been done regarding problems of other governmental units in the area.

Even though the research on school districts was undertaken with limited initial objectives, the schedule designed to collect the data was sufficiently comprehensive to secure information from each district on such factors as total assessed value, assessed value per pupil in average daily attendance, tax rates, income, expenditures, state aid, number of years of instruction offered, number of units of high school credit available, area, and pupil enrollment.

Numerous factors contributed to the decision to concentrate attention on proposed changes in the school districts in St. Louis County. The school district in the City was certainly large enough to offer an adequate educational program measured by any established standards. *Your School District,* a report of the National Education Association, recommended that school districts should have an enrollment of from 10,000 to 12,000 pupils to provide an adequate program; the school system in the City has an enrollment approximately eight times this range. Moreover, it has an AAA rating, the highest given by the state department of education. If the Survey had decided to recommend the consolidation of the other governments in the City and the County, it would have been consistent to consider also the consolidation of school districts in these areas. When the decision against consolidation of the other governments was made, no good reason could be advanced to consider combining school districts in the City and the County.

Legal problems would also be encountered if an attempt were made to merge the City and County school districts. The state school district reorganization law under which districts in the County can be consolidated does not apply to consolidations involving both the City and the County. Furthermore, the predominant existing legal opinion indicated that a City-County board of freeholders did not have authority to include schools in a plan to adjust City-County governmental relationships.[3]

DECIDING TO MAKE RECOMMENDATIONS

Analysis of the comparative data on school districts in St. Louis County revealed four important findings conclusively indicating that these units of government should be studied further and possibly recommendations should be made about them. First, wide disparity exists among the districts in the amount of financial support given to the public schools.[4] One district, for example, spends over five times more per pupil in average daily attendance than another. The range is from $112.88 to $638.09. Moreover, the wide difference among school districts in amount spent is present despite the recent adoption of a new state foundation program designed to provide some degree of equalization of educational opportunity, whether students lived in poor or rich districts.

Second, variations among districts in expenditures per pupil reflect differences in financial ability and not in willingness to support an adequate educational program. The measure of willingness to support education can be observed in the tax rates voted by the districts for school purposes; any tax levy above $1 must be approved by the voters. These rates range from $1.68 to $3.58 on the $100 of assessed valuation. Significantly, the district with the lowest tax rate spends the most per pupil for schools; the district with the highest tax rate is second lowest in the amount spent per pupil.

Differences in the value of property within districts make it possible for some of them to spend more than others and still keep tax rates low. General property taxes constitute about the

---

[3] Since the issuance of the Survey's recommendations, some legal opinion has arisen to the effect that merger of the governments of the City and County under the first alternative in the constitutional section authorizing the adjustment of City-County relations would automatically effect a consolidation of all school districts. This opinion, even if valid, would not have altered the Survey's approach to the school district problem in view of its decision to recommend a metropolitan district rather than a single municipal government for the area.

[4] Figures for the latest available school year, 1955–56, were used in making the analysis; figures for 1956–57 demonstrate the variations to be as great. Comparisons were based on current operating expenses excluding debt service, as they indicate the actual amount spent for educational effort. The addition of debt service and capital expenditures could easily have biased the comparisons; older districts had already constructed their physical plants and in some instances most of these facilities were already paid for.

only local source of revenue for school districts, and the uneven distribution of commercial and industrial properties in St. Louis County has resulted in widely varying tax bases. The range of assessed valuation per pupil in average daily attendance extends from a low of $2,201 to a high of $37,521. Only three districts in the County have an assessed value per pupil as high as the school district in the city of St. Louis. Thirteen of the 29 districts in the County have assessed valuations of less than $10,000 per pupil in average daily attendance while three have valuations in excess of $20,000 per pupil.

Third, the quality of the educational programs offered by the districts in the County differs markedly. Classification ratings, assigned by the state department of education and based upon quality of instruction and breadth of program offered, furnished evidence of this disparity. The ratings from the top are AAA, AA, and A. School districts not meeting the minimum requirements are rated either U or APP; U rating means the school is unclassified while APP means that the school is approved for credit only.

The school district in the city of St. Louis and some of the systems in the County have AAA ratings. Five of the 26 districts in the County which maintain high schools are below AAA, and two are approved for credit only. Three districts in the County maintain elementary grades only. Furthermore, the number of high school credits available to students varies from 31½ to 69½ credits. It became apparent that the smaller districts have the least adequate educational programs.

The large share of the total local property taxes received by schools was a fourth finding that was important in the decision by the Survey to study school districts more intensively. For example, 62 per cent of the total tax rate in the fifteen most populous incorporated areas in the County is devoted to school district use.

PREVIOUS REFORM EFFORTS

Consolidation of existing school districts has been possible under a general state law since 1931. This law provided for a board in each county to plan practical consolidations. The proposals were then to be filed with the county clerk who would publish them for public inspection. The board, however, had no authority to initiate a vote; such an election could be held only if petitions were signed by at least fifty voters in each school district involved, and separate majorities in each district were required to accomplish a consolidation. Not a single consolidation proposal was recommended by the board during the many years this law was the only means of bringing about change.

No successful realignment of County school districts was accomplished until adoption of the state reorganization law in 1948. The number of school districts had remained relatively stable from 1910 to 1947, never being less than 86 or more than 91. In 1949, just before the effective date of the new law, there were 86 school districts in the County.

Under the new law a county board of education was created to plan a general reorganization of school districts in each county. This board consists of six members selected by vote of the members of all the local district school boards of the county. This county board within a specified time had to submit a comprehensive reorganization plan to the state board of education, which had to return the plan with its approval or with reasons for disapproval. If the original plan was not approved, the county board had to submit a revised plan taking the objections into account.

This second plan was to be submitted to the voters, whether or not it was acceptable to the state. The statutes provided, however, that no plan could be submitted to popular vote without state board approval if it provided for any district with less than 200 pupils unless it included at least 100 square miles of area.

A simple majority of votes within the proposed reorganized district was required for approval. If all the proposed reorganized districts were not approved in the first election, the county board was required to prepare a second plan and submit it to the state board. If this plan was not approved by the state, a revision was to be submitted, and then presented to the district voters, even without state approval. The state law required only two rounds of reorganization proposals, but it did make the county board a permanent institution with power to make further proposals for reorganization at any time. The county board of education has been handicapped by lack of sufficient funds to conduct studies necessary to plan reorganization programs.

By 1954 the number of school districts in St. Louis County had been reduced from 86 to 29 and all but three were maintaining high schools. The 1948 law was not, however, directly responsible for all the changes. Many small elementary districts were annexed to other districts under the still-available old law. Seventeen districts were annexed to larger districts between the time of the elections on the first and the second reorganization plans.

These annexations were brought about indirectly by the reorganization law. Leaders in small elementary districts knew that a reorganization proposal would attach them to a larger high school district not necessarily of their choosing; by annexation a district could negotiate for inclusion in the larger district of its choice, often one that possessed a high assessed valuation. In one instance 11 small districts annexed to a city district containing a number of large commercial and industrial properties. An important consideration in evaluating the reorganization success in St. Louis County is that 19 of the 29 existing districts were not changed by any of the reorganizations.

The success achieved by the 1948 reorganization act is attributable to three of its features that differ from the earlier consolidation laws. First, the reorganization act insured that a vote would be held on proposed plans. Under the consolidation law of 1931, the county board did no more than make public its proposals; initiative petitions were required to bring them to a vote. Second, the county board of education created by the reorganization act is permanent. The board under older laws made only one set of proposals. The newer law required at least a second plan if the first was not completely successful, and it made possible the submission of additional plans at any time. Third, the vote required for approval of a new reorganized district was only a simple majority within the entire area in the proposed district. The older laws required a majority vote in each district involved in a proposed consolidation.

Controversy and Misunderstanding

Immediately before the Survey published its first report, *Background for Action*, the press carried a number of articles dealing primarily with suggestions for revision of the home rule charter of the County. Emphasis was focused on the organization of the regular governmental machinery, but the County supervisor in a report to the County council submitted to the press included a statement about the school districts of the County. Although neither he nor the council has authority to alter school districts, his report suggested the consolidation of the 29 school districts into one, chiefly for greater fiscal economy.

The County supervisor subsequently appeared before the County board of education and urged its members to give the people a chance to vote on his proposal. Press interviews with a number of school superintendents reported strong opposition in the wealthier districts. Other superintendents were noncommittal. The County board of education indicated that a complete study of the proposition was necessary and it had no funds for such research.

The metropolitan and local press gave extensive space to the section of *Background for Action* that presented information about school districts. The newspaper accounts stressed the inequities in tax rates and amounts spent for education, the lowness of the school tax in the City in comparison with various parts of the County, and the smallness of many County districts on the basis of the National Education Association standards.

Although *Background for Action* made no recommendations, its contents were freely interpreted to mean need for change. Certainly numerous school officials concluded that specific Survey recommendations concerning school districts would be forthcoming.

Through individuals directly associated with school officials, the Survey staff learned that many district superintendents were very unsympathetic toward what they assumed the Survey was planning to do. A staff member received permission to appear at the next meeting of the organization of superintendents to present the position of the Survey. The antagonism, obvious from the beginning of the meeting, stemmed from the mistaken assumption that the Survey had already decided to recommend the consolidation of all school districts in the County into a single district. When the superintendents learned that no recommendations had yet been determined, all ill feeling was dissipated; the organization voted to have its executive committee meet with the Survey staff to consider possible recommendations about school districts.

WEIGHING ALTERNATIVES

The Survey favored making recommendations for changes in the 29 school districts in the County on the basis of the inadequacies brought forth by its research. Three major alternatives were considered before a final decision was reached.

One County district. The creation of a single school district throughout the County was especially attractive for a number of reasons. It insured a uniform tax rate for school purposes. The tax base of large industrial establishments and concentrated commercial areas thus would be spread so as to benefit all pupils regardless of place of residence. Some school districts were standing the expense of educating the children of parents who were employed in industrial plants located outside the boundaries of the particular districts. Moreover, this proposal would create a district large enough to offer an expanded high school program, provide education for the handicapped, and make a junior college possible. In addition, with the entire county as a tax base, adequate physical facilities could be constructed for a first class school system.

The idea of a single district was rejected by the Survey after extended discussion among the staff members and with community leaders. The most compelling reason for discarding the proposition was the virtual certainty that it would not be accepted. Almost without exception, community leaders expressed either active opposition or lack of support. Furthermore, most superintendents of the local districts were definitely hostile. Publicly announced support for a single district by the County supervisor had a negative effect on professional school leaders; they looked with misgivings on a proposal emanating from an official of the County government.

Disregarding the chances of its acceptance, there were other reasons against a single district. The approximately 500 square miles of the County would constitute an extremely large area as a single administrative unit. A large part of the area is and will continue for some time to be agricultural in character. The sparsity of population in the outlying sections means that in any election the municipalities would be assured a dominant position. As all directors would be elected from the County at large, the larger urban centers would be given a dominant voice in decisions of the board.

Another important objection to a single district was the certainty that the educational level would be lowered in a number of areas. Some equalization would result—as poorer districts were brought up, others would of necessity be brought down. The staff could see little possibility that the level for the entire County would be brought up to what already existed in the better systems.

Six districts. A second proposal considered by the Survey was the consolidation of the 29 County school districts into a small number of larger districts, preferably six. While this approach was being formulated, the staff was considering a proposal to consolidate the ninety-six municipalities in the County into six larger cities. If these two propositions had been made into recommendations, the boundaries of the school districts and municipalities would have been identical.

This arrangement offered certain advantages. Because municipal and school district boundaries were not coterminous, considerable confusion arose among the County residents. For example, each of five different municipalities lay in four different school districts. Creation of six districts, moreover, would result in units with sufficient student population to furnish, according to a study by the National Education Association, an adequate educational program at reasonable cost.[5]

The decision against recommending six districts hinged on a number of considerations. The practical problem of fixing district boundaries so as to equalize the tax base was very difficult. The rich districts are in geographical proximity, and the poor districts are similarly clustered. Public reaction to the idea of six districts was also influential. During the time the staff was considering this question, the County supervisor created another stir in the political atmosphere. In a public speech given prominence in both the metropolitan and local press, he urged that the County be divided into six governmental districts that would replace the existing municipalities. Later, in an interview with a reporter, he stated that these districts would also operate the public schools. This suggestion, which was in no way prompted by the Survey, acted as a trial balloon, permitting the Survey staff to judge public sentiment on its own proposed six-district plan. Almost all public reaction to the supervisor's proposal was negative. School officials were quick to comment unfavorably and municipal officials also expressed opposition. Public criticism had to be interpreted as opposition to the plan in general, for the supervisor had not specified the exact boundaries of his proposed districts. No doubt additional criticism would have been stirred up if these boundaries had been set forth.

Also, the Survey's research on factors affecting the cost of education found no conclusive evidence that larger districts would result in substantial economies if quality of education were kept constant. The staff had assumed that a large school district could maintain a certain level of educational opportunity at a lower unit cost than a small district could. Lower unit cost was to be a major argument to support the six-district approach.

Some staff members were not convinced that the techniques

[5] *Your School District*, National Commission on School District Reorganization (Washington: National Education Association, 1948), p. 87.

used to measure quality of education were sufficiently valid to justify the conclusion that unit costs in large districts were not less than in small districts. Only those elements of quality that were mathematically quantifiable could be used in arriving at a measure of quality. Certainly many less tangible factors are significant, such as degree of parental interest, intellectual climate of the classroom, the relationship between students and teachers, the relative emphasis on various subject areas, and the kind of classroom discipline maintained, but they cannot be easily reduced to statistical measures. The significant point on which the staff had general agreement, however, was that no positive statistical evidence supported the conclusion that substantial economies could be expected from the creation of large districts.

The practical difficulty of drawing boundaries for six large districts, the unmistakable opposition of powerful individuals and groups to such a proposal, and the failure to discover any statistical evidence of economies from such consolidation led the Survey staff to reject this solution to the school problem in the County.

County-wide equalization. A third possibility considered by the Survey was County-wide equalization based on existing districts. The staff reviewed its school objectives; basically they were to insure educational opportunity at a satisfactory level for every child of school age in the County regardless of his place of residence, and to equalize the school tax burden by spreading the advantages of the assessed valuation of large commercial and industrial establishments over the entire County.

The recommendations ultimately proposed by the Survey are adaptations of equalization proposals used in a number of states. The County board of education would determine what was to be considered a satisfactory level of education, measured in terms of dollars per pupil in average daily attendance. A tax rate uniform throughout the County would then be set to produce the revenue required to sustain this level of education. Sources of income from state aid and other County taxes would be considered in setting the County-wide rate. The tax would be collected by the County collector and distributed to the local districts.

Besides satisfying the objectives established by the staff, these recommendations had certain favorable features not found in the other two types of proposals. First, no school district would have its level of education lowered. Second, each district would receive from the County-wide tax and the state sufficient revenue to provide the standard of adequacy fixed by the County authority, but would remain free to extend its program beyond this standard if its patrons so desired. The extra revenue would be obtained by the local district board levying upon property within the district a tax rate in addition to the County levy. This would avoid absolute uniformity in the educational offering throughout the County.

This arrangement would also promote additional district reorganization within the County. Local school officials readily admit that some districts are too small to finance a balanced school program, but under existing laws none of the larger districts will support a reorganization plan to include them, principally owing to the low assessed valuations of these small districts. When a tax rate is set on a County-wide basis and every district is insured a fixed sum for every pupil, the small district would no longer be such a drain upon the finances of a larger district to which it might be attached. Although the Survey emphasized County-wide equalization, it also recommended further use and strengthening of the current reorganization law. It called for the attachment of any district with an enrollment of less than 1,500 to a larger district, leadership by the County board of education in encouraging public support for other consolidations, and amendment of the state law to permit the board to make expenditures to study the need for additional reorganization.

Recent developments in the County have emphasized the importance of altering the existing school situation in the near future. Very little land available for commercial and industrial development remains in the city of St. Louis and a number of large developments have already started in the County; others can be expected soon. This means that a few school districts will reap the benefits of the new tax base and often will assume very little additional educational burden. The more this takes place, the more determined the opposition of the wealthier districts will become toward any proposals for change.

Certain objections to the Survey plan were anticipated and discussed. The districts with high assessed valuation object to paying taxes to educate pupils in other districts. This represents serious opposition, for districts falling into this class have large voting populations and can be very influential in any County-wide election. It is interesting to note in this respect that the high valuation property in a specific district is usually owned by persons who do not live in the district, and these owners, whose children are not educated in the district where the taxes are paid, would have no reason to object if such taxes were spread over a wider area. In many instances, existing transport facilities, topography, and County planning and zoning actions have determined present commercial and industrial locations.

Some individuals and groups argue that equalization of educational opportunities is a state rather than a county responsibility. This may be true in general practice, but experience in Missouri indicates that the level at which the state will equalize opportunity is far below that desired by school districts in St. Louis County. This argument would have seemed more pertinent to the staff if the adoption of a County equalization plan would in any way hinder the development of a better state-wide program, but the suggested County equalization arrangement dovetails into the present state program. If the state should decide to base its equalization program at $200 per pupil rather than the present $110, this would simply mean that the amount to be raised by a County tax would be reduced by the amount of the increase in state aid.

After considering proposals to create a single school district in the County, consolidate the twenty-nine present districts into six large districts, and establish County-wide equalization, the Survey staff felt the last-named was best suited to the specific needs and desires of the people of St. Louis County.

THE CITY OF ST. LOUIS

The Survey did not make many recommendations that related only to the city of St. Louis. This was due both to official activity then under way in the City and to the large amount of time the Survey necessarily spent on deciding whether the City should be absorbed into a consolidated government.

Major changes in the charter of the City could have been recommended. The charter dates back to 1914 and the basic governmental structure has not been subsequently altered. Substantial agreement among the staff about the nature of such charter changes could have been reached without difficulty. But there was already public recognition of the need for such changes and steps were being taken to accomplish them. During the time the Survey was at work, an official commission, a board of freeholders, was preparing a draft of a new charter for the City. This proposed charter would have to be submitted to a popular vote very near the time the recommendations of the Survey were to be presented to the public.

If the Survey report contained specific recommendations for charter revision which did not conform to changes incorporated into the freeholders' document, the charter opponents might have used them to help defeat the charter. If the Survey recommendations agreed substantially with proposals in the charter and it was defeated at the polls, the possibility of acceptance of at least some of the Survey recommendations on other governments might lessen.

The staff had confidence in the charter commission and felt its proposals would generally be sound. Furthermore, the Survey report would not be available in time to alter the decisions of the charter commission. Consequently, the staff decided to refrain from making suggestions for changes in the internal structure of the government of the City.

This decision was wise; the proposed charter was decisively defeated by the electorate. The Survey was not connected in any way with charter revision in the public mind and therefore was unaffected by the defeat.

On functional problems, the Survey concentrated its efforts on the City-County area and the County. Structural changes concerning them could be expected to result in both improved and more economical service. If after extensive research and discussion the Survey had recommended City-County merger, major internal problems of the City, which could not be appreciably aided by internal structural reorganization through charter reform, would have become the concern of the consolidated government. The Survey's decision to urge the establishment of a multipurpose metropolitan district meant that practically all the existing internal problems of the City would continue to be the responsibilities of the City. When the decision on the preferable City-County governmental arrangement had finally been made, there was not sufficient time left to focus on any internal problems of the City. In retrospect, it is clear that it would have been beneficial to study certain basic difficulties of the City, the most crucial of which is its tax structure.

The City is faced with serious financial difficulties. Approximately one-sixth of its revenues is derived from an earnings tax levied on all residents and on those nonresidents who work in the City. This tax is levied under authority of a state law that applies only to the city of St. Louis. To meet the increased need for revenue, the mayor has tried unsuccessfully to secure authority from the state legislature to increase this tax. The property tax rate in the City is near the constitutional maximum, and very little additional revenue can be expected from this source.

The recommendations of the Survey which call for the establishment of a metropolitan government affect the City in several important ways. The City would no longer be responsible for the performance of three—assessment, civil defense, and traffic control—of the seven functions proposed as proper activities of this larger governmental unit. The metropolitan government would constitute a new taxing authority and it would assume some of the financial burden which the City carries alone.

Another problem confronting the City received attention from the Survey. The flight from the City of both population and industry was analyzed, particularly in terms of how this exodus to the County was producing significant changes in the City. In general, higher income families, most noticeably in the younger age brackets, have been moving to the suburbs. The dwelling units thus vacated are subsequently filled either by lower income groups coming from rural areas outside the City or from less desirable parts of the City. This change has been resulting in deterioration of neighborhoods and new rings of blight. These areas increase the costs to the City of providing health and welfare services, combating crime and juvenile delinquency, and maintaining adequate fire protection. They also make the City a less attractive place to live and work, thereby further stimulating the movement to the suburbs.

Fortunately, by the time the Survey was in progress, the City had embarked on major slum clearance and housing projects, and the planning commission was developing improvement programs in a number of neighborhoods. The Survey recommended the vigorous execution of these projects and the inauguration of others.

One major shortcoming of the governmental structure of the City requires state legislative action. Under the present interpretation of the state constitution, the City must support a set of county officers to carry out county functions within its boundaries. The method of selection, salaries, and terms of these offices are provided by state laws, whereas the charter and City ordinances provide for City offices. This dual set of offices weakens the position of the mayor; a portion of the total budget is administered by officers over whom his control is limited. Various public officials, organizations, and individuals have called attention to the advantages of combining City and county offices in the City, but the state legislature has never acted favorably on these suggestions. The Survey recommended the enactment of a state law authorizing the City to integrate its county functions with its other functions and to assign them to a single set of officers.

The City will benefit from adoption of the Survey's recommendations. It will be relieved of problems with which no government that does not have jurisdiction over the entire City-County area can adequately cope. It will intensify its slum clearance, public housing, and rehabilitation programs, which are of growing significance in the light of the changing nature of the central city. It will become a highly integrated unit of government, freed from the harassments and inefficiencies of numerous independent offices now required by state law. Two large shortcomings will remain, however—the attainment of an improved organizational structure through adoption of extensive charter amendments or a new charter, and the formulation and state legislative acceptance of a better tax system for the City. The installation of all these changes will provide the means for a high level of performance of a wide range of public services in one of the nation's major urban centers.

AN OVER-ALL VIEW

The Survey's approach to formulating a plan of government for the St. Louis area was unique in two major respects. First, the supporting research was interdisciplinary in character, utilizing the services of sociologists and economists as well as political scientists. Second, its objectives were broader than the presentation of recommendations for restructuring the local governmental pattern. The Survey not only examined the immediate public problems of the St. Louis area and the means for their solution, but it also probed deeply into the nature of a metropolitan community as a political, economic, and social organism. This general approach was based on the conviction that local government in a metropolitan area should be studied in the context in which it operates.

Metropolitan reform, as viewed by the Survey, involves more than mere tinkering with the machinery of government. Modifications of the governmental pattern may be ineffectual or even harmful if they are made without a basic understanding of the metropolitan community. It is unlikely that such comprehension can be attained by an administrative management type of study or one that is concerned primarily with organizational aestheticism and administrative effectiveness. Combining governmental units, creating new levels of local government, and reorganizing existing agencies may be conducive to the better operation of a metropolitan complex in terms of efficiency and economy. Standing alone, however, such changes give no assurance of beneficial effect on other community values and objectives.

As the research work of the Survey proceeded, the problem that presently confronts action-oriented research in the metropolitan field became more evident. On the one hand, the assembled evidence showed the urgent need for some type of governmental reform. On the other hand, there was little experience with metropolitan models to draw on and only a modicum of previous research to aid the staff in its work. Only in recent years have social scientists begun to examine empirically the metropolitan community as a political, economic, and social phenomenon. Faced with a close and irrevocable time limit, the Survey was unable to analyze fully the comprehensive data on the St. Louis area complex that it had collected. Even so, its political, economic, and social studies were most helpful in indicating the direction that governmental reorganization in the local area should take. And apart from their immediate pragmatic value, they and other studies subsequently derived from the data should contribute to a better understanding of metropolitan areas and lessen the grossly inadequate knowledge about them.[6]

Metropolitan reorganization should be based on political engineering preceded by careful investigation and analysis. The Survey included comprehensive research in an action setting, but it did not entail widespread citizen involvement during the progress of the studies. Numerous public officials and community influentials were consulted, group interviews were held with representatives of business, labor, civic associations, and political parties, and many informative talks were given to local organizations by staff members. None of these individuals or groups, however, participated in the recommendation drafting process. Nor was any citizens' committee established to review the plan of

---

[6] After the completion of the Survey in 1957, further analysis of certain data was made expressly for this book. And additional analysis and writing, based on Survey research, have been undertaken or are contemplated by several former Survey members.

government before its release to the public. The Survey was conducted under joint university sponsorship. As in other university-sponsored research, the heads of the universities and their governing bodies were not involved in the Survey's recommendations. Ultimate responsibility for the recommendations rested with the two directors on the board of control (one from each university), the executive officer–director of research, and the two associate research directors (again, one from each university).

Would greater citizen involvement in the study process and the drafting of recommendations have created a better climate of receptivity for the proposals? This question is difficult to answer. By excluding outside control, the Survey was able to proceed more rapidly with the research and to formulate recommendations on the basis of its findings and judgments. Thus, it was not forced to compromise or to reshape proposals in order to satisfy the various public officials and private citizens who may have been involved in the studies.

This does not mean that the Survey's work was done in complete isolation from political reality. Every proposal was carefully considered in the light of information derived from the interviews with groups of leaders, the survey of citizen opinion, and the many individual consultations. Possibly there is one serious weakness in this procedure; the existence of a broadly based citizens' committee that has participated in all stages of the studies gives reasonable assurance of a knowledgeable and motivated group to promote the action program once the research is completed. Whether the absence of such a committee during the research work on the St. Louis area was a mistake is debatable.

8

Post-Recommendation Activities

WHAT HAS happened since the Survey made its recommendations, which call for important changes at several levels of government in the City-County area? [1] Considerable study and action have taken place along a number of lines. The most widespread interest and support centered on recommendations for a metropolitan district government.

METROPOLITAN DISTRICT GOVERNMENT

Five days after the release of the Survey's proposals in late August, 1957, the Citizens' Committee for City-County Coördination filed its petitions to establish a board of freeholders to draft a plan adjusting City-County governmental relations. The petitions filed in the City easily qualified, but those in the County were insufficient, according to the local election board, which determined they lacked about one-third of the needed number of legal signatures. Although the committee filed thousands of signatures in excess of the requirement in both the City and County, only 37 per cent deposited in the County were found to be valid.

The attorney general ruled that supplementary petitions to make up the shortage in the initial filing could not be circulated, and consequently the committee had to start all over again the

---

[1] This chapter covers the principal developments during the period from late August, 1957, through early February, 1960. Editorial support by the metropolitan newspapers, which has been widespread, has not been included in the presentation.

task of collecting signatures in the County. About seven months
after the first effort, a new set of petitions were filed with County
election officials, who certified them as containing an adequate
number of valid signatures.

THE FREEHOLDERS AT WORK

The Metropolitan Board of Freeholders was organized in early
May, 1958, and had one year in which to complete its work. It
consisted of nineteen members, nine from the City selected by
the mayor of St. Louis and the St. Louis circuit judges, nine from
the County chosen by the County council and the County circuit
and probate judges, and one from elsewhere in the state designated by the Governor. The board was composed of nine Demo-

Fig. 11. "Interesting piece of goods. Think we can
make a suit out of it?"

crats, eight Republicans, and two independents, drawn from a diversity of occupations, including law (seven lawyers, one of whom was a leader of the City's Negro community), labor, business, and education. Two members were women.

After hearing from numerous people about various problems in the City-County area and discussing several alternative approaches, the board, shortly before the midpoint of its year of existence, voted to develop two plans in detail simultaneously. One was the district plan, involving the creation of a new metropolitan district government to handle certain area-wide services. The other was the merger plan, involving the consolidation of the municipal government and county offices of the City and the municipal and County governments of the County into a single unit. Seemingly early in their yearlong deliberations, the freeholders agreed some form of governmental reorganization was necessary, but at least from the time of the decision to draw up drafts of two proposals, the members became sharply divided over the extent of changes necessary.

About a month after its decision to proceed with two plans, the board voted ten to eight (one member was out of town) to prepare only the merger draft. In the next month, however, it again reversed itself by a fourteen-to-four vote (one member was absent owing to illness) and decided to draft two plans, appointing two committees, each to formulate one proposal. Finally, in mid-

FREEHOLDERS' VOTING ON METROPOLITAN DISTRICT PLAN
BY PLACE OF RESIDENCE AND PARTY AFFILIATION

	For	*Against*
City	4	5
County	6	3
Outstate	0	1
Democrats	4	5
Republicans	4	4
Independents	2	0
City Democrats	2	2
City Republicans	1	3
City Independent	1	0
County Democrats	2	2
County Republicans	3	1
County Independent	1	0
Outstate Democrat	0	1

April, 1959, about three weeks before the expiration of the board, the freeholders chose the district plan over the rival merger plan by the narrowest possible margin, a ten-to-nine vote. One member, originally a supporter of merger, sent his vote in favor of the district proposal by messenger from a hospital, where he was scheduled to undergo an operation on the following day. The decision was in doubt until the final vote was recorded in a roll call.

The vote did not divide along either geographical (City-County) or political party lines. Fourteen of the nineteen freeholders signed the metropolitan district plan at their fifty-sixth and last meeting, held eight days before the end of the board's existence, and signed copies were transmitted to the election officials in the City and the County.

SURVEY RECOMMENDATIONS

The metropolitan district plan, submitted to the voters by the freeholders, adhered in large part to the Survey's recommendations. The district was authorized to perform seven services. Six of them had been suggested by the Survey:

1) control and construction of arterial roads;

2) regulation and, if necessary, ownership of local transit facilities;

3) sewerage and drainage;

4) comprehensive area-wide planning, requiring local zoning and subdividing to be consistent with the comprehensive plan;

5) economic development, principally through acquiring and developing tracts for lease or sale for manufacturing and business purposes; and

6) civil defense.

In the words of one of the freeholders who helped to draft the district plan, "We tried to include in the district plan all functions recommended by the Metropolitan St. Louis Survey, but one is absent." [2] The assessment of property, the seventh function recommended for the metropolitan district by the Survey, was omitted from the official plan because the freeholders' legal counsel doubted the constitutionality of granting it to the district. The one type of power vested in the district by the freeholders' plan which had not been recommended by the Survey related to certain central police services—communications system, uniform crime reporting, police academy, and crime laboratory.

---

[2] *St. Louis Post-Dispatch,* March 15, 1959.

The major organizational aspects of the official district plan also followed or resembled the Survey's recommendations. A strong executive, called the president, was to be elected at large for a four-year term. (Some Survey members, who believed strongly that the ultimate success of the metropolitan government might depend upon vigorous leadership, appraised this suggestion as one of the most important made by the organization.) The governing body was to consist of fifteen members, four elected at large and eleven from single-member districts, serving four-year terms. The Survey suggested a board of fourteen (fifteen if the council named an outside chairman), composed of twelve members elected for four-year terms (three at large and three by districts from both the City and County) and two appointed members, selected by the mayor of St. Louis and the County supervisor, respectively, and serving at their pleasure.

The official district plan ran counter to the Survey's suggestions in two important respects. Elections were to be on a partisan basis. (In retrospect, some Survey staff members concluded the Survey should have been silent on the subject of partisan or nonpartisan elections, leaving the matter open for decision by the board of freeholders.) Amendments to the plan would have to gain the separate approval of voters in the City and County. (The Survey felt its proposal for making amendments subject only to over-all majority vote, although sound in that a metropolitan electorate would be created with the establishment of a metropolitan district, might be subject to a court test; the state constitution made no reference to the amending procedure and no supporting or opposing judicial precedents existed.)

CAMPAIGN AND ELECTION

The special election on the metropolitan district plan, which was termed as important as any conducted locally in the last quarter-century, was scheduled for November 3, 1959, approximately six months after the plan was filed. The campaign was appraised by the *St. Louis Post-Dispatch* as among the most intensive and hardest fought political battles ever witnessed in the area on an issue not involving candidates. Two groups of proponents, the City-County Partnership Committee, which succeeded the Citizens' Committee for City-County Coöperation, and the League of Women Voters of St. Louis and St. Louis County, made up of nine units in the City and County, filled requests for speakers at more than 600 meetings. The league received more requests for information on the district plan than for any proposal on which it had previously taken a stand. Opponents of the plan explained their points of view at more than 300 meetings. The St. Louis educational television station presented a number of discussions, and metropolitan and community newspaper coverage was broad.

In the campaign, the expected opposition to the district plan by those who favored the status quo crystallized quickly. What

Courtesy: St. Louis Post-Dispatch

Fig. 12. "Eek!"

had not been expected—at least before the deliberations of the board of freeholders—was the unbending position of a large number of the mergerites, many of whom apparently decided that retention of the status quo was preferable to adoption of the district system. (It had been thought by the Survey, in view of the results of its sampling of citizen opinion and participation, that many mergerites, as well as those advocating reëntry of the City into the County and consolidation of County municipalities into a smaller number, would favor the metropolitan district idea over status quo when presented with the two alternatives.)

The intransigent attitude of the mergerites was demonstrated by several who had served as freeholders and who took an active part in the campaign against the district plan. About two months after the completion of the freeholders' work, one of them said, "The best thing that could happen would be rejection of the district plan by the voters, clearing the way for appointment of a new Board of Freeholders to try for merger." [3] Caught in the cross fire and stiff opposition of advocates of merger and the status quo and lacking a sufficient number of highly motivated proponents who could successfully counter this onslaught, the plan never mustered sufficient strength in the campaign.

The metropolitan district plan went down to resounding defeat. It failed to gain either required majority, losing by two-to-one in the City and three-to-one in the County. The vote in the City was 21,450 for and 43,237 against, with only 21 per cent of the registered voters participating, which was less than had been predicted by election officials. The vote in the County was 27,633 for and 82,738 against; larger than anticipated, this was about 40 per cent of the total registration. The proposal carried in only two of twenty-eight wards in the City and in only thirty-nine of the County's 353 precincts.

The election defeat was followed immediately by an announcement of plans for a campaign on behalf of City-County merger. One leader in the movement indicated that an effort would be made to get a constitutional amendment adopted, one clarifying the freeholders' power to draft a consolidation plan and substituting an over-all majority for the separate City-County majorities required for adoption. Within a week, six pro-merger members of the recent board of freeholders, along with a number of other people, including the 1956 Republican candidate for Governor, the Democratic national committeeman for Missouri, and the president of the St. Louis Labor Council, met to organize a group to work for merger. The former chairman of the board was selected temporary chairman. The movement proved to be short-lived.

MUNICIPAL AND COUNTY GOVERNMENTS

A committee on municipalities and services in the County, formed by joint action of the County council and the St. Louis County League of Municipalities shortly after the release of the

---

[3] *St. Louis Post-Dispatch*, July 14, 1959.

Survey's recommendations, issued its proposals about a year later. Many suggestions of the committee were identical to or closely resembled those of the Survey. Examples are the initiating role of the County governing body in the consolidation and disincorporation of municipalities and the consolidation of fire protection districts, the preparation of a uniform fire prevention code, and tax refunds by the County government to municipal police departments meeting minimum standards determined by the County government, provision by the County government of five types of specialized police services—special criminal investigation, central uniform record keeping, central dispatching, training, and a crime detection laboratory—to all municipal police forces in the County, and the collection of property taxes for all municipalities by the County government.

At a subsequent meeting of the league of municipalities, its members reacted to the committee's proposals with overwhelming approval of all except the one relating to consolidation and disincorporation.

INTEREST IN PROPOSALS

The proposals pertaining to a County-wide police tax and refund program, central law enforcement records, and tax collection by the County government have generated the most interest. Several months after the committee's report, the County supervisor announced that state legislation would be sought to authorize the County government, after local approval, to levy a special police tax up to twenty cents. One-half of the tax would be refunded to municipalities having their own police force or contracting with the County government for police protection. A bill permitting such a tax passed the lower house of the state legislature in the 1959 session, but failed in the Senate. In late 1959, the same official stated that efforts would be renewed for a similar bill at the next session.

Support for a central records system came in 1959 from the prosecuting attorney, coroner, sheriff, and constables of the County government. Later in the same year, the County justice department, of which these officials are members, passed a resolution approving establishment of a central records and communication center and asked the County council to set aside $25,000 in the 1960 budget for these activities.

Collection of municipal property taxes by the County government has had a favorable reception. The method employed involves contracts with individual municipalities. Although it is utilized on a basis that is far from County-wide, its rapid acceptance is impressive. At the time of the Survey's recommendations, the County government collected taxes for only one municipality. The number increased to seven in the following year and tripled in 1959. More than one-fifth of the municipalities now contract for tax collection.

Further action on Survey recommendations about County municipalities and the County government may be forthcoming. Promptly after the November, 1959, election on the metropolitan district plan, the St. Louis County League of Municipalities organized a number of committees to study and work for adoption of certain recommendations contained in the report prepared fifteen months earlier under its cosponsorship. Among the matters to receive attention are annexation and consolidation laws, police and fire protection, property assessment and collection, and reorganization of the County government.

COUNTY REFORM EFFORTS

There have been sporadic efforts to obtain structural reorganization of the County government. In December, 1957, the County council submitted its proposals for change. Although the suggestions generally were far less comprehensive than those advocated by the Survey, some of them contained elements compatible with Survey objectives: the elimination of the elective status of the coroner, highway engineer, assessor, and tax collector; strengthening of the office of County supervisor through increasing its duties; establishment of an independent audit of County governmental finances; extension of the merit system to any County agency by ordinance action; and creation of the post of budget director.

The report containing the proposals was signed by all except one council member. It urged that such amendments to the County charter as were finally agreed upon after a series of public hearings be placed on the ballot in early 1958. The hearings, which were well attended by County officeholders, employees, and political party workers, brought forth many expressions of opposition to any major alteration. A leading metropolitan newspaper observed in its editorial columns that "Dominating the scene is the distinct impression that the political professionals of both parties—and especially the Democrats who think they smell victory in the wind for next November—

seem to be against any administrative changes sufficiently broad to be effective." [4]

After five hearings were held, a member of the County council criticized the proposed changes as being politically inspired to reduce the number of elective County offices held by Democrats. He suggested the withholding of further changes until the metropolitan freeholders completed their work. (At this time the board of freeholders, which would function for one year, had not yet been organized.)

The early 1958 target date established for submission of amendments to the charter passed without action at the April County primary elections. In August, a councilman announced his intention to introduce bills to authorize presentation at the November election of most changes proposed in the council's report of the previous December. Within a few days, however, he gave up on his effort, deciding there was insufficient time to have the proposals drafted and presented to the council. In October, the same councilman cosponsored seven bills to be submitted as charter amendments at a special election in the spring.

Another member of the council was elected County supervisor in November, 1958, and publicly announced his opposition to charter revision; he favored a two-year trial and then a board of freeholders, if needed. The councilman who had twice initiated actions to get the reorganization proposals on the ballot then moved that the bills be dropped from the council's agenda. He stated that he could not justify the special election cost of about $50,000 since the new administration had promised economies could be realized by enforcing the present charter. His motion was approved by a six-to-one vote. Thus, almost a year to the day after the council had approved a report containing more comprehensive proposals than those in the bills, the same members voted to drop the measures from further consideration.

A flurry of activity, resulting from a breakdown in the mailing of tax bills by the tax collector, finally developed in early 1960. A bill to be presented as a charter amendment in the August primary election was introduced in the County council. It called for abolition of the elective offices of assessor and tax collector and the transfer of their functions and the tax responsibilities of the County clerk to a new department of revenue. The bill stipulated, however, the election of the departmental director.

Meanwhile, a citizens' committee for charter reform was or-

---

[4] *St. Louis Post-Dispatch*, January 18, 1958.

ganized in support of two charter proposals that it drafted—
the appointment of the director of the revenue department and
the inclusion of all employees of the department in the County
merit system. The chairman of the citizen group subsequently
warned the council that unless it adopted the two proposals for
submission to the voters, petitions would be circulated to qualify
them for the November ballot.

SCHOOLS AND BI-STATE AGENCY

The Survey's major recommendation about school districts
urged the establishment of a County-wide financial equalization
plan to assure an adequate level of opportunity in all school districts. A bill, identical in concept and in many details to the Survey's proposal, was introduced in the regular biennial session of
the state legislature in 1959. Relating only to St. Louis County,
the bill provided for an equalization quota, the total required to
provide all districts with a predetermined amount per pupil in
average daily attendance when added to the contributions from
the state and County governments. It directed the County board
of education to establish a minimum level of financial support for
each district and authorized it to certify the total amount required to pay the quota in full.

An organization of school officials in the County had a somewhat similar bill presented in the same session. It also contained
an equalization plan, but required a $3 tax rate by a district as a
condition for full participation in the equalization program.
(Only three of the twenty-nine school districts had such a tax
rate at the time of the Survey's full-time research; it would be
extremely difficult for a number of districts with low per pupil
assessed valuation to levy such a rate.) Neither bill passed.

Of less general importance to the improvement of school programs, but still significant, was the Survey's recommendation
favoring the consolidation of school districts of less than 1,500
enrollment with other districts. All five districts enumerated in
the Survey's proposal were included in a plan presented by the
County board of education in November, 1958, and later approved
by the state board of education. The plan called for these financially poor districts to be attached to more prosperous ones,
thereby resulting in four enlarged districts to replace nine. Four
separate elections were held in the following February. Each proposal failed to get the necessary over-all majority in the affected

area. In all instances, the wealthier and larger districts voted decisively against the proposition; in one, the vote was 8 for to 2,260 against.

The Survey, along with a number of other groups and individuals, advocated removal of restrictions on the power of the Bi-State Development Agency to finance projects through the sale of revenue bonds. In 1959 the state legislatures of Missouri and Illinois agreed to a revised compact, later approved by Congress. One of its provisions made revenue bonds of the agency negotiable and available for purchase by trust and guardianship estates, thus eliminating the principal obstacle to adequate financing. It had taken six years for the revision to be approved by the Missouri state legislature.

The use of the Survey's recommendations as a springboard for discussion and action and as a continuing point of reference for interested individuals and organizations has exceeded the most optimistic hopes of the Survey. All the major suggestions have received support, although only that for the metropolitan district government could be predicted in advance. Moreover, support for certain proposals, such as those regarding municipal services in the County, has been renewed after the initial surge of interest did not materialize in successful action. Extremely encouraging and satisfying are the newspaper editorial references to the Survey's findings and recommendations which continue to be made in the metropolitan press well over two years after their issuance.

Part Three
CITIZEN PARTICIPATION AND ATTITUDES

9

An Overview:

The Metropolitan Citizen and His Local Governments

PART THREE of the book focuses on citizen participation in and opinions about local public affairs. It presents many results of the extensive, systematic interviews conducted with a large, representative cross section of the adult population of the City-County area. The sample survey findings analyzed here pertain to three matters important in developing a better understanding of metropolitan areas and in the preparation and effectuation of recommendations for governmental improvement. They are participation in local government through voting for officials; citizen relations with local governments, including extent of dissatisfaction with services; and opinions about the desirability and possibility of change in the governmental arrangements of the area.

Initially, these three subjects are discussed in terms of the total population sampled. A broad range of questions relating to the adult population of the City-County area are considered: How many people have ever voted in a local election? How many in specific types of elections? How much overlap is there among participants in different types of elections? How does the electorate for local government compare with that for presidential elections? How many people are dissatisfied with specific local governmental services and how many rate the over-all performance of their local governments as good, fair, or poor? How many people complain about their local governmental services to a particular individual or agency? Why do some people, despite dissatisfaction, never register a complaint? How many see the area as sharing common problems, want the governments to work together to solve them, and favor some type of governmental reorganization? And how many want the governmental pattern in the City-County area left unchanged?

PARTICIPATION IN THE ELECTORAL PROCESS

VOTING IN LOCAL ELECTIONS

Even when the total electorate for local government is defined very broadly—as those ever having voted in any local election while residing in their present community—it includes only about two of every three adults in the St. Louis City-County area. Five per cent are ineligible to vote, presumably because of recent migration into or within the area; 28 per cent, although eligible, have never voted in a local election since living in their present community; and 67 per cent have voted in some local election.[1] Moreover, the total electorate for local elections is somewhat smaller than that for presidential elections; 75 per cent voted in the 1956 presidential contest.

But a person can be eligible to vote in some types of local elections and not in others. For example, a resident of an unincorporated part of the County cannot participate in municipal elections. Residents of the city of St. Louis cannot take part in electing County governmental officials in St. Louis County. And

---

[1] The percentages computed for the City-County area as a whole, which appear primarily in this chapter of part three, are based upon a weighted average of the sample survey results for the City and the County, as the City sample was drawn from one in each 400 dwelling units and the more intensive County sample from one in 100 dwelling units. The basic sample included 515 interviews in the City and 1,285 in the County. When interviews were weighted proportionately to the total population for the area (by dividing 4 into 1,285), the County sample was then weighted as 322 persons. However, the specific percentages for the County portion of the combined sample were computed for the total of 1,285 cases, and were then weighted by 322, while City interviews were weighted by the 515 cases. Thus, the number of cases or interviews appearing for City-County totals was rounded to 837; however, for County residents the findings are more reliable than this number indicates. Confidence limits for a sample of 837 underestimate the degree of confidence that can be placed in these estimates. Tables for computing the reliability of differences and the sampling error of estimates are contained in Appendix C.

many County residents as well as all City inhabitants do not live within the boundaries of fire districts and therefore are legally unable to vote in such elections. This leads to the question of what proportion of those eligible to vote in various kinds of local elections do so.

The extent of voting by eligible persons varies considerably according to the type of local government. For example, a difference of 19 per cent exists between the proportion of eligibles who have ever voted in County elections and school elections. Although wide variance is present in participation in different types of local elections, only 70 per cent of the eligible individuals have ever voted for the officials of any type of local government.

TABLE 13

VOTING BY THOSE ELIGIBLE IN THE
CITY-COUNTY AREA

Type of election	Voted	N[a]
Any local	70%[b]	795
County	67	1,169[c]
Municipal	64	740
Fire district	50	330[c]
School	48	795

[a] Throughout the tables, N represents the number of persons interviewed.
[b] All percentages in tables in part three are rounded to the nearest whole number.
[c] For elections held in the County only, the total County sample was used.

To what degree do the various local electorates consist of the same people? There is much overlap; individuals who vote in one type of local election are likely to provide most of the electorate for other local units. A substantial number are generally oriented to local government and politics; a smaller number never vote in any local election. Those who vote selectively, participating in one type of local election but not in others, are a small minority (D1).[2]

The conclusion that local government is of some importance to a substantial portion of the citizenry is further supported by replies to this question: "A good many local elections aren't im-

---

[2] Tables supporting a number of statements in the text of part three are contained in Appendix D. Parenthetical references to these appendix tables appear in the text (e.g., D1, D2).

portant enough to bother with. Do you agree or disagree?"[3] Seventy-four per cent disagreed, 24 per cent agreed, and the remaining 2 per cent were undecided. Although such agreement is not a clear indication of future political action, it runs counter to the frequently held notion that most people do not care about local elections and politics.

LOCAL ELECTIONS AND NATIONAL ELECTIONS

What is the overlap between the electorate in local elections and that in national presidential elections? Does the presidential election select from within the electorate for local elections, or does it include many who do not vote in local elections? Does the local electorate comprise many persons who do not participate in national elections?

Those who voted for a presidential candidate in 1956 are five times as likely as the nonparticipants to have voted in each type of local election, despite the variations in the number eligible to vote in the different kinds of local elections and the proportions who did vote. Thus a preponderant majority of the electorate in national presidential elections also vote in most local elections, and a very small minority of the nonvoters in the national elections vote for officials in local government.

TABLE 14

PERCENTAGE VOTING IN LOCAL ELECTIONS BY VOTING
IN THE 1956 PRESIDENTIAL ELECTION

Type of local election[a]	Voted in 1956 (N = 639)	Did not vote in 1956 (N = 198)
Municipal	76	16
County	75	14
Fire district	58	12
School	57	12

[a] Those ineligible to vote are necessarily omitted as propensity to vote is being determined.

With very few exceptions, those who vote in local elections also vote in presidential contests; approximately 95 per cent of the local electorate is part of the national presidential electorate.

_____

[3] This item is adapted from one in the sense-of-political-duty scale in Angus Campbell, Gerald Gurin, and Warren E. Miller, _The Voter Decides_ (Evanston: Row, Peterson, 1954), pp. 187–194.

However, of those who have not voted in local elections, a much smaller majority (from 50 to 70 per cent) voted in the presidential election of 1956.

Such findings suggest that voting in local and national elections may be arranged along a scale according to frequency of participation. Those who vote in the least popular local elections —school elections—also vote in the more popular elections, of which the most popular is the national presidential election (D2).

THE CITIZEN AS A CUSTOMER OF LOCAL GOVERNMENTS

Do residents of the City-County area feel that important public needs are not being met adequately by local governments? Several measures of dissatisfaction were used in the sample survey. The first was based on replies to two open-end questions (inquiries containing no check list of items) relating to changes or improvements in the person's own local community and in the entire City-County area, and they preceded any discussion of specific local governmental services.

DESIRED CHANGES

The number of changes or improvements desired by people varies considerably, both for the community of residence and the entire City-County area. Regarding the local community, 20 per cent had no suggested changes, 32 per cent had one, 28 per cent had two, and 21 per cent stated three or more.

Most local community improvement suggestions fell into two large categories. The first and larger group pertains to maintaining and improving the "livability" of the community; it includes concern for the condition of residential streets, the character of the neighborhood (land use, space, maintenance of structures), improving parks and playgrounds, and improving sewerage and drainage systems. All these changes refer to neighborhood environmental conditions that are important to the individual household. The second major category of change centers on the improvement of traffic conditions and public transportation facilities.

No other local governmental activity elicited suggestions for change from as much as 5 per cent of the respondents. Schools, police protection, fire protection, water supply, waste collection, library services, and taxes individually are negligible portions of the total public problems mentioned.

A similar pattern emerges with respect to suggestions for changes or improvements in the entire City-County area. Again, there is considerable range in the number of suggestions. Twenty-nine per cent had none, 37 per cent offered one, 22 per cent made two, and 12 per cent desired at least three changes. The majority of suggestions focused upon bettering the means of getting around in the metropolitan area; three of the four most frequent suggestions dealt with transportation—traffic conditions and parking, condition of streets and roads, and public transportation.

A substantial number of the residents also suggested changes

Local   community

Condition of residential streets	49%
Character of neighborhood (maintaining and improving)	21%
Traffic conditions	18%
Parks and playgrounds	12%
Various non-governmental services, such as private utilities and employment practices	10%
Sewerage and drainage systems	7%
Public transportation	6%

City-County   area

Traffic conditions and parking	30%
Condition of streets in entire area	17%
Character of residential neighborhoods (maintaining and improving)	13%
Public transportation	11%
Area-wide air and water pollution	8%
Area-wide police protection	6%
Sewerage system	5%
Parks and playgrounds	5%

Fig. 13. Suggested types of improvements in local community and City-County area. (A number of respondents wanted more than one type of change. Suggestions made by fewer than 5 per cent of the respondents are omitted.)

that help to maintain and improve the character of the residential neighborhoods. Smaller numbers mentioned changes aimed at preventing air and water pollution and improving the area-wide police and sewerage systems, as well as betterment of parks and playgrounds. Changes in many other important governmental activities were mentioned by only a negligible percentage of the residents: water supply, fire protection, schools, race relations, taxes, general governmental efficiency, and waste collection seldom elicited suggestions for improvement.

Several general characteristics of these responses deserve mention. One is the absence of widespread concern about many basic local governmental services. Clearly, in the public's estimation, such services as fire and police protection have not reached a critical condition. On the other hand, the suggested changes generally call for extension of local governmental services beyond their present scope. This desire may take the form of an increase in the amount of a service now provided, such as traffic control and street maintenance, or the inauguration of certain types of governmental activity, such as parks, playgrounds and public swimming pools, or neighborhood conservation. Either type of alteration in service demands that governmental resources must be increased. Certain changes, such as the improvement of traffic flow in the City-County area, and frequently in the local community, necessarily require functional and territorial powers beyond those now held by any local government in the metropolitan community.

The amount of interest in improved leisure facilities and a more adequate urban environment for community, neighborhood, and dwelling is not a crisis response. It reflects not a functional breakdown but rather a desire to extend the range and quality of provided governmental services. At the same time, there are few suggestions about the cost of local government. Only 1 per cent suggested the lowering of taxes as a change they want to see made.

In view of the extent of publicity given to the need for better schools and the amount of the local tax dollar spent for education, it is indeed remarkable that less than 5 per cent of the citizenry suggested changes or improvements in the schools. Although this result does not mean changes are unnecessary, it does reveal that the "crisis in education" has not been effectively communicated to the public in the City-County area.

EVALUATION OF GOVERNMENTAL SERVICES

The second type of question asked consisted of a series of structured (closed-end) inquiries concerning each of a number of governmental services. The respondent was asked to indicate his satisfaction or dissatisfaction with eleven major services according to response categories on a printed card. The objective of this check list was to obtain judgments on every important local governmental service, particularly because the respondent might not immediately think of at least some of them in response to the open-end questions. The structured questions guarantee coverage, although they do not guarantee the importance of the opinion to the particular subject. On the other hand, the open-end questions provide a check of the saliency of the specific subject in the mind of the respondent; they help guard against overinterpretation of what may be very casual judgments.

The responses to closed-end or structured queries show considerable agreement with those to the open-end questions. Public concern is most widespread about traffic and transportation, neighborhood streets, and parks and playgrounds. Sewage disposal, police protection, and garbage collection were considered unsatisfactory by a substantial number of residents. The largest percentage of discontent about sewage disposal was in the south

Traffic control and facilities	50%	11	35	4
Public transportation	39%	20	32	10
Condition of street	35%	22	42	1
Parks and playgrounds	31%	29	32	9
Police protection	16%	39	42	3
Sewage disposal	16%	41	39	4
Garbage collection	15%	46	36	3
Libraries	9%	44	27	20
Schools	8%	43	37	13
Water supply	7%	67	26	*
Fire protection	4%	58	33	5

☐ Dissatisfied, very dissatisfied   ▨ Fairly satisfied

■ Very satisfied   ▦ Don't know

* Less than one-half of 1 per cent.
Note: These percentages were compiled from answers to the closed-end question, "How do you feel about ——— ——— in this area (or around here) ?" Two of the response categories (Dissatisfied and Very Dissatisfied) have been combined for purposes of this analysis.

Fig. 14. Evaluation of local governmental services.

part of the County. Similarly, police protection was regarded as inadequate chiefly in the city of St. Louis. Other local governmental services brought forth expressions of dissatisfaction from not more than 9 per cent of the population in any large section of the City-County area. These results indicate that the citizens felt little need for changes and improvements in services such as fire protection, schools, libraries, and water supply.

COMPLAINTS ABOUT SERVICES

A third type of question asked was whether the respondent had ever felt like complaining about local services. Thirty-eight per cent answered affirmatively, but only 40 per cent of those who have wanted to complain have actually done so to a public or private person or agency. Thus, only one-seventh of the persons interviewed have personally tried to improve at least one local governmental service.

Fifty-four per cent of those who complained had objected to sanitation services (refuse collection, sewage disposal) ; 31 per cent spoke about utilities (water supply, electric supply, condition of streets) ; 8 per cent, about inadequate protection of person and property; and the other 7 per cent, about educational and cultural facilities. The overwhelming proportion of complaints dealt with breakdowns in the functional necessities for the household. Very few complaints demanded an extension of services into new spheres. Although traffic and transportation are the most important areas of citizen dissatisfaction, only a small proportion of citizens have ever personally attempted to put pressure upon the agencies of local government to improve these services.

Complaints are made, then, only where there is a well-defined governmental responsibility. However, as the earlier discussion of suggested changes and improvements indicates, many services desired by the persons interviewed are not the current responsibility of any governmental agency. Consequently, the aspirations of the citizens cannot be proven through a study of "what they have done about it," for there is no channel for action short of petitioning, running for office, or the like. In contrast, where there is an established agency with responsibility for a particular service (as in fire or police protection, for example), the individual with a complaint has a channel for expression.

THE WORTH OF LOCAL GOVERNMENT

When proposals are made for either extending or improving governmental services, or doing both, certain counterarguments often appear. Seemingly the most constant is thrift, the value of not spending money for taxes and the value of conserving the tax dollars already levied. It is frequently assumed that the great majority of citizens are extremely tax-conscious and are enthusiastic about any move to lower taxes. Such an assumption implies that the citizen is skeptical about the worth of governmental services he receives. Because it is important to know just how much credit local government has in the opinion of the citizens, the Survey designed a series of questions to elicit judgments of worth.

One question was worded as follows: "Some people feel that they pay more local taxes than they should, considering what they get from their local government; others think they get a good bargain for their tax dollar. How do you feel? Do you think that local taxes are too high, about right, or too low?" The answers were: "too high," 40 per cent; "about right," 52 per cent; "don't know," 7 per cent; and 1 per cent, "too low." Thus only a minority, although a substantial one, believes local taxes are too high. Slightly more than half the population feel they get a good bargain for the tax dollar.

EVALUATION OF GOVERNMENTS

What are the public's evaluations of specific governments in the City-County area? There is no strong criticism of any of the governments evaluated (D3). Only in the County is a government —the metropolitan sewer district—considered to be performing poorly by as many as 10 per cent of the residents. If, however, the very positive evaluations (very good and good) are considered, there is more variation in the appraisals of different governments.

The most interesting aspect of these findings is the good repute enjoyed by the government of the city of St. Louis: about three-fifths of the respondents in both City and County consider it good or very good. Apparently the picture of the City as decaying and the rumors of its corruption and domination by political party bosses and trade unions are not taken seriously by a large majority of either City or County residents. A second interesting aspect is the difference in favorable evaluations of local units according to governmental level. The municipal level, in both the County and the City, gets a very good mark from many people. The St. Louis County government much less frequently receives popular esteem.

These findings have validity as a measure of the general images of governments; however, over 40 per cent of the City residents have no opinion on either the County government or County municipalities, and one-fourth the residents of both the City and County make no evaluation of the metropolitan sewer district. It is, therefore, useful to consider judgments in terms of those with opinions.

When those without opinions about local governments are excluded, the evaluations of specific units by City and County residents are quite comparable (D4). The appraisal of the St. Louis City government is identical in City and County. The judgments about other governments are very similar, with one exception. Of those with opinions in St. Louis County, 21 per cent think the Metropolitan St. Louis Sewer District has done either a poor or a very poor job. This principally reflects the difficulties this agency has encountered in taking over a sewage disposal system that was highly inadequate in certain sections of the County.

METROPOLITAN PROBLEMS AND SOLUTIONS

Eighty-one per cent of the residents feel that the City and the County share major problems. Of those who answered affirmatively, one-fourth listed three or more difficulties, one-fourth named two, one-fourth specified one, and one-fourth could not name any particular problem.[4] The most frequently cited difficulties are traffic and transportation. In total, the problems mentioned are very similar to those indicated for the City-County area. In view of the general feeling that the City and County have mutual problems, what are the opinions of residents about various kinds of governmental change—coöperation and integration—aimed at bringing about improvements?

OPINIONS CONCERNING EXISTING
GOVERNMENTAL ARRANGEMENTS

The first question in the sequence dealing with coöperation among local governments was both an introductory inquiry and a test of whether the lack of an esthetic local governmental system, caused by the multiplicity of units, has any public significance. (Lack of symmetry and unity in a governmental system, essen-

---

[4] Sixty-three per cent believe there are major problems involving both the City-County area and the East Side, which is the urban complex on the Illinois side of the Mississippi River; only 36 per cent named at least one specific problem.

tially esthetic defects, are the major targets of some governmental reform efforts.) The question was "We have discussed some of the most important things that local government does for the people in this area. Now, as you probably know, the St. Louis City-County area is divided into 97 different cities and villages, and some people think there are too many, while others think there are not too many. What do you think?"

A majority (51 per cent) agreed that 97 governments are too many; however, 39 per cent did not think so, and another 10 per cent did not know. The argument that 97 cities constitute an excessive number has an appeal to many persons but not to an overwhelming majority.

Following this question, the interview turned to coöperation among these local governments. A substantial majority of the residents in the City-County area believed that some measure of governmental coöperation is desirable. In answer to the question, "Do you believe it would be to your community's advantage or not to join with others in handling some of these [governmental] services?" two-thirds said "Yes," 23 per cent said "No," and 10 per cent did not know.

The most frequently mentioned value of coöperation is the extension and improvement of governmental services in an effective manner—in short, more government. Thus, certain popular beliefs about what arguments will sell governmental reform are not borne out by the reasons given by a majority of the people who favor governmental coöperation. Cheaper government and lower taxes, often considered the more persuasive rewards that can be offered, rank a poor second among the reasons advanced. Interestingly, a small proportion think the main advantage accruing from coöperation is to stimulate public participation and interest.

Replies to the question of what services should be coördinated

TABLE 15

ADVANTAGES TO LOCAL COMMUNITY RESULTING FROM GOVERNMENTAL
COÖPERATION IN THE CITY-COUNTY AREA

Efficiency, coördination, more and better services	51%
Cheaper government, lower taxes	18
Both cheaper and more efficient	13
More participation and interest in government	8
Advantage, but don't know what	10
	(N = 558)

were vague and scattered. Only police protection, mentioned by 14 per cent, was named by more than one-tenth of the people. Most laymen do not possess the technical knowledge required for a detailed answer of this type. They may feel generally that more coördination is desirable, but they are vague as to its nature. In the absence of an extensive campaign of public education, it is unlikely that many citizens will have firm opinions on such matters.

WILLINGNESS TO ACCEPT GOVERNMENTAL INTEGRATION

Five alternatives, four for bringing about the integration of government and one for continuing the status quo, were presented in popular terms, and people were asked if they liked or disliked each possibility. The alternatives in their order of presentation were:

A. Make St. Louis City a part of St. Louis County, so that all the cities in this area would still exist but would have one single County government.

B. Make a federal system, keeping all the cities but letting a metropolitan government take over such jobs as traffic control.

C. Merge the city of St. Louis, St. Louis County, and the County cities into one big unified city.

D. Leave the present governments of St. Louis City, St. Louis County, and the County municipalities just as they are.

E. Consolidate the 96 cities of St. Louis County into a smaller number.

The various changes, or lack of change in the case of D, range from the most extreme form of integration (complete merger of all general-purpose local governments) to the opposite extreme, status quo. All reorganization alternatives are legally available to the City-County area. Merger into one government, a federal system (through establishing a multipurpose metropolitan district), and reëntry of the City into the County can each be realized by obtaining separate dual majorities in the City and the County. Consolidation of County municipalities into a smaller number requires separate popular majorities in each municipality involved. As emphasized in an earlier part of this book, "Formulating a Plan of Government," only merger or a federal (district) system provides an adequate area-wide mechanism that can immediately deal with metropolitan problems.

Residents were asked if they liked or disliked each proposal. The federal system was most generally liked and the status quo most generally disliked. More people liked than disliked three of the alternatives—the federal system, municipal consolidation in the County, and merger. Reëntry of the city of St. Louis into the County was disliked by a close margin and a substantial majority rejected retention of the status quo.

TABLE 16

RESPONSE TO VARIOUS GOVERNMENTAL ALTERNATIVES

Proposal	Like	Dislike	Don't know
Merger (C)	49%	45%	7%
Reëntry of City into County (A)	44	47	9
Federal system (B)	54	35	12
Municipal consolidation in County (E)	49	41	10
Status quo (D)	39	54	7
(N = 837)			

Of those with definite opinions, 61 per cent liked a federal system as against 42 per cent in favor of the status quo. A fairly even split appears between persons favoring and opposing the other types of governmental integration. Slightly more than half favored merger and consolidation of County municipalities, and slightly less than half favored reëntry of the City into the County.

Such an analysis does not yield the basis for a meaningful rank order of preference among the various proposals as it is unlikely that respondents make automatic comparisons of the different options. To develop a rank order, the respondent held a card describing the various proposals while he was asked, "Which of these do you like the most?" and "Which do you really dislike the most?" A majority of both the favorable and unfavorable responses fell into the two most contrasting possibilities— merger and status quo. The public expressing opinions about governmental change in the City-County area apparently consists of three groups of persons—the two polar classes, consisting of the advocates of merger and the supporters of status quo, and the intermediate class or classes, composed of those who choose among the less extreme alternatives.

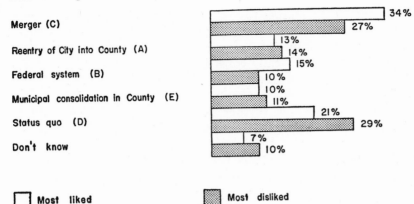

Merger (C)

Reentry of City into County (A)

Federal system (B)

Municipal consolidation in County (E)

Status quo (D)

Don't know

☐ Most liked   ▨ Most disliked

Fig. 15. Most liked and most disliked proposals for governmental change.

CONSISTENCY OF OPINION ON CHANGE

The evidence that there are three classes of persons with opinions about governmental change is reinforced by cross-tabulation analysis.

As indicated in column 1 of table 17, a consistent increase in the percentage most disliking merger occurs in proceeding from those most committed to integration (row 1) to those least committed (row 5). Conversely, as shown in column 5, the proportion most disliking status quo, there is a consistent decrease from

TABLE 17

ASSOCIATION BETWEEN MOST LIKED AND MOST DISLIKED CHOICES
AMONG PROPOSALS FOR GOVERNMENTAL CHANGE

	Most liked proposal	Most disliked proposal						
		1	2	3	4	5	6	
		Merger	Reënter County	Federal system	Municipal consoli- dation	Status quo	Don't know	N
1	Merger		16%	14%	14%	52%	3	280
2	Reënter County	25%		15	16	37	7	112
3	Federal system	34	16		15	32	2	128
4	Municipal con- solidation	48	14	12		23	4	86
5	Status quo	54	20	9	10		7	176
6	Don't know	5	0	4	0	9	82	55

those who prefer merger to those who prefer leaving the governments unchanged. In short, personal preferences range from complete integration to a very high degree of local autonomy. The opinions are logically consistent from the question ranking the alternative most liked to that indicating the proposal most disliked.

This consistency is further demonstrated when table 17 is analyzed from the row position, that is, the most liked proposal. Sixty-six per cent of those preferring merger dislike most intensely the two alternatives that do not involve integration of the City and County (status quo and municipal consolidation in the County). Eighty-three per cent of those who prefer the existing governmental arrangements most dislike the three propositions that involve some kind of City-County integration. In both instances, the bulk of the cases falls at the extreme—over half of those who prefer merger most dislike status quo as an alternative; similarly, more than half who prefer the status quo most dislike merger.

In contrast, persons whose preference is the federal system are most frequently opposed to one of the two extreme positions —66 per cent dislike merger or status quo more than the other four proposed alternatives. This is true of those preferring any one of the three moderate proposals. In each instance, a majority dislikes the two extremes most.

Approximately two-thirds of all persons interviewed can be categorized on the basis of reaction to the governmental alternatives. One group, which can be called the mergerites (22 per cent of the adult population), likes merger best and most dislikes either status quo or municipal consolidation in the County. A second group, the local autonomists or advocates of status quo (16 per cent), prefers status quo to all other alternatives and most strongly disapproves of either merger or reëntry of the City into the County.[5] A third category, the moderate integrationists or moderates (26 per cent), likes best either the federal system, reëntry of the City into the County, or municipal con-

---

[5] "Local autonomists," used throughout this part of the book, although not an ideal term, seems about as accurate as any available, unless "status quoers" is to be coined. It is not completely precise. Although people who believe in the continuance of the status quo are advocates of extreme local self-government (and thus are autonomists), they oppose reëntry of the City into the County, which would not affect the local self-government of the City nor any local government in the County. The term "isolationists" might be more appropriate, but its wide use in other contexts would render it too confusing here.

solidation in the County, and most dislikes one of the two extremes.

SUPPORT FOR THE FEDERAL SYSTEM

The federal system is liked most by only 15 per cent of the people, but is disliked most by merely 10 per cent, the lowest among the five options. A majority of the opponents of each of the four alternatives liked the federal system (D5). Particularly large majorities favored it among those most hostile to municipal consolidation in the County and status quo. The opponents of merger also liked it by a substantial majority—64 per cent of those with opinions were favorable.

Proponents of most other governmental alternatives also tended to like a federal system. Of those with opinions, a majority of the advocates of each alternative favors the federal system, with the exception of those who most preferred status quo. Sixty per cent of them disliked the federal system.

TABLE 18

OPINIONS OF THE FEDERAL SYSTEM BY THOSE MOST LIKING
THE OTHER ALTERNATIVES

Most liked proposal	Opinions of the federal system			N
	Liked	Disliked	Don't know	
Merger	50%	44%	6%	280
Reëntry of City into County	62	31	7	112
Municipal consolidation in County	50	42	8	86
Status quo	33	53	14	175

EXCLUDED: 56 respondents who could not make up their minds.

OPINIONS CONCERNING CHANGE

At the conclusion of the sequence of questions dealing with the alternatives, individuals were asked if they thought there should be an election on one of the proposals in the next year (D6). Seventy per cent stated that they thought so; 24 per cent said no; 6 per cent did not know. These results had probably been influenced by the interview process. Certainly the persons interviewed had been indoctrinated to some degree about governmental problems and solutions by the series of questions; they had been stimulated to an interest probably atypical of the total adult population. They were much more positive about holding such an election than about the probability of voter approval of any proposed change. When asked "Do you think any changes are likely to take place in the near future?" 44 per cent thought changes are probable, 44 per cent thought otherwise, and 12 per cent did not know (D7). Proponents of each type of change favored holding an election on the matter of reorganization in the near future.

Similarly, although to a much smaller degree, those most favoring each of the alternative types of change tended to believe some kind of reorganization is likely to materialize. Only individuals who judged status quo as best generally viewed reorganization as improbable. Of persons having an opinion, a slight majority most liking each option except status quo regarded change to be likely.

SUMMARY: VOTING, SERVICES, AND REORGANIZATION IN THE CITY-COUNTY AREA

The electorate for local government in the St. Louis City-County area is slightly smaller than that for national presidential contests. Considerable overlap occurs between the electorates for different kinds of local elections. Quantitatively, the important distinction is between those who do not vote in any local election and those who vote in several different kinds.

Most citizens believe local elections are important, but a substantial minority have never voted in any local election since living in their present community. As most adult residents of the City-County area can vote in some local elections, lack of opportunity is no explanation. Almost all who vote in local elections also participate in presidential elections, but the reverse does not hold. However, a majority of the voters in national elections have voted in some type of local election.

A large majority of the citizens suggested at least one change or improvement for their community and also for the City-County area as a whole. Community improvements emphasized the livability of the area for householders, whereas suggested area improvements concentrated heavily on traffic and transportation. Nevertheless, there was no great consensus concerning what needs improvement; while 49 per cent mentioned improving the condition of residential streets and 30 per cent spoke of traffic and parking, other services were mentioned by only 20 per cent or less. Many major services elicited practically no suggestions for improvement.

In general, the public does not feel a crisis situation regarding the provision of local governmental services. The desire for faster traffic flow, more leisure facilities, and cleanliness and order indicate aspiration, but not an incessant demand, for improved urban living. This is indicated by the very small proportion of people who have ever personally complained about even one governmental service to the responsible agency.

More striking is the large proportion of citizens expressing favorable evaluations of the various local governments in the City-County area. Suburban municipalities and the city of St. Louis alike received strong votes of confidence. Nevertheless, a majority of the citizens mention common problems shared by the various governments and indicate that coöperation is desirable. When they are presented with several types of governmental reorganization possible in the area, they manifest little consensus as to the most desirable kind. Reorganization is preferred to status quo, but opinion is scattered among four categories nearly equal in size—mergerites, moderates, local autonomists, and those with no consistent opinion. The extreme proposal, that for City-County merger, produces considerable antipathy. The only proposal more generally disliked is to leave the present governments of St. Louis City, St. Louis County, and the County municipalities unaltered.

Most people would like to see an election held on some reorganization proposal. Only a slight majority of those with opinions, however, think such an election is likely to result in the adoption of reorganization.

10

The Citizen and
His Local Governments:
Central City and Suburban County

IN THIS CHAPTER, participation in local government through voting, citizen relations with local governments, and opinions about the desirability and likelihood of governmental reorganization are analyzed for the City and County separately. The intervening governmental boundary and the socioeconomic differences of the people in the City and the County make comparisons between the central city and suburban county theoretically interesting and practically important.

Is electoral participation disproportionately concentrated in the County where local governments are smaller and thus supposedly closer to the people? Are the service dissatisfactions in the aging central city quite different from those in the rapidly growing suburbs? Is a favorable opinion of governmental reform largely concentrated in the central city or is it widespread in both sections? The answer to the last question is extremely important, for the acceptance of a plan of governmental reorganization for the City-County area depends upon obtaining a separate affirmative majority popular vote in both the City and the County. Thus, the attitudes found in both the City and the County are crucial to the chances of any plan formulated and submitted to the voters.

PARTICIPATION IN THE ELECTORAL PROCESS

VOTING IN LOCAL ELECTIONS

Although many more poorly educated people reside in the City and such persons are more likely to be nonvoters, the total electorate is similar for the two areas. Sixty-nine per cent of those eligible in the City and 72 per cent in the County have voted in some local election since living in their present community.

A much larger proportion of the City electorate has voted for municipal officials, but this is partly owing to the ineligibility of many County residents who live in unincorporated sections. When the percentages of those eligible who have voted in the municipal and school elections are considered, however, clear differences between central city and suburban county remain. A higher proportion has voted for municipal officials than for school officials in both City and County, and a substantially higher proportion has voted in both types of elections in the City.

TABLE 19

VOTING FOR MUNICIPAL AND SCHOOL OFFICIALS

Residence	Per cent voting for				Per cent of eligibles voting for			
	Mu-nicipal officials	N	School officials	N	Mu-nicipal officials	N[a]	School officials	N
City	65%	515	48%	515	67%	495	50%	495
County	44	1,285	40	1,285	57	970	44	1,196

[a] In City-County comparisons, the interviews in the basic sample are used (515 in the City and 1,285 in the County). The N column is omitted from many subsequent tables which contain the entire basic sample. Regarding the weighted sample employed for percentages on the City and County considered together, see chapter 9, footnote 1.

It is evident that a large proportion of residents of the County municipalities either do not know they live within a municipality having municipal elections, or else they are confused about the matter. One-fifth of the people in the County municipalities thus are politically incompetent in their knowledge about municipal elections, as against 5 per cent of the City residents. In general, the suburban municipalities, often regarded as being more viable governmental units than the central city, apparently fail to communicate to a significant proportion of their electorate that municipal elections take place and people can vote in them.

TABLE 20

VOTING FOR MUNICIPAL OFFICIALS: CITY AND COUNTY MUNICIPALITIES

Residence	Voted	Did not vote	Could not vote	Did not know	N[a]
City	67%	28%	*	5%	490
County	57	22	14	7	975

[a]The number of cases includes only those who say they are eligible to vote in local elections and reside in incorporated municipalities.
* In all tables an asterisk denotes an entry of less than one-half of 1 per cent.

The question upon which these findings are based was worded as follows: "Which of these officials can people vote for here?" and the show card included as the first category, "Officials in a *City* Government." When the findings emerged, it became apparent that the word "city" may have confused some people who reside in municipalities legally classified as villages. For this reason, the respondents in the County were grouped by type of municipal unit in which they lived—233 lived in villages, 738 in cities. When the two types of municipalities were compared, village residents much more frequently said they did not know, or that they could not vote for city officials. Thirty-five per cent gave such responses.

Seventeen per cent of those living in cities in the County, however, made similar responses; this proportion is significantly much higher than the 5 per cent in the city of St. Louis. Moreover, it is by no means certain that the greater proportion of "don't know" and "can't vote" responses in the villages resulted from confusion over what was meant by officials in a city government. Of village residents who said they could vote, a significantly greater proportion have never voted in their municipal elections.

Even larger proportions of eligible voters in both the City and the County either believe they cannot vote or do not know whether they can vote in school elections. And again, as is true

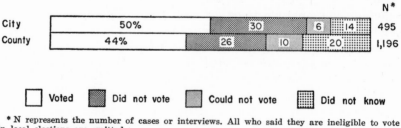

* N represents the number of cases or interviews. All who said they are ineligible to vote in local elections are omitted.

Fig. 16. Voting in school elections: City and County.

in municipal elections, a much larger percentage in the County do not know they have a right to participate in school elections.

These findings, which show the more extensive knowledge of residents of the city of St. Louis about municipal and school elections, cannot generally be accounted for by the recent movement of many residents into the County. Only individuals who said they were eligible to vote in local elections were included in the tabulations. Furthermore, the findings on another type of local election in the County—for officials in the County government—are quite different. Sixty-six per cent of the County residents report they have voted in County elections, and 25 per cent have not voted but know they could. Only 3 per cent say that they cannot vote for County officials, and 7 per cent that they do not know. Thus the difference between City and County in political competence with respect to municipal and school elections stands as an important finding. The suburban communities fail to mobilize as large a portion of the citizenry to vote as the central city and this failure is chiefly owing to the greater political incompetence of their residents.

There are no comparable data for the percentage of County eligibles who voted in fire district elections because the residence of the individual in a fire district was not determined. (Such districts operate in only certain parts of the County and not at all in the City.) Fifty per cent of all County residents who said they were eligible to vote in this type of election stated they had done so on one or more occasions. (It is possible that the percentage of County residents who are really eligible is considerably lower.)

The rank order of voting in elections in the County is: elections for County governmental officials, 66 per cent of those eligible; municipal elections, 57 per cent; fire district elections, 50 per cent; and school elections, 44 per cent. The rank order in the City is municipal elections, 67 per cent, and school elections, 50 per cent.

As shown in table 21, there is much overlap in both the City

TABLE 21

MULTIPLE VOTING IN FOUR DIFFERENT TYPES OF LOCAL ELECTIONS
BY THOSE EVER VOTING IN A LOCAL ELECTION

Residence	One	Two	Three	Four	None	N
City	24%	71%	0	0	5%	341
County	5	2	72	19	3	862

and the County in the electorate that takes part in different types of local elections. Of approximately 70 per cent in City and County who have ever voted in any local election, 71 per cent in the City and over 90 per cent in the County have voted in at least two kinds of elections, and most County voters have voted in three or more kinds. Two kinds of elections constitute the maximum number (municipal and school) for which residents of the City can be eligible.[1] All County residents who can qualify to participate in local elections can vote in at least two types (County and school). Many others can take part in a third type (municipal elections), and still others, a fourth (fire district) (D8).

The amount of multiple voting in both City and County indicates that voting in local governmental elections is a general practice for many people in both areas. This conclusion is reinforced by responses to the question about whether or not local elections are of consequence. In response to the statement that "A good many local elections aren't important enough to bother with," the percentage disagreeing in the County (82) was substantially higher than that in the City (68). Although verbal agreement as to the importance of local elections is greater in the suburban county than in the central city, the proportion of eligible voters who have exercised their right is greater in the City for both municipal and school elections. The greater assent to the verbal statement of value could be a result of educational differences between City and County; the greater proportion who have voted in the City must stem from other differences between the two populations.

LOCAL ELECTIONS AND NATIONAL ELECTIONS

In the preceding chapter, which contained findings about the City-County area as a whole, it was shown that most people who vote in local elections also voted in the 1956 presidential election (95 per cent), and a large majority who voted in this presidential election had voted in one or more local elections (83 per cent). Very few who did not vote in the presidential election voted in local elections, but 17 per cent of those who did vote in the presidential election did not vote in local elections.

---

[1] Because of judicial interpretation, the City is required to elect certain "county" officials, but it does not have a full-fledged county government (no county governing body, for example). It thus has no county elections comparable to those in the County and can be said to hold elections involving only two types of local governments, municipal and school.

There is very little difference in these relationships between the central city and the suburban county. For City and County alike, a majority has voted both in local elections and the 1956 presidential election (D9). The minority that has voted in neither type is a slightly larger part of the City electorate than the County. Another small proportion voted in the presidential election but never in local elections. Only about 4 per cent in either City or County have voted in local elections but failed to vote in the 1956 presidential election.

THE CITIZEN AS A CUSTOMER OF LOCAL GOVERNMENTS

DESIRED CHANGES

Residents of the County consistently suggested a larger number of changes or improvements in their local community (D10). More than one-half in the County (53 per cent) and somewhat less than one-half in the City (45 per cent) desired two or more community improvements. However, substantial percentages in each area mentioned no changes or only one change.

The sharpest difference in dissatisfactions between City and County occurs in the frequency of two particular suggestions— maintaining or improving the character of the neighborhoods and improving sewage disposal systems. Almost three of ten City residents want changes related to neighborhood conservation or rehabilitation, as compared to less than one of twelve in the County. The frequency of such suggestions in the City undoubtedly indicates concern about the extent of aging structures and blighted areas in its older portions. They also provide a broad basis of support for the present programs of neighborhood renewal. Mention of improvement of sewage disposal came almost exclusively from County residents; this reflects the relative degrees of adequacy of this service in the City and the County. Such concern in the County prompted the adoption of the proposal that created the metropolitan sewer district in 1954. The percentages citing various other improvements are approximately the same for City and County, with a larger percentage in the County suggesting most of them.

The City residents are more concerned with problems stemming from the age of their neighborhoods, but the County inhabitants worry more about problems emanating from rapid

TABLE 22

Suggested Types of Improvements in Local Community: City and County

Type of improvement desired	Percentage of persons suggesting type of improvement [a]	
	City	County
Condition of residential streets	47%	53%
Character of neighborhood (maintaining and improving)	29	8
Traffic conditions	17	20
Parks and playgrounds	11	13
Various nongovernmental services such as private utilities and employment practices	10	9
Sewage disposal system	*	18
Public transportation	4	8
Public schools	3	8
Police protection	5	4

[a] Suggested changes are ranked by frequency of their occurrence for the City-County area as a whole. The last two changes that appear here are not listed in figure 13. They are suggested by at least 5 per cent in either City or County separately, but not by 5 per cent in the City and County together.

suburban growth and inadequate public facilities. In each area a large percentage is bothered by the condition of residential streets, and other large numbers want improvements in traffic conditions and park and playground facilities.

As is true of problems in the local community, a major difference between the City and County residents is that a larger percentage of County people name three or more improvements for the entire City-County area (D11). In terms of City-County problems, this may reflect the generally higher social rank of County residents; the much sharper difference in naming problems in the local community may indicate the greater commitment of suburban residents to their local neighborhood. It may also demonstrate that suburban communities have more local problems and many City-County problems are felt more severely in the suburban county.

Traffic is the area-wide problem most often cited in both the City and County, but agreement on the rank order of area-wide difficulties ends there. Condition of streets and character of neighborhoods stand second and third in the City. Public transportation, air and water pollution, and condition of streets are of about equal importance, after traffic, in the County. These variations are consistent with the known differences between City and County as places to live and the nature of their respective populations. County residents are apparently more aware of the truly metropolitan problems—those that are area-wide and call for area-wide solutions—whereas City inhabitants are more interested in the effects of structural decay and blight in their aged neighborhoods.

The answers to the closed-end questions about satisfaction and dissatisfaction with a specific list of services are quite similar to the answers to the open-end question about what changes or improvements should be made (D12). The rank order of dissatisfaction is approximately the same.[2] Traffic, condition of streets, and parks and playgrounds all produced high propor-

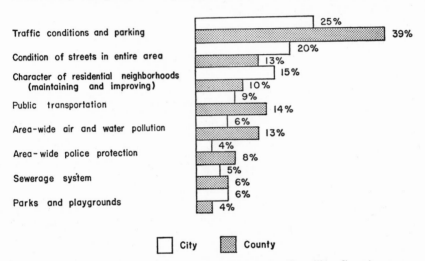

Traffic conditions and parking — City 25%, County 39%

Condition of streets in entire area — City 20%, County 13%

Character of residential neighborhoods (maintaining and improving) — City 15%, County 10%

Public transportation — City 9%, County 14%

Area-wide air and water pollution — City 6%, County 13%

Area-wide police protection — City 4%, County 8%

Sewerage system — City 5%, County 6%

Parks and playgrounds — City 6%, County 4%

☐ City   ▨ County

Fig. 17. Suggested types of improvements in the City-County area: City and County residents. (Suggestions follow the order of presentation of the lower half of fig. 13, p. 186.)

tions of responses that they are public problems. However, public transportation, which was mentioned by only 4 and 8 per cent of the City and County residents, respectively, in an answer to the open question, elicited the second highest percentage of unfavorable judgments (34 and 44 per cent, respectively) when particular services were presented in a list.

In response to the list, services with which City and County residents are dissatisfied vary most sharply in ranking police protection and sewage disposal. Over one-fifth of the City residents

---

[2] The item on maintaining and improving the character of the neighborhood is not comparable as it was not included in the closed-end questions, although it was mentioned frequently in responses to the open-end question.

are dissatisfied with their police protection, as against one-tenth in the County. More than one-fourth of the County residents are concerned about sewage disposal as compared to one-tenth of the City residents. These findings are similar to the variation found in answers to the open-end question.

City residents indicate more dissatisfaction with garbage collection, police protection, and the condition of the residential streets. Residents of the County, on the other hand, demonstrate more dissatisfaction with sewage disposal, parks and playgrounds, public transportation, and traffic conditions (although many persons in the City are also dissatisfied with these services). There is little variation in dissatisfaction between City and County people about libraries, schools, water supply, and fire protection.

COMPLAINTS ABOUT SERVICES

The same percentage (38 per cent) in the City and the County felt like complaining about one or more services. A majority who wanted to complain in the County (54 per cent) did so to a person or agency, but a majority in the City (68 per cent) did not. There is little difference in the types of services about which the residents of City and County complained. Somewhat fewer City residents complained about sanitation (49 per cent as compared to 57 per cent in the County), and somewhat fewer County residents about streets and utilities (27 per cent as against 35 per cent). Practically all complaints dealt with immediate necessities of the household. The only exceptions were a few relating to protection of person and property (about 7 per cent in each area) and educational, cultural, and recreational facilities (5 per cent in the City, 9 per cent in the County).

Forty-two per cent of the complainants in the County lodged their complaints with a specific person or officeholder, as against 25 per cent in the City. The most pronounced difference between the City and County is in the number of persons who communicated directly with elected officials (D13). One-fifth making complaints in the County did so, four times as many as in the City, where the recipient was likely to be a "faceless" agency or "City Hall." These findings support the belief that government is more personalized for the resident of the small suburban community than for the citizen of the central city.

Are citizen complaints effective? A majority indicated their efforts failed (D14). On the other hand, a very sizable minority succeeded in getting conditions changed. This does not conform to the image of practically all citizens being helpless in the face of a bureaucratic structure immune to their pressure.

Equally interesting are those persons who said they have wanted to complain, but have never done so. Commonly held images of the citizen's relationship with local government imply an impotence on his part to influence local governments, either from a lack of personal power, which occasions a cynical attitude toward the agency responsible to its constituents, or from the lack of knowledge regarding to whom the citizen should complain. With such considerations in mind, the answers to "How does it happen that you've never complained?" were placed in four categories.

1) Rational inaction: includes such answers as "It was only a minor problem, and was hardly worth the bother," or "They had started work on it anyway."

2) Naïveté: indicates a lack of personal confidence as well as the application of personalized norms—"It's not my place to complain," "I wouldn't want to get anybody in trouble," or "Nobody else complained."

3) Ignorance: persons who said they did not know to whom they should complain.

4) Cynicism: individuals said, in one form or another, "It wouldn't do any good for me to complain; nothing can be done about it."

There are differences, although not pronounced ones, in the reasons given for not complaining by City and County residents. More County residents claimed ignorance, more City residents expressed naïveté and cynicism (D15).

The reasons are not mutually exclusive. For example, those whose naïveté influences their reason for not complaining may also have been ignorant of the proper agency or person to receive the complaint. Nevertheless, the over-all impression remains that cynicism (or lack of faith in government) is not a common rationalization for failure to express complaints. The bulk of the rationalizations manifests either a reasonable inaction or incompetence to deal with the local situation (naïveté and ignorance). Forty-three per cent in the City and 46 per cent in the County give naïveté and ignorance as reasons. More than one-third in both City and County give answers that can be classified as rational inaction.

THE WORTH OF LOCAL GOVERNMENT

No great differences between the City and County were expressed in opinions about local taxes. However, County residents more frequently judge local taxes to be excessive. People in the County, which faces steeper tax increases in the near future, are almost equally divided in believing taxes are and are not too high.

TABLE 23

JUDGMENTS ABOUT LOCAL TAX RATES

Residence	Too high	Satisfactory	Too low	Don't know
City	37%	54%	1%	7%
County	45	49	1	7

EVALUATION OF GOVERNMENTS

Virtually no difference exists between City and County in their evaluations of any governments other than the metropolitan sewer district. Many more County residents judge this government to be doing a poor job. County residents living in incorporated municipalities generally appraise their municipality somewhat higher than the residents of the city of St. Louis evaluate their own municipal government.

Residents in both City and County gave the City a majority of favorable (very good or good) evaluations, the County municipalities (other than the one in which various respondents lived) a substantial minority, and the St. Louis County government a smaller minority. Only one government, the metropolitan sewer district, was rated poor by more than one-fifth of the people in either area, in this instance, the County.

METROPOLITAN PROBLEMS AND SOLUTIONS

County residents more often state that there are problems shared by the City and the County. Over 63 per cent in the County mentioned one or more specific mutual problems as compared to 47 per cent in the City. More City than County residents said there were no such problems (22 per cent versus 14 per cent), and twice as many in the City as in the County (24 per cent as against 12 per cent) said there are such problems but do not know what they are. Of those who said there are major problems, 87 per cent in the suburban county could name specific problems; only 69 per cent could do so in the City.[3]

OPINIONS CONCERNING EXISTING GOVERNMENTAL ARRANGEMENTS

As might be expected since practically all municipalities are in the County, somewhat fewer City residents have a definite opinion on whether 97 municipalities in the City-County area constitute an excessive number (D16). More important is the difference in the proportions within City and County who think there are too many municipalities. Only a minority of the City residents agree, but just under three-fifths in the County think so. County residents have more direct knowledge of the fragmented governmental pattern and they experience more service inadequacies resulting from it.

TABLE 24

ADVANTAGES TO LOCAL COMMUNITY RESULTING FROM GOVERNMENTAL COÖPERATION IN THE CITY-COUNTY AREA

Advantages	City	County
Efficiency, coördination, more and better services	51%	51%
Cheaper government, lower taxes	19	17
Both cheaper and more efficient	10	18
More participation and interest in government	9	7
Advantage, but don't know what	12	7

There is little difference in the proportions of City and County residents who believe it would be to their own community's advantage to join with others in handling some local governmental services. Most people in both sections feel it would be advantageous. The only important variation is in the percentage who do not know—13 per cent in the City and 6 per cent in the County.

The largest single category of reasons why governmental coöperation would be advantageous hinges upon more and better services and a more adequate governmental organization. Only a comparatively small minority in both City and County mention lower taxes. The coördination of local public services appeals to most persons because of its potentiality to extend governmental services.

---

[3] More than 60 per cent in both City and County believe there are major problems involving the City-County area and the East Side in Illinois. Only 31 per cent in the City and 41 per cent in the County can name at least one specific problem.

WILLINGNESS TO ACCEPT GOVERNMENTAL INTEGRATION

Substantial variations between the City and County appeared in opinions about alternative plans of governmental reorganization. In general, County residents are less friendly to alternatives that involve some degree of integration of County and City and more favorable to the status quo.

A majority of the residents of the City favor every proposal

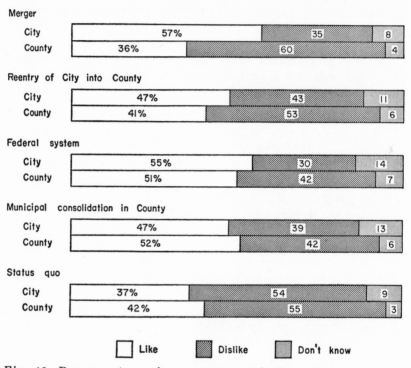

Merger

City	57% · 35 · 8
County	36% · 60 · 4

Reentry of City into County

City	47% · 43 · 11
County	41% · 53 · 6

Federal system

City	55% · 30 · 14
County	51% · 42 · 7

Municipal consolidation in County

City	47% · 39 · 13
County	52% · 42 · 6

Status quo

City	37% · 54 · 9
County	42% · 55 · 3

☐ Like   ▨ Dislike   ▨ Don't know

Fig. 18. Response to various governmental alternatives: City and County.

for integrating the governments in the City-County area, from City-County merger to consolidation of County municipalities. At the same time they oppose status quo. In the County, there is a sharp reversal of the prevailing City attitude about merger and reëntry of the city of St. Louis into the County; strong majorities of County residents oppose both alternatives. Over half the County residents, however, state that they like both the federal system and the consolidation of the ninety-six County municipalities into a smaller number. A larger percentage in the County opposes status quo, a result in part of the fact that more County people have an opinion on this alternative.

The consolidation of County municipalities is not directly relevant to City residents; if elections for such a change take place, they would have no vote on the matter. This proposal would not affect City-County relationships directly, but a rather substantial majority (55 per cent) of County residents with opinions on the proposal favor it.

The intensely held opinions for residents of the City-County area as a whole cluster about the two extremes, City-County merger and status quo, but there is important variation between City and County. Two-fifths in the County most dislike merger, as compared to about one-fifth in the City; however, about two-fifths of the City residents prefer merger to all other suggestions. At the other extreme, the largest percentage of City residents dislikes status quo more than any other alternative, while the second largest percentage of County residents likes this proposal best.

TABLE 25

Most Liked and Most Disliked Proposals for Governmental Change

Proposal	Most liked	Most disliked
Merger		
City	38%	19%
County	26	40
Reëntry of City into County		
City	13	15
County	14	11
Federal system		
City	15	10
County	15	9
Municipal consolidation in County		
City	6	13
County	17	8
Status quo		
City	19	30
County	24	28
Don't know		
City	9	13
County	3	5

The weight of each distribution is in favor of some type of change. Although 40 per cent of the County residents most dislike the merger solution, another 26 per cent prefer it above all others.

And with respect to the status quo, almost as many County as City people dislike it most.[4]

TABLE 26

ASSOCIATION BETWEEN MOST LIKED AND MOST DISLIKED CHOICES AMONG PROPOSALS FOR GOVERNMENTAL CHANGE

Most liked proposal	Most disliked proposal						
	1	2	3	4	5	6	
	Merger	Reënter County	Federal system	Municipal consolidation	Status quo	Don't know	N
1 Merger							
City		19%	13%	15%	49%	4%	196
County		10	17	11	59	2	337
2 Reënter County							
City	21%		18	18	33	10	67
County	31		12	15	41	1	179
3 Federal system							
City	38	18		15	27	2	79
County	56	14		9	17	4	195
4 Municipal consolidation							
City	32	16	16		29	7	97
County	56	13	10		19	2	221
5 Status quo							
City	42	24	10	13		10	31
County	70	17	6	5		3	314
6 Don't know							
City	4	0	2	0	9	84	45
County	8	0	5	0	13	74	39

Within the City and County separately, there is consistency in ranking. As indicated in table 26, the proportion most disliking merger generally increases in proceeding down column 1 toward status quo, and the percentage disliking the existing governmental arrangements generally decreases in moving down column 5 toward status quo. However, little difference was expressed in the extent of negative judgments about merger and status quo between the proponents of municipal consolidation in the County and the proponents of the federal system. It is possible, then, that these two proposals have approximately the same meaning to

---

[4] The relatively small percentage that has no opinion on these questions of the most liked and most disliked proposals for governmental change indicates the extent of public interest in them. But the questions occurred in the middle of an hour and a half interview and the respondent had been stimulated. Nevertheless, for such complex choices with a random sample, a range of 3 per cent to 13 per cent who do not know is small.

their adherents—they represent some, but not too much, integration. More supporters of each moderate proposal dislike merger than status quo.

The general tendency for City residents to favor change over the existing state of affairs is clearly apparent. They are, however, less consistent in their opinions and less polarized. The County resident who chooses a form of City-County governmental integration is more frequently hostile to the milder approach of municipal consolidation in the County or to the status quo than is the City resident. On the other hand, if the County resident is most favorable to these latter alternatives, he will be much more often hostile to merging the City and the County. Additional support for the hypothesis of greater polarization in the County appears in the percentage of those who do not know which proposal they most dislike. Aside from the proponents of the federal system, County residents have a lower percentage of persons without opinions on each type of governmental alternative.

A categorization of people into three types of consistent holders of opinions—mergerites, moderate integrationists, and local autonomists—was undertaken for City and County residents separately. The first group includes those who most prefer City-County merger and who dislike most either municipal consolidation in the County or status quo—proposals that do not involve City-County integration. The moderates prefer either municipal consolidation in the County, a federal system, or reëntry of the City into the County, and most dislike either status quo or merger. The local autonomists prefer the status quo to all other proposals and most dislike either merger or the reëntry of the City into St. Louis County.

In each type, the adherents of a proposal are twice as likely to oppose its most contrasting alternative. For example, of those who prefer merger, 49 per cent in the City and 59 per cent in the County disapprove status quo most strongly; these percentages are more than twice as high as those for greatest dislike of any other alternative by people who like merger best. The most imprecise type consists of the moderates, but it seems valid and consistent because it involves preference for some degree of governmental integration and opposition to extreme alternatives. Persons whose responses do not fall into one of these three consistent patterns may be called "no type" (identified as "all others" in table 27).

An absolute majority of the County residents come within

TABLE 27

THREE TYPES OF PERSONS HOLDING CONSISTENT OPINIONS
ABOUT GOVERNMENTAL ALTERNATIVES

Residence	Mergerites	Moderates	Local autonomists	All others
City	24%	21%	12%	43%
County	19	34	21	26

either the extreme or moderate integrationist categories. The largest single category in the County is composed of the moderates. In the City, however, the distribution of types is more heavily loaded toward merger.

Also important is the larger proportion of holders of consistent opinions in the County. If the three types are considered to exhaust the possible consistent positions on the issue, County residents are much more definite and consistent.[5] Over 73 per cent of them fall into one of the three types, as against slightly over 57 per cent of the City inhabitants.

TABLE 28

OPINIONS OF FEDERAL SYSTEM BY PERSONS MOST DISLIKING
THE OTHER ALTERNATIVES

	Opinions of federal system			
Most disliked change	Liked	Disliked	Don't know	N
Merger				
City	62%	25%	13%	97
County	55	38	7	683
Reëntry of City into County				
City	54	35	10	79
County	52	46	2	143
Municipal consolidation in County				
City	67	28	4	67
County	70	27	3	98
Status quo				
City	76	19	5	152
County	54	41	5	355

The percentage of local autonomists is higher in the County, but it is not a very large proportion (21 per cent) and is almost matched by the mergerites (19 per cent). If the proponents of City-County merger could be expected to support a moderate proposal, then the local autonomists in the County would be out-

[5] There is one other consistent position that contains relatively few people —those who do not know what they like and dislike most.

numbered, even though they might be joined by most or all of the residual, "no-type" holders of opinions.

SUPPORT FOR THE FEDERAL SYSTEM

A majority among those who are strongly opposed to each alternative says it likes the federal system. The percentages preferring it are similar for each group of City-County residents with opinions with one major exception—County residents most opposed to the status quo are considerably less favorably disposed toward the federal system than are the opponents of status quo in the City. In connection with this exception, it is worth recalling that a larger proportion of the County residents are polarized and consistent in their opinions of the various proposals. A proponent of merger might very well dislike the federal system, which leaves all local governments in existence, as a halfway step. And, among residents of the County, mergerites dislike halfway measures more consistently than their counterparts in the City do.

Further support for this position is exemplified by table 29, which presents opinions of the federal system by each class of proponents. Those who hold the extreme positions are the only classes of County residents in which a majority of those with opinions dislike the federal idea.

TABLE 29

OPINIONS OF THE FEDERAL SYSTEM BY PERSONS MOST LIKING
THE OTHER ALTERNATIVES

	Opinion of federal system			
Most liked proposal	Liked	Disliked	Don't know	N
Merger				
City	55%	38%	8%	196
County	39	57	4	337
Reëntry of City into County				
City	64	28	7	67
County	59	35	6	179
Municipal consolidation in County				
City	52	39	10	31
County	49	44	6	221
Status quo				
City	33	49	18	97
County	33	56	10	314
Don't know				
City	18	7	76	45
County	18	16	67	39

OPINIONS CONCERNING CHANGE

Little variation is present between City and County on whether an election should be held on one of these plans of governmental reorganization in the near future. About 70 per cent in both think so. Moreover, a majority who most prefer each type of change (and almost the same percentage) want such an election; those who prefer merger or reëntry of the City into the County are overwhelmingly for an election (82 and 85 per cent in the City and County, respectively). Smaller, but still impressive, percentages preferring the federal system (76 per cent in the County, 81 per cent in the City), or consolidation of County municipalities into a smaller number (77 per cent in the County, 55 per cent in the City) want an election soon. However, of those who prefer status quo, 49 per cent in the County and 46 per cent in the City oppose an election, whereas 42 per cent in the County and 43 per cent in the City are in favor. Thus, among proponents of governmental reorganization, adherents of consolidation of County municipalities represent the only significant difference in the City and County regarding the desirability of an election.

TABLE 30

BELIEF IN PROBABILITY OF GOVERNMENTAL REORGANIZATION

Residence	Change likely	Change unlikely	Don't know
City	46%	41%	14%
County	40	50	10

There are differences between City and County regarding belief in the probability of change in the near future (D17). City residents are somewhat more optimistic. This is consistent with their tendency to view all reform alternatives as desirable. Among proponents of every type of change, there are more City residents who believe change is likely, and a majority choosing each plan believe it probable. In the County, with equal consistency, a majority with opinions discount the likelihood of change, no matter what their personal preference is for the future.

SUMMARY: VOTING, SERVICES, AND REORGANIZATION IN CITY AND COUNTY

In both City and County, those who vote in one local election are likely to be the same persons who vote in others, and almost all the electorate for local contests vote in the national presidential elections. In the suburban county where some citizens may vote in as many as four different local contests (County, municipality, school district, and fire district), most voters participate in at least three kinds. In the City, most persons vote in the two local elections (municipal and school) that are available to them.

A larger percentage in the County disagree with the statement that local elections are unimportant. However, in the City a larger percentage have voted than in the suburban county. Whether this reflects the importance of the metropolitan daily newspapers, political party organization, or simply the size and importance of the single central municipality and a single school district, the fact remains that political participation is more common in the local government of St. Louis City than in the suburban county.

More suburban residents are unable to say whether they and their neighbors can vote, and more state that they cannot vote (when, in truth, they can). The widely held assumption that governmental fragmentation results in a lower voter competence seems firmly supported by this finding, particularly when the higher average educational level in the County is kept in mind.

Suburban residents are more likely to suggest needed changes or improvements in their local community and to suggest more of them. Moreover, they are more frequently dissatisfied with a larger number of services already provided. Their complaints differ from those made in the City in several respects. More emphasis is placed by County inhabitants upon improving the condition of residential streets, traffic conditions and public transportation, park and playground facilities, sewage disposal, and public schools. Residents of the City are more frequently worried about maintaining and improving the character of the neighborhood, indicating that such functions as zoning, neighborhood conservation, and urban renewal are extremely important. Suburbanites are more aware of problems shared by City and County, and suggest more changes and improvements for the City-County area as a whole.

A majority of the people in both City and County have never felt like complaining about any of the local services they had been asked to evaluate. Of those who have felt like complaining, however, a much larger proportion in the County had done so. But there is little difference in the extent of complete success with their complaints. A much larger percentage of those who complained in the County did so to specific individuals. Of those who have felt like complaining, but had never done so, similar proportions in City and County alike have failed to complain. Evaluations of the various local governments differ very little between City and County.

A large majority in the County believe there are too many municipalities in the area, practically all of which are in the County. Most people in both City and County believe it would be to their community's advantage to join with others in handling some public services.

City residents are more favorable to every proposal involving City-County governmental reorganization—merger, reëntry of the City into the County, or a federal system. County residents, however, favor some form of governmental change, one type of which, consolidation of County municipalities, would involve only the County. Three types of holders of opinions about reorganization—mergerites, moderates, and local autonomists—account for almost three-fourths of the County residents, but for less than three-fifths of the people in the City. This indicates that County residents are more consistent and more polarized in their reactions to suggestions for change.

A majority of those hostile to all alternative proposals say they like the federal system, which would be a multipurpose metropolitan district under the legally available options. Supporters of most other proposals, with the important exceptions of those in the County who are proponents of the extreme positions, merger and status quo, also state that they like the federal system.

11

The Electorate
for Local Government

ARE DIFFERENCES in political participation and governmental attitudes between central city and suburbs largely explained by differences in the prevailing social and economic characteristics of
their residents? Are responses on various matters approximately
the same for the same type of people, regardless of whether they
live in the City or County? These questions are investigated
extensively in this chapter and the two that follow in terms of
five clusters or groups of social and economic attributes. Grouping makes possible the comparison of relative effects of socioeconomic distinctions with residence in central city and suburbs.

The five clusters of attributes are: biologically based status
(age and sex), social rank (education, income, and occupation),
ethnic background, mobility and migration, and commitment to
place. Each of them deserves elaboration at this point.[1]

1) *Biologically based status.* Age and sex differences are universally important as differentiators of human behavior, for they
are basic determinants of roles. The male role involves a different
set of rights and duties, including in American society economic
and political acts not nearly so important in the female role. Age
is important, for it yields an index of the individual's position in
the family life cycle. The residents are grouped into five age

---

[1] In general, only the significant findings relating to these attributes are
presented.

classes, corresponding roughly to (a) young adults, unmarried, childless, or with small children—ages 21–29; (b) younger family people, usually married with children in the home—ages 30–39; (c) older family people, with children who are in the higher grades of high school or who have left home—ages 40–49; (d) postparental people whose children are outside the household—ages 50–64; and (e) the oldsters, disproportionately female and widowed—age 65 and over.

2) *Social rank.* Determinants of life chances, prestige, and rewards have effects upon political interest, association, and action. *Education* is a clue to the individual's frame of reference, his technical equipment for understanding governmental affairs, and his likely associates. Six categories for education are used: (a) those with less than an eighth grade education, persons who, even in a less "school oriented" society, achieved less than the average amount of schooling; (b) those who completed the eighth grade, frequently in a society (rural or ethnic or foreign) where this was considered adequate, though it is a measure of inadequacy in America today; (c) those who had some high school education but did not finish, including many persons who were compelled to stay in school but not to finish (or even to learn); (d) those who finished high school, the contemporary average education; (e) those with some college training; and (f) those who completed the bachelor's degree or even had further formal educational training.

Income directly indicates some of the rewards the individual has had allocated to him; it also tells something of his objective interests (as they might be determined by an economist) and his capabilities to produce. A fourfold breakdown of income classes has been employed: (a) the very poor, with annual incomes under $3,000 for the entire household; (b) the average poor, with incomes from $3,000 to $4,999; (c) the average "middle class," from $5,000 to $6,999; and (d) the more prosperous, with incomes above $7,000. The last category has a wide range, and on occasion will be subdivided for the County population; in the City it is too small for subdivision.

Occupation of a working person furnishes an index of the kinds of skills he possesses and the types of persons he associates with, and is, indirectly, a measure of his education and income. Adults are divided into five classes: (a) lower blue-collar workers, those who are classified as laborers or factory operatives—in general, the least skilled; (b) upper blue-collar workers, mainly foremen and craftsmen; (c) lower white-collar workers, principally sales personnel and clerical workers; (d) upper white-collar workers, including professionals, semiprofessionals, managers, officials, and proprietors; and (e) inappropriate—those who are not in the labor force, chiefly the retired.

Each of these three aspects of social rank—education, income, and occupation—is related to each of the others; they tend to vary together. For some kinds of behavior, however, education is a better discriminating attribute than income, and in other cases, the reverse is true. What these three measures have to tell, both singly and in common, is of interest.

3) *Ethnic background.* Nationality of origin, although that "origin" may be years and generations in the past, continues to affect present behavior. Closely associated with nationality background is religion, and it may sometimes make a difference. The population has been classified into four ethnic contingents: (a) persons whose original background, or family background, was in the British Isles or northern or western Europe, except Germany —the Old Americans; (b) those whose family originally came from Germany (Germans do not necessarily have a lower prestige rank than Old Americans, but the large concentration of Germans in the St. Louis area makes it advisable to treat them as a separate ethnic category; they sometimes behave differently); (c) persons whose family origin was in southern or eastern Europe —the Italians, Slavs, Jews, and others of the "new migration"; and (d) Negroes. By religion the people have been grouped into Catholic and all others. The latter will be referred to as "Protestant," which they are in 90 per cent of the cases.

4) *Mobility and migration.* The movement of population, whether through migration or in daily cycles, is characteristic of modern urban society. The number of years since migration into the metropolitan area has been used as a measure of migration history, and the categories consist of persons who have been in the area (a) less than five years, the new migrants, (b) between five and twenty years, composed chiefly of the wartime migrants, (c) twenty years or more, the old predepression and depression decade migrants, and (d) a lifetime, the natives. An associated measure is living on a farm during the first twenty years of life, as many migrants to urban areas came originally from farms. Finally, the effects of fluidity, or movement within the area, are investigated through the analysis of those living in the suburbs and working in the central city.

5) *Commitment to place.* The type of dwelling unit in which a person lives, whether a single-family house or an apartment building, is an approximate index of his social relations with his neighbors. In general, this relates to neighboring, identification, and commitment to the neighborhood as a social fact. Type of occupancy is also related to commitment; those who own their homes have a "real" or economic stake in the neighborhood. Finally, years of residence in the dwelling unit is major evidence of commitment.

The three measures of commitment to place—type of dwelling unit, type of occupancy, and years of residence in dwelling— seemingly possess an increasing degree of precision. Type of dwelling unit is the crudest, years of residence the most valid. The first requires a chain of inference from the dwelling unit to the neighborhood and back to the individual (although this is usually justified because of the concentration of apartment houses); the second more directly measures his liking for the neighborhood (he did not move away) and his opportunities to identify and become involved with the place. Because of the likelihood that it represents a good composite index of commitment, people have been grouped into six classes by their period of residence in their present dwelling unit: (a) new arrivals, less than one year; (b) new residents, one but less than three years; (c) three but less than five years; (d) five but less than ten years; (e) ten but less than twenty years, and (f) twenty years or more.

This chapter is concerned with the electorate for local government. Who are the voters? Are they more likely to be old or young, male or female, Negro or white? How does the composition of the electorate vary among those who have voted in a national presidential election and several types of local elections? Who believes in the proposition that a local election is important? How does this belief relate to electoral participation? Finally, how much of the difference between City and County residents can be attributed to variations in socioeconomic background?

THE LIMITS OF THE TOTAL ELECTORATE

The total electorate for local government, determined according to those eligible to vote who have ever voted in any local election since living in their present community, amounts to 69 per cent in the City, 72 per cent in the County. Although there are important variations by most of the socioeconomic factors used, the most striking are associated with age, migration, history, and commitment to place.

AGE AND SEX

The single most powerful estimator of ever having voted in a local election is age. In the City there is an increase in the percentage having voted from the 21–29 year class to the 30–39 year class, and from the 40–49 year class to the 50–64 class with a slight decline among those 65 years and over (D18). In the County sharp increases are incurred between the three lowest age categories, reaching a plateau from age 40 onward, with no variation in percentage having voted. Proportions voting are very similar for City and County, except in the class 40–49.

Variations by sex are not nearly so important; however, in City and in County, men are more likely to have voted in some local election. Seventy-one per cent of the males in the City have voted, as against 62 per cent of the females; 73 per cent of the males in the County, as compared to 63 per cent of the females.

SOCIAL RANK

Measures reflecting socioeconomic stratification do not have nearly the predictive power regarding local election voting that might be expected from studies of national elections. Taken separately, each makes a difference, but not a striking one. The relationship between voting in any local election and education is neither very strong nor very consistent; the most dependable finding is the increase in voting with some college education (D19).

The proportion of people who have ever voted locally does not increase consistently or significantly through the various levels of income. In both City and County 60 to 66 per cent of the three lowest income classes have voted. A much larger proportion of the very highest income class, however, has voted; three-fourths in the County have done so and 84 per cent in the City. The relatively larger size of this class in the County accounts for the slightly larger over-all percentage of County residents who have ever voted in local elections.

Similar findings emerge regarding occupational levels, but they are of even less magnitude than differences by income classes. In both City and County, 73 per cent of the upper white-collar category have voted, compared with 65 per cent in the two blue-collar categories. A larger proportion of City clerical workers have voted than their counterparts in the County, although the difference is not significant (70 per cent as against 63 per cent). The difference between the voting of professional persons and all others in the County is significant; in the City the variation is slight and not significant.

ETHNICITY

Ethnicity is of consistent importance in voting. Both color and nationality background must be considered and in many instances religion. In the central city all "minority" populations are more likely to have voted in a local election than the Old Americans, although the percentages of Negroes and Old Americans are virtually the same; in the County, however, the proportions of Negroes and persons with southern or eastern European backgrounds who have voted are smaller. In both City and County those with German backgrounds rank very high. The ranges for City and County in percentages voting among the various ethnic classes are wide—61 to 80 per cent in the City, and 57 to 71 per cent in the County. In other words, the decline in voting with ethnic status, from those with Old American and German background to Negroes, is consistent in the County, but in the City the low-ranking ethnic populations outvote the Old Americans, and those from southern and eastern Europe stand first.

TABLE 31

ETHNIC IDENTITY AND VOTING IN ANY LOCAL ELECTION

Residence	Old American	German	Southern and eastern European	Negro
City	61%	77%	80%	62%
	(200)[a]	(124)	(49)	(116)
County	68%	71%	82%	57%
	(626)	(425)	(148)	(51)

EXCLUDED: City 26 and County 35 "don't know" or "other."

[a] The figures in parentheses here and in following similar tables represent the number of interviews in each category. When certain interviews are excluded, the reasons are given in a footnote to the table.

In the City a much larger proportion of Catholics have voted than Protestants. Seventy-eight per cent reported they have voted in some local election, as against only 60 per cent of the Protestants. In the County, however, the difference is slight—70 per cent

Catholic against 66 per cent Protestant. The difference in the City may be related to the fact that Catholics are mostly of German or Italian background (the two populations with the highest percentages voting), whereas Protestants are apt to be Negroes or Old Americans. In the County the typically Catholic populations do not vote as frequently, but the Old Americans there vote more often than in the City.

MIGRATION

The number of years the individual has lived in the metropolitan area bears an important relationship to likelihood of voting. Length of residence summarizes the effects of the individual's age, number of opportunities to vote, and involvement in the political processes and crosscurrents of interest in the metropolitan community. In the St. Louis area this factor ranks with age as the two most powerful predictors of having voted in a local election.

The proportions of the newest migrants who have voted are comparable for City and County. A much larger percentage of County migrants who have been in the area between five and twenty years have voted, however. This may reflect the different social rank of migrants in the City and in the County; it also suggests that migrants to the area now living in the suburbs may be of higher social rank than the natives in the suburbs. The difference in voting between natives in City and County is pronounced and significant.

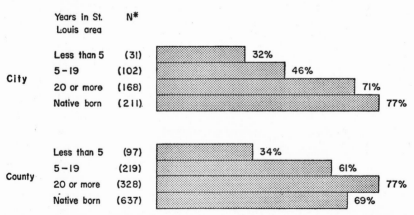

* N represents the number of cases or interviews. Excluded: City 3 and County 4 "don't know."

Fig. 19. Time in metropolitan area and voting in any local election.

Another measure of migration is the individual's rural experience, determined by residence on a farm between birth and age twenty. A substantial portion of the population in both the City and the County had some childhood experience on a farm, and in the City this does relate to whether or not they have ever voted in local elections. Only 55 per cent in the City of rural background have ever voted in a local election while living in their present community; 73 per cent who had no early farm experience have voted. In the County, the difference is negligible—65 per cent and 67 per cent, respectively, have voted.

Although County residents with a farm background have voted more often than City residents with a similar past, individuals in the City without a farm background are more likely to have voted (73 per cent compared to 67 per cent). Or, from another point of view, City residents can be divided into the "farm boy in the City" and the urban resident; this dichotomy does not hold for the suburban population. The higher percentage of voting among City residents without a rural background compensates for the much lower rate of voting by those with a farm background and for the somewhat large proportion of "farm boys" in the City population.

COMMITMENT TO NEIGHBORHOOD

There are important differences between people who have and have not ever voted locally according to type of dwelling, type of occupancy, and years lived in present residence.

The difference in voting between those living in single-family and multiple-family dwelling units is striking. In the City, 15 per cent more single-family residents have voted (76 per cent and 61 per cent) and in the County, 10 per cent more (68 per cent and 58 per cent). Larger percentages of City residents in both types of dwellings have voted, but the preponderance of single-family residents in the County results in the slightly higher rate of voting there.

Type of occupancy further divides the single-family residents. Almost all homeowners live in single-family residences. Some people who live in these units, however, are renters and, if the assumption is correct, they are likely to be less committed to the locality, just as some persons living in multiple-family units are owners of these units (chiefly duplexes) and consequently more committed than renters. The differences by type of occupancy are even sharper than by type of unit; 26 per cent more owners in the City (82 per cent compared with 56 per cent), and 25 per cent more in the County (71 and 46 per cent) have ever voted in a local election. Again, a substantially larger proportion in each category have voted in the City, but 60 per cent of the City residents are renters, compared with 10 per cent in the County.

The number of years the individual has lived in his present dwelling unit is another measure of commitment to neighborhood or place. It is the strongest factor distinguishing voters and nonvoters (D20). Very few persons who have lived in their present dwelling unit less than one year have voted in any local election; many, but not all, of these persons are new to the metropolitan area. Only about one-half of those who have lived in their present home between one and three years have ever voted. Over 90 per cent of those who have lived in their present location for twenty years or more have voted in local elections.

The steady increase after the 3–4 year category indicates that more is involved than simply the opportunity to vote. Stability and homeownership, which are most characteristic of persons living in single-family dwelling units, are associated with participation in the local electoral process.

VOTING IN MUNICIPAL ELECTIONS

A substantially larger proportion of the City than of the County electorate has voted in municipal elections. Considering only County residents who live in municipalities and are entitled to vote in such elections, and eliminating those who said they are ineligible to vote, only 57 per cent have ever voted in municipal elections in their present community as compared to 67 per cent in the City. This ratio in voting is more than accounted for by the difference in incompetence between City and County. Incompetence is measured by the percentage of individuals who state that (1) people in their neighborhood cannot vote for city officials, or (2) they do not know if people can vote when, in fact, they can. Twenty per cent of the County residents living in municipalities are incompetent, compared with only 5 per cent in the City. Of those who are competent, however, a somewhat larger per cent have voted in the County.

In general, as with the electorate for local government, the percentages of those who are eligible to vote in municipal elections who do so vary most sharply by indexes associated with migration background, commitment to neighborhood, and age. Social rank is of more importance, however, in predicting the per cent voting in municipal elections than that ever having voted in any local election, particularly in the County. For the most part, the factors have similar effects in City and County, although the variations tend to be somewhat greater in the City.

AGE AND SEX

Voting in municipal elections is most common among older-age populations. The age curve is typically one in which participation increases sharply between the youngest age class and the 30–39-year-old category, increases less sharply but consistently to the 50–64 category, then declines somewhat with the population aged 65 and over (D21). These changes in voting participation are explainable: the youngest persons are not yet as involved in family, neighborhood, and community networks of communication and responsibility; the oldest group has begun to find many bonds falling away with the dissolution of the family and the relative isolation of old age.

Most striking are the increasing disproportion between City and County in voting with increasing age and the much greater incompetence among most age classes in the County. Only 4 per cent more have voted in the City among the 30–39 age class, but 20 per cent more have voted among those 65 and over. Persons between the ages of 30 and 39 are the only ones in the County who are nearly as competent as the similar City population. This age class, the most competent in the County, is the least competent in the City. For those aged 40 and over in the County, the proportion that is incompetent is very high, between one-fifth and one-third of all residents of the municipalities—compared with 2 to 5 per cent in the City.

Sex differences in voting are negligible in the City; however, most of the incompetence is among the women. Eight per cent of the women do not think people in their neighborhood can vote for municipal officials, compared with 2 per cent of the men. In the County men more often vote (66 per cent compared with 50 per cent) and are less frequently incompetent (15 per cent and 26 per cent, respectively). Men in the suburbs are about as likely to have voted in municipal elections as women in the City. Considering sex and residence together, however, the difference is pronounced; 71 per cent of the men in the City have voted in such elections and 50 per cent of the County women.

SOCIAL RANK

The higher the social rank, the greater the probability a person has voted in municipal elections. Particularly in the County, the three measures of social rank indicate broad differences in municipal election participation. Education and income differentiate similarly in City and County, but occupation is much more important in the County. Among each educational class, except the college-educated, 15 per cent more have voted in the City. And, in the County, the college-educated are almost twice as likely to be incompetent as individuals in the City who did not finish the eighth grade.

TABLE 32

EDUCATION AND VOTING IN MUNICIPAL ELECTIONS

Voters	Years of education completed					
	0–7	8	9–11	12	13–15	16 or more
Voted						
City	60%	66%	70%	71%	68%	77%
County	46	47	55	55	71	66
Have not voted						
City	33	26	27	26	29	23
County	15	26	23	24	17	21
Incompetent						
City	7	7	3	3	4	0
County	40	26	22	21	12	12
Number						
City	(110)	(122)	(110)	(96)	(28)	(26)
County	(68)	(155)	(180)	(287)	(134)	(144)

EXCLUDED: City 3 and County 2 "don't know."

The increase in voting with an increase in education is not substantial in the City. In the suburbs, however, the increase is regular and considerable. About 45 per cent without a high school education, 55 per cent with some high school, and 70 per cent with some college education, have voted. There is a similar decline in incompetence, from 40 per cent of those who did not finish the eighth grade, to one-eighth of those who finished college.

Education obviously makes a substantial difference in voting in the County; however, area of residence seems even more important. People in the City who have finished the eighth grade vote as often as individuals in the County who have completed college. Only in the college-educated classes are County residents approximately as likely to vote as are all City residents.

Similar conclusions may be made about income (D22). The City-County differences in voting and competence are considerable for every income level. Incompetence in the City is confined to those with less than $5,000 annual income; in the County, even the highest income class has a large proportion who are incompetent. (When those with incomes of $10,000 and over are considered separately, 14 per cent are still incompetent in the County, but none are incompetent in the City.) Despite the impressive City-County differences, income classes differ in voting within each area. Individuals from households with annual incomes of $7,000 and over consistently have voted more and are less often incompetent than those with household incomes of less than $3,000.

The relations of voting and occupational classes yield similar results. Higher-ranking occupational classes in the County are more likely to vote (66 per cent compared to 51–54 per cent) and less likely to be incompetent (13 per cent and 26 per cent). In the City, incompetence is limited to blue-collar workers and those out of the labor force (5 and 11 per cent), whereas from 65 to 74 per cent of all occupational classes have voted in City elections. And in the County, even individuals from households whose head is in a professional or managerial occupation are over twice as likely to be incompetent as City people from the households of laborers and operatives (13 and 5 per cent).

ETHNICITY

Proportionately more Old Americans than other ethnic groups in the County have voted in municipal elections (D23). In the City, however, they have voted no more frequently in such elections than the Negro residents and less frequently than the Germans or southern and eastern Europeans.

The Old Americans have voted in municipal elections to about the same extent in City and County, although there is a difference in competence between these segments of the two populations. With the Germans and the "minority" ethnic contingents, the pattern is very different. Negroes are more likely to have voted in the City by 18 per cent, Germans by 24 per cent, and southern and eastern Europeans by 30 per cent. The higher proportion of the City population with such ethnic backgrounds (about 60 per cent, compared with 50 per cent in the County) does not account for the higher voting rate in municipal elections in the City. It is attributable to the much larger percentage of persons with these ethnic backgrounds who vote in the City.

Greater percentages of both Catholics and Protestants have voted in City municipal elections. Seventy-eight per cent of the Catholics have done so (compared with 60 per cent in the County) and 62 per cent of the Protestants have voted (compared with 56 per cent in the County). Catholics have a slightly higher rate of voting than Protestants in the suburbs; in the City this difference is substantial—16 per cent more Catholics have voted. It will be remembered that Negroes and Old Americans, usually Protestants, have the lowest per cent voting in the City.

MIGRATION BACKGROUND

The number of years the individual has lived in the local metropolitan area is significantly related to whether or not he has voted in municipal elections (D24). In both City and County, proportionately more old migrants have voted than newer migrants; in fact, those living in the area twenty years or more are about as likely to have voted as the natives in the metropolitan area.

Political incompetence in the City is largely confined to the newer migrants; people in the City who have been in the metropolitan area twenty years or more almost always knew they could vote for municipal officials. Although there is similar variation in the County, still about one-fifth of the natives did not know they could vote in such elections. Although County residents are consistently more incompetent regarding municipal elections than City inhabitants, regardless of the length of residence, persons who migrated between five and twenty years ago have voted more often. (It is possible that wartime migrants, who come within this category, are significantly different for City and County.) In all other classes, more City residents have voted; the chief City-County differences, however, are between old migrants and natives, the two heaviest-voting categories. In both of them, significantly larger percentages of City residents have voted.

Rural background is of some importance in differentiating the voters and nonvoters in each area. In the City 72 per cent without farm experience have voted, compared with 60 per cent who spent at least part of their childhood on a farm. The comparable County percentages are 59 and 53. These comparisons tend to support the assumption that the characteristics of City migrants differ from County migrants, even when both are rural. Nevertheless, rural migrants to the City have voted in municipal elections to about the same extent as County residents without rural experience.

COMMITMENT TO NEIGHBORHOOD

Type of dwelling unit, type of occupancy, and years of residence in present dwelling unit are all important in differentiating those who have voted in municipal elections and those who are competent about them. The first named is the least significant of the three; the last named, the most important.

Residents of single-family dwelling units are more likely to have voted—by 15 per cent in the City (77 per cent and 62 per cent), 9 per cent in the County (58 per cent and 49 per cent). Thus, the City residents of single-family units are more likely to have voted than are their County counterparts by 19 per cent; similarly, City residents living in multiple-family units are more likely to have voted by 13 per cent. There are, however, no important differences in the rate of competence between occupants of the two types of houses. But the City-County differences are very large, and in favor of the City—18 per cent more are incompetent in the County for each type of dwelling unit (2 per cent incompetent compared to 20 per cent in single units; 6 per cent against 24 per cent in multiple-family units).

Homeowners more often have voted and are informed about their eligibility. The difference in voting between homeowners and renters is 23 per cent (81 per cent and 58 per cent) in the City and 18 per cent (59 per cent and 41 per cent, respectively) in the County. The differences in competence are 6 per cent in the City (7 per cent and 1 per cent incompetent) and 7 per cent in the County (20 per cent compared with 27 per cent incompetent). In the City incompetence is virtually confined to those who rent. It is higher among such residents in the County, but one-fifth of the homeowners do not know they can vote in municipal elections.

The percentage who have voted increases steadily with years of residence in the present dwelling unit (D25), but the proportion is higher for each category in the City; the City-County difference is 19 per cent for those residing less than a year, 22 per cent for twenty years or more. The proportion of those who know they can vote and do not do so diminishes steadily with years of residence in both City and County—from 53 per cent to 5 per cent in the City, from 48 per cent to 9 per cent in the County. Incompetence does not decline as consistently in the latter area; over one-fifth of those who have been in their present dwelling units for ten years or more do not know that they can vote for municipal officials.

VOTING IN SCHOOL ELECTIONS

The important differentiators between the voters and nonvoters in school elections are age, migration, and commitment to neighborhood. Ethnicity and social rank are of lesser importance, but still represent important differentiation in the City. As noted in chapter 10, a higher percentage of the City residents have voted in school elections (50 per cent compared to 43 per cent), and more County residents are incompetent, saying "people in their neighborhood could not vote in school elections" or they "did not know whether they could vote" (30 per cent in the County as against 19 per cent in the City). These differences persist for every important cluster of socioeconomic attributes.

AGE AND SEX

Age is the most important factor in differentiating those who have and have not voted in school elections in City and County, (D26). Much of the preponderance of voters in City school elections, however, comes from the greater percentage of voters in the older-age brackets. The rate of increase in voting is most marked between the youngest age class and the 30–39-year-old category; however there is continued increase to the 50–64 class, and a decline in voting by those aged 65 and over.

The variation in incompetence is particularly interesting; in the City it declines from over 30 per cent to 11 per cent at the 40–49 age group; in the County it declines from over 50 per cent to about 24 per cent at this age class. Incompetence is higher in the County for all classes except the 30–39 age class; voting is higher in the City for most classes, but particularly for those over 50. The percentage who have not voted in school elections (but know they can) is higher in the City. The lower rate of voting in the County thus is largely among those who do not even know they are eligible.

Sex is of some importance in differentiating voters from nonvoters. Men are more likely to vote in the City (54 per cent compared to 47 per cent for women), and in the County (49 per cent and 39 per cent).

SOCIAL RANK

Dividing the people by level of education yields no significant difference in voting or competence with respect to school elections. Those with less than an eighth-grade education and those who have completed college vote in about the same proportions. Nor is income of consistent importance, although the very highest income class has a much higher rate of voting in both City and County. In the City the difference is from 21 to 29 per cent (71 per cent in the $7,000 and over class, compared with 42 to 50 per cent for other categories); in the County the comparable difference is from 6 to 10 per cent (49 per cent compared with 39 to 43 per cent). People in the highest income group are also somewhat less likely to be incompetent, but the difference is neither consistent nor significant. There is more voting and less incompetence at each income level in the City.

In terms of occupational level, proportionately more higher white-collar workers in the City have voted in school elections than any other occupational category (66 per cent compared with 46 to 49 per cent). In the County there is no significant variation among the three highest occupational categories, and even the lowest (blue-collar operatives and laborers) are significantly different only from the very highest occupational class. The greatest difference between City and County, however, is at this highest level, where 19 per cent more in the City have voted (66 per cent compared with 47 per cent). The percentage incompetent declines very slightly with an increase in the occupational level in either area (36 per cent to 30 per cent in the County, but no consistent difference in the City). This is an important finding. Political incompetence, lack of knowledge of eligibility to vote in school elections in this instance, is usually thought to be closely associated with low social rank, but this factor does not explain much of the variation in the City-County area. Differences between the highest and the lowest ranks are negligible compared with City-County differences.

ETHNICITY

The pattern of ethnic variation in school election voting is similar to that for ever having voted in a local election. Old

Americans and Negroes are the lowest, Germans and other Europeans the highest two participants in the City, the first two groups having 46 and 49 per cent voting, the last two, 60 per cent. In the County the latter two are relatively lower, Old Americans relatively higher. There is little marked difference by ethnic background in the County except for the low percentage voting among those from southeastern Europe (33 per cent compared with 43 to 47 per cent) ; in the City both those of German and southeastern European backgrounds are 10 per cent higher than Old Americans and Negroes.

Incompetence does not vary among the ethnic contingents of the City. In the County the only variation is, surprisingly, the low rate of incompetence among Negroes; they are by far the most competent ethnic segment in the County (17 per cent compared with 30 to 34 per cent). Their percentage incompetent is, in fact, lower than that for the City as a whole.

The variation by religion is sharp only in the City. Proportionately more Catholics are competent and have voted in the City, but the reverse is true in the County. In the City 60 per cent of the Catholics but only 45 per cent of the Protestants have voted; in the County the comparable percentages are 40 and 45. Similarly, more City Catholics are competent (17 per cent and 21 per cent incompetent), more County Protestants (30 per cent and 37 per cent) incompetent. This reversal is not to be explained simply by the large proportion of Negroes among the Protestants in the City, for the Catholics in the County vote at a rate only two-thirds that for City Catholics, but the rates are even for Protestants. Religion here is related to social rank and ethnicity, and City-County differences may well be related to differences in generation of migration. At the same time, the use of parochial schools may be relevant. Irrespective of the explanation, the sharpest difference is between the Catholic contingents of City and County; 20 per cent more voted in the City (60 per cent and 40 per cent). This is identical with the difference in the percentages of incompetence—37 per cent of the County Catholics are incompetent with respect to school elections, as compared with 17 per cent of the Catholics in the City.

The only difference between City and County in percentage voting is among Catholics. (Forty-five per cent of the Protestants voted in each area.) Both Catholics and Protestants, however, are more incompetent in the County.

MIGRATION

No matter how long they have been in the metropolitan area, County residents are more likely to be politically incompetent— do not know they can vote in school elections (D27). Incompetence declines only between the first two categories (less than five years, 5–19 years) for the County, but it declines through the "twenty years or more" category for the City. At the same time, voting increases steadily in the City, from one-sixth of those who have been in the area less than five years to 61 per cent of those native to the metropolitan area. Voting increases also in the County, but the natives of the area are less likely to have voted than those migrants who have been in the area for more than twenty years.

Rural background is of considerable importance in differentiating the voters in the City, but of no significance in the County, indicating again that rural experience is not sufficient explanation for the City-County differences between migrants. In the City proportionately more of those with rural experience during childhood are incompetent (25 versus 16 per cent), and proportionately fewer have voted (40 and 57 per cent). Neither proposition is true in the County. The City preponderance in voting is attributable then to the voting by those without any rural experience— 14 per cent in favor of the City.

COMMITMENT TO NEIGHBORHOOD

There are no differences in rate of voting in school elections in the County between those living in single-family and multiple-family dwelling units. In the City, however, those living in single-family units are more likely to have voted by almost 20 per cent (62 per cent compared with 43 per cent) and are less likely to be incompetent (13 as against 23 per cent). Voting and incompetence are very similar for those living in multiple-family units in City and County. The sharp difference is among those who live in single-family residences; half again as many have voted in the City.

Larger percentages of both owners and renters in the City have voted in school elections, and smaller percentages are incompetent (D28). Five per cent more of the renters voted in the City, but 23 per cent more of the owners voted. And proportionately more of those who rent in the City are politically competent than those owning their homes in the County.

As in the case of variation in ever having voted in any local election, the number of years the person has lived in his present dwelling unit is the most powerful predictor of participation in school elections. And, at each level, there is a larger percentage of persons in the City who have voted and a larger percentage of County residents who are politically incompetent.

Both the increase in voting and the decline in incompetence with years of residence in the present dwelling are clear-cut and consistent (D29). However, the City residents even with the shortest period of residence are much more competent than County residents, just as they are more likely to have voted.

Variation in voting for school district officials between City and County cannot be explained as a result of recent in-migration or greater mobility in the County.

VOTING IN COUNTY ELECTIONS

Residents of the suburban county are much more likely to have voted in elections for County officials than in any other local elections. The proportion voting, 66 per cent, is almost identical with the proportion who have voted for City officials in the city of St. Louis. Furthermore, political incompetence in the County declines to 10 per cent when County elections are concerned. The County government is more meaningful and produces more participation than any of the smaller governments of the suburbs—school districts, fire districts, or municipalities.

The higher rates of competence and participation among people in the City may be the result of the greater size of its two local governments, the municipal government and the school district. They spend extensive sums of money, hire thousands of employees, and receive much coverage from the mass media of the metropolitan area. They loom very large in comparison with the tiny municipalities of the County (the biggest of which, University City, is only a small fraction of the population size of the City). The multiplicity of governmental units in the County may also produce confusion and thus contribute to incompetence and nonparticipation.

If this assumption is valid, it follows that participation by suburbanites in their County government should be most analagous to the relationships of City residents with the municipal government of the city of St. Louis. The County government is also a large-scale unit, with a population of 600,000 under its jurisdiction, and with continuing attention from the mass media. In addition, and perhaps most important of all, the County government is partisan in its elections, as is the municipal government in the City. The traditional political parties contend for public offices, patronage, and policy-making prerogatives. Through such partisanship the greater political interest in national elections may be associated with the campaigns for County office. If local elections in the County suffer from the multiplicity of governmental units, this situation is least true of elections involving the County government because this unit encompasses all the territory of the County.

With these considerations in mind, the participation of various important segments of the County residents in elections for officials of the County government is compared with the City residents' vote for municipal officials. As this is done, it will be possible to gauge the extent to which these two kinds of elections are analagous in their importance to the citizens.

The most important variations are associated with age, sex, and commitment to the local neighborhood. Social rank is of moderate but consistent importance.

AGE AND SEX

The percentage voting in County elections increases consistently with age up to those 65 and over (D30) ; this segment has a lower percentage, as was true in the previous analyses of voting in any local election and voting in school elections. The over-all difference between the youngest age class and those aged 50–64 is an impressive 32 per cent. A larger proportion of County residents are incompetent than City residents, but the difference is much less than for other elections and does not appear among those aged 30–39. Furthermore, in all age classes under 50, County residents are more likely to have voted for County officials than are City residents in municipal elections.

Men are much more likely to have voted in County elections (74 per cent compared with 61 per cent) and women are more likely to be incompetent (15 per cent and 6 per cent). These differences parallel variations by sex with respect to voting in municipal elections in the City. Although there is little difference in the proportion of each sex voting in City and County, the difference in competence still remains. Proportionately more City residents know they can vote, even if they do not do so. In the

County, one in seven women and one in sixteen men do not know they can vote in elections for County officials.

SOCIAL RANK

Voting does tend to increase with education, but the group with less than eighth-grade education has a surprisingly high percentage voting in County elections (D31). Proportionately more County residents have voted than City residents at the lowest level and the college level. However, between the eighth grade and completion of high school, residents of the City are consistently more likely to have voted in municipal elections.

At each educational level, County voters are at least twice as likely to be politically incompetent regarding elections for County officials as City residents concerning municipal elections.

With respect to variations by income, much larger percentages of County residents are politically incompetent. The percentage is twice as large at the lower levels (15 and 14 per cent compared to 7 and 5 per cent). At the upper income levels there are less than 2 per cent incompetent in the City, but 11 per cent for County residents in the $5,000–6,999 class and 7 per cent in the class having an income of $7,000 and over.

Little variation by income shows in the County or City until the $7,000-and-over class is considered; proportionately more individuals with this comparatively high family income have voted in County elections than other groups of County inhabitants (72 compared with 61 to 64 per cent), fewer are politically incompetent about them (7 per cent compared with 11 to 15 per cent). The increase in the City is similar (81 and 63 to 68 per cent). It is apparent that income differences do not produce City-County variation; instead, the greater percentage voting at each income level in the City compensates for the much higher average income in the County.

The chief variation by occupational class in voting for County officials is the sharp increase in proportion of participants from households of professionals, managers, proprietors, and officials (75 per cent compared with 63 to 65 per cent). There is no important difference in voting among other occupational classes. Very few persons from professional or managerial households are incompetent with respect to County elections—7 per cent compared with 14 per cent who were incompetent regarding municipal elections and 30 per cent regarding school elections. Little variation in competence exists among the other occupational classes. Nor is there a significant City-County variance in the percentage of different occupational categories who have voted in County elections and City municipal elections, respectively.

Thus, social rank differences are measurable, but not striking, in their effects upon voting in County elections. Education is most important, but is not a consistent factor, because a larger proportion of the least educated have voted than any class except the most educated. Income and occupation are important only in discriminating between people with the highest social rank and all others.

ETHNICITY

Ethnic background is of very little importance in differentiating the voters for County offices. From 62 to 69 per cent of each major ethnic contingent have voted in County elections, with the exception of the Negroes; only one-half of them have ever voted for County offices. Competence varies little.

There is more likelihood that Old Americans in the County have voted for County officials than those in the City have voted for municipal officials (68 and 62 per cent, respectively). Negroes and those with backgrounds from Germany or southern and eastern Europe are consistently more likely to have voted in the City.

No significant difference arises in the proportion of Catholics and Protestants who have voted for County officials; this is in marked contrast to City elections, where Catholics have voted more often by 17 per cent.

MIGRATION BACKGROUND

Only one important variation is associated with migration background; those migrants who have been in the metropolitan area for less than 5 years are significantly more incompetent and less likely to have voted in County elections. Twenty-eight per cent are incompetent, compared with 9 per cent of the other residents of the County; only 45 per cent have voted, compared with 67 per cent of the older migrants and natives. County residents who spent part of their childhood on a farm are somewhat less likely to have voted (67 per cent compared with 76 per cent), but no more likely to be incompetent with respect to County elections.

COMMITMENT TO NEIGHBORHOOD

There is no significant difference between occupants of single-family dwelling units and duplexes or apartments. Type of occupancy is more important. Fifty-two per cent of those who rent have voted in County elections, but 69 per cent of the home-owners have voted. The difference between the two classes in knowledge of these elections is negligible, however. The renters know about their right to participate in County elections; they simply do not vote in them.

Length of time in the present dwelling unit is by far the most powerful factor of the three relating to commitment to neighborhood (D32). The range is from 30 per cent of those who have lived for less than a year in their present home to 79 per cent of those residing there for 20 years or more.

Omitting persons who have lived in their present dwelling unit for less than a year, the increase in voting and competence with an increase in length of residence is still striking. One-half the people in City and County have lived in their present dwelling for 5 years or longer. Eight of every ten such persons have voted for municipal or County officials. In contrast, only six of ten of the more recent residents and three of ten of the very newest residents have voted.

Thus, variations among major segments of the population with respect to voting for County officials are very similar to those in voting for municipal officials in the City, and participation in County elections is more analogous to municipal elections in the City than to municipal elections in the County.

VOTING IN THE 1956 PRESIDENTIAL ELECTION

Participation in the 1956 presidential election varies, in general, with the same factors as voting in local elections; the most important are age, time of migration, and commitment to the neighborhood. Differences in social rank and ethnicity, however, are much more noticeable for the suburban county than for the central city in presidential voting. (In local elections these factors are much more important in the City.)

AGE AND SEX

Age difference is considerably more important than sex difference. The peak of participation is in the 50–64-year class, with a slight decline in the class aged 65 and over. Larger proportions of men voted—77 per cent in the City as against 71 per cent of the women; 85 per cent in the County compared with 77 per cent of the women.

TABLE 33

AGE AND VOTING IN THE 1956 PRESIDENTIAL ELECTION

Residence	21–29	30–39	40–49	50–64	65 and over
City	53% (96)	74% (94)	76% (107)	86% (131)	77% (87)
County	63% (228)	81% (363)	86% (302)	87% (278)	83% (114)

SOCIAL RANK

The social rank variables, significant as they are in differentiating political party affiliation, are considerably less important in discriminating between voters and nonvoters. Education is most important, with college-educated persons most likely to vote in each area. The percentage voting in a presidential election tends to be higher in the County, indicating that the lower rate of participation in local elections is not the result of a "less politically oriented" population. The differences in presidential voting between City and County are not, however, very great.

TABLE 34

EDUCATION AND VOTING IN THE 1956 PRESIDENTIAL ELECTION

Residence	Years of education completed					
	0–7	8	9–11	12	13–15	16 or more
City	70% (113)	70% (125)	76% (114)	74% (103)	89% (28)	86% (29)
County	71% (90)	74% (233)	78% (238)	81% (393)	86% (167)	91% (162)

EXCLUDED: City 3 and County 2 "don't know."

Differences in presidential voting according to income are larger and more consistent within the County than the City. And, while County people in income classes of $3,000 and above report more voting than individuals in the City, lower-income City residents have voted substantially more than their counterparts in the County.

TABLE 35

HOUSEHOLD INCOME AND VOTING IN THE 1956 PRESIDENTIAL ELECTION

Residence	$0–2,999	$3–4,999	$5–6,999	$7,000 and over
City	74% (123)	68% (155)	79% (117)	80% (75)
County	66% (98)	74% (203)	79% (341)	86% (510)

EXCLUDED: City 45 and County 133 "don't know" or refused to supply information.

The higher rates of voting for upper social rank people in the County holds when the occupation of the head of the household is the factor under consideration. Among both upper and lower white-collar households in the County, 86 per cent voted compared with 76 per cent in the blue-collar classes. The City, however, shows little difference by occupation.

ETHNICITY

Ethnic variations differ markedly between County and City. The range in the County is 20 per cent; in the City, 15 per cent. The most interesting differences are those between Old Americans in City and County (10 per cent higher in the County) and between Negroes in the two areas (7 per cent higher in the City). Germans and those from the "new migrations" vote at a similar rate in City and County.

TABLE 36

ETHNICITY AND VOTING IN THE 1956 PRESIDENTIAL ELECTION

Residence	Old American	German	Southern and eastern European	Negro
City	71% (200)	81% (124)	86% (49)	72% (116)
County	81% (626)	83% (425)	84% (148)	65% (51)

EXCLUDED: City 26 and County 35 "don't know" or "other."

Religion is a less important factor. Proportionately more Catholics voted in both the City (81 per cent compared to 71 per cent of the Protestants) and the County (84 per cent and 76 per cent).

MIGRATION

Length of time in the metropolitan area is of great importance in differentiating the voters from the nonvoters in the presidential election (D33). At each level, more County residents voted. The percentage of difference is very slight, however, for the old migrants and the natives; these two groups voted at a similar rate in both City and County.

Rural experience is of importance in the City and of less importance in the County. Larger proportions of those without rural experience have voted in both areas. In the City 80 per cent of those without rural experience voted, 66 per cent of those with rural experience. In the County the comparable percentages are 83 and 75.

COMMITMENT TO NEIGHBORHOOD

All three measures of commitment to neighborhood are important differentiating factors. Not only is there a significant difference in voting by type of dwelling unit, but also those living in similar dwelling units have comparable rates of participation in the two areas. The percentage of those living in single-family units who voted is identical in City and County (82 per cent) and multiple-unit dwellers are very close (70 and 73 per cent in City and County). The somewhat higher over-all rate for the County reflects the larger proportion of single-family units in the County.

Differences in percentage voting are even clearer on the basis of type of occupancy. Eighty-six per cent of the owners voted in the City, 83 per cent in the County. Of the renters in the City only 67 per cent voted and, in the County, 68 per cent. The percentage voting is very similar for those occupying the same type of dwelling in City and County.

In the City percentage voting consistently increases as length of residence in present home increases (D34). In the County, however, there is an increase only to the class that has lived in the dwelling between three and five years; after this point, longer residence makes little difference.

OPINIONS OF LOCAL ELECTIONS

A larger percentage of City residents vote in local elections involving municipal and school officials, but more City than

County residents agree with the statement that many local elections are unimportant. One possible reason for this contrast between action and belief could be that response to "attitude" questions (in which people are asked what they feel or think) are more likely to be related to their social rank, while responses to "action" questions (in which people are asked what they have done) are more related to the structure and available channels of activity. It can then be assumed that political activity is easier in the City, owing to the large-scale organization of local issues and elections, via political parties and the press.

What are the differences among major population segments in percentage disagreeing with the proposition that many local elections are unimportant? Are the social rank factors relatively more important in explaining attitudes toward participation than explaining past voting?

AGE AND SEX

Age is important in differentiating between those who believe and disbelieve that local elections are important, just as it is in discriminating between voters and nonvoters. However, there is a significant difference: age is positively related to having voted in all kinds of local elections (in general, the older the age group, the greater the rate of voting), but it is negatively related to belief in the importance of local elections (D35). The differences are consistent for both City and County. The discrepancy between attitude and voting may, of course, reflect a change of mind since the individual last voted. It seems more plausible, however, to interpret age classes as reflecting great variation by education. As will be seen, education is positively related to disagreement with the statement that many local elections are unimportant.

Sex is of no consequence in response to this question. As with age classes, all categories are more apt to disagree in the County than in the City.

SOCIAL RANK

Education, income, and occupation are the factors that most sharply differentiate responses to this question. There is an increase up to the class that completed high school; after that, no consistent variation (D36). The difference between those who did not complete the eighth grade and those who graduated from college is 37 per cent in the City, but only 17 per cent in the County. The per cent disagreeing is higher for all classes in the County, and there is less variation by education. Whatever the education of the resident, common interests and cultures seem to produce a leveling off of ideological differences.

Income is even more important (D37). Again, differences are more striking and consistent in the City, whereas the County has a higher percentage disagreeing at each income level.

A similar pattern emerges when occupational classes are analyzed (D38). However, the white-collar workers do not differ as much between City and County as the higher income classes. The greatest differences between the suburbanites and the residents of the City are at the craftsman and operative levels and among the retired ("other"). For the latter, it is likely that the disparity in income for retired persons in the two areas, with more old-age pensioners in the City, is closely related to their response.

ETHNICITY

Ethnicity is of much less importance than social rank, although the differences do have some significance. Once again, there is more variation by ethnic background in the City (17 per cent in the City, 9 per cent in the County). There is more disagreement by all ethnic contingents in the County. The correlation between the ethnic "ranking" (from Old American to Negro) and belief in the importance of local elections is quite clear; such a correlation does not appear between ethnic ranking and voting. Religion is of no importance in differentiating belief and disbelief.

MIGRATION

The number of years of residence in the local metropolitan area, a powerful predictor of voting, makes absolutely no difference regarding belief in the importance of local elections, nor does having or not having lived on a farm. Migration does not seem to affect belief in the importance of local electoral participation.

COMMITMENT TO NEIGHBORHOOD

These factors, most important in differentiating voters and nonvoters, are of little significance with respect to belief in the importance of local elections. Neither the type of dwelling unit nor the length of time in it makes any difference. Type of occupancy has some "cutting power" in the City, but is of no importance in the County: 64 per cent of the renters in the City disagree with the proposition, as against 76 per cent of the owners; 81 per cent of County renters and owners disagree.

The City-County differences remain for each category based on commitment to neighborhood. However, as with respect to type of occupancy, single-family-unit dwellers and more stable populations differ less between City and County than do renters. Only one in ten County residents rents his home, but 60 per cent in the City are renters. If, then, the same percentage were home-owners in both areas, the difference in agreement would be much less. Of course type of occupancy is correlated with many other aspects of population, and the resulting neighborhoods cannot be understood by concentrating upon individual attributes. Type of occupancy, type of dwelling unit, and stability of the people are indicators of the character a social environment will manifest.

SUMMARY: DIFFERENCES IN LOCAL ELECTIONS

Three major findings emerge from this analysis of variations in political behavior among the major segments of residents in City and County. The most important finding is the persistence of broad City-County differences for each major segment of the population. The five clusters of socioeconomic attributes do make a difference in voting behavior within the City and the County (and sometimes a very dramatic one), but they do not eliminate the City-County differences for each category. A second major finding is the relative importance of commitment to place as a predictor of voting: this is far more important than social rank and ethnicity factors. A final important conclusion is that belief in the general importance of local elections is not clearly related to participation in such elections.

CITY-COUNTY DIFFERENCES

City-County differences in voting and competence are very sharp for municipal and school elections, the two comparable types. They remain clear for each major segment of the population. There is little difference, however, in the proportions who have ever voted in any local election and who voted in the 1956 presidential election.

Thus it is not the City-County dissimilarity in social rank, ethnic background, or migration history which accounts for the much higher rate of voting in the City and the more widespread incompetence in the County. Negroes in the City are as likely to be voters as are whites in the County; those with household incomes under $3,000 a year in the City have as high a proportion voting as those with $7,000 and over in the County. The ethnic enclaves, poor people, and rural migrants, who are disproportionately concentrated in the City, are typically considered to be less active politically,[2] yet the City has a livelier political process than County communities.

One explanation is based upon the idea that political activity is a consequence of governmental organization and the channeling of citizen participation, and this may exert more influence as a predictor of voting and competence than the individual attributes of the citizens. Three characteristics of the municipal government in the City may be decisive—its size, the open partisanship of its elections, and, derived from these two, the extent of public interest reported in and stimulated by the mass media.

This proposition was tested by comparing County participation in the election of County officials with that of City residents in the election of municipal officials because the two governments are comparable in size and in the partisanship of their elections. To some unknown extent the evidence is weighted against the hypothesis (for county governments are not usually as effective in interesting and mobilizing citizens as city governments); nonetheless a great similarity in voting showed up. However, when City residents do not vote, they are aware they could; County residents are not nearly as knowledgeable about County officials. This may very well reflect the difference in popularity between County and City governments.

SOCIAL DIFFERENCES AND VOTING

The residents of the City and the County vary most sharply in their local (as well as 1956 presidential) election participation according to commitment to neighborhood, age, and migration history rather than according to social rank and ethnic background.

Type of house, type of occupancy, and length of residence in the present dwelling bear important relationships to electoral participation. The last is the most powerful, apparently because it summarizes economic, prestige, and community consequences of commitment. Certainly participation in local elections continues to increase from very new residents to those of twenty

---

[2] Genevieve Knupfer, "Portrait of the Underdog," *Public Opinion Quarterly*, XI, 103–114.

years or more. Type of dwelling unit has consistent discriminating power in the City, but less in the County. Type of occupancy is consistently important, and homeowners are in all instances more likely to vote.

Between the youngest age group (21–29) and those at the peak
age for political participation (50–64), differences in voting for
each local election usually ran between 35 and 50 per cent. Age
is much more important than sex, although proportionately more
men have voted in each kind of local election.

The new migrants and the wartime migrants are consistently
less likely to have voted, but regional origin is a very weak
factor. Migration background is more effective as a predictor
of voting in the City: older migrants and natives are more than
twice as likely to vote in local elections generally and in school
elections; there is slightly less difference in municipal elections.
In the County the differences are smaller. Migrants with rural
backgrounds are less likely to have voted in the City; they are
equally likely to have voted in the County.

Ethnic background is generally much more important in the
City in differentiating the electorate. The "minority" ethnic
contingents (Germans, southern and eastern Europeans, and
Negroes) consistently participate more actively than Old Americans. In the County, in contrast, Germans and Old Americans
are most likely to vote, and other ethnic groups less likely to do
so.

Education, income, and occupation are the least important and
least consistent factors in differentiating voters and nonvoters.
In general, the very highest levels ($7,000 or more annual in-
come, professional and managerial people, college-educated) are
clearly more likely to vote, but in no consistent order by social
rank. Curiously, participation in school district elections is not
related to education of the voters.

Each of the five clusters of socioeconomic attributes has a
similar differentiating power with respect to incompetence, particularly in the County. People least likely to vote are most likely
to be uninformed about local elections. None of the factors, however, identifies a category of County people who are as competent as the comparable City population about either municipal
or school elections.

The number of socioeconomic factors that are important varies
by elections, with those who have voted in any local election
most often and most sharply differentiated from those who have

never voted, followed by voters and nonvoters in municipal, school, and County elections.

The variations in proportions of important segments of the population voting in the 1956 presidential election are very similar to variations in the electorate in local elections. Interestingly enough, however, County residents are more likely to have voted in the presidential election than City residents. Commitment to the neighborhood, migration background, and age are once more the most important variables. Social rank and ethnicity are consistent but less important.

The participation in the presidential election affords one possible explanation of City-County differences—the "machine vote." The higher City vote for local elections might have resulted from the activities of the Democratic party machine. This explanation seems to be supported by the greater proportions of ethnic minorities voting in the City, but does not agree with the other attributes of people most likely to vote in City local elections—old residents, homeowners, and those in single-family dwellings. Nor does it seem plausible that a machine able to "get out the vote" in a City election would be less effective than the suburban national party branches in a presidential election. Thus, a crude "machine vote" explanation of City-County differences in electoral participation and competence is as yet doubtful.

IDEOLOGY AND ACTION

The individual's belief in the importance of local elections differed noticeably from his actual participation. By far the most important factors are social rank, ethnicity, and age, whereas commitment to neighborhood and migration background are not significant. Those of higher social rank are consistently more likely to disagree with the statement that "many local elections aren't important." Disagreement also increases consistently from Negroes to Old Americans, and is strongest among the younger age groups.

This opinion question exposes the interesting dichotomy between ideology and action. The residents of the City are less likely to agree verbally to the importance of all local elections, but they are more likely to have voted in each type.

12

Local Government and
Its Customers

BROAD DIFFERENCES exist between City and County in dissatisfaction with local public services, in access to governmental agencies, and in acceptance of the taxation level of local government. Certain services arouse widespread dissatisfaction in one area but little in another. A much larger proportion of the County residents have not only felt like complaining about services, but have also done so. The belief that local taxes are not too high is much more common in the City.

These differences might plausibly be explained through the population differences between central city and suburbs. Perhaps the City's belief in the worth of government merely reflects the appreciation of government aid, which is often assumed to exist among ethnic minorities and the poor. Perhaps the greater willingness of County residents to complain to local governmental agencies simply indicates a stronger self-confidence among those who are more highly educated and have better incomes. The evidence for such an explanation is examined in this chapter by comparing the responses of those with similar socioeconomic characteristics in City and County.

Attention is also given to the responses among different categories of the population in each area because of the clues they provide explaining the demand for local governmental services. Who are the dissatisfied and the satisfied for each major governmental service? How does dissatisfaction relate to ethnicity, age and sex, commitment to neighborhood, social rank, and migration background? What inference can be made from these factors concerning the distribution of services and service needs?

Also, how does dissatisfaction with a service relate to action with respect to the responsible local governmental agencies? Who merely complains and who acts? And what does this tell about the access of various types of people to governmental agencies? How much division of opinion and action, which exists in local voting, also takes place in citizen relations with local government?

Finally, who are the citizens who feel they do not get full value from their local taxes? And who are the people who believe that government is well worth its cost? Do these attitudes arise from the nature of the services provided or from the standards held by the citizens?

LOCAL CHANGES AND IMPROVEMENTS SUGGESTED BY RESIDENTS

Seventy-nine per cent and 83 per cent of the City and County residents, respectively, mention one or more changes they would like to see made in their local area. These figures relate to interest and involvement in the immediate neighborhood or community, not for the City-County area as a whole. A substantial minority in the City (45 per cent) and a majority of the County residents (54 per cent) name two or more specific changes they desire in their immediate local area. The proportion specifying two or more changes is the best single indicator of the distribution of changes mentioned; it is used as an index of general service dissatisfaction in this section.

The City-County difference in percentages naming two or more changes is substantial but not startling. The same is true of the variation among major segments of the populations of City and County. The most important differentiating factors are social rank, ethnicity, age, and sex. In general, County residents in each segment are more likely to offer two or more suggestions for their neighborhood.

AGE AND SEX

In both City and County, the largest proportions suggesting two or more changes are people in the middle age brackets (D39). The percentages are similar only for those aged 65 and over; for the other ages the County inhabitants more often name two or more changes.

The early peak and continuous decline according to increasing age of the proportion suggesting changes are probably related to the life cycle. During the peak ages, 30 through 39, proportionately more persons are parents of children living at home and they are, therefore, involved in local neighborhood activities and problems.

Sex is of less importance than age in this context. In the City, men more frequently name two or more changes (52 per cent compared with 38 per cent of the women). In the County there is little difference (56 per cent for men, 52 per cent for women). There is little difference between City and County men suggesting changes; differences among women are much larger (14 per cent). This may be related to the higher incidence of marriage and parenthood among County women, for such social ties bring into prominence, especially for women, the characteristics of the neighborhood and local community as a setting for the major portion of everyday life.

SOCIAL RANK

Social rank factors reflect both the individual's objective situation (that is, how good his local governmental services as well as his neighborhood are) and his aspirations. It might be expected that certain crosscurrents would affect the naming of two or more needed local community improvements: (1) the more education, the more people expect, (2) the more income, the more material goods they have, (3) the higher either their educational, occupational, or income level, the higher the other two are likely to be. The poor have, objectively, more to complain about; yet, as will be seen, they are not consistently the category of people most anxious for improvements.

Education is a significant factor only in the City; there the better-educated more often suggest improvements. Less than 40 per cent do so among those with eighth-grade education or less in contrast to about 50 per cent with partial or completed high school education. Of those with some college, 61 per cent suggest two or more changes. In the County there is no consistent variation—50 to 60 per cent of all education classes name two or more changes. A larger proportion of each class in the County suggest changes, with the exception of the two most highly educated groups, which are the same in City and County.

The very lowest income classes are least likely to name two or more changes in either the City or County. In the City less than 40 per cent do so, compared with 48 to 51 per cent of the higher income brackets; in the County, 45 per cent compared with 53 to 57 per cent. Again, for every income class the County has a larger proportion who name two or more changes they would like to see made.

Occupation does not differentiate consistently or sharply in either area. In the City, those at the extremes of occupational rank differ noticeably from similar populations in the County. Only 40 per cent of the upper white-collar category in the City name two or more changes, compared with 56 per cent in the County. Similarly, 46 per cent of the operatives in the City do so, compared with 56 per cent in the County. For the middle occupational range there is very little City-County difference.

If both aspiration and objective conditions of the neighborhoods are affected by this measure of social rank, then the "fit" is best among the very highest and lowest status City populations. In truth, the latter are frequently slum dwellers (in contrast to their counterparts in the suburbs), while proportionately more of the professional and managerial workers in the City live in the apartment-house neighborhoods where there is little basis for complaint. Each of these two extreme categories of City people may be less involved in their neighborhood and less interested in its improvement.

ETHNICITY

Ethnic identity shows little important variation. About 45 per cent of practically all ethnic categories in the City name two or more improvements, with the Negroes having a somewhat higher percentage (52 per cent). In all ethnic categories in the County, approximately 52 per cent name two or more, except Negroes who are again slightly higher (61 per cent). Although Negroes have lower educational and income levels, they also have more to criticize in their neighborhoods, and in the County Negroes have a larger percentage naming two changes than any specific income class.

MIGRATION

Differences associated with migration are of little importance in the County with respect to suggesting changes in the neighborhood. Rural experience does not differentiate among the City population, but the length of time in the metropolitan area does. Proportions suggesting two or more community improvements are: new migrants, 29 per cent; wartime migrants, 38 per cent; old migrants and natives, 48 and 47 per cent. In the same four categories, County people run higher (57, 53, 55, and 53 per cent); the difference is particularly marked for the newer migrants. In the City, however, only natives and those having lived twenty years or more in the metropolitan area suggest changes and improvements as often as the newest County migrants. In fact, the finding of most import here is the lack of variation among the categories in the County. If the naming of two or more community improvements judged to be needed is a measure of identification with community, the process requires little time in the County.

COMMITMENT TO NEIGHBORHOOD

Factors relating to commitment to neighborhood are more important in the naming of two or more improvements in the County than in the City. Although only 10 per cent of the County residents live in multiple-dwelling units, they are much less likely to name two or more improvements in the neighborhood than single-family dwellers (38 per cent compared with 56 per cent). In the City, however, the difference is negligible; apartment dwellers are as likely to name two or more local community changes as residents of single-family dwellings and they are more likely to name two changes than their counterparts in the County (43 compared with 38 per cent). The last-named situation is reversed for those who live in single-family dwellings, however (56 per cent in the County and 43 per cent in the City), suggesting that the City apartment houses contain a different type of population (probably a larger proportion of Negroes and poor people).

Differentiation by type of occupancy also varies between City and County. It is markedly important in the County, where 56 per cent of the owners suggest two or more changes, compared with 43 per cent of the renters. In the City the difference is, again, insignificant; the percentages practically duplicate those based upon house type.

Length of residence makes little difference. In the County about 54 per cent for all categories of residents suggest two or more improvements. In the City there is some increase through the 5–10-years bracket (from 35 per cent to 62 per cent), but smaller proportions of the older residents suggest improvements (49 per cent and 41 per cent).

There thus is very little variation according to socioeconomic factors in the naming of two or more local community improvements. In the County the only significant variations are by age and types of dwelling unit and occupancy; the younger owners of single-family units are most likely to suggest this number of changes or improvements. Migration, sex, and social rank are more important in the City. Over all, a consistently larger proportion of County residents name two or more local community or neighborhood improvements they would like to see made. It is conceivable that the more prevalent naming in the County is not largely a measure of ease and promptness in getting identified with the local community. It may indicate principally the more widespread existence of problems in the County.

DISSATISFACTION WITH SPECIFIC LOCAL SERVICES

Persons interviewed were asked to state their satisfaction or dissatisfaction with eleven important local public services—schools, police protection, water supply, fire protection, condition of own residential streets, library services, garbage collection, parks and playgrounds, sewage disposal, public transportation, and traffic control and facilities. Services that elicited considerable dissatisfaction are discussed in detail in this section; others receive briefer consideration. Dissatisfaction is high in both City and County with traffic conditions, public transportation, condition of residential streets, and parks and playgrounds. There also is much dissatisfaction with police protection and garbage disposal in the City, and with sewage disposal in the County. The amount of dissatisfaction with these services is analyzed for the major segments of the population, classified according to social and economic characteristics.

TRAFFIC CONDITIONS

Forty-five per cent of the City residents and 57 per cent of the County residents express dissatisfaction with traffic conditions, which varies significantly with age, sex, social rank, and ethnicity.

As to *age* and *sex*, larger proportions of younger persons (21–39) in City and County alike are dissatisfied with traffic conditions (D40). Probably this level of dissatisfaction is affected by the higher percentage of drivers among younger people, but it may very well result from their higher aspirations regarding standards of service. Those under 40 years of age are most dissatisfied, and those 65 and over, least dissatisfied. However, less variation occurs in the County, and a substantially larger proportion of County residents are dissatisfied at each age level, except those 65 and over. (The last category is a relatively small part of the interview sample.) Both automobile ownership and the driving habit are much more widespread in the County, due to suburban distances and higher social rank.

Men are consistently more dissatisfied with traffic conditions (51 per cent in the City as against 40 per cent of the women; 63 per cent of the men in the County, 52 per cent of the women). This, again, probably reflects driving habits. Even when women drive regularly, proportionately fewer drive in the congested areas during rush-hour traffic.

By education, income, and occupation, the three measures of *social rank*, those on a higher level are more likely to be dissatisfied. They are, of course, more likely to be automobile owners and drivers, and also may have higher expectations of service. The variations based on educational level (D41) are more consistent as well as more pronounced in the County, which does reflect in part the small number of interviews in the college categories in the City, but it may also imply a less consistent use of automobiles by more educated persons in the City.

In both City and County the biggest difference according to income is between the very low income class (which depends heavily on public transit) and the remainder of the population (D42). In the County dissatisfaction increases as income increases. (If those with incomes of $10,000 or more are considered separately, over 70 per cent are dissatisfied.)

Occupational level produces similar variations (D43). They are again more consistent and of greater magnitude for the County, and the major difference is between the very lowest occupational level and the others. In the City the only consistent difference by occupational level is that clerical and professional workers are even less dissatisfied than are the middle levels. (The chief negative instance of clerical workers seemingly reflects the high incidence of women in these jobs—and women are less dissatisfied.) In the County the increase in dissatisfaction is consistent and significant; professionals are dissatisfied much more frequently than operatives.

Ethnicity produces important differentiations in the County among those most likely to be dissatisfied with traffic conditions.

All ethnic contingents in the City are 43 to 49 per cent dissatisfied, except those from southern and eastern Europe (31 per cent). However, County dissatisfaction is correlated with the ethnic rank order: Old Americans, 63 per cent; Germans and southern and eastern Europeans, 53 per cent; Negroes, 39 per cent. In general, the Old Americans are most dissatisfied, the minority Americans least so, and the Germans in between but closer to the Old Americans. Except for Negroes, each County contingent is more dissatisfied; Negroes are slightly more dissatisfied in the City.

Migration does not differentiate a dissatisfied population; neither years in the area nor rural experience is effective. *Commitment to neighborhood* (number of years in the present dwelling, type of occupancy, and type of dwelling unit) is not a significant factor.

PUBLIC TRANSPORTATION

Dissatisfaction with public transportation in the area is widespread. Forty-four per cent of the County residents and 34 per cent of the City residents are not pleased with transit service and facilities. Public transportation, it should be noted, is much more adequate in the City and is used as the only means of transport by a much larger proportion of the people; in the County the automobile is overwhelmingly more often utilized.

Dissatisfaction with public transportation does not vary as widely among the population segments as does dissatisfaction with traffic. However, certain measures are important, including social rank (particularly income), ethnic background, and migration. Factors associated with neighborhood type and commitment are of some importance; age and sex differences are of little importance.

Educational level, one determinant of *social rank*, bears little upon reaction to public transportation. Only on the part of the college-educated is there about a 10 per cent higher degree of dissatisfaction. Differences by occupational level are not great and are not consistent. The higher the income, the more dissatisfaction: the income level difference is paradoxical. Those who depend upon public transportation are chiefly in the lower income groups, but dissatisfaction is more common in the higher levels (D44). An explanation, in part, is that public transportation service tends to be more adequate in low-rank neighborhoods; the volume of traffic justifies more facilities and better scheduling.

At the same time, expectations of service may be higher among the more prosperous. That better facilities in middle- and high-social-rank areas would result in increased use is, however, a doubtful proposition.

Dissatisfaction varies by *ethnic background:* in both the City and County the Old Americans are least dissatisfied, and Germans and those whose families were from southern and eastern Europe are most dissatisfied (D45). And, in each ethnic contingent, County inhabitants are substantially more dissatisfied than City residents.

Migration differences are important among the City residents, but much less so in the County. The longer a person has lived in the metropolitan area, the more he is likely to be dissatisfied with public transportation. While the differences increase consistently in the City with an increase in length of residence, the only major difference in the County is between the newest migrants and the remainder of the population (D46).

Rural background is also important in the City; 38 per cent without any farm background are dissatisfied as opposed to 23 per cent with it. Rural experience does not affect County attitudes.

Commitment to neighborhood, as measured by length of residence in present dwelling unit, is of no importance in either area. However, differences show between those who lived in multiple- and single-family dwelling units, and between renters and owners.

A larger percentage of apartment dwellers express dissatisfaction in City than in County, but those who live in single-family units express more dissatisfaction in each area (37 per cent compared to 32 per cent in the City, 45 compared to 34 per cent in the County). Thus, those living in single-family units in the County constitute the group most dissatisfied with public transportation (and are in fact more likely to have poor service). Correspondingly, homeowners are more dissatisfied than renters in each area (39 per cent against 30 per cent in the City, 45 against 36 per cent in the County). It is probable that variations do exist in the service provided to different types of neighborhoods. Length of time in present residence is of little importance.

CONDITION OF RESIDENTIAL STREETS

Street lighting, street cleaning, and condition of pavement in the individual's neighborhood produced the third highest proportion of dissatisfied responses. Thirty-eight per cent of the City residents and 30 per cent in the County express such dissatisfaction. These responses vary by social rank and ethnicity; other factors are of little importance.

Social rank has more effect in the County. In general, the higher the social rank, the less dissatisfaction with the streets. This is in contrast to dissatisfaction with traffic and public transportation. These latter two services do not improve with the social rank of the neighborhood, but the condition of the streets may well do so, especially in St. Louis County with its multitude of municipalities providing services for populations of diverse economic status. In the County the decrease in dissatisfaction with streets is indeed consistent with an increase in education (D47), but in the City dissatisfaction is generally high with no significant variation by educational level. The most pronounced differences between City and County thus are between the more highly educated classes. The differences are less striking for income classes (D48).

The highest occupational classes are least dissatisfied with the conditions of their residential streets in both City and County (34 per cent and 26 per cent, respectively). For the three lowest City classes dissatisfaction runs between 39 and 44 per cent. In the County, however, the break in satisfaction is at the "collar line"; individuals from white-collar households are less dissatisfied (25 and 26 per cent, compared with 32 and 39 per cent of the blue-collar workers).

Ethnicity is the factor providing the sharpest differentiation of all and it does reflect the importance of residential segregation in limiting the environment of ethnic minorities (D49). Negroes are the group most dissatisfied with the condition of their streets in City and County alike. Fifty-one per cent express dissatisfaction in each area, compared to 31 through 38 per cent of other groups in the City, 27 through 38 per cent in the County. Such a response indicates that the segregated are no more adjusted to their civic lot with respect to this important governmental service in the County than in the City.

PARKS AND PLAYGROUNDS

Recreational facilities are another focus of discontent. Twenty-nine per cent of the City residents and 34 per cent in the County express dissatisfaction with these services. Important variations are based on age, commitment to neighborhood in City and County, and ethnicity in the City only.

Age bears an important relationship to dissatisfaction with parks and playgrounds in City and County. The interaction of the life cycle with concern over these child-oriented facilities is evident; for the younger age groups, the percentages dissatisfied are identical in City and County (D50). Dissatisfaction is highest in the 30–39-year bracket and thereafter declines consistently. The young married persons with children are the chief customers for this governmental service: few persons 65 years old and older are concerned.

Ethnicity differentiates the dissatisfied in the central city, but not in the suburban county. In the City the range dissatisfied is from 21 per cent of those with German backgrounds to 41 per cent of the Negroes. Twenty-nine per cent of the Old Americans and persons from southern and eastern Europe are dissatisfied.

Each of the three indicators of *commitment to the neighborhood* has some predictive power of dissatisfaction. Type of dwelling unit is important in the County; 36 per cent of the residents in single-family units, as compared to 18 per cent of those in multiple-family units, are dissatisfied with parks and playgrounds. In the City, however, the difference by type of dwelling unit is negligible. As for type of occupancy, a slightly higher proportion (5 per cent) of City renters are dissatisfied with parks and playgrounds. In the County, however, 36 per cent of the homeowners are dissatisfied, compared with 22 per cent of the tenants.

These City-County differences may be a reflection of the facilities available to apartment dwellers in the two areas. Many multiple units in the County are near Forest Park, which is a large area in the City but bordering the City-County boundary, whereas the dense apartment areas of the City are often far from any kind of recreational facility.

The percentage dissatisfied in City and County is identical for new residents (D51). The oldest residents in the City, however, are least dissatisfied with parks and playgrounds, while those having lived in their present County dwelling unit twenty years or more are among the most dissatisfied. This indicates that such facilities are no more available to the stable, homeowning population in the County than to apartment dwellers in areas of high residential mobility. In short, concern for these facilities is much more widespread among the various categories of people in the County

—although each substantial class in the City, except the older-age population and the very long-time residents, has a large proportion expressing displeasure.

POLICE PROTECTION

Dissatisfaction with the police is largely expressed by City residents—20 per cent, as against 9 per cent in the County. Because of the small variation for major segments of the population in the County, this discussion will be chiefly concerned with the City. The 20 per cent in the City who are dissatisfied are disproportionately concentrated in the low income classes, the Negro population, and the multiple-family dwelling unit neighborhoods; in other words, dissatisfaction is most evident in the areas of segregation and congestion. At the same time, the most recent residents are more likely to be displeased with police protection; age and sex are of no importance.

Social rank differences show up most importantly by income classification; occupation and education are of slight importance. (For example, the very lowest education class is most dissatisfied —26 per cent; the next lowest, however, is least dissatisfied—17 per cent.) The discrepancy between education and income for Negroes probably explains some of the difference between these two measures of social rank for, as will be shown, ethnic identity is the most important factor differentiating dissatisfaction with police.

Between the highest income class ($7,000 and over) and the others, the difference is sharpest (15 per cent of the former, compared to 20 through 24 per cent of the others). This relationship remains consistent when the very high and very low income classes are further divided; 26 per cent of those with less than $1,000 income express dissatisfaction and only 12 per cent of those with over $10,000 income do so. Income thus is a consistent predictor of dissatisfaction with police protection in the City. Both criminal and police activity center in neighborhoods of low social rank.

Ethnicity is the most important differentiating factor of dissatisfaction with police protection. The range in the City is from 15 per cent dissatisfied among the Germans, southern and eastern Europeans, and Old Americans, to more than one-third of the Negroes. It is evident that a disproportionate percentage are Negroes; they are twice as likely to complain as any other ethnic group. Nevertheless, for each ethnic group City residents are at least half again as likely to express dissatisfaction with police as County residents.

Migration differences probably reflect the fact that proportionately more Negroes are migrants, and migrants with a rural background. Twenty-two per cent of the migrants are dissatisfied, as against 17 per cent of the natives. And, 25 per cent of those with a rural background are dissatisfied, as against 18 per cent of those who have lived only in cities and towns.

Commitment to neighborhood, as measured by length of time in the present dwelling unit, has little effect upon dissatisfaction with police. Much more important, however, is type of dwelling unit. Only 14 per cent of those living in single-family units are dissatisfied with police protection (compared with 9 per cent in the County), but 23 per cent of those living in multiple-family units express dissatisfaction. Dissatisfaction with police is concentrated in the more urban neighborhoods of the City.

GARBAGE DISPOSAL

There is greater dissatisfaction with garbage disposal in the City, where 17 per cent express discontent as against 11 per cent in the County. Variation by segments of the population is also much more marked in the City. Important factors are social rank and commitment to neighborhood. They seemingly indicate a disproportionate concentration of complaints in the blighted areas of the City.

As to *social rank* factors, education and occupation are of no importance. Income, however, does make a difference. Of the very lowest income class ($0–2,999), 22 per cent are dissatisfied. This decreases to 11 per cent of those with incomes of $7,000 and over. The poor are twice as likely to be dissatisfied with garbage collection, implying a general decrease in the quality of this service as the social rank of the neighborhood declines.

Commitment to neighborhood is important as a predictor of dissatisfaction; undoubtedly, these factors reflect the general character of the neighborhood and the quality of services supplied. Each indicator has some power to predict dissatisfaction. Proportionately more of those who live in multiple-family dwelling units are dissatisfied (19 per cent compared to 14 per cent); a larger percentage of those who rent are dissatisfied (21 per cent compared to 12 per cent); and a larger proportion of those who have lived the shortest period of time in their present dwelling unit are dissatisfied. Of those who have lived in their dwelling less than five years, 20 to 22 per cent express dissatisfaction, compared to 15 per cent of the five-through-nineteen-year residents, and only 7 per cent of those who have been in their present dwelling twenty years or more. These latter findings may reflect the nature of people who move frequently; they probably also reflect the quality of services. Neighborhoods of long-time homeowners are least likely to be dissatisfied with garbage collection, and those densely inhabited areas of the City with a large mobile population, most likely to express dissatisfaction.

SEWAGE DISPOSAL

Twenty-six per cent of the County residents indicate dissatisfaction with sewers, as against 9 per cent in the City. Sewage disposal services are generally less adequate in the County; the chief impetus behind the creation of the Metropolitan St. Louis Sewer District in 1954 was the lack of sufficient facilities in many suburban areas, a deficiency that takes time to correct completely. Attention here thus is largely on the County. However, dissatisfaction with sewage disposal is quite high among certain segments of the City population, differentiated primarily by social rank, but also commitment to neighborhood. Ethnicity, migration background, age, and sex are of little importance.

Social rank differences are evident for education, less important for income. Dissatisfaction declines somewhat with increasing education in the County (34 per cent dissatisfied among those with less than eight years of schooling to 20 per cent with sixteen years or more). In the City the tendency is the opposite; the more educated the individual, the more likely he is to express dissatisfaction (3 per cent compared to 17 per cent).

Differences by income class are not impressive in the County. About 29 per cent of all classes in the County, except the highest (at 24 per cent), express dissatisfaction. In the City there is a reversal: the higher the income, the greater the dissatisfaction. The range is from 9 per cent dissatisfied in the lowest income class to 19 per cent of those with incomes of $7,000 and more. Occupational classes differ slightly in the County only; 23 per cent are dissatisfied in white-collar households, compared to 31 per cent in others.

Ethnicity is of only a slight importance; in the County, the most dissatisfied group consists of Negroes (31 per cent dissatisfied), and the least, the Old Americans (24 per cent). In the City, however, Old Americans and Negroes are both much more dissatisfied than the other groups (12 compared with 6 per cent).

Commitment to neighborhood is important in the County, but of no importance in the City. In the County, homeowners, persons living in single-family units, and those who have lived longest in their present dwelling are most apt to be dissatisfied with the sewage disposal system. The unimportance of these factors in the City may be based on the generally uniform and acceptable level of sewerage services.

In the County, of those who live in single-family units, 28 per cent are dissatisfied, compared with only 14 per cent in the multiple-family units, whereas homeowners are more likely to be dissatisfied by a much lower margin (27 per cent compared with 21 per cent). Those who have lived more than three years in their present dwelling are more dissatisfied than those who have lived there less than three years (about 30 per cent dissatisfied in each of the longer residence categories, as compared with 21 and 22 per cent of the newer residents). The sharpest measure here—type of dwelling unit—may summarize both condition of facilities and concern or disinterest of the people in the neighborhood. Clearly, type of unit is much more important than either type of occupancy or years of residence in present dwelling.

SCHOOLS, LIBRARY SERVICE, WATER SUPPLY, AND FIRE PROTECTION

Dissatisfaction about other local services specified in the interview is not widespread. They do not bring forth expressions of dissatisfaction from as many as 10 per cent of the people in either City or County. The very few significant differences in discontent over any of these services among the major segments of the population are briefly summarized.

For schools the most striking variation is among age classes in the City. In the youngest age class (21–29 years) 23 per cent are dissatisfied with the schools, compared with approximately 5 per cent in each of the other categories. This difference is highly significant and therefore cannot be explained by the relatively small sample. Many of the youngest age group in the City have finished their schooling there in recent years and are parents of preschool-age or school-age children, and they are by far the most concerned with the condition of the public schools of any segment of the population in City and County.

Library services produce disproportionate expressions of dissatisfaction among only two major segments of the population—

the younger persons and the Negroes in the City. Dissatisfaction declines steadily from 16 per cent of the youngest age class to only 2 per cent of those aged 65 and over. For the major ethnic groups, 5 per cent of the Italians and Germans are dissatisfied, 9 per cent of the Old Americans, but 18 per cent of the Negroes.

There is no significant dissatisfaction with water supply or fire protection according to any social or economic factor.

SERVICE DEMAND AND POPULATION TYPE

In explaining the variations in service demand among major segments of the population, it is important to look more closely at the meaning of the social and economic indexes used to analyze the City and the County. These indexes can be placed into two clusters. The first, combining social rank and ethnicity, reflect variations in access to the material goals of urban life. Insofar as these goals are differentially available to the citizenry, persons of higher social rank and of German or Old American background are likely, on the average, to have more of whatever is considered desirable. The second, combining age and sex and commitment to neighborhood, reflect variations in the needs of the residents and therefore the consumption norms which are applicable. They indicate something of the role, commitments, and style of life of individuals.

ACCESS TO GOODS AND SERVICES

Education, occupation, and income, the measures of social rank, are intercorrelated and each is a basis for estimating the individual's share of the material rewards of the society. However, education tends to emphasize the individual's awareness of standards and his verbal ability, just as income emphasizes his access to goods and services available on the market. Ethnic background is a separate dimension; the most important ethnic difference occurs between Negroes and all others. Negroes are limited in their access to residences, regardless of their income, and are differentially treated in many social relationships, regardless of education, occupation, or income. Each of these measures, then, are the limits in access to the valued goods or services provided by the society.

NEEDS AND SERVICE NORMS

Age and sex and commitment to neighborhood measure, each in a different way, the general requirements of the individual, including his needs for governmental services. Age indicates the position in the life cycle, whether on the average the population is unmarried, married but childless, married with small children or with grown children, or postparental. Sex indicates on the average the jobs, commitments, and focus of activity associated with the culturally specified roles of housewife and breadwinner. House type, type of occupancy, and length of residence in dwelling unit indicate the individual's commitment to a specific location in a particular neighborhood; in studying the type of dwelling, however, the kind of neighborhood is being measured in the aggregate, for both apartment houses and single-family units are concentrated and spatially segregated in urban areas. Zoning ordinances and the economics of location determine this.

The effects of these two clusters of indexes upon average satisfaction or dissatisfaction with services are now considered.

INDEXES REFLECTING ACCESS TO GOODS AND SERVICES

1) Educational differences are important in both City and County, but the effects are not identical. In the City, the more highly educated persons are more dissatisfied with traffic conditions and sewage disposal; the effects of education on satisfaction with streets are inconsistent. In the County, however, although persons with higher education are also more likely to be dissatisfied with traffic, they are considerably less dissatisfied with the condition of their residential streets and sewage disposal.

2) Income differences are more consistent between City and County, but again they vary by services. The higher the income, the greater the dissatisfaction with traffic and transportation in both City and County, and the lower the dissatisfaction with residential streets in the County, with police protection and garbage collection in the City. Whereas income does not affect dissatisfaction with sewage disposal in the County (all classes are very discontented), such dissatisfaction increases with income in the City.

3) Negroes are least dissatisfied and Old Americans most dissatisfied with traffic. However, Negroes are much more dissatisfied than any other ethnic group with the condition of their residential streets and police protection in both City and County, and with parks and playgrounds and library facilities in the City.

INDEXES REFLECTING GOVERNMENTAL SERVICE NEEDS

1) Age differences are important and consistent. Younger persons are more dissatisfied with traffic conditions and parks and

playgrounds in City and County than any other group. And, in the City, younger persons are much more dissatisfied with schools, libraries, and the condition of residential streets.

2) A larger proportion of men are dissatisfied with traffic conditions in both City and County.

3) In the County, those who live in single-family dwelling units are more likely to be dissatisfied with public transportation, parks and playgrounds, and sewage disposal. In the City they are less dissatisfied with police protection than residents of multiple units.

4) Proportionately more homeowners in both City and County express dissatisfaction with public transportation. They are more likely to be displeased with the parks and playgrounds in the County; they are less likely to be dissatisfied with garbage collection in the City.

5) Those who have lived longest in their present dwelling constitute the group in both City and County most favorable toward traffic conditions. In the City only, they are the group most satisfied with parks and garbage disposal. In the County the older residents represent the group most dissatisfied with sewage disposal.

Many of these indexes are far from accurate indicators of the effect any one dimension has upon attitudes about governmental services, for they tend to reflect several dimensions at once. Further analysis is required to test the propositions, but the following initial interpretation may be offered.

First, the assumption is made that some services have a relatively uniform quality throughout the City-County area. (Traffic control is the most important.) Second, some services are relatively uniform within the City and some within the County. (These services may be relatively poor, as with public transportation in the County and garbage disposal in the City, or relatively good, as with water supply in the County and sewage disposal within the City.) Third, some services are likely to vary with the type of neighborhood in City or County. (Included here are condition of residential streets and police protection.)

For services that are relatively uniform throughout an area, variations in dissatisfaction reflect the norms or standards of service expected by particular types of people. Where the services vary in quality, the indexes may reflect that quality (if needs and norms are relatively uniform); on the other hand, the indexes may reflect variations in both need and quality of services, in which case, of course, nothing very definitive can be said at this point.

In general, where only social rank indexes are effective, it may be hypothesized that there is variation in quality of services. If the chief differentiating indexes are associated with age and neighborhood type, it may be hypothesized that the variation is in the nature of service needs or norms (particularly if service is uniform). When all indexes are effective, it may be hypothesized that there are complex interrelations of needs or norms and services; when none of the indexes makes any difference, it may be hypothesized that the norms and services "fit" and an inquiry about satisfaction or dissatisfaction with a particular service has no relevance. (And indeed, for services that elicit low proportions of dissatisfaction, there tends to be little variation among major segments of the population.)

If this framework of analysis is adopted, the following interpretations are possible.

1) Traffic conditions are relatively uniform for most of the area, and the chief variations in dissatisfaction relate to automobile ownership and usage. Younger persons, males, those who live in the County and work elsewhere, and higher income groups are most likely to rely mainly upon automobile transportation. They are the segments of the population which are most dissatisfied with traffic conditions.

2) Public transportation is relatively uniform within the City and within the County, although it is much better in the City. It is most adequate in the low-income and apartment-house neighborhoods. Residents of these areas express the least dissatisfaction with the service; they are also the most frequent users of public transportation.

3) The condition of residential streets varies greatly with the general social rank of the neighborhood, and the most important factors associated with dissatisfaction are those reflecting social rank and ethnicity. Persons with low education and low income levels and Negroes are most likely to be displeased with the condition of streets. None of the indexes that reflect life-cycle stage or way of life is of importance in differentiating between dissatisfied and satisfied persons.

4) Availability of parks and playgrounds is fairly uniform to each general type of County neighborhood; in the City, parks are less accessible to the highly urban population. The principal factors that differentiate dissatisfaction with these facilities are

related to life cycle and way of life. In the County it is the younger people, who own their homes and have lived for some time in the present dwelling unit, who are dissatisfied. In the City younger persons are also dissatisfied; however, the discontent tends to be more widespread among those living in their present home a shorter while and renting, and among Negroes. It is likely that many of these younger people in the City are young Negro families with children, living in densely settled areas having few park and playground facilities.

5) Dissatisfaction with police protection varies little in the County but is highly concentrated in the City. It is disproportionately common among persons of low income and Negroes. It is also more common among the residents of multiple-family units. These areas need more police protection in order to meet the norms and less effective policing may be given them.

6) Dissatisfaction with garbage collection is disproportionately concentrated in the highly urban, low social rank neighborhoods. Persons who rent, who have lived a relatively short time in their area, and who live in multiple-family dwellings are most likely to be dissatisfied; they are also poorer people. The norms or standards expected for garbage collection are assumed to be uniform; if so, these indexes reflect inadequate services in certain areas.

7) Persons who have lived longest in their present dwelling and those who live in single-family units are most likely to be dissatisfied with sewage disposal in the County. This seemingly reflects variations in the quality of service provided, for the multiple-family units are concentrated in the City and probably have adequate sewage facilities. Consistent with the view that variation in dissatisfaction with sewage disposal in the County reflects variation in service is the fact that the higher social rank people are less dissatisfied.

In the City, however, while there is no variation in dissatisfaction with sewer service by any index related to family status or style or way of living, those with higher educational achievements and higher family incomes tend to be more dissatisfied with this service. This anomaly leads to the suspicion that social rank is also related to norms or expected standards of service. If performance is uniform in the City, those with higher standards, on the average, should be more dissatisfied.

8) The major variation in dissatisfaction with schools is related to age. The youngest class in the City is highly dissatisfied

with the schools, reflecting the greater concern of young parents with schools. This service evokes little expression of dissatisfaction from other major segments of the population. Evidently the norms tend to fit with the service provided for most of the residents in the area.

9) Library services bring forth a disproportionate amount of dissatisfaction among the young adults in the City. This may reflect their greater personal aspirations and their greater need for libraries in raising children. One other group, however, is dissatisfied with this service—Negroes. The other segments are not differentiated in judgments of library service.

Three general conclusions can be made. (1) Variations in dissatisfaction with traffic and parks and playgrounds in both City and County, and with City schools and libraries are chiefly the product of the different needs and expected standards of the various segments of the population. (2) Variations in dissatisfaction with public transportation, police protection, and the collection of waste (sewage and garbage disposal) are largely based on differences in the services provided different segments of the population in City and County. (3) There is little variation in need or services regarding water supply and fire protection.

COMPLAINTS TO LOCAL GOVERNMENTS

Although 38 per cent of the residents in both City and County had felt like complaining, a far larger proportion in the County have actually complained to a governmental official, employee, or agency (21 per cent compared to 12 per cent). Each major cluster of social and economic attributes is of some importance in separating those who have complained from those who have not complained.

Age and Sex

Age is important as a predictor of both desire and action regarding complaints (D52). The proportions who felt like complaining and the proportions who have complained decrease from the 30–39-age class to those over 64 in both City and County. When, however, those who complained are taken as a proportion of those who felt like complaining, the percentage increases with age. Older persons (those 40 and over) are less likely to feel like complaining, but if they have felt like complaining, they are more likely to have done something about it. These trends are quite clear and consistent; they well may reflect increasing ability to file a complaint and to get results with greater maturity.

The differences between City and County for the proportion that have actually complained are striking. In the County, a majority of those who felt like complaining have done so in each age class, except the youngest. Only a minority of these persons in any age class have ever done so in the City. Although age differences are important, they' do not account for City-County differences.

Sex is not an important factor. Proportionately more males have complained in each area, but the City-County differences for each sex are much more important.

SOCIAL RANK

In the City both education and income are important factors regarding those who have felt like complaining; they are less important in the County. Their importance for actual complaints made is substantial but not very consistent. In the City the proportions of those who wanted to complain and of those who did tend to increase with education (D53). In the County, education has little effect on the former, but for the latter, there is a consistent increase from the eighth-grade level to those who completed college. When the complainers are taken as a proportion of those who wanted to express discontent, there is no very consistent trend, except that the college-educated in the County are more likely to have complained if they felt like it.

There is a consistent increase up to the highest income class in the proportion who felt like complaining in the City, and in the County those with incomes of over $5,000 are more likely to feel like complaining. Similarly, the percentage of those who have actually made their service dissatisfaction known increases with an increase in household income (D54), from 8 to 23 per cent in the City and from 13 to 26 per cent in the County. When complaints are a proportion of those who ever felt like complaining, there is some increase with income; the most significant variation is the sharp increase evident for residents with incomes of $7,000 and over.

No significant variation in those who felt like complaining appears by occupational level, with the single exception that the operative households in the County are remarkably low (26 per cent compared with 39 to 41 per cent). Some consistent increase does appear by occupational level in actual complaints made (9 to 17 per cent in the City, 13 to 24 per cent in the County). And there are very sharp increases in complaint-making by those who had felt like doing so. This is more consistent, however, in the County, where it varies as follows: lower blue-collar, 43 per cent; upper blue-collar, 56 per cent; lower white-collar, 53 per cent; and upper white-collar, 60 per cent. The chief variation in the City is that between laborers or factory operatives (22 per cent) and others (37 through 42 per cent).

Social rank indexes differentiate in a fairly consistent fashion between those segments of the population who are likely to complain and those who are not. However, City-County differences remain. Particularly in the populations of lower social rank, the County resident is more apt to have complained. And even though the better-educated, higher-income City residents are about as likely to have complained as similar populations in the County, they are much more likely to have felt like complaining. The disproportionate percentage complaining in the lower social rank categories of the County means that social rank differences do not account for the much larger proportion of County residents who have actually complained to local governments about their services.

ETHNICITY

In both City and County, a larger proportion of Negroes have wanted to complain about their services. However, there is little variation in actual complaints by ethnic background (D55) in the City (except for the tiny proportion of the southern and eastern European sample), and in the County the only real variation is the relatively low proportion of Negroes who have complained. For Negroes alone, the percentage who have actually complained is the same in City and County; in all other ethnic groups a larger percentage of the County residents has complained.

When those complaining are taken as a percentage of those who felt like doing so, the Negro percentage is very low in each area. This is also true of the percentage with southern and eastern European backgrounds; particularly in the City, they are much less likely to have complained even though they felt like doing so, and Old Americans and Germans are substantially more apt to have acted. In the City all ethnic groups are less likely to have complained than in the County. Interestingly, Negroes who feel like complaining are more likely to do so in the County. Although

Negroes, segregated and concentrated residentially, are better organized and have more access to local government in the City, a larger proportion of them have actually complained in the County.

MIGRATION

Length of residence in the metropolitan area, but not rural background, is of some importance in relation to actual complaints. There is no City-County variation in the proportion who felt like complaining. For the City, however, the differences in those who did complain are significant, ranging from no action at all by the most recent migrants (in the area less than five years) to 15 per cent for the native-born residents. In the County, the most recent migrants have not complained as much as other groups (16 per cent compared with 20 to 24 per cent), but there is little variation among the wartime migrants, old migrants, and natives.

For both City and County, differences in the percentage complaining of those who felt like doing so are related to years of residence in the area. The patterns are not the same, however. In the City a regular increase from nothing by the newest migrants builds to 40 per cent of the natives. In the County, on the other hand, there is little variation among those who have been in the area for at least five years (53 to 59 per cent); only the most recent migrants differ (43 per cent of those who felt like it have complained).

COMMITMENT TO NEIGHBORHOOD

Although homeowners are much more apt to have complained if they so felt, nevertheless the City-County variance is so large that homeowners in the City are only about as likely to have complained as renters in the County. Differences in type of occupancy are important (D56): City-County differences are of equal importance.

Longer years of residence in the present dwelling unit is another factor enlarging the proportion who have complained and the percentage of those who say they have felt like complaining and acted (D57). The former is especially evident in the County. In the City, however, those who have lived in their present dwelling ten years or more are less likely to have spoken up than shorter-term residents. The percentages that have felt like complaining and have done so increase with even more consistency according to length of residence in the present dwelling unit.

Residential stability and homeownership are closely related to people's propensity to go to local governments with criticisms and complaints. Newcomers and renters are less likely to register dissatisfaction with a government.

THE WORTH OF LOCAL GOVERNMENT

Thirty-seven per cent of the City residents and 45 per cent of the County residents believe local taxes are too high, considering the services provided. Responses to this question about the level of local taxation demonstrate an evaluation of both tax rates and governmental services. They also identify those who resent taxes, and those who have a more sanguine attitude. Some persons have more faith in government than others; they are more aware of the necessity for governmental services and of the inevitable costs.

Resentment of local taxes is largely confined to the less educated residents. The major breaks occur between grammar school,

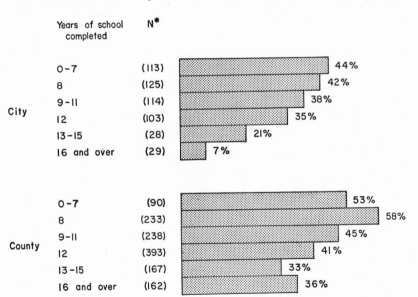

* N represents the number of cases or interviews. Excluded: City 3 and County 2 "don't know."

Fig. 20. Education and belief in worth of government: percentage agreeing taxes are too high.

some high school, and some college. For each level of education, however, the County contains a larger proportion who believe that taxes are too high.

Income is a less powerful and less consistent differentiating factor of belief in the economic worth of local government. The highest income bracket ($7,000 or over) in the City has the smallest proportion of people who agree that taxes are too high (27 per cent compared with 36 to 42 per cent). At all income levels except the $3,000–4,999 bracket, City residents agree less often with the statement that taxes are too high. In the County the only variation of significance is between the lowest income class (under $3,000) (54 per cent agree) and the rest (40 to 46 per cent).

The major difference by occupational class is the low percentage of the professionals, managers, and proprietors who believe local taxes are too high. Nineteen per cent agree in the City, compared to 32 per cent of the lower white-collar workers, 45 per cent of the craftsmen, and 41 per cent of the operatives. In the County all classes except professional and managerial households are about the same; 38 per cent of the latter agree, as against 47 to 49 per cent of the other job levels. County residents in all occupational classes are more likely to agree that taxes are too high.

The consistent tendency for the poorest and least educated portion of the population to bear greatest resentment to local taxes is an interesting commentary on the differences in knowledge about local government. Such persons tend to pay lower local taxes in proportion to their benefits, and some would consider them major beneficiaries of local government. However, they do not evidence greater faith in government, as measured by this question, but rather the contrary. And, as was indicated in chapter 11, they are more inclined to believe that many local elections are unimportant. There are, consequently, grounds for believing that resentment of taxes is more closely related to knowledge about local government, as measured by education, than to either the objective level of local services or ability to pay.

In both City and County, Negroes are most likely to believe taxes are too high, while Old Americans and Germans are least likely to agree (D58). In the City there are sharp differences between ethnic groups. In the County the only striking difference is the very high percentage of Negroes who agree. The most striking City-County difference arises between persons with German backgrounds; in the County they are almost twice as likely to agree that local taxes are too high. Such persons are a large percentage of the total populations (one-fourth in the City, one-third in the County) and this difference is significant.

Factors associated with social rank and ethnicity are the only ones that make a difference for both City and County residents. In the County, however, the three measures associated with commitment to neighborhood are all significantly related to belief that taxes are too high. Of persons who live in single-family dwelling units, 47 per cent agree, but in the multiple-family units only 28 per cent concur. And, for homeowners, the percentage is again high—48 per cent—in contrast to only 25 per cent of the renters. (Fifteen per cent of those in multiple-family units and 21 per cent of those who rent say they do not know, compared with less than 5 per cent of the owners and the residents of single-family units.) Differences by period of residence in present dwelling unit are significant only between those who have lived there less than one year (18 per cent do not know) and the other groups.

SUMMARY: THE METROPOLITAN CITIZEN AS CUSTOMER

None of the principal differences between City and County in opinion and behavior regarding local governmental services disappears when the major social and economic factors are controlled. There are proportionately more County residents who suggest changes and improvements in their local area, who have personally complained to local public agencies about services, and who believe their local taxes are too high in relation to the benefits they derive. Factors associated with age, sex, social rank, ethnicity, migration, and commitment to neighborhood differentiate within both City and County, but variations between City and County still remain.

In analyzing the demand for governmental services, as reflected in the discrepancy between the norms for service and the services provided, dissatisfaction varies sharply by type of service and, more importantly, the socioeconomic factors affecting demand vary by services. For some services the poor are the chief objectors; for others, the rich; for still others, social rank seems irrelevant and factors associated with age, sex, and commitment to neighborhood are most important.

Dissatisfaction with specific services of local government occurs in three major patterns. Variations in dissatisfaction with traffic conditions, parks and playgrounds, and, in the City, schools and libraries, reflect differences in the needs of various segments of the population. Variations in dissatisfaction with public transportation, police protection, sewage disposal, and garbage collection reflect different levels of service for the neighborhood of residence. There is little variation and little dissatisfaction relative to fire protection and water supply; the levels of these two services are regarded adequate for the needs of the residents.

Those who have felt like complaining about one or more of these various services are younger persons, with higher social rank. They are more likely to be Negroes than any other ethnic group. In general, feeling like complaining does not differ significantly or consistently among the major segments of the population. Those who have complained to a governmental agency, however, are disproportionately concentrated among people who own their homes, have lived in their present dwelling for a relatively long period of time, and are of higher social rank. When those who have in fact complained are taken as a proportion of those who have said they have felt like complaining, most of these variations become even clearer. (There is one reversal—older persons who felt like complaining are more likely to have done so.)

Belief in the economic worth of local government, as indicated by the proportion agreeing or disagreeing that taxes are too high in view of the services provided, varies sharply by education and less sharply by income and ethnicity. Those who say taxes are too high (a percentage larger in the County than City) are more often poorly educated, of lower income, and of backgrounds other than Old American or German. Other factors make little difference, except that in the County those most committed to the neighborhood are most likely to believe local taxes are excessive.

In general, the most supportive public for local government consists of those with more education, a higher income, and higher occupational levels—that is, those of higher social rank. Such persons are most likely to suggest changes or improvements for their neighborhood, complain to local agencies about inadequate services, and believe that local taxes are not disproportionately high considering the benefits. They are more likely than others to be dissatisfied with traffic conditions, public transportation and, in the City, sewage disposal.

Persons of lower social rank, as well as the "ethnic minorities" (Negroes and persons with southern or eastern European backgrounds), probably have greater needs. Proportionately more of them are dissatisfied with police protection, the condition of residential streets, and in the City, garbage collection—conditions suggesting congested or blighted neighborhoods.

Persons who live in neighborhoods of families, own their own homes, and have lived in the present dwelling unit for a long period of time are most likely to be dissatisfied with parks and playgrounds, traffic conditions, and, in the County, sewage disposal. Younger adults are most likely to be dissatisfied with schools, libraries, traffic conditions, and parks and playgrounds. Young married people with families, who own their own home in an area of similar families, are concerned about services and facilities necessary for their type of existence. Their needs are quite different from those of the apartment dwellers and, particularly, those who live in the tenements of the blighted areas.

13

Metropolitan Governmental Change:
Support and Opposition

WHETHER sprawling metropolitan complexes are in any real sense "metropolitan communities" depends upon more than the presence of many persons and organizations in close physical proximity. Community presupposes an interdependence of action in everyday life, the resulting flow of communication, and the development of normative standards. Certainly there is large-scale interdependence between the City with its work opportunities and the labor force residing in the County, between an industry and its urban setting, suburban workers, and various subcontractors. However, in order to speak of an over-all St. Louis metropolitan community, it is important to have some measure of interdependence and identification at the grass-roots level.

The proximity of hundreds of thousands of people in the City-County area results in political, economic, and social interdependence that can be objectively specified by the analyst. But only as this unity affects the lives of the citizens does it become the basis for statements about general welfare and political decisions integrating the area. Governmental interdependence is implicit in the need for area-wide control of traffic and transportation; traffic engineering studies, for example, make this clear. Economic interdependence is evident in the fact that a majority of employed County residents work in the City (and they are the persons with a disproportionate share of the better-rewarded jobs). Social interdependence is evident in the results of political and economic ties; the bifurcation of work and residence forces thousands of persons to cross governmental boundaries two or more times a day—to fight their way through the web of traffic from suburb to suburb to downtown, and back again. In the process they are not crossing alien territory; they are binding the separate governmental and spatial fragments into a single metropolitan "field of action." This unity is reinforced by their tendency to find many of their closest associates—in fact, a majority of their close friends and relatives—outside their immediate local community.

Such interdependence should result in a broader awareness of the metropolitan scene as a unity, and of its problems as general to the City and the County. Awareness should be greatest among those who require the widest field for their activities—those who live in the County but pursue their crucial work activities in the City, those who are of higher social rank, those who are males, and those in the prime of life, the middle years.

These people, then, should be the chief supporters of metropolitan governmental change. They are expected to experience governmental fragmentation most concretely in their daily round of activities. At the same time, clear-cut norms and sharply focused definitions of the metropolitan community and its problems should not be expected. The "community," after all, lacks any universally encompassing structure. And, insofar as governmental boundaries and corporate images define the metropolitan area for the resident, "the City-County area" is simply a summary term for the scores of units in City and County. Thus there is interest in the emergence of a metropolitan image out of experience, of metropolitan problems out of the day-to-day problems of the residents.

This chapter examines the nature of the public for metropolitan governmental change. Consideration is given first to variations among major segments of the population with respect to their awareness of problems shared by City and County, their opinions of various kinds of governmental reorganization, and their division into major types of opinion-holders. In the process some of the views about the probable supporters of governmental reform are investigated.

After a consideration of all residents and their different opinions of change in relation to their socioeconomic characteristics, the chapter divides the population into those who seem most relevant to an election situation (those who have ever voted) and those who have never participated in local elections. These two groups are briefly compared, but the chief purpose of this division is to isolate those who care at all about local government and thus to determine who constitutes the electorate. The opinions of these people concerning proposed changes are then analyzed on the assumption that these attitudes provide a dependable clue to the thinking of the politically effective citizenry. Finally, the degree to which active dissatisfaction with present services is related to willingness to accept major governmental change is scrutinized.

In the process the nature of the opposition to governmental change will also be presented. In the past, this opposition has usually turned out to be very strong in an election involving proposed metropolitan governmental reorganization. Little is known about such opposition. Its nature will be clarified and interpretations about its reasons for existing will be made.

AWARENESS OF PROBLEMS SHARED BY CITY AND COUNTY

The ability of residents to suggest changes or improvements for the City-County area as a whole is taken as an indicator of interest in and awareness of metropolitan problems, regardless of the individual's competency to diagnose the situation objectively.

There is little difference between City and County in the percentage suggesting changes. Awareness of metropolitan problems does vary sharply by social rank and significantly by age and sex. There are important variations according to indexes associated with migration in the City, and ethnic identity is of some importance in the County. A very significant variation is associated with differences in the location of the person's job.

AGE AND SEX

In both the City and the County, the awareness of City-County problems decreases as age after 40 increases (D59). The range is from around one-half to around 80 per cent of the residents suggesting one or more changes in each area. As is true of many other socioeconomic factors, the effect of age increases between the youngest adult class and those in their thirties; from there it drops. Such a decrease is consistent in the City but in the County there is a disproportionate decline between those aged 50–64 and those 65 and over.

Age variations may very well reflect differences in the objective

needs of the residents and their problems resulting from inadequate area-wide facilities. Variations by sex certainly support
this assumption; a larger proportion of men than women suggest
changes. Seventy-eight per cent of the men in the City suggest
area-wide problems, compared with only 63 per cent of the women.
In the County, the difference also occurs, with both sexes somewhat more likely to suggest changes—82 per cent of the men
and 67 per cent of the women.

Other evidence supports the hypothesis that awareness of
metropolitan problems is greater for those whose daily routine
exposes them more to the metropolitan network of activity. When
County residents are divided into those who are not in the labor
force, those who work in the County, those who work in the city
of St. Louis, and those who work in both City and County or in
localities adjacent to the City-County area, a consistent increase
appears in the percentages suggesting specific changes or improvements for the City-County area (64, 75, 83, and 92).

There is thus a variation in the way the economic interdependence of the area is reflected in the lives of the citizens. Age, sex,
and work location indicate sharp differences in awareness of
metropolitan needs for those who are exposed in varying degrees
to resulting metropolitan problems. (A similar analysis is not
possible for the City, as only a very small percentage of the residents work outside the City.)

SOCIAL RANK

A larger proportion of people of high social rank have occupations that direct their attention to broader horizons. Professionals, entrepreneurs, and managers are all occupationally led
to see interrelationships among separate aspects of society. At
the same time, better-educated persons are more likely to have
a frame of reference emphasizing interrelations and normative
standards. Income, in turn, should be related to and reinforce
these tendencies. In short, awareness of metropolitan problems
should increase with social rank, and it does.

Differences based on education are very sharp and clear (D60).
The one negative case (City residents having 13 through 15
years of schooling) is probably a result of the small number of
interviewees in this category. Otherwise, those without high
school education are much less likely to mention City-County
improvements than those with some high school. In turn, fewer
of the latter suggest changes than those who have completed

high school, and almost all who have completed college suggest at least one change.

Income is a less significant factor (D61), but there are large differences between the various income classes in ability to suggest changes. Those in the three highest income classes are much more likely to be aware of possible improvement. The sharpest differences are between the lowest income class and the middle income classes and, in the County only, between the latter and the highest.

ETHNICITY

In the City, ethnic variations are of no importance in naming City-County changes. All ethnic groups are close to the average. In the County, Negroes constitute the smallest proportion suggesting changes, and Old Americans the largest. The gap in social rank between Negroes and others in the City, particularly for education, is much less than in the County, and these findings seemingly reflect that fact.

MIGRATION

City migrants do not suggest changes as frequently as natives. Only 52 per cent residing in the area between one and five years and two-thirds of the older migrants as against three-fourths of the natives of the metropolitan area can specify desired improvements. This suggests variance in knowledge of the area's problems—but those who have been in the area twenty years or longer still suggest improvements less frequently than natives. A smaller proportion of persons with rural experience (64 per cent) than of those raised in urban areas (74 per cent) mention one or more metropolitan problems. In the County, the same proportion of migrants and nonmigrants, and of those with and without farm experience, suggest City-County changes.

Variations in awareness of metropolitan problems, as measured by ability to suggest changes or improvements in the area as a whole, are greatest by social rank and factors that relate to an individual's personal experience with the results of metropolitan interdependence and inadequate governmental arrangements. Migration background differences are important in the City but not in the County, and, in the latter, ethnic variation has some significance.

While only certain factors consistently make a difference in metropolitan awareness, they make very sharp and clear differences. Younger persons, males, those of higher social rank, and those who live in the County and work in the City are most likely to suggest changes or improvements in the City-County area as a whole.

OPINIONS ABOUT METROPOLITAN
GOVERNMENTAL REFORM

Elections on metropolitan governmental reorganization present the voters with only two alternatives—to accept a specific proposal or to vote for "no change." In an effort to estimate the support for various types of reorganization, the four alternatives legally available to the City-County area, together with the fifth possibility that nothing be done, were presented to the residents. They are (1) merger of all general governmental units into one, (2) reëntry of the City into St. Louis County, (3) establishment of a federal system through continuing all general governments and creating a metropolitan government to handle the most pressing area-wide problems, (4) consolidation of municipalities in the County into a smaller number, and (5) retention of the existing governmental pattern. The last option represents resistance to any type of change; the last two alternatives do not produce any City-County integration. The other three represent different degrees of City-County integration.

In general, County residents are more favorable than City residents to nonintegration of City and County, especially to status quo. City residents are much more favorable to merger. However, only a minority in either City or County favors the status quo; a majority of the residents of both prefer some form of change to no change at all.

What is the relative importance of socioeconomic characteristics and area of residence in differentiating the supporters of the various alternatives? Can the greater support for merger in the City be accounted for by the larger proportion of urbanites, Negroes, and persons of lower social rank? Can the more extensive preference for the status quo in the County be explained by the presence of large upper-middle class enclaves?

What are the independent effects of each cluster of socioeconomic indexes as differentiating factors of the supporters and resisters of governmental reorganization? What is the general relationship between social rank and willingness to support change? What kind of change? And how does this vary between

City and County? What about the Negroes? They are accused of desiring merger so that they can increase their access to the suburban municipalities, and desiring no change at all in order to preserve their relative political influence within the central city. Which is correct, if either?

In this section responses to the questions on liking or disliking each of the five governmental alternatives, responses to the ranking questions (proposal most preferred and one most disliked), and, finally, belief among the major population segments in the likelihood of change, are discussed.

REACTIONS TO GOVERNMENTAL ALTERNATIVES

The substantial variations in the residents' liking for various governmental alternatives are caused by many different factors. (The indicator used to measure reactions is the percentage who say they like a specific proposal.) The most important relate to age and sex, social rank, and ethnicity. In the City those related to migration history and commitment to the neighborhood are of considerable weight; this is not true of the County. Population segments vary more in the City by practically all factors.

Age and sex, it will be recalled, are factors clearly associated with the individual's awareness of metropolitan problems; persons in the middle span (30 to 64) and males are most likely to offer suggestions for City-County improvements (D62). These people are also more apt to favor extreme governmental integration; the percentage who prefer merger increases with age in both City and County. Aside from this, age offers no significant variation. Even the status quo is liked by about the same percentage at each age in the County. Interestingly enough, the youngest age group in the County likes it least, whereas the youngest in the City likes it more than other age groups.

Men in the City are friendlier to the two extreme integration proposals, merger and the reëntry of the City into the County (D63). Women in both City and County more often like the status quo. Sex differences are sharpest in the City; men are much more likely to favor governmental change, women, the status quo. In the County the clearest difference is in the percentage who like the latter; although men are slightly more favorable to every action alternative except the federal system, they are much less favorable to the proposal that nothing be changed (16 per cent difference). The male role in American society prescribes more mobility and more political interest and action for men, which is probably the basis for these differences. Women generally are less exposed to problems, less interested, and less knowledgeable with respect to politics.

Social rank differences are important for responses to each of the two polar proposals, merger and the status quo. Approval for merger increases with education in the City; in the County it declines (D64). Thus, although more choose merger at each educational level in the City, the difference between City and County increases consistently with educational level, from 12 per cent for those with seven years or less to 30 per cent for the college graduates.

Educational level only slightly affects the response to proposals for a federal system or the reëntry of the City into the County. However, the proposal to consolidate the municipalities of the County into a smaller number finds increasing approval among the more educated in both City and County. The range in the County is 23 per cent; in the City it is less sharp and less consistent.

Between the most highly educated and the least educated people of City and County looms a large difference in the percentage who like retention of status quo (24 per cent and 46 per cent in the City; 23 per cent and 48 per cent in the County). Once more, the role of the educated person is important. He is expected to take more interest in, have more opinions on, and be more knowledgeable about politics. He is also likely to have more widespread interest and activities. A desire for change does not necessarily mean competency in local governmental affairs. However, those who consistently wish to retain the present system come from the population segments least likely to know whether they and their neighbors can vote and are themselves least likely to vote.

Income produces less variation. However, in the City proportionately fewer in the most affluent class approve status quo (20 per cent compared to 39 through 42 per cent), and in the County approval declines in the two highest income classes (the range is 47 to 35 per cent). The sudden decline with the $7,000-and-over category probably indicates a substantial increase in education and "middle class" occupations; larger percentages of blue-collar workers and persons with little education have incomes ranging from the bottom to the next to highest income category. (Those earning $10,000 or more, when separated in the County, are less likely to approve the existing system than those earning $7,000 to $9,999.)

The highest income class in the City is not only most likely to dislike status quo, but it also is most likely to prefer merger. Seventy-six per cent of these people like merger, compared with 52 to 55 per cent of the other income groups. Only with respect to consolidation of County municipalities is the income of County residents positively related to approval; between the very lowest income class and the highest, the proportion of those liking the proposal increases from 38 to 58 per cent, and the middle income classes fall at 54 and 51 per cent.

For most major population segments, County residents are much less likely to have a favorable opinion of merger than City residents. Approval of status quo, however, does not vary sharply by area of residence, and there is little variation in response to other alternatives.

In the City the Negro population is less favorable to merger than those with other *ethnic backgrounds* and, in the County, tends to like the status quo more than do those of Old American and German backgrounds (D65). Negroes and whites with backgrounds in southern and eastern Europe are the ethnic groups in both City and County most likely to approve the present system. Old Americans and Germans (whose opinions about the various alternatives are generally identical) in both the City and County are least likely to have a favorable opinion of the existing governmental arrangements.

Beyond this area of agreement, however, City and County differ greatly. These latter two ethnic groups in the City are most likely to prefer total merger, but in the County are least likely. In the County they are also more apt to dislike the idea of the City reëntering the County, but are the ones most favorable to consolidation of County municipalities.

The Negroes in the City highly approve both a federal system for the City-County area and the reëntry of the City into the County. Their overwhelming support for the federal system is difficult to understand; it may be that simple association with the federal system of national-state relations accounts for it. There is some supporting evidence for this hypothesis in the analysis of social rank and opinions about reform; the very lowest income class and those with a high school education or less are most likely to favor a federal system.

Clearly, the City population most favorable to outright merger is not disproportionately made up of Negroes. In fact, the Old Americans and Germans are most attracted to the proposal—and their ethnic background is the same as most County residents'. In both City and County they must often look with disfavor upon retaining status quo.

The number of years since *migration* to the local metropolitan area, and the kind of background, whether rural or urban, are important factors in shaping attitudes about the various types of governmental alternatives. Older migrants and natives are most apt to approve of merger.

In the City, old migrants and natives differ strongly from other categories in support for merger (61 and 60 per cent respectively, compared to 48 per cent of wartime migrants, 35 per cent of the new migrants) ; in fact, the majority of opinion favoring merger comes from these first-mentioned two groups. Even in the County, a slightly higher percentage of these categories supports merger (39 and 38 per cent, compared to 35 and 23 for wartime and new migrants). These same people are most friendly to the federal system in the City, and least supportive of the City's reëntry into the County. In the County the chief difference is that the newest migrants are most likely to have a favorable opinion of status quo (49 per cent), whereas all others are less well disposed toward it (39 to 43 per cent).

Those in the City with rural experience are less likely than those without to approve of merger, and in both City and County they are more likely to hold a favorable opinion of the status quo (D66). In the City they are more apt to like reëntry of the City into the County and the federal system. In both areas they are less approving of consolidation of County municipalities. The differences in the City may be partially explained by the number of Negroes among those with rural experience; however, as 76 per cent of the Negroes favor the federal system, compared with only 53 per cent of the persons with farm backgrounds, it is apparent that ethnicity does not explain all differences.

The differences are much less marked for the County residents, but generally parallel those for the City people. Again, differences between City and County with respect to merger and the status quo remain for each population segment.

The three factors under *commitment to the neighborhood* lead to the same general conclusion—people committed to their home and neighborhood are most likely to approve of merger and least likely to accept status quo as satisfactory.

The people living in single-family detached residences are more favorable to merger, particularly in the City, and less favorable to status quo (D67). In the City they are less disposed toward reëntry of the City into the County and toward the federal system, but in the County they are more favorable to the federal system than are the apartment dwellers. Apartment dwellers in the City are more likely than their counterparts in the County to approve of consolidation of County municipalities.

City-County differences remain very great, however. A little more than one-third of those County residents who live in single-family units like merger, but almost two-thirds of the similar population in the City approve it.

These variations are almost identical to the type-of-occupancy factor. City and County homeowners are more favorable to merger and less likely to approve of status quo. The differences are of the same magnitude as those produced through comparison by type of dwelling unit.

Number of years in the present dwelling makes little difference. City residents who have lived longest in their present dwelling are most apt to prefer merger and consolidation of County municipalities (by margins of 5 and 8 per cent from the groups least liking these two alternatives) and much less likely to have a favorable opinion of the status quo (by 16 per cent).

In general, the segments of the population favoring status quo are those who most frequently answer "don't know," and they are also the persons least likely to vote. Those who are most competent and interested differ in their opinions of action proposals by area of residence; in the City but not in the County they are the most frequent supporters of merger.

PREFERENCE AMONG GOVERNMENTAL ALTERNATIVES

Consideration now turns to the questions in which the proposals are ranked: "Which of these do you like most?" and "Which do you dislike most?" Because reactions to the three moderate alternatives—reëntry of City into County, the federal system, and consolidation of County municipalities—"scatter" so much, the major differences here are in the proportions who most prefer or dislike the two extreme proposals, merger or status quo. Since, furthermore, each person had only one vote among the five possibilities, the percentages are much lower than in the preceding analysis. Nevertheless, they are probably more significant. Those who dislike a proposal most of all are conceivably the hard core of political resistance; those who choose a proposal from among the five are presumably strong adherents of that program.

With respect to the individual's first choice, the findings are generally consistent with the earlier responses on liking or disliking the options. Similar segments of the population prefer merger on one hand, the existing governmental arrangements on the other.

Age and sex. Older persons are more likely to prefer merger in both areas, but particularly in the County; younger persons are more likely to prefer status quo only in the City. In the County, younger persons are more apt to prefer the federal system. These differences are not striking.

Sex is a more important factor (D68). Men are more favorable to governmental integration and women more often prefer status quo. Sex differences are more important than City-County differences regarding the choice of the status quo. As to merger, women in the City choose it in equal proportions to men in the County. Opinions on merger thus are sharply different in the two areas.

Social rank. The adherents of merger tend to be concentrated in the higher social rank populations of the City, while those who choose the existing system are rarest in these segments of City and County populations alike. A large percentage of City residents at all educational levels prefers merger, but it increases from 28 to 48 per cent; in contrast, only about one-fourth of the County residents at all educational levels prefer merger. The less educated County residents are much more apt to choose status quo than those of similar education in the City. City-County differences are not great, however, for those who have been to college.

Although it is not one of the most popular proposals, preference for the consolidation of the County municipalities increases regularly with education and one-fifth of the college graduates in the County prefer it above all others. Choice of the federal system is also most popular among the better-educated in the County, with one-fourth of the college graduates preferring it. The increase in the percentage choosing these two moderate proposals as education increases is consistent and striking in the County; 21 per cent at the lowest level choose them, 44 per cent at the highest level.

There is no similar increase in support for these proposals in the City. The consolidation of suburban municipalities, of course, is of little concern to the residents of the City, regardless of whether they are politically interested and competent. In the City, the chief shift with education is from support of leaving the present system unchanged to choice of merger. Thus, support for

TABLE 37

Education and Preference among Governmental Alternatives

Proposal	Years of education completed					
	0–7	8	9–11	12	13–15	16 or more
Merger						
City	28%	39%	39%	44%	39%	48%
County	26	24	29	26	27	25
Reëntry of City into County						
City	15	13	12	13	14	10
County	13	14	13	14	16	13
Federal system						
City	12	15	20	15	25	3
County	10	14	12	16	13	24
Municipal consolidation in County						
City	3	3	8	9	4	14
County	11	15	15	18	22	20
Status quo						
City	24	18	16	17	18	17
County	30	29	30	23	20	14
Number						
City	(113)	(125)	(114)	(103)	(28)	(29)
County	(90)	(233)	(238)	(393)	(167)	(162)

Excluded: City 3 and County 2 "don't know."

programs of moderate integration increases with education in the County, resulting in a much wider dispersion of choice among the better-educated, but in the City there is an increasing concentration of preference for merger in the most highly educated classes.

A somewhat similar pattern holds for income classes. Support for merger increases by income in both City and County. In fact, while lower income classes are more likely to prefer status quo than merger, the higher income classes are more likely to prefer merger by similar margins. Support for the moderate proposals is similar for all but the lowest income class in the County. Again, the City is more likely to prefer merger by a wide difference at each income level. Ninety-one per cent of the City residents with incomes of $7,000 or more choose some form of City-County

TABLE 38

HOUSEHOLD INCOME AND PREFERENCE AMONG GOVERNMENTAL ALTERNATIVES

Proposal	$0–2,999	$3–4,999	$5–6,999	$7,000 and over
Merger				
City	35%	30%	40%	60%
County	21	22	26	29
Reëntry of City into County				
City	11	15	14	13
County	20	14	15	13
Federal system				
City	16	17	14	17
County	10	14	16	17
Municipal consolidation in County				
City	7	18	6	1
County	11	21	19	19
Status quo				
City	18	21	23	8
County	29	29	23	20
Number				
City	(123)	(155)	(117)	(75)
County	(98)	(203)	(341)	(510)

EXCLUDED: City 45 and County 123 "don't know" or refused to supply information.

integration, compared with 60 per cent among County residents.

Ethnicity. The strongest protagonists of merger in the City are the Germans and Old Americans; there is little variation in the County. Negroes are least apt to choose merger in both areas (28 per cent compared with 37 to 43 per cent in the City; 22 per cent compared with 26 to 31 per cent in the County). Support for consolidation is somewhat higher among the "majority" ethnic population of the County (18 to 19 per cent compared with 12 to 13 per cent) and support for the federal system is highest among the Negroes in the City (28 per cent compared with 10 to 16 per cent). All other variations do not seem significant.

Migration. Those with rural backgrounds most often prefer status quo and are least favorable to merger. A stronger factor is the number of years of residence in the metropolitan area. The most striking aspect of these findings is the consistent increase in support for merger, between the newest migrants and the natives, in both the City and the suburbs. Half again as many of the natives support merger as do the newest migrants. Yet this difference is not reflected in any consistent variation among the adherents of other proposals.

TABLE 39

YEARS IN METROPOLITAN AREA AND PREFERENCE
AMONG GOVERNMENTAL ALTERNATIVES

Proposal	Less than 5	5–19	20 or more	Native
Merger				
City	29%	29%	37%	44%
County	16	24	25	29
Reëntry of City into County				
City	10	17	15	9
County	11	14	12	15
Federal system				
City	6	14	15	17
County	22	18	12	15
Municipal consolidation in County				
City	6	11	4	6
County	23	15	19	17
Status quo				
City	32	19	18	18
County	25	26	29	21
Number				
City	(31)	(102)	(168)	(114)
County	(97)	(219)	(328)	(691)

EXCLUDED: City 3 and County 4 "don't know."

Support for merger remains higher for each class in the City. Support for status quo, while higher for most classes in the County, is even higher in the City for the newest migrants.

Commitment to neighborhood. These differences are consistent with those reported on likes and dislikes earlier in this chapter. Those who live in single-family dwellings are more likely than apartment dwellers to choose merger and less likely to choose status quo; the difference in each instance is about 6 per cent in both City and County. Those who own their own homes are more favorable to merger in the City (44 per cent compared with 34 per cent), but there is little difference in the County. In both areas renters are more likely to choose status quo (by only about 5 per cent, however).

Work-residence location. It was noted earlier that County residents who work in the City are more apt to suggest area-wide improvements than either those working in the County or those who are not in the labor force. Such individuals also more often manifest a liking for merger, and less often a liking for status quo. Their choice among the alternatives is consistent with these findings; 21 per cent of County residents who do not work prefer merger, as against 27 per cent of those who work in the County and 33 per cent of those who work in the City. In contrast, status quo is preferred by 29 per cent of those who do not work at all, compared with 23 per cent of those working in the County and only 19 per cent of those working in the City. These findings reflect more than the effects of place-of-work, however; those who do not work at all are usually women, and those who work in the City but live in the County are likely to have higher social rank. Further analysis is necessary to indicate the independent importance of work location.

THE PROPOSAL MOST DISLIKED

Residents were also asked which proposal they would least like to see put into effect. Variations in response are not nearly so sharp and consistent as is the case with the choices of proposals that are most liked. The only sharp differences relate to the two extreme proposals. The results therefore will be summarized very briefly.

Dislike for merger is most common among younger persons, women, and those who live in multiple-family units that they rent. In the County only, the more educated persons, those who work in the County, and those who have lived the shortest period of time in the metropolitan area disproportionately select merger as the proposal they most dislike.

Dislike for status quo is concentrated among older persons, males, and those who live in single-family dwelling units. In the City only, those without farm experience are likely to oppose status quo, while those with a high school education or more are also disproportionately opposed. In the County, the older inhabitants of the metropolitan area and those who work in the City are more likely to oppose the proposal.

These results are consistent and reflect the same polarities that appeared earlier. Those segments of the population most apt to say they like one of the two polar proposals—merger or status quo—are most apt to choose it as the one they like best and to choose its opposite as the one they like least. Further light may be shed on this variation by analyzing the types of holders of consistent opinions regarding the governmental alternatives.

TYPES OF CONSISTENT OPINION HOLDERS
AMONG IMPORTANT POPULATION CATEGORIES

The residents have been divided into three classes of holders of logically consistent opinions. They are (1) the mergerites, those who like merger best of the five proposals and most dislike either of the two proposals that produce no City-County integration (consolidation of County municipalities and local autonomy), (2) the moderate integrationists or moderates who like one of the three intermediate proposals best (consolidation of County municipalities, the federal system, or reëntry of the City into the County) and dislike most either of the two extremes, merger or status quo, and (3) the local autonomists, who like best status quo and most dislike either merger or reëntry of the City into the County.

The distribution of the categories in City and County is discussed in chapter 10. The City people consist of one-fourth mergerites, one-fifth moderate integrationists, one-eighth local autonomists, and slightly more than two-fifths fall into none of these three types (and thus are termed "no type").[1] In the County, about one-fifth are mergerites, more than one-third moderate integrationists, one-fifth local autonomists, and slightly over one-fourth are no type. The mode of the City distribution is in the no type category; that of the County distribution is in the moderate integrationist category. Thus, in the County as a whole there is more interest and more logical consistency of opinion.

The distribution of these categories varies significantly for most of the major segments of the population.

There is no consistent increase or decrease in the proportions of mergerites with increasing *age*. The percentage of local autonomists decreases with age in the City, while that of moderate integrationists decreases in the County. Those who do not fall into any type increase, although not consistently, with age in the City. In the County the increase is consistent though not of great magnitude.

Sex again is a more important and consistent factor. The local

---

[1] Persons who said they did not know in response to either question are classified as "no type"; it is assumed that this category indicates the same lack of consistent opinion as contradictory answers.

autonomists are disproportionately concentrated among the women, while the mergerites are much more common among the men. Surprisingly little difference appears by sex in the percentage not fitting into any of the three types. The proportion of men who are consistent merger adherents in City and in County is quite similar. The most impressive City-County differences are still in the percentage of each sex who are moderate integrationists, and the percentage who are none of the three types.

TABLE 40

SEX AND TYPE OF OPINION HOLDERS

Opinion holders	Men	Women
Mergerites		
City	28%	21%
County	23	14
Moderates		
City	21	19
County	36	33
Local autonomists		
City	8	16
County	16	25
No type		
City	42	43
County	25	27
Number		
City	(232)	(283)
County	(581)	(704)

With increasing *social rank* there is a decrease in the percentage that does not fall into one of the three constructed types. The protagonists of merger increase consistently among the more educated in the City. In the County, however, there is no such tendency. Instead, the moderate integrationists increase—from 23 to 46 per cent. By the same token, local autonomists decrease with education in the County, particularly among those who have had some college education. The percentage in the no type category declines somewhat with higher education.

Income is not a very powerful predictor of opinions on governmental reform. A simple economic class interest might dictate opposition to all change in the prosperous suburbs of the County and rational support for local autonomy. The large, prosperous suburbs provide excellent services and also provide "status pro-

TABLE 41

EDUCATION AND TYPE OF OPINION HOLDERS

Opinion holders	Years of education completed					
	0–7	8	9–11	12	13–15	16 and more
Mergerites						
City	21%	21%	26%	27%	32%	31%
County	21	18	23	15	20	18
Moderates						
City	27	22	24	20	25	14
County	23	30	27	35	42	46
Local auton- omists						
City	14	12	10	13	7	17
County	22	25	26	21	17	11
No type						
City	47	46	39	40	36	38
County	33	26	24	29	20	24
Number						
City	(113)	(125)	(114)	(130)	(28)	(29)
County	(90)	(233)	(238)	(393)	(167)	(162)

EXCLUDED: City 3 and County 2 "don't know."

tection" to their residents. However, the more affluent in the County are the least likely to support status quo, and most likely to support moderate integration. On the basis of annual incomes of $10,000 or more, 41 per cent are moderate integrationists and 16 per cent are local autonomists. Nor, at the other extreme, are the very poor in the City overwhelmingly in favor of merger. A much smaller proportion of them than of those with incomes of $7,000 or more are merger adherents.

Differences among occupational classes are similar to those for education and total household income, although not as large nor as consistent.

Ethnic backgrounds result in little variation in the distributions of types of holders of consistent opinions regarding governmental alternatives. These variations tend to parallel those for social rank, with Old Americans and Germans similar to the higher social rank classes. However, Negroes are considerably more likely than others in the City to favor moderate integration (37 per cent compared with 14 to 17 per cent) and less likely to fall into the no type category (34 per cent compared to 44 per cent for each of the other categories). Negroes are more likely

TABLE 42

HOUSEHOLD INCOME AND TYPE OF OPINION HOLDERS

Opinion holders	$0–2,999	$3–4,999	$5–6,999	$7,000 and over
Mergerites				
City	23%	20%	23%	40%
County	17	17	18	20
Moderates				
City	20	24	20	20
County	25	36	37	36
Local autonomists				
City	11	14	12	7
County	24	25	18	18
No type				
City	45	41	45	33
County	33	23	26	26
Number				
City	(123)	(155)	(117)	(75)
County	(98)	(203)	(341)	(510)

EXCLUDED: City 45 and County 123 "don't know" or refused to supply information.

to favor the federal system and less likely to prefer merger; apparently they do so in a consistent fashion.

The natives and the older *migrants* are consistently more likely to be mergerites in the City; they are slightly more likely to fit into one of the three types. The proportion of mergerites increases consistently, from 16 per cent of the newest migrants to 27 per cent of the natives. The percentage coming within none of the types declines from 48 per cent to 40 per cent. There are no significant or consistent variations by migration background in the County.

Commitment to neighborhood does not play a strong role. In the City larger proportions of the owners are mergerites or fall into none of the three types and a smaller proportion are moderates. In the County, a larger percentage of them are moderate integrationists, and smaller percentages are local autonomists, or fall into a type. None of these differences is as great as 10 per cent, however.

BELIEF IN PROBABILITY OF GOVERNMENTAL CHANGE

The population varies by age, sex, and education, although not sharply, in its optimism concerning governmental reorganization. There are slight differences by ethnicity, migration, and religion, while commitment to the neighborhood is of no importance. Because these differences are nowhere substantial, they will be summarized briefly. Belief in the likelihood of change decreases as age increases and is much more consistent in the County, declining from 46 per cent for the 30–39 age class to 25 per cent for those past 64. One plausible reason is the tendency for older City persons to be more favorable toward extreme integration and therefore to predict what they would like to see occur. Certainly the difference between those aged 50 to 64 and those over 64 in the City (40 and 42 per cent) is insignificant, whereas that for the same age classes in the County is very marked (38 and 25 per cent). A larger proportion of City residents in each of five age categories, beginning with the 21 to 29 class, believe change is probable.

Men and women are not very different in either City or County in their opinions on the matter; however, women in both City and County are more likely to say that they do not know (16 per cent of the women compared with 11 per cent of the men in the City, 13 per cent compared with 6 per cent in the County). Of those with opinions, a majority of each sex in the City believes change likely, but comparable majorities in the County believe it unlikely.

With increasing education, a larger percentage believes change improbable, especially in the County, and a declining percentage does not know. The percentages in the City who do not expect change range from 30 per cent for those with less than grammar school to about 50 per cent for the two highest categories. Those in the County range from 40 per cent to 61 per cent of persons who went to college; however, individuals who completed college are significantly less likely to say change is improbable (52 per cent) than those who attended college. The percentage not knowing is disproportionately concentrated among persons having a grammar school education or less. For those with some high school and more, the undecided proportion is relatively constant. Income and occupation differentiate in approximately the same fashion as education, although less sharply.

Old Americans are the least likely to believe change possible in both City and County, although each ethnic group is more optimistic in the City. Italians and Negroes are markedly more optimistic in the City; other variations are slight. Catholics in both City and County are more likely to believe change is probable, 50 per cent of those in the City think so (compared with

44 per cent of the Protestants), and 44 per cent think so in the County (compared with 38 per cent of the Protestants).

Those who have been in the area between one and five years, lacking the knowledge of previous campaigns to unite City and County, may have concluded that the present situation has always been generally acceptable. At any rate, older migrants and natives, who are more favorable to change, are also more optimistic about its probability.

Variations among the people of City and County based upon commitment to neighborhood, work-residence locations, and other background factors are of little or no importance in sorting the optimistic from the pessimistic.

THE ACTIVE ELECTORATE AND METROPOLITAN REFORM

One of every three adults has never voted in a local election while living in his present community. These citizens may be considered less involved and less important in determining the outcome of elections on metropolitan governmental reorganization. Although some of them have moved recently and presumably will vote in future elections, and although others may vote in an election on reorganization despite never having voted before, it is plausible to expect them to take little interest in and have little influence on reorganization efforts.

To divide the population into participants and nonparticipants improves the sample for purposes of assessing support for and opposition to reform. The opinions of those who have never been a part of the local electorate may "mask" important differences between voters and nonvoters, for the latter are likely to be less competent about local government and less involved in it.

Those who have not voted are disproportionately concentrated among certain types of people—those with less commitment to neighborhood, lower social rank, younger age, female sex, and fewer years in the metropolitan area. These same segments are disproportionately represented among those in the City who oppose merger, among County opponents of consolidation of County municipalities, and among those in both City and County who like status quo. Therefore, it can be expected that the active electorate takes opposite positions, and it does.

The voters in both City and County are significantly less friendly to the existing governmental arrangements than nonvoters. Voters in each area are also much more favorable to the consolidation of County municipalities and slightly more favorable to the federal system. There is, however, no difference in support for the reëntry of the City into the County between the two categories. The difference in opinion between City and County with respect to merger is accentuated when voters are considered separately: 60 per cent of the City voters like merger, but only 36 per cent in the County have the same opinion.

TABLE 43

SUPPORT FOR GOVERNMENTAL ALTERNATIVES
AMONG VOTERS AND NONVOTERS

Alternative	Voters	Nonvoters
Merger		
City	60%	48%
County	36	39
Reëntry of City into County		
City	46	46
County	41	40
Federal system		
City	57	49
County	51	49
Municipal consolidation in County		
City	50	40
County	56	43
Status quo		
City	34	45
County	40	46
Number		
City	(341)	(154)
County	(862)	(334)

EXCLUDED: City 20 and County 89 ineligible.

The establishment of a federal system is the only proposal involving any degree of City-County integration which has major support in both areas. The support remains about the same when nonvoters are eliminated, indicating the federal system is not disproportionately the choice of the less politically competent and less active part of the citizenry. Moreover, this proposal has the highest proportion of voters in each area saying they do not know if they like it (11 per cent in the City, 7 per cent in the County), and thus the lowest proportion of opposition of any proposal looking to City-County integration—27 per cent in the City, 42 per cent in the County.

RANKING OF PROPOSALS BY VOTERS AND NONVOTERS

More than two-fifths of the City voters favor merger over all governmental alternatives; almost twice as many persons there who have voted prefer merger as those who have never cast a ballot in a local election. In the County, however, only about one-fourth of the voters prefer merger, a somewhat smaller proportion than the nonvoters. There is little variation between voters and nonvoters in preference for other proposals. Voters in the County more often choose consolidation of County municipalities, and the difference in support for status quo is consistent, although not pronounced. Much more important is the variation in the

TABLE 44

PREFERENCE FOR GOVERNMENTAL ALTERNATIVES
AMONG VOTERS AND NONVOTERS

Alternative	Voters	Nonvoters
Merger		
City	44%	23%
County	26	28
Reëntry of City into County		
City	12	16
County	15	12
Federal system		
City	15	16
County	14	15
Municipal consolidation in County		
City	6	6
County	19	15
Status quo		
City	18	23
County	24	26
Don't know		
City	6	16
County	2	4
Number		
City	(341)	(154)
County	(862)	(334)

EXCLUDED: City 20 and County 89 ineligible.

proportion that does not know; it is higher among the nonvoters in each area, and strikingly so in the City.

Analysis of the active electorate compared with the potential voters thus indicates that the City-County differences are not owing to any greater concentration of support in the City for merger among the inactive, or in the County for status quo, among the same type of people. City-County differences become even sharper when only the voting population is considered. Among the nonvoters, however, 39 per cent in the City and 30 per cent in the County either do not know which alternative they prefer, or prefer no change. Among the voters, the comparable percentages are 24 and 26.

TYPES OF HOLDERS OF CONSISTENT OPINIONS

It is assumed that the clarity and strength of a person's commitment to a specific choice of governmental alternatives are indicated in ascending fashion by his general liking or disliking for a proposal, his required choice of the proposal he likes best, and the consistency between the choice he likes best and the one he likes least. The rationale for the three major types of holders of consistent opinions—mergerites, moderate integrationists, and local autonomists—as well as the nature of the "no type" individuals was presented earlier.

What is the distribution of types among the active electorate and among those who have never voted? Voters are more frequently one of the types. The change in the proportion coming within a specific type among the voters is 8 per cent in the City, 10 per cent in the County. Most of the difference among City residents is reflected in the much larger proportion of voters who are mergerites; among County voters it is reflected in the larger proportion of moderate integrationists.

The elimination of the nonvoting residents results in even sharper City-County differences of opinions about governmental alternatives. County voters are more consistent in their opinions and the largest proportion of them prefers moderate City-County governmental integration. About one-half of the City voters who have consistent opinions favor merger.

SERVICE DISSATISFACTION AND SUPPORT FOR METROPOLITAN REFORM

A frequent assumption about the impetus for governmental reorganization in a metropolitan area is that it is based on wide-

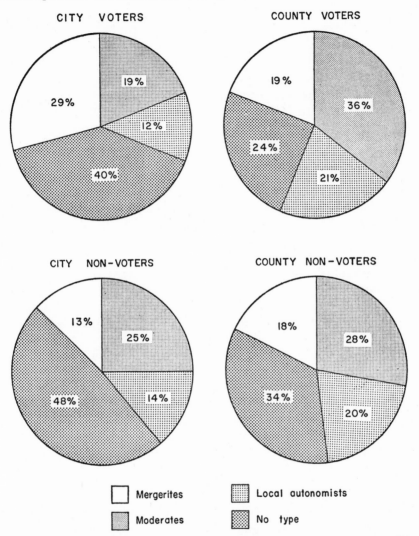

CITY VOTERS

COUNTY VOTERS

CITY NON-VOTERS

COUNTY NON-VOTERS

☐ Mergerites ▦ Local autonomists

▦ Moderates ▦ No type

Note: Number of interviews: City voters 341; County voters 862; City non-voters 154; County non-voters 334. Excluded: City 20 and County 89 ineligible.

Fig. 21. Major types of opinion makers among voters and non-voters.

spread dissatisfaction with services. But such widespread dissatisfaction does not exist in the City-County area, although it is evident from the Survey's research on governmental services that there are many inadequacies. Only a few major services produce expressions of dissatisfaction from as much as 10 per cent of the population. The major sources of dissatisfaction are traffic, residential streets, parks and playgrounds, police protection (in the City only), and sewage disposal (in the County only).

There remains the possibility of dissatisfaction so scattered that one segment of the population is thoroughly dissatisfied with police but not residential streets, another, with the streets but not police. In such an event possibly all residents are very dissatisfied, but with different services. In testing this hypothesis, the major sources of dissatisfaction that are strictly local and refer to the immediate neighborhood or local community (residential streets and parks and playgrounds in each area, police in the City and sewage disposal in the County) have been selected from all local services as key indicators. Together, they account for a very large majority of all expressions of dissatisfaction. How many voters are dissatisfied with none of these services? [2] If the above hypothesis is correct, very few would be satisfied with all three.

In fact, only slightly over one-half the voters are dissatisfied with any of the services—48 per cent in the City, 49 per cent in the County, registered no dissatisfaction. The second largest category in each area consists of those dissatisfied with only one service (30 and 31 per cent in the City and County, respectively); about one-fifth of the residents are dissatisfied with two or three of the services (22 per cent in the City, 20 per cent in the County). Thus there is sufficient piling up of dissatisfaction among a small part of the population to invalidate the notion of a patchwork pattern of dissatisfaction corresponding to the patchwork pattern of service inadequacy. What difference does dissatisfaction make in the willingness to accept governmental change?

DISSATISFACTION WITH LOCAL SERVICES AND SUPPORT FOR CHANGE

Because of interest in the politically effective, this analysis is confined to those who have ever voted in any local election while living in their present community. They are divided into those dissatisfied with none of the three most widely criticized local services and those dissatisfied with from one to all three of them. Each "dissatisfaction" category is then divided into the consistent supporters of change (the mergerites and the moderate integrationists), the opponents of change, and those who are inconsistent.

---

[2] Voters only are considered in order to facilitate the later investigation of the relation between dissatisfaction and probable support for reform.

Reading across the rows in table 45, from those dissatisfied with none of the services to those dissatisfied with all three, the difference that dissatisfaction with services makes in support for a specific proposal can be assessed. (Thus, in the City 27 per cent of those dissatisfied with no service support merger, 37 per cent of those dissatisfied with all three.) And, by reading down the columns, the comparative distributions of those with different degrees of dissatisfaction can be studied.

TABLE 45

Service Dissatisfaction and Type of Opinion Holders

Opinion holders	Number of "dissatisfied" responses			
	0	1	2	3
Mergerites				
City	27%	33%	22%	37%
County	16	22	16	27
Moderate integrationists				
City	19	15	25	10
County	35	36	44	34
Local autonomists				
City	13	14	7	10
County	24	20	16	14
No type				
City	40	38	45	42
County	25	22	24	25
Number				
City	(164)	(103)	(55)	(19)
County	(425)	(271)	(102)	(64)

In brief, there is little indication that satisfaction or dissatisfaction makes much difference in opinions about governmental reform. The percentage of mergerites does increase between zero and three judgments of dissatisfaction, but in an extremely inconsistent way, and only by 10 per cent in the City, 11 per cent in the County. If all those dissatisfied with any or all services are grouped and compared with those dissatisfied with none, the differences are negligible. The moderate integrationists fluctuate in the same way.

If the grouping is done in a different fashion, taking the local autonomists together with those who are not one of the consistent types (indicating indifference or incompetence) there is no variation for the City, but in the County there is a decline in the percentage (from 49 per cent to 39 per cent) with increasing dissatisfaction. This is entirely accounted for by the decreasing proportion who support status quo. Thus the most that can be said is this: in the suburbs only, the proportion of consistent advocates of local autonomy or status quo decreases somewhat (from 24 per cent to 14 per cent) as service dissatisfaction increases. Persons of this persuasion, however, account for only one-fifth of the total voters. For the other 80 per cent there is no significant variation by dissatisfaction.

In short, an analysis of the dissatisfaction with major services supplied to the residential neighborhoods, and thus presumably of immediate interest to the residents of the City-County area, indicates that four services in general account for the great majority of dissatisfaction in City and County. When only those who have ever voted in a local election are analyzed, however, there is very little indication that dissatisfaction with services is related closely to support of governmental change. In consequence, the general proposition that from dissatisfaction with fire protection, police protection, sewage disposal, residential streets, parks and playgrounds, and other services emerge a widespread general discontent with the existing structure of government, and a willingness to support governmental reform, is not supportable by the evidence.

On the other hand, it was advanced earlier that awareness of metropolitan problems might conceivably be a precondition for agreement to metropolitan solutions. It thus is possible that the kinds of services specific to the neighborhood or local community are irrelevant to support for metropolitan reform, but services that are necessarily metropolitan in character are quite relevant. One such service is now considered.

DISSATISFACTION WITH METROPOLITAN SERVICES AND SUPPORT FOR CHANGE

The largest percentage of dissatisfied responses relate to traffic conditions in the City-County area. It therefore is used as the best single indicator of awareness of and dissatisfaction with services of area-wide impact. Again, only those who have ever voted are considered and their distribution in opinion types, by their degree of dissatisfaction, is noted.

It is clear that dissatisfaction with traffic is a much more powerful indicator of support for change than the localized services combined. If the mergerites and moderates as consistent sup-

TABLE 46

DISSATISFACTION WITH TRAFFIC AND TYPE OF OPINION HOLDERS

Opinion holders	Very satisfied	Fairly satisfied	Dissatisfied	Very dissatisfied
Mergerites				
City	21%	28%	26%	40%
County	26	15	18	21
Moderates				
City	19	19	23	15
County	21	32	40	43
Local autonomists				
City	16	10	14	10
County	38	23	21	15
No type				
City	44	43	36	34
County	14	30	22	21
Number				
City	(43)	(129)	(99)	(58)
County	(65)	(272)	(277)	(237)

EXCLUDED: City 12 and County 11 "don't know" or don't ride.

porters of change are grouped, the percentage increases regularly with increasing dissatisfaction, from 40 per cent to 55 per cent in the City and from 47 per cent to 64 per cent in the County. Those who support status quo also decline with increasing dissatisfaction in the County, from 38 to 15 per cent, and to a lesser extent in the City (from 16 to 10 per cent). The proportion belonging to no type also declines consistently in the City, from 44 to 34 per cent, but not in the County.

The hypothesis that support for metropolitan changes rests upon dissatisfaction with metropolitan services thus appears tenable. However, the practice of lumping together all those services considered inadequate by outside observers and deriving a theory of widespread reform sentiment from these inadequacies would seem not only crude, but in serious error. The local services considered may be in numerous instances inadequate by many standards, and they do elicit much dissatisfaction; they do not, however, relate meaningfully to sentiment for governmental reorganization. Dissatisfaction with traffic conditions does relate meaningfully to the desire for reorganization.

This analysis should not be taken to mean that the support for change is completely accounted for by dissatisfaction with metropolitan services. It should be kept in mind that almost one-half of those satisfied with traffic conditions support reform in the City and in the County, while even among the very dissatisfied a substantial proportion either opposes change or has no consistent opinions. Support for governmental reform is a much more complex matter than the simple rational response to perceived problem situations. It is, however, related to such problems when they are metropolitan in scope.

SUMMARY: SOCIOECONOMIC DIFFERENCES AND METROPOLITAN GOVERNMENTAL CHANGE

The people of the St. Louis City-County area differ widely in awareness of area-wide problems, in willingness to accept governmental reorganization, and in the kind of change preferred. The differences between the central city and the suburban county are of considerable magnitude for the kind of change preferred. Differences in age, sex, social rank, ethnicity, migration history, and commitment to neighborhood are also important.

The public for local governmental reform includes a disproportionate number of men, and persons in the prime of life (30 to 64 years of age). It is composed of a disproportionately large number of persons from households of higher social rank and Old American or German ethnic background, older migrants or natives to the metropolitan area, and stable homeowning people in single-family dwelling units. This public is generally more involved in metropolitan activities, more committed to the metropolitan area and the immediate neighborhood, and more adequately equipped (through education, income, and occupation) to participate in governmental change.

These persons express an awareness of metropolitan problems and a willingness to see governmental reorganization take place in order to improve the metropolitan community. They differ in the City and County, however, in the reorganization they would accept. In the City merger is more popular than any other specific alternative among all major categories of people, and it is most popular with the high social rank population. By the same token, the most staunch supporters of merger in the City are the Old Americans and Germans; Negroes are much less favorable.

In the County the population categories most likely to constitute the public for governmental change are not particularly interested in merger. Instead, they express strong preferences for the moderate programs—the federal system and the consolidation of County municipalities. One-half of those with opinions among the most highly educated population prefer one of these two alternatives. The small homeowner of the County does not jealously guard his local autonomy; there is, in fact, somewhat more sentiment for change among such persons. In general, the County population is friendly to change, but it is moderate change.

When people are divided into three types of holders of consistent opinions about reorganization and those who are inconsistent in their position, the City tends to divide into two major categories—those who are in favor of merger and those who are inconsistent. It is plausible to see the City residents as either not very concerned with the question of reorganization or else firmly committed to the belief that merger is the best solution. In the County, however, the three consistent positions—merger, moderate integration, and status quo—each has substantial support, and only a minority adopts an inconsistent position. The most popular position in the County is moderate governmental integration while status quo attracts only a minority. If, in fact, the mergerites and the moderates are taken together as constituting the forces for change, the County consistently has more sentiment for reform than the City. This is true for each segment of the interested public. For example, 59 per cent of the men in the County favor change, compared with 49 per cent in the City; 63 per cent of the college-educated favor change, compared with only 51 per cent in the City; 53 per cent of the homeowners are mergerites or moderate integrationists, compared with 41 per cent in the City.

These findings may be summarized in one statement—governmental change is a more salient question for the County resident, no matter what his degree of political competence, but he is much less attracted to merger than his counterpart in the City. Those who have pictured the movement for metropolitan integration as chiefly a response to the needs and problems of the central city have probably underestimated the suburban response to the problems of urban expansion. And, within the City, the people most interested in metropolitan integration are most similar to the inhabitants of suburbia—the Old Americans, the higher rank population, the homeowners, the natives of the metropolitan area.

From the preceding discussion it is possible to conjecture a popular image of the City-County area, the socioeconomic city, in political fragments, and a certain yearning for reintegration among the people of the City. Reform movements for metropolitan governmental integration in the past have certainly played upon the citizen's desire to see his metropolitan area as a commanding quantitative whole. The persistent relationship in the City between persons of older age and support for merger may thus reflect a nostalgia for the past era when most of the socioeconomic city lay within the geographical boundaries of the political city—the city of St. Louis.

In the suburban neighborhoods, however, merger has much less appeal. Concern there for change seems to be related functionally to the breakdown of services incident to unplanned expansion, particularly such area-wide services as traffic facilities and control. The suburbanites have accommodated themselves to an image of the City-County area as a loose confederation of neighborhoods and industries within a complex network of government. Their concern is to create a minimal order within that network and between its constituent parts, one that will make possible more adequate housekeeping services and the capital investments necessary for the preservation of their communities.

Part Four
MEASUREMENT AND ECONOMIC STUDIES

14

Factors Affecting Local Governmental Expenditure Levels

THE STUDY of factors influencing local governmental expenditure levels consisted of several inquiries. Separate analyses were first undertaken to identify and measure the factors that affect the per capita expenditures for each of five types of services—public education in primary and secondary schools, fire protection, police protection, refuse collection, and street service. A composite analysis then was made of combined per capita expenditures for four of the more closely related services—fire, police, refuse collection, and street.

PURPOSES

The Survey expected this study to be useful in several ways. It would provide (1) an explanation of the variations in governmental expenditures for specific functions, (2) a background for projecting governmental expenditures, and (3) insights into economies of scale as a possible aid in formulating policies for structural and functional reorganization of governments. These three purposes deserve consideration.

VARIATIONS IN GOVERNMENTAL SPENDING

It is common knowledge that different governmental units provide different amounts of the same service. Differences in expenditures probably exist insofar as community X is noted for its schools, community Y is recognized for its fine police, and community Z has excellent refuse collection. What is less well known, however, is the factors accounting for the differences. It could be that occasionally the variations in the level of expenditures are based on chance, although few would assume this. Thus, the Survey sought to ascertain the effect of various factors on the level of services. It will be seen, for instance, that assessed valuation of real property, a reasonably good indicator of how much communities can afford, is indeed an important factor in explaining differences in educational expenditures.

Consider another important question. Larger cities spend more on governmental services and evidence indicates that the larger the city, the greater the per capita governmental expenditures. With increasing urbanization this relation is the source of a problem. Cities faced with limited tax resources and growing populations are confronted with increases in per capita expenditures, not just increases in total expenditures. An important question arises: Is this a result of increasing population or is it a result of other differences? It was subsequently discovered, and will be explored in detail later, that population alone is not a particularly strong factor in accounting for variations in per capita spending for most services.

Projecting Governmental Expenditures

In order to project future governmental expenditures, it is necessary first to understand the interrelations of the factors influencing the current expenditures. Suppose, for example, the population of the St. Louis area is expected to increase by 20 per cent during the next decade. What does this imply for governmental expenditures? An answer calls for some empirical estimates of the relation between population and per capita governmental expenditures. A further question might be asked: How would governmental expenditures be influenced were a large part of this increase in population nonwhite? Again to anticipate a finding, it does indicate greater proportional expenditures may be expected for police services.

Clearly, this study is necessary as an understanding of the factors affecting today's expenditures is a prerequisite for a projection of tomorrow's.

ECONOMIES OF SCALE

Economies of scale concern the relationship of unit costs as output increases. In the private market, it is generally assumed to be "U" shaped for firms. In other words, unit costs fall as output expands and, as the firm becomes unwieldy, rise as output becomes quite large.

This same concept is important when governments provide services. For example, it is often argued that large sanitary districts offer economies of scale, that as more and more areas come under the district the cost per unit of sanitation goes down. In turn, the cost to the taxpayer is lowered. Smaller plants are inefficient. On the other hand, it may be that for hospitals larger units (plants and districts) raise unit costs. Were this the case, diseconomies of scale would exist.

The Survey recognized the difficulties involved in measuring economies of scale. The available data gave actual expenditures for the five specific services studied. Many factors other than those resulting in economies or diseconomies of scale enter into the determination of levels of expenditures by local governments. Yet, to the extent that these factors can be held constant by statistical techniques, it might be that the presence or absence of economies of scale would be revealed. Thus the Survey could evaluate the possibilities of consolidation of various types and numbers of govermental units so that residents might receive more service at lower per unit cost.

The other side of the economies-of-scale coin should also be understood. The Survey was looking not only for economies of scale, but diseconomies as well. Do costs rise with increasing output? If the study had shown that diseconomies exist, the Survey would have been hesitant in recommending, among other matters, a larger role for the County police department. In more general terms, if diseconomies of scale do not exist, it cannot be said that larger governmental units are more inefficient than smaller units.

METHOD OF STUDY

This study of factors affecting governmental expenditures is, to the knowledge of the Survey, unique in two major respects. It is the first to apply certain statistical techniques—multiple correlation analysis[1]—to an analysis of local governmental expenditures in a specific metropolitan area.[2] In addition, the Survey's study attempted to devise a service-quality index to measure the quality of the service rendered and relate it to expenditures.

The Survey encountered difficulties in the application of multiple correlation techniques in the St. Louis City-County area because relevant data were available for only a few years, thus ruling out time series analysis, and the number of governments in the area was relatively small, thus confining cross-section analysis to a comparatively small sample.

A small number of cases or sample units always presents problems in statistical analysis. The smallness of the sample in this study, relative to what would be desirable, stems in part from two factors: (1) the state government in Missouri does not require local governments, except in the field of public education, to file comprehensive, comparable data. This lack of a central source of information compelled the Survey to collect data for several research projects through extensive field work. In this process of data collection, some governments refused to supply the needed facts, some could or would furnish only part of the data, still others supplied the data in noncomparable form. (2) Some of the coöperating governments do not furnish one or more of the services considered in the statistical study. Consequently, the number of governmental units that could be included varied from twenty-seven to eighty-seven in the investigations of individual services, and in the composite analysis only seventeen governmental units could be utilized.

The population distribution of governmental units used in the study is uneven. The overwhelming majority of municipalities, for example, have fewer than 2,500 residents. The largest has approximately 850,000 people, whereas the next largest has an

---

[1] Multiple correlation analysis is associated with multiple regression analysis. Regression analysis shows how items are related, positively or negatively, and to what degree. Correlation analysis asks whether or not the relations are statistically significant, that is, how much confidence can be put into the statistical findings. This distinction will be amplified in the expository discussion that follows.

[2] Two other similar investigations have been conducted recently, however, on municipalities of more than 2,500 people in one state and on selected types of municipalities in the nation as a whole. Stanley Scott and Edward L. Feder, *Factors Associated with Variations in Municipal Expenditure Levels: A Statistical Study of California Cities* (Berkeley: University of California Bureau of Public Administration, 1957); and Harvey E. Brazer, *City Expenditures in the United States* (Washington: National Bureau of Economic Research, 1959).

estimated population of only 53,000. Lopsided distributions are also present in school and fire protection districts.

For purposes of statistical analysis, it was assumed that the per capita expenditures for a particular governmental service are affected by three broad factors: (1) the characteristics of the area served, (2) the quality of the service, and (3) the willingness and ability of the area to pay for the service. The first factor relates to the cost of supplying a service and seeks to determine some of the variables related to such costs. Quality recognizes that although two communities, virtually alike in most respects, may offer the same service, one of the communities may provide it far more adequately than the other. It is important to account for these differences. The ability of an area to pay for a service sometimes helps explain the demand for such a service. If, for example, a community desires and can afford a fine educational system, per pupil expenditures will tend to be relatively high.

Having decided that these are the important broad groups of factors that influence the per capita expenditures for specific services, the Survey began to identify their components and reduce them to measurable quantities. In each specific analysis, the per capita expenditures were considered the dependent variable, or the magnitude to be explained. The goal, then, was to identify which specific factors or independent variables determine per capita expenditures, that is, to develop a working hypothesis. For each of the services a specific set of measurable factors had to be selected in such a manner that the relationship to the dependent factor made theoretical sense. This selection process and the logic behind each selection will be given later.

FORMAT AND INTERPRETATION

MULTIPLE REGRESSION AND CORRELATION ANALYSIS

The basic ingredients of multiple regression and correlation analysis are best illustrated by a simple example. For present purposes, skip ahead to one of the findings and consider the following problems.

Suppose you are interested in the per capita expenditures for fire and police protection, street service, and refuse collection combined, hereafter called "combined services." You note that this figure varies from community to community. Can some of this variation be accounted for? On what factors does it depend?

Knowledge of governmental expenditure patterns suggests many factors or variables. A hypothesis can be stated, involving three strong candidates for which data are available. They are (1) the size of the night-time population, (2) a service-quality index, and (3) the average per capita assessed valuation of real property in the community. Hypotheses are also stipulated for the relations between these factors. For example, per capita expenditures for the combined services increase as the average assessed valuation of real property increases. Multiple regression and correlation analysis provides statistical tests of these hypotheses.

First, this statistical technique can help to indicate how much of the variation in the per capita expenditures for the combined services is accounted for by the three factors—technically, the coefficient of multiple determination. A perfect accounting would be 100 per cent. This kind of relation falls under multiple correlation analysis.

Second, the technique can help to test hypotheses about the nature of the relation between each of the three factors (the independent variables) and the per capita expenditures for combined services (the dependent variable). For example, it turns out that increases in average per capita assessed valuation of real property are associated with increases, not decreases, in per capita combined expenditures. Technically speaking, the net regression coefficient is positive. This kind of relation falls under multiple regression analysis.

Multiple correlation analysis takes care of a third question. As there is positive relation between per capita assessed valuation and per capita expenditures for combined services, is it significant or could it have happened by chance? The partial correlation coefficient provides information on this score.

In presenting findings on correlations and regressions, the amount of variation explained by the regression equation is given. Then the association of the statistically significant factors is presented. In terms of the example: "about 71 per cent of the variation in per capita expenditures for combined services is explained by the three factors studied." Further, increases in per capita expenditures for combined services are associated with

increases in　(1)　size of night-time population
　　　　　　　(2)　per capita assessed valuation

Note that the service-quality index has been omitted. Why? Because it is not significant. The relation could easily have happened by chance.

The general procedure, then, for each specific service will be to state (1) the dependent and independent variables and why they were chosen, (2) the nature of the sample studied, (3) the multiple regression and correlation findings, and (4) the conclusions. Readers interested in additional detail with regard to the statistical results are referred to Appendix E.

PUBLIC EDUCATION: FACTORS SELECTED

Of the numerous factors that might affect expenditures for public education, only those deemed most relevant should be tested. For the task of evaluating the appropriate factors, the help of school officials and other educators was enlisted. On the basis of a number of discussions and meetings, the following variables were judged to be most important and quantifiable.

DEPENDENT VARIABLE

The dependent variable to be measured was *total expenditures for public education in primary and secondary schools per pupil in average daily attendance (ADA), including the cost of debt service.*[3] In other words, this is the dependent variable whose level is to be determined as a result of other factors.

In the St. Louis City-County area, public school expenditures are met from local and state sources. By far the bulk of the funds are raised locally. During the period under analysis, the state of Missouri contributed very little to the local school districts on an equalization basis—less than $60,000 to the school districts in St. Louis County and nothing at all to the St. Louis City School District in 1954–55.

It was also possible to estimate factors responsible for various subcategories of total expenditures per pupil in average daily attendance. They include expenditures for general controls such as administrative salaries; instruction; auxiliary services, such as bus transportation; plant operation and maintenance; and payments to cover fixed charges, such as insurance contributions.

---

[3] An analysis of subcategories of the total expenditure for public education is given. In analyzing these subcategories, the cost of debt service is excluded.

INDEPENDENT VARIABLES

The following were assumed to be the independent factors influencing the level of expenditures.

Number of pupils in average daily attendance in primary and secondary schools. This factor indicated the school district size and, in general, per pupil expenditures may be expected to vary with the size of the school district. To the extent that larger school districts have larger schools, there may be some savings, especially in general control and plant costs. One major difficulty with the education study was the inability to get information on school plants within school districts. Although some economies may come about because of the size of the individual school, the data will not show this. It should be explicitly noted that this study does not deal with school plants; rather it deals with districts. Thus a second factor that may affect the expenditures for education in school districts is the number of pupils squared. In the nature of the mathematics of multiple regression analysis, this will account for any "U" shape in the average expenditure pattern; that is, as population increases from zero to larger and larger numbers, other things constant, per capita expenditures fall and then rise.

In general, the schools are small in small school districts. There does not appear to be much difference in the size of schools within medium and large school districts.

High school pupils in ADA as a per cent of all pupils in ADA. There are many indications that pupil-teacher ratios are smaller in high schools than in primary schools. Furthermore, salaries are often higher and equipment more expensive in high schools than in primary schools.

Number of public school pupils in ADA per square mile. When pupils live far from their school, they require transportation, and if a school bus is used, school expenditures increase. Density of pupils can be assumed to reflect the relative proximity of pupils to schools. The lower the density, the farther away some children live.

Per cent increase in public school pupils in ADA, 1951–1956. The assumption is that young and rapidly growing areas incur relatively high per pupil expenditures: in particular, the debt service charges of such areas are apt to be high.

Quality of public education. Education is not a homogeneous commodity; there are good schools and poor ones. It is important, therefore, to try to account for differences by construction of a service-quality index. In this respect, the Survey's study was unique in its attempt to account for differing qualities of service. The construction of the service-quality index warrants discussion.

Because no single factor can properly measure the quality of educational services, an index is needed. In all indexes two main problems occur: what should be included and how heavily should each component be weighted.

The following six components, or subindexes, were agreed upon:

> number of teachers per 1,000 pupils in ADA,
> per cent of high school seniors entering college,
> number of semester hours of average teacher in college,
> average teacher salary,
> per cent of teachers with more than ten years of experience, and
> number of units of high school credits.

The Survey attempted to include in the index a subindex reflecting the amounts of money earmarked by different school districts to supply supervisory services. Unfortunately, such data were impossible to get as the financial records of the St. Louis City-County school districts lump the data together with other items in the category of "General Control." It also would have been advantageous to use the results of intelligence and achievement tests. Unfortunately, no uniform achievement test is given in the various school districts.

Some components of the service-quality index will appear, on first glance, to be highly correlated with either per pupil expenditures or fiscal ability to afford services (average assessed valuation). For instance, it is widely assumed that whether a high school student enters college depends very heavily on the financial position of his parents. If this were true, the inclusion of per cent of high school seniors entering college would not be a useful component of the service-quality index. However, a statistical check does not support this assumption. (Technically, the rank correlation coefficient measuring the relation between per cent of high school seniors entering college in 1955 and average assessed valuation of the twenty-seven school districts is +0.34. This is barely significant at an α of 0.05.) At least three reasons can be cited for this low correlation. College education has become more and more universal and is no longer primarily available to the sons of the well-to-do. Also, school districts are not entirely homogeneous in regard to property values. And finally, assessed valuation is not wholly the product of residential property values; instead, it is heavily affected by the relative importance of commercial and industrial property within the district.

Similarly, the number of teachers per 1,000 pupils and average teacher salary can be expected to be correlated with the general level of expenditures. An analysis revealed that the simple correlation coefficient, while high, was far from perfect. It was +0.71 for teachers per 1,000 pupils and +0.68 for average salary. The inclusion of these two factors in the service-quality index appears warranted.

The weighting problem is no less difficult. Who can confidently predict that as a service level gauge the number of teachers per 1,000 pupils is as important as or more important than the number of high school credits offered by the school? No good basis could be found to give each of the six factors specific differential weights and, consequently, each was given equal weight. Fortunately, with six components to the index, the weighting system is no longer so very crucial. Doubling the weights of any one or two of the components will not greatly affect the magnitude of the index numbers.

The specific numbers arrived at by means of the service-quality index were subjected to a test designed to check on their general reliability. A number of educators who are well acquainted with the public schools of the St. Louis City-County area were interviewed separately and asked to rate the various school districts in terms of excellent, good, medium, poor, or very poor. These ratings, when compared with the quality index numbers, showed very close consistency. In no case was a school district with an index number above 1.00 given a subjective rating of poor or very poor, and vice versa. In the few instances with differences in the rating, the index number was equivalent to excellent while the subjective rating was good. If the index numbers are inaccurate, they are off by no more than 5 to 10 per cent either way. Discrepancies, if they exist, are likely to be randomly distributed, so no bias appears to have crept into the index.

Assessed valuation. How much the various school districts can spend per pupil on public education depends partly on their tax base. In general, the assessed valuation of real property gives some indication of the wealth and, to a lesser degree, income of the school district. It may be argued, however, that assessed valuation is high where expenditures are high. The higher expenditures give rise to the need for tax monies and, in turn, give rise to high assessed valuations. Despite the merit of this argument, the logic and the weight of evidence indicate the reverse, as assumed by the Survey, is true; that is, higher expenditures occur where the tax base is larger. This last independent variable, then, is *average assessed valuation of real property per pupil in ADA.*

The same set of factors will not necessarily have a bearing on each individual subcategory of expenditures for education. Thus, different factors could be considered for each expenditure element. It was simpler to include for each subcategory all the various factors that might have an impact and let the analysis indicate their relative importance. For this reason the same independent variables were used in every case.

PUBLIC EDUCATION: FINDINGS

Twenty-seven school districts could be utilized in the study of educational expenditures—the St. Louis City School District and twenty-six districts in St. Louis County. Three of the twenty-nine County school districts operating during the 1954–55 school year were excluded from the analysis because they provided only elementary education. In order to increase the sample size, the Survey used information for two school years, 1951–52 and 1954–55, and thus doubled the number of observations. To the extent that 1951–52 and 1954–55 data are not closely tied—that is, there is little serial correlation—the method produces a genuine increase in the size of the sample.

As noted, public education was the only service for which a breakdown of internal expenses on a comparable basis was available. Consequently, it was the only service in which the component parts of the expenditures (here, less the cost of debt service)—instruction, auxiliary services, general control or administration, plant operation and maintenance, and fixed charges —could be analyzed. Influential factors varied with the particular subcategory of total expenditures under consideration. For example, a high pupil density in a school district had the effect of decreasing general control expenditures per pupil, but had no measurable effect on instructional expenditures per pupil.

Multiple Regression and Correlation Results

The six independent variables explained 82 per cent of the variation in total current per pupil expenditures, including debt service, and the same percentage when debt service was excluded. The inclusion of debt service in the dependent variable thus made no difference. When current spending is divided into subcategories and analyzed, the six independent variables explain 45 per cent of the fixed charges; 55 per cent of plant operation and maintenance; 57 per cent of general control; 72 per cent of auxiliary services; and 79 per cent of the expenditures for instruction. (Technically, in all cases these percentages were statistically significant at an α of 0.05.) This suggests with respect to the expenditures for plant operation and maintenance, fixed charges, and general control either that important factors were missing as variables in the analysis or that these expenditures are more randomly determined.

Three independent variables of the six tested appear to have a statistically significant influence on total per pupil expenditures for public education. They are related as follows. Increases in total current per pupil spending plus debt service are associated with

increases in   (1) per cent of total attending high school
                (2) service-quality index
                (3) per pupil assessed valuation

The above statement indicates that the three partial correlation coefficients are significant and positive. No statistically significant negative influences appear to operate to decrease total per pupil expenditures.

FACTORS INFLUENCING SUBCATEGORIES
OF PER PUPIL EXPENDITURES

Instructional expenditures. Seventy-nine per cent of the variation in per pupil expenditures for instruction in the school districts was explained by the factors used in the multiple regression analysis. Per pupil expenditures for instruction are influenced to a considerable degree by the quality of service rendered, per pupil assessed valuation, and the proportion of the pupils enrolled in high school. Stated differently, increases in per pupil spending for instruction are associated with

increases in   (1) service-quality index
                (2) per cent of ADA enrolled in high school
                (3) per pupil assessed valuation

It is not surprising to find the same factors accounting for expenditures on instruction and total expenditures per pupil. Expenditures for instruction make up a large part of total expenditures.

Auxiliary services expenditures. Multiple regression analysis of auxiliary services—which includes such miscellaneous items as transportation, school lunches, and school nurses—accounted for 72 per cent of the variation of this per pupil cost among the school districts studied.

Increases in per pupil spending for auxiliary services are associated with

increases in   (1) per pupil assessed valuation
                (2) density of pupils per square mile
decreases in   (3) service-quality index

These relationships seem logical since the less densely settled districts have to spend more on transportation and usually offer a lower service level (as density increases, service level increases).

General control expenditures. Approximately 57 per cent of the variation in per pupil expenditures for general control of administration was accounted for by the factors tested in the multiple regression analysis. Increases in per pupil expenditures for general control are associated with

increases in   (1) per pupil assessed valuation
decreases in   (2) total number of pupils in ADA

The first relation may indicate that more "administrative luxuries" or aids are obtained where the resources are available to pay for them. The second relation suggests some possible economies of large scale operation.[4]

The negative relationship between the number of pupils served and per pupil spending for general control does not appear to apply, however, to the largest units in which per pupil expenditures for general control rise with an increase in the size of the population served.

Plant operation and maintenance expenditures. Fifty-five per cent of the variation in per pupil expenditures among the school districts studied was explained by the six independent variables employed. Only two factors, assessed valuation and proportion of the total students attending high school, showed significant influence on per pupil spending for operation and maintenance.

---

[4] Economies of scale also appeared in a simple correlation and regression analysis of general control spending (administrative and legislative salaries) in twenty-two municipalities.

Increases in per pupil spending for plant operation and maintenance are associated with

increases in   (1) per pupil assessed valuation
               (2) the proportion of total pupils enrolled in high school.

It would appear from (1) that the wealthier districts spend more on operating and maintaining physical facilities. The second relation suggests that the physical facilities necessary for secondary education are more expensive to operate and maintain than those used in the primary grades.

Fixed charges. Less success was achieved in the analysis of fixed charges—rents, insurance, and retirement contributions—than for the other four parts of total current spending. Only 45 per cent of the variation in per pupil expenditures among school districts was explained by this equation. Only one variable was statistically significant, that of per pupil assessed valuation. Increases in per pupil expenditures for fixed charges are associated with

increases in   (1) per pupil assessed valuation

SUMMARY OF FINDINGS ON PUBLIC EDUCATION

The two most important determinants of per pupil spending for public education are the resources available to pay for the service (per pupil assessed valuation of real property) and the level at which the service is rendered. The proportion of pupils in ADA who are enrolled in high school tends to increase per pupil expenditures since secondary education is more expensive to provide. Assessed valuation has an important influence on all five parts of total current per pupil spending—instruction, auxiliary services, general control, plant operation and maintenance, and fixed charges.

An increase in the service population, or pupils in ADA, has the effect of decreasing general control expenditures on a per pupil basis (the most efficient size would be about 44,000 pupils), but does not significantly affect the other parts of total current spending. A high density of pupils decreases per pupil spending for auxiliary services. The increase in pupils served from 1950–51 to 1955–56 did not significantly affect current per pupil expenditures, although a separate analysis of capital outlay indicated that the increase in number of students has and will continue to have some influence on such spending.

FIRE PROTECTION: FACTORS SELECTED

The coöperation and advice of a number of fire chiefs, directors of public safety, and personnel in the fire insurance rating section of the Missouri Inspection Bureau helped lay the groundwork for formulating hypotheses about the variables that explain the per capita expenditures for fire protection. As with education, the Survey considered fire protection by entire governments—municipalities and fire protection districts—rather than by individual fire house precincts.

DEPENDENT VARIABLE

The dependent variable to be measured was *per capita total current expenditures plus debt service for fire protection.* It thus consisted of current spending for fire protection services, plus debt service for fire equipment and facilities. When fire equipment was purchased out of balances or receipts, its cost was pro-rated over the expected life of the equipment.

INDEPENDENT VARIABLES

The following were assumed to be the independent factors influencing the level of expenditures.

Night-time population. It is important to distinguish between night-time and daytime population. The former is closely related to the number of dwelling units. A major excess of daytime over night-time population in an area can usually be traced to commercial and industrial activity, a factor that is best treated separately.

Area in square miles. The distance from the fire station to the property farthest removed is an important consideration. Larger areas requiring a number of stations make for a more efficient placing of fire stations. In addition, administrative overhead may be spread.

Density of dwelling units per square mile. Density of burnable property within an area is likely to increase the fire hazard as well as the difficulty of fighting fires.

Night-time population increases, 1950–1955. The general assumption is that young and rapidly growing areas encounter relatively high per capita expenditures in rendering services. This is true in part because of the relatively heavy and expensive capital outlays necessary in rapidly growing areas, involving substantial debt retirement payments.

Combined receipts of wholesale, retail, and service establish-ments. Commercial establishments harbor burnable property and therefore affect the expenditures for fire protection. Receipts of establishments appear to be a better yardstick than number of establishments. The same is true to a lesser extent for industrial concerns. Medium-sized and large industrial firms often have only a minor effect on per capita expenditures for fire protection; many have their own fire department. Then, too, their location is often more accessible than crowded downtown commercial proper-ties. As data for industries are not readily available and their effect is presumed to be minor, industrial activity is not included in this factor.

One reason speaks against the inclusion of receipts of com-mercial establishments as an independent variable. Average per capita assessed valuation of real property reflects not only resi-dential property values, but commercial and industrial activity as well. On the average, the assessed valuation of an acre used by commerce or industry is higher than that used for residential purposes. Thus, a difficulty arises in connection with the effort to measure the relation between per capita expenditure for fire protection and commercial activity, while holding constant other factors, including per capita assessed valuation. In fact, it is vir-tually impossible to conceive of changes in commercial activity without concomitant changes in assessed valuation.

Quality of fire protection. In the St. Louis City-County area the Missouri Inspection Bureau attempts to quantify many of the factors that reflect need for fire protection and quality of service rendered. The bureau collects these data to rate fire insurance risks. About 90 per cent of the private insurance firms base their premiums upon these ratings. If the demand for fire protection were uniform—the kinds of buildings, area, density, and so forth —the ratings would serve as a straightforward index of quality of fire departments. Because this uniformity does not exist, the ratings reflect the difference between difficulty of protection and the actual amount of protection provided. Depending on this quality of fire protection, the Missouri Inspection Bureau rates by classes numbered from 1 to 10, the insurance premium increas-ing with the number.

The difference in the kinds of physical structures among gov-ernmental units poses the further task of limiting an index of quality to a similar service problem in all units, independent of other variations in demand. For this purpose, the Survey decided to focus on a typical residential structure. A reasonable assumption for a typical single-family brick structure in the St. Louis City-County area is a market value of about $15,000, with $10,000 worth of insurance for the structure and an additional $3,000 coverage for its contents. Using insurance rates for buildings and contents for each class of inspection bureau ratings, the necessary premium was computed for each governmental unit providing fire protection.

For further convenience in interpretation, the Survey took two additional steps. First, the inverse or reciprocal value of the premium was computed for each area. This produces a manageable set of numbers which also has the advantage of assigning the highest numerical value to the area with the most favorable rating. Finally, in order to provide a clearer ranking among the units studied, an index was derived from the inverse of the premium. The mean of these ratios for all units was computed. The rating for a given unit was then divided by this mean value, a procedure equivalent to setting the mean for all units equal to 1.00. The use of the index in the multiple regression analysis deals with the separate units providing fire protection; in table 47 these units are grouped by Inspection Bureau classes for convenience as well as to show more clearly the consequences of a shift in ratings.

Assessed valuation. Average per capita assessed valuation of real property indicates both the ability of a community to pay for

TABLE 47

INDEX OF FIRE PROTECTION QUALITY FOR GOVERNMENTAL UNITS IN ST. LOUIS CITY-COUNTY AREA, GROUPED BY MISSOURI INSPECTION BUREAU CLASSES

Class[a]	N[b]	Total premium[c]	Inverse of premium[d]	Index[e]
1 & 2	2	$10.90	.0918	1.94
3 & 4	0	13.20	.0758	1.60
5 & 6	26	17.40	.0578	1.22
7 & 8	12	20.00	.0500	1.05
9	9	27.80	.0360	.76
10	15	33.00	.0304	.64

  [a] Classes with identical insurance rates are combined.
  [b] Number of municipalities and fire districts in 1952 and 1955 within each class. Some are approximations, since a few districts contain areas with different ratings. In this table, they were assigned to the class closest to their average rating. The two cases in class 1 represent St. Louis City in 1952 and 1955. Selection of governmental units is explained later in this section.
  [c] Based on insurance rates for assumed single-family brick structure insured for $10,000 with an additional $3,000 for contents.
  [d] For example, 1/$10.90 = .0918.
  [e] Index equals inverse premium for a given class divided by mean inverse premium for 64 districts and municipalities (.0475).

services and the value of property to be protected against fire. Whereas it would have been desirable to include the valuation of personal property, the absence of data made it impossible. The indications are, however, that real and personal property values are highly correlated.

FIRE PROTECTION: FINDINGS

During 1955, 16 municipalities, including St. Louis City, and 18 special-purpose districts furnished fire protection services in the St. Louis City–St. Louis County area. As in the analysis of public education, data for a previous year, 1952, were included. As only 14 fire protection districts operated in 1952, this made a total of 64 cases with which to work.

There also were a few private, or nongovernmental, volunteer fire-fighting units that operated on a subscription basis; data were not available for this last-named group.

MULTIPLE REGRESSION AND CORRELATION RESULTS

The seven variables or factors analyzed in this study explained 82 per cent of the variation in per capita spending. Five of the seven factors analyzed have an important impact on the per capita expenditures on fire protection in the St. Louis City–St. Louis County area. They are population, area, commercial activity, service level, and resources. Population growth and dwelling unit density have little measurable impact.

Stated differently, increases in per capita spending (current, plus debt service) for fire protection services are associated with

increases in   (1) service-quality index (based on Missouri Inspection Bureau rating)

               (2) per capita assessed valuation (which is also a measure of burnable property)

decreases in   (3) area served in square miles

               (4) commercial activity (as measured by total sales and receipts of wholesale, retail, and service establishments)

               (5) total population (this relationship is curvilinear)

The first relation reflects the fact that a higher quality of service leads to greater expenditures for fire protection. The second relation indicates that wealthier communities are able to provide more fire protection.

As negative influences, remember that (3) also implies larger districts have lower expenditures. This suggests the possibility that larger districts may be able to spread costs and thus reduce the expenditures per person. It should be pointed out, however, that larger districts may be associated with less urban communities and, in turn, lower assessed valuations.

Increasing the number of persons served, under (5), also has the effect of decreasing spending on a per capita basis. The relationship found to exist in this case is not straight-line but curvilinear or curved-line correlation. In other words, per capita expenditures decrease with increases in total population served up to a certain point, in this case 110,000 people, and then per capita expenditures begin to increase. The decrease is small ($1.24) as the population increases from 1,000 to 110,000. The increase in per capita expenditures is substantial as the population increases from 110,000 to 300,000 ($3.62) and from 300,000 to 500,000 ($12.26). Thus, up to a point, small economies of scale seem to be present in fire protection.

Commercial activity has the effect of reducing the per capita expenditures for fire protection. See (4). However, the relation is barely significant.

SUMMARY OF FINDINGS ON FIRE PROTECTION

There is some decline in per capita expenditures up to a population of 110,000 and thereafter a substantial expenditure increase. Smaller governments, covering smaller geographic areas, have some difficulty reaching an optimum size in terms of the location of the fire station and the combination of equipment purchased.

POLICE PROTECTION: FACTORS SELECTED

Determining the factors affecting police protection presented many problems. A number of police chiefs as well as other experts in the field of police protection provided considerable information that helped the Survey to establish hypotheses about the various factors that might influence expenditures.

DEPENDENT VARIABLE

The dependent variable to be explained was *per capita total expenditures for police protection*. This figure encompasses all current expenditures including the purchase of equipment. A substantial part of the equipment used by police departments, the most expensive of which is police cars, is replaced on an annual or biennial basis. Most larger police operations buy new cars each year. There were no other major capital outlays during 1955.

INDEPENDENT VARIABLES

Night-time population. See the preceding discussion on fire protection.

Total miles of streets. The presumption is that more patrolmen on the beat and more motorized patrols are needed where more street mileage is to be protected.

Night-time population density per square mile. It is generally recognized that congestion breeds crime.

Per cent of nonwhite population. Police experts voiced the opinion that the nonwhite population requires more police service than does the white. Much of this can seemingly be traced back to the economic status of this group. While economic status is reflected in the assessed valuation figures, it was decided also to include this ethnic variable.

Per cent of night-time population under twenty-five years of age. Juvenile delinquency seems to pose serious police problems in many metropolitan areas and for this reason the age factor is included. The analysis is complicated by the fact that crime does not stop at municipal boundaries and that juveniles from one municipality may and do commit crimes in another.

Combined receipts of wholesale, retail, and service establishments. See the preceding discussion on fire protection.

Number of wholesale, retail, and service establishments. From the viewpoint of providing police protection, commercial activity poses problems related to both dollar volume and number of establishments. Police work related to traffic congestion is best measured by the dollar volume. Police work in connection with night-time closing and protecting of commercial property is best measured in terms of the number of establishments.

Quality of police protection. As in education and fire protection, the quality of police protection can be measured by two different approaches. One way is to assess its net impact upon the community. To attempt to compare the crime potential with the crimes committed is no easy undertaking. It assumes that a community's crime potential can be assessed and compared with the effectiveness with which it is combated. Moreover, because not all crimes are of equal severity, a serious weighting problem presents itself.

An alternate approach would be an attempt to measure the various ingredients that produce good police protection, such as policemen's pay, the number of police, and so forth. Interestingly enough, it was found that the annual salaries of full-time patrolmen in the various police departments in the St. Louis City-County area were about the same. However, there were wide variations in the number of patrolmen that the different departments hired either per 1,000 inhabitants or per $1,000 of property protected. Supposedly, except for inefficiencies, the more men and equipment available to protect a given complex, the better the service.

It would be ideal, then, to establish an index of the number of policemen, police cars, and motorcycles per protection unit, adjust for efficiency, and come up with an index that defines the relative quality of a police department. The chances of assessing the efficiency of a department are slim. Thus, the index constructed did not take into account the efficiency with which men and equipment were utilized.

To construct this index, the Survey had to make certain assumptions about factors affecting expenditures for police protection and in a sense assume the knowledge that the index is ultimately designed to seek. The assumption was made that the number of policemen required depends upon the size of the nighttime population, assessed valuation of real property, street mileage, and receipts by wholesale, retail, and service establishments.

Data suggested that five part-time police officers are equivalent to one full-time officer. Computations were then made for each department to establish the number of officers per 1,000 inhabitants, $1,000 assessed valuation, mile of streets, and one million dollars' worth of commercial receipts, respectively. These four figures were averaged to give the number of policemen employed in a department and assigned to protect one unit of this protection complex. A similar computation was made for police cars and motorcycles. The three averages—officers, cars, and motorcycles —of each department were then weighted by the relative expense associated with a policeman, car, and motorcycle, that is, 52, 32, and 11, respectively.

The resulting number testifies to the quantity of men and equipment used by a department within a given protection complex. The larger the figure, the more men and equipment are used, and, except for inefficiencies, the better the police protection. In spite of their limitations, these calculations produced some helpful results, which will be discussed subsequently.

In recognition of the various difficulties of this method, experts were asked to rate the sixty-four police departments in the St. Louis City-County area for which expenditure data were available. The experts were given the following instructions:

1) Rate department as to how well it copes with its police problems, using a rating of 1.00 as very poor, 2.00 as poor, 3.00 as satisfactory, 4.00 as good, and 5.00 as very good.

2) Take into consideration the qualifications and leadership ability of police chief; qualifications, training, and strength of police force; supporting equipment; morale of police force; and basic conditions bearing on the magnitude of policing problems.

A panel of three highly qualified police experts gave its joint rating for each department. In addition, the police chiefs of two of the finest police departments in the area each separately made a further rating. By and large, the three ratings coincided, and in instances of difference, averages were assigned.

When this subjective index was compared with the one based on number of men and equipment per protection unit, some systematic discrepancies appeared. They largely disappeared, however, after the index of men and equipment was subjected to three adjustments.

1) Instead of giving population, assessed valuation, street mileage, and commercial receipts equal weights, street mileage was assumed to be three times more important than either of the other factors. Therefore street mileage was given a weight of three and each other factor a weight of one.

2) Commercial activity was neglected unless it was in excess of two million dollars a year; it was given a 1.0 weight if annual receipts were between $2 and $17.5 million, and a 1.5 weight if they exceeded $17.5 million.

3) Police cars used on a part-time basis, primarily in small departments with part-time officers, were given a weight of 10 instead of 32, the weight of cars in full-time use.

Once these adjustments were made, many large differences disappeared. Because of the empirical problems involved, however, the index of quality of police protection in this analysis is based almost exclusively on the subjective rating of experts.

Average per capita assessed valuation of real property. See previous discussions of this variable.

POLICE PROTECTION: FINDINGS

Sixty-two County municipalities, the city of St. Louis, and the St. Louis County Police Department (the latter rendering services only to the unincorporated areas and a few contracting municipalities) were providing police protection services in the St. Louis City-County area during 1955. As a total of sixty-four cases was available, only the data for one year were inserted in this analysis.

MULTIPLE REGRESSION AND CORRELATION RESULTS

Two regression equations were estimated for police protection. The first sought to account for variations in per capita expenditures for police protection in terms of the foregoing nine factors. Only four of the factors were significant. It therefore seemed advisable, by the nature of statistical tests, to determine a second regression equation using only the significant factors. Further, in the second analysis, attention was focused on governmental units in St. Louis County, thus omitting the city of St. Louis.

The first regression equation, using nine factors to explain variations in per capita expenditures, explained 94 per cent of the variation. The second analysis, which excluded St. Louis City, explained 87 per cent of the variation.

In the first analysis, only three of the items showed significant relationships to per capita spending for police protection services —per cent of nonwhite population, quality of service, and per capita assessed valuation. All of the significant relationships were positive. In other words, increases in per capita expenditures for police protection are associated with

increases in   (1) per cent nonwhite
                  (2) service level
                  (3) per capita assessed valuation

In the first test, the correlation between police expenditures and per cent nonwhite is barely significant. In the second test, the per cent nonwhite is not quite significant.

An interesting by-product of the service-quality index should be mentioned. When communities under 4,000 are tested for quality of service, the following results appear.

Service-quality index rating	*Number of communities under 4,000 population*
0.00 to 2.50 (very low)	30
2.51 to 3.50 (low)	5
3.51 to 4.50 (high)	2
4.51 to 5.00 (very high)	0
	$\overline{37}$

These data suggest that smaller communities have difficulty in providing adequate police protection.

SUMMARY OF FINDINGS ON POLICE PROTECTION

Differences in per capita expenditures for police protection are largely associated with assessed valuation and the quality of service.

REFUSE COLLECTION: FACTORS SELECTED

The refuse collection function, as the term is used here, includes both garbage and rubbish. Various municipal officials who deal with refuse collection problems as well as a number of private contractors were consulted in establishing hypotheses about the factors that affect expenditures for refuse collection.

DEPENDENT VARIABLE

The dependent variable to be measured was *per capita total expenditures for refuse collection.* In all but six municipalities refuse is picked up by private collectors who usually have contracts with or are licensed by the municipal government, and the charges of private collectors are most likely higher than their costs to allow for a profit. The expenditures of city-operated refuse collection include current expenditures plus equipment purchased in a specific year, 1955. The Survey assumed that the same amount of equipment is purchased annually. Some minor items that could be charged to the refuse collection department, such as office space and parking facilities for equipment, are probably not included in the figures of municipally operated refuse collection, thus tending to make expenditures appear somewhat lower than they actually are.

INDEPENDENT VARIABLES

Night-time population. The amount of refuse that requires collection is highly correlated with the size of the night-time population. Large commercial and industrial establishments usually provide their own refuse collection. Unfortunately, the boundaries of areas served by a private collector do not coincide with municipal boundaries. Quite often one collector picks up a city's rubbish and another collects its garbage. Likewise, often more than one collector handles a city's garbage and yet each one may also collect in other cities or parts of them. For these reasons, the night-time population of municipalities is not too good an indicator of the scale of refuse collection.

Density of dwelling units per square mile. Density is more reliable than population size as a measure of the scale at which refuse collection takes place in cities with city-operated refuse collection. Supposedly the greater the density of dwelling units, the smaller the expense in moving equipment and men from one collection stop to the next.

Number of persons per dwelling unit. This factor interrelates to some extent with the preceding problems. It is generally assumed that the larger the family, the more refuse accumulates and needs to be picked up.

Number of wholesale, retail, and service establishments. This factor was included because refuse pickups are made at commercial establishments as well as residences.

Index of collection arrangements. There are four general types of arrangements for the collection of refuse.

> *Municipal operation:* the municipality uses its employees and equipment to collect refuse and either bills those served or levies a property tax to cover the cost of the service.

> *Municipal contract:* the municipality contracts with private refuse collectors for the service and either uses one of the above two methods to raise the money or charges the private operator a fee for operating in its jurisdiction and the oper-

ator in turn collects his fees. In either instance, the municipality regulates the charge the collector can impose.

Municipal license: the municipality requires the private refuse collector to obtain a city license. Regulation and control are usually less stringent than under city contract.

Private arrangement: the municipality neither stipulates any conditions nor enters into any arrangement.

A preliminary analysis of the data suggested that charges are affected by the type of arrangement in use. Thus, when per capita charges for refuse collection are weighted by the number of persons coming under the arrangement, the per capita charge for refuse collection in 1955 was for

Municipal operation	$2.78
Municipal contract	$3.28
Municipal license	$4.87
Private arrangement	$5.21

Although these per capita figures are likely to be affected by such additional forces as scale of operation, quality of service, and density of dwelling units, the first two types of arrangement apparently mean lower charges than the latter two. The first two types were combined and given the value 1 and the latter two, the value 2. In a sense, therefore, this index of contractual arrangements testifies to the type of arrangement that is being used.

Quality of refuse collection. Of the information that ideally should go into an index of the quality of refuse collection, only data on the type and frequency of collection were readily available. In some instances garbage and rubbish are collected separately and in others jointly. Also, the frequency of pickup varies between summer and winter. Using the convenience of the householder as the criterion, the following weighting system was applied in constructing an index.

Based on this rating the average weighted index for the City-County area in 1955 was 4.95, for St. Louis County, 4.85, and for St. Louis City, 5.00.

This simple approach to measuring the quality of refuse collection was used in testing the hypothesis under consideration. It would have been possible to improve the service-quality index by inclusion of data on the place of refuse collection, had they been available. Refuse collection costs can apparently increase by as much as 65 per cent depending on whether refuse is picked up in

Rating and weight	Type of collection	Frequency of collection per week Garbage	Rubbish
0.0	. . .	0	0
1.0	combined collection	1	1
1.5	garbage only		
	(a) summer	2	0
	(b) winter	1	0
2.0	garbage only	2	0
2.5	separate collections		
	(a) summer	2	¼*
	(b) winter	1	¼*
3.0	separate collections	3	¼*
4.0	combined collection		
	(a) summer	2	2
	(b) winter	1	1
5.0	combined collection	2	2
	separate collections	2	1
6.0	combined collection	3	3

*One rubbish collection each month.

the street, the alley, or behind the house. A study of the operation of a number of municipal and private refuse collectors revealed that in-street collection was 35 per cent and in-alley collection 40 per cent less expensive than rear-of-dwelling collection.

Average per capita assessed valuation of real property. See previous discussion under other services.

REFUSE COLLECTION: FINDINGS

Data on type, frequency, and expenditures for collection were available for eighty-seven municipalities, including St. Louis City, during 1955. As noted, one of the more important limitations of this analysis was that data were not available by service area for all municipalities inserted in the equation. In other words, some private collectors serviced areas that were not coterminous with municipal boundaries. Some served parts or all of several municipalities, while others served only part of one governmental jurisdiction. It had to be assumed that the service area was coterminous with municipal boundaries for purposes of this analysis.

MULTIPLE REGRESSION AND CORRELATION RESULTS

The six variables used explained only 35 per cent of the variation in per capita spending for refuse collection.

Significant factors which influence the expenditures for refuse collection are related as follows. Increases in expenditures for refuse are associated with

increases in (1) index of collection arrangement
               (2) service-quality index
decreases in (3) density of dwelling units

The two positive associations are not surprising. The nature of the collection arrangement index postulates a positive relation. Again, expenditures are positively associated with the level of service. As stated earlier, lower density should provide for easier collection. Perhaps the most interesting finding is the lack of importance of assessed valuation. Evidently, this indicator of financial resources and the demand for refuse collection are not highly correlated.

SUMMARY OF FINDINGS ON REFUSE COLLECTION

This is one service that is rendered rather uniformly in the City-County area without reference to ability to pay, as measured by per capita assessed valuation. On the average, private collection costs from 50 to 90 per cent more than public collection per person. Due to the limitations on available data, it is impossible to determine if economies of large-scale operation are present. Per capita expenditures are lower in areas where dwelling units are closely spaced than in more sparsely settled communities.

STREET SERVICE: FACTORS SELECTED

During meetings with state, county, and city highway engineers, problems connected with street construction, maintenance, lighting, and storm sewers were considered in detail.

DEPENDENT VARIABLE

The most immediate problem was which items should be included in the dependent variable, street service. After lengthy discussions over what to consider in an analysis, the Survey decided to include maintenance (repair, painting, cleaning, and snow removing), street lighting, street signs and electric signals, and street construction prorated over a ten-year period.

It is very difficult to separate expenditures for street construction and maintenance from those for storm sewers. Often streets and storm sewers are built at the same time and by the same construction crew. Similarly, the same crew that cleans streets often cleans storm sewers. Nevertheless, because many smaller municipalities do not have storm sewers, the Survey attempted to obtain expenditure figures, excluding those for storm sewers, in order to have comparable data. This is also desirable from another point of view. In the City-County area the Metropolitan St. Louis Sewer District assumed responsibility for operating and maintaining sewers on October 1, 1955. Since 1954 and 1955 data were to be used for the analysis, the assumption of this responsibility by the district would have made municipal sewer expenditure data more difficult to use. Also, since 1955, sewers, unlike streets, are not a municipal responsibility. Understanding expenditures for street service alone is thus quite important.

The dependent variable to be measured was *per capita total expenditures for street service less the county road fund allotment*. This includes current expenditures for street maintenance, street signs, electric signals, and street lighting together with a ten-year prorate of the construction cost. As a general rule, all recurring expenditures were included, while major capital outlays were prorated over a ten-year period. Thus, if every year an almost equal amount of money is spent for new street signs and electric signals, the annual figure was included. To remove the influence of large variations in annual capital outlays, all expenditure data were averaged over the two years 1954 and 1955.

A number of St. Louis County communities have within their boundaries private subdivisions that build, maintain, and clean their own streets. For purposes of this analysis, municipalities with more than 10 per cent of their streets under the jurisdiction of private subdivisions were excluded.

One further complication deserves mention. In St. Louis County, the County government levies a property tax on all real and personal property. The receipts are entered into a road fund with a separate account for each municipality. Half a municipality's account can be drawn against it by not later than two years after the money has been collected. To obtain its share of the road fund, the municipality must only produce an invoice stating that a certain amount had been spent on roads. Because of this arrangement, of which virtually all municipalities make use to the limit, municipalities receive money from the County road fund directly in proportion to their personal and real property assessment valuation. Inclusion in the expenditure figures of County road fund allotments would tend to produce a spuriously high correlation between expenditures and assessed valuation. The correlation would be high because of institutional factors— that is, virtually forced expenditures amounting to a fixed per cent of assessed valuation. It is best, therefore, to exclude from the expenditure figure the portion derived from the County road fund allotment.

INDEPENDENT VARIABLE

Night-time population. See discussion on fire protection.

Area in square miles. See discussion on fire protection.

Night-time population increases, 1950–1955. The presumption is that the more rapidly growing municipalities are the younger ones and need much new street construction, but relatively little maintenance.

Total miles of streets adjusted for type of street. Streets that are built and maintained by the municipal government are of three main types: primary streets, access roads, and secondary streets. The first type costs about two and one-half times as much to build and maintain as do the latter two. Consequently the mileage of primary streets has been multiplied by 2.5 before being added to that of the other streets and roads to yield the total street mileage of the municipality.

All thoroughfares and arterial roadways not maintained by state, county, or private funds have been considered primary city streets. Measurement of street mileage was made with the help of detailed area maps furnished by the St. Louis County Planning Commission and of a map measurer.

Quality of street service. Ideally the index should measure the quality of all aspects of street service, that is, the quality of road-bed, painting, cleaning, lighting, as well as the network of streets and the extent of electric signals. It soon became clear that there was little chance to measure these various characteristics. Instead, the decision was made to pick a few important ones. It was assumed that (1) street mileage adjusted for type of street on a per square mile basis testifies to some extent to the scope of the street network, and (2) street lighting in terms of candle power per square mile indicates the quality of the lighting system.

On the basis of the cost of these two services, the subindex of street mileage was given seven times the weight of the candle power index.

Average per capita valuation of real property. See previous discussions.

STREET SERVICE: FINDINGS

The empirical results of this study were most disappointing. Merely 12 per cent of the variation in per capita street service expenditures was explained by the various factors that were tested. Only the fiscal ability of the community as measured by assessed valuation had a significant effect on expenditures.

COMBINED SERVICES: FACTORS SELECTED

DEPENDENT VARIABLE

After the five local government services had been separately studied, the Survey thought it desirable to draw on this knowledge and investigate the factors affecting *combined per capita expenditures for the four municipal services: fire protection, police protection, street service,* and *refuse collection.* Public schools were not included because in Missouri they do not come under municipal jurisdiction and in virtually no instance are municipality and school district coterminous. Seventeen of the larger municipalities in the City-County area, all offering the four services and varying in size from 6,000 to 865,000 in 1955, were included in the investigation. (Refuse collection was either carried out by the municipal government or was contracted for by the government.)

An analysis of the combined expenditures were undertaken with two main questions in mind.

Which factors significantly affect the combined expenditures of these four municipal services and what is their relative importance?

Do per capita expenditures, as the scale of output increases, fall, or fall and then rise? In other words, are there economies of scale?

INDEPENDENT VARIABLES

Owing to the relatively small number of observations—only seventeen municipalities—it was not useful to work with a large number of independent variables; the results tend to become un-reliable because too many degrees of freedom are lost. Therefore, the main emphasis was placed on learning more about expenditure patterns than about the factors that affect expenditures.

Three independent variables were selected. The two variables *quality of service* and *average per capita assessed valuation of real property*, were chosen because they had proven to be the most important ones in the separate analyses. *Size of the night-time population* was used to measure the scale of the operation. The results of the first regressions indicated no significant relation between the service-quality index and expenditures. This was surprising and may be based in part on the difficulty of construct-ing a combined index for the four services and the lack of success in constructing an adequate index for street service. A second regression analysis was run off, using the *area in square miles* as the measure of scale of output instead of *night-time population*.

COMBINED SERVICES: FINDINGS

MULTIPLE REGRESSION AND CORRELATION FINDINGS: FIRST ANALYSIS

The variables included in the analysis accounted for 71 per cent of the variation in per capita expenditures. Fiscal ability and size of the night-time population significantly affect per capita ex-penditures for these four services. Quality of service has no significant effect on combined expenditures. Stated alternatively, increases in per capita expenditures for these combined services are associated with

    increases in   (1) size of night-time population
                         (2) average per capita assessed valuation of real property

The most surprising finding is that the size of the night-time population has a significantly positive effect on the combined expenditures for the four services. The seventeen cities included in the analysis had night-time populations of 6,000 to 865,000. As (1) indicates, the larger the city, the higher the per capita ex-penditures for the four services—fiscal ability and quality of service held constant.[5] This finding, however, does not rule out

---

[5] However, excluding St. Louis (which has about sixteen times the popula-tion of the second largest city in the sample) and Kinloch (a small com-

the possibility that cities with a population of less than 6,000 have higher or lower per capita expenditures than those with more than 6,000.

There is no clear evidence that the quality of the four services significantly affects combined expenditures. This finding is inconsistent with the results of the separate analysis, where in three of four services significant relations between service level and expenditures were found. This discrepancy is of importance, since it emphasizes the usefulness of analyzing each service separately. It shows that aggregation can conceal important relations.

MULTIPLE REGRESSION AND CORRELATION FINDINGS: SECOND ANALYSIS

In the second analysis, using square miles as the measure of scale, 93 per cent of the variation in per capita expenditures could be explained. Increases in per capita expenditures for combined services are associated with

increases in   (1) the municipality's square mileage
             (2) per capita assessed valuation

The quality of service, as measured by the service-quality index, is below the significance level in the second analysis.

In conclusion, on *a priori* grounds it would be surprising to find large economies or diseconomies of scale. If economies or diseconomies were present in combined services, the data—however inadequate—might be expected to reveal them. When economies of scale are not large and do not account for much of the change in expenditure levels, more refined data would be needed to indicate their presence.

SUMMARY AND CONCLUSIONS

RESULTS PERTAINING TO INDIVIDUAL SERVICES

A summary of the measurable effect on per capita spending— in terms of multiple regression analysis—of the various factors tested for the five selected services are presented in table 48.

---

munity with a high tax rate and a very inadequate tax base), simple correlation analysis indicates that as population increases, per capita expenditures for these combined services decrease. Although a statistically weak correlation, it serves as a qualification to the finding in the first multiple regression analysis that per capita expenditures for these combined services are associated with increases in population.

TABLE 48

SIGNIFICANT FACTORS: MULTIPLE REGRESSION ANALYSIS

Service	Factors influencing per capita spending[a]	Direction of the effect on per capita spending
Public education	High per pupil assessed valuation	Increase
	High service level rating	Increase
	High percentage of total enrolled in high school	Increase
General control	High per pupil assessed valuation	Increase
	Large number of pupils in ADA	Decrease
Instruction	High service level index rating	Increase
	High percentage of total enrolled in high school	Increase
	High per pupil assessed valuation	Increase
Auxiliary services	High per pupil assessed valuation	Increase
	High service level index rating	Decrease
	High pupil density per square mile	Decrease
	Large numbers of pupils in ADA	Decrease
Plant operation and maintenance	High per pupil assessed valuation	Increase
	High percentage of total enrolled in high school	Increase
Fixed charges	High per pupil assessed valuation	Increase
Fire protection	High per capita assessed valuation	Increase
	Large service area in square miles	Decrease
	Large service population	Decrease
	High service level index rating	Increase
	Large amount of commercial development	Decrease
Police protection	High per capita assessed valuation	Increase
	High service level index rating	Increase
	High per cent of resident population nonwhite	Increase
Refuse collection	High service level index rating	Increase
	High density of dwelling units per square mile	Decrease
	High index rating of contractual arrangement	Increase
Street service	High per capita assessed valuation	Increase
	Large service area in square miles	Decrease

[a] The factors influencing per capita spending are listed for each service on the strength of their partial correlation coefficients being statistically significant.

RESULTS PERTAINING TO A COMBINATION OF SERVICES

For a particular set of services—police and fire protection, refuse collection, and street service—per capita assessed valuation seemingly is the most important determinant of per capita spending. The results relating to population appear to be highly inconclusive.

GENERAL CONCLUSIONS

Recognizing that the analyses are limited to available data for a single metropolitan area, extended generalizations are not justified, but certain patterns do emerge. It should be emphasized that the statements made here apply only to the St. Louis City–St. Louis County area during the 1951 to 1956 period. In one sense, this is a case study of a metropolitan area, based on certain statistical tools that have not previously been applied in this manner. The success was varied.

The use of a single metropolitan area had both advantages and disadvantages. Some environmental factors could be either controlled or accounted for, a measure of available resources obtained, and at least a rough measure of quality of service utilized. The use of local governmental units in Missouri was advantageous since few state aids and grants are present to complicate fiscal analysis. Corresponding limiting factors were encountered, however, such as the size and distribution of the sample used, the desire for better measurements of quality of service, and the need for more comparable and uniform financial information. It would also be beneficial to analyze services in terms of subfunctions. For example, in police it would be worthwhile to analyze separately items such as traffic control, crime detection, and laboratory facilities.

Three conclusions are relevant to the Survey's recommendations about government: (1) the importance of assessed valuation; (2) the significance of the service-quality index; and (3) findings that give insights into the presence or absence of economies of scale.

In the analyses both of specific services and of combined services, assessed valuation was an important factor. The expenditures reflect what communities can afford, insomuch as assessed valuation indicates their fiscal ability. Negatively stated, the expenditures of some communities are low because they cannot afford more. Yet, in a metropolitan area it is essential to provide an adequate level of at least certain basic services for all residents. Thus, means must be found to bring needed services to communities that cannot afford them.

Consider the importance of quality of service. In each service studied, except street service, higher quality was associated with larger per capita expenditures. This is not a surprising finding, but it is nevertheless important to the Survey's recommendations. Not only must communities be helped in providing services, they must have services that meet quality standards.

The final over-all pattern that emerged related to economies or diseconomies of scale. If major diseconomies of scale had appeared in certain services, the Survey would have been reluctant to suggest their transfer to a larger unit, unless faced with other compelling reasons. If economies could have been shown, support is implied for consolidation. However, since no major economies or diseconomies are apparent, this factor could not be used as an argument for or against consolidation.

These three findings from the study of factors affecting expenditure levels gave support to a number of the Survey's governmental recommendations. The provision of an adequate expenditure level to bring about a satisfactory quality of specific basic services is an important element in a healthy metropolitan community. The Survey felt reorganization could achieve this goal, and could do so, as the evidence suggests, without encountering diseconomies.

15

Measuring Local Services

A MAJOR OBJECTIVE of the Metropolitan St. Louis Survey was to analyze services and expenditures of all governmental units in the City-County area and, on the basis of the analysis, to make specific recommendations about the governmental pattern. The Survey deemed the measuring of specific governmental services so important to making certain recommendations that it used another and simpler approach at the same time its statistical study of factors affecting governmental expenditures, reported in chapter 14 of this book, was under way.

A general inventory of each government produced data on its number of services and employees and its expenditures. Meaningful analysis of these data required some kind of measuring device to enable the making of significant comparisons among various governments. Without such a device, the only comparison possible was a numerical count of the services being provided by each. Although information about quantity is of some significance, comparisons that take adequacy or quality of service into account are much more meaningful. Consequently, a tool is needed to make it possible to express services rendered by each government in terms of a common denominator. Only then can comparisons be made about the quality or level of service supplied by various governmental units.

A unit of measure is also essential in order to make comparisons of service expenditures. It would be fallacious to conclude that it costs more to perform a specific public service in a large city than in a small community unless the quality of service performed by each city can be compared against a common standard. Once a unit is devised for measuring such quality or level of service, costs per unit can be computed for all municipalities and significant comparisons can be made.

A unit of measure for local governmental services reduces the need for value judgments about the adequacy of services being rendered by particular governments. If specific recommendations for changes in governments are contemplated, substantial evidence of the need for such change is essential. It must be shown that either some existing governments are not supplying essential services at an adequate level or the services are being maintained at a satisfactory level only by a per unit expenditure substantially above that of other local governments.

The literature dealing with measurement of public services reveals a great deal of information about the difficulties involved in making valid measurements, but it furnishes few practical measuring devices or techniques. One of the best treatments of this problem suggested four distinct kinds of measurements which might be attempted—measurement of costs, efforts, performance, and results.[1]

Governmental costs can be expressed in terms of cost per person served, such as the cost of street cleaning or fire protection per resident of the city. This measure does not take into consideration variations in the difficulty of performing the service or differences in the quality or effectiveness of the service rendered. One city may show a low cost per capita for supplying police protection mainly because of the social and economic characteristics of the locality, or the low cost may be due to the very low quality of police protection actually provided.

Measures of effort expended can be useful for comparative purposes. These measures indicate the number of man hours or machine hours applied to the performance of a specific public service. The inadequacy of such measures is that they furnish no indication of the results achieved by the application of a given number of man and machine hours; when used alone, they do not reveal either the differences in difficulties faced by various governmental units in performing a service or the efficiency in terms of results with which the effort is expended.

Measures of performance can be used in comparing certain

---

[1] Clarence E. Ridley and Herbert A. Simon, *Measuring Municipal Activities* (2d ed.; Chicago: International City Managers' Association, 1943).

types of governmental services. Street construction can be accurately tabulated in terms of square yards of pavement laid. Number of fires extinguished is a criterion of performance for fire departments, and number of arrests made in relation to crimes committed can be used to indicate police performance. To be meaningful, performance must be used in conjunction with other standards if comparisons of governments are to be made. Because of the nature of the terrain in one city, the laying of a square yard of pavement may require more man and machine hours than in others. Similarly, the problems involved in extinguishing a fire in one community may be quite different from those elsewhere.

The most significant measure of service is one that expresses results achieved by the expenditure of a specific amount of effort toward the achievement of a previously established objective. Data are readily available to show effort expended and results can be observed in some instances. Application of such a measure requires clear statements of the objectives, and it is extremely difficult to state these objectives in numerical terms. For example, if the goals of public education are stated as "training for citizenship" or "producing sound minds in sound bodies," they are not readily subject to quantification. Difficulties also arise in attempts to measure results of police services. If the chief objective is to prevent crime, a low number of crimes committed may be accepted as a measure of success, but if the chief objective is to arrest violators and bring them to trial and conviction, an entirely different guide must be used.

MEASURES USED AND SERVICES SELECTED

The Survey staff kept constantly in mind that its study was oriented toward an action program. The kind of measures used to compare services performed by the various governments therefore had to be understandable and meaningful to residents of the City-County area, and had to reveal significant differences in either the nature of the services or the expenditures.

A decision was reached to use measures that would indicate the effort expended to perform a service in terms of the need for the service. Effort could be measured simply by number of persons employed. The need for a service was to be ascertained by the use of factors that were quantifiable and generally recognized as indicative of service needs. Population and area thus were assumed to be determinants of the number of policemen needed by a city.

A standard of adequacy for fire and police services was established by averaging the present service level in eight and nine, respectively, of the most populous cities in St. Louis County. This kind of standard can be readily understood by citizens living in the area since it is based on actual performance in communities with which they have some familiarity. The Survey did not propose that its specific suggested standards be necessarily adopted; it was more interested in providing a methodology that responsible authorities could readily use.

The time and staff available compelled the Survey to select a limited number of public services for comparison. Police protection, fire protection, and public education were chosen for analysis. A number of factors prompted the decision to concentrate on these three services: they account for a major portion of expenditures from local taxes; they are generally supplied in all urbanized areas of the City and County and are considered by citizens to be essential local government functions; moreover, they represent activities of different kinds of governments. Police protection is regularly performed by municipalities in the area, public education is a responsibility of school districts, and fire protection is supplied by both municipalities and special-purpose fire protection districts.

MEASURING POLICE PROTECTION

The measure of police protection was based on the assumption that a number of factors for which information was available demonstrated the need for the level of service. The first factor included was area, expressed in square miles. Consultations with police chiefs revealed that a substantial part of police work demands the maintenance of motorized patrols. The number of patrol vehicles and policemen required for regular patrol duty is determined in part by the total area to be covered, and costs such as motor fuel, tires, and vehicle repair and maintenance are directly affected by territorial size.

A second factor that showed the extent of required police service was population. In municipalities with approximately equal areas, the level of police service needed would be assumed to be greater in the one with the larger population. The number of police calls is affected by the number of people requiring police protection, and, similarly, the number of private cars on the streets is closely associated with population and the magnitude of the traffic problem. Using both area and population to determine a measure of police protection takes into account whatever effect density may have.

Assessed valuation of property was used as a third criterion. It furnishes an indication about the amount of property requiring police protection. High property valuations usually signify commercial rather than residential development. The type of property is important since a higher concentration of policemen is generally required in commercialized areas.

Number of miles of streets in a municipality was also considered influential. This factor influences regular patrol assignments and serves as an indicator of traffic control requirements.

The fifth and final factor used in the measurement was total annual receipts from retail sales and services in the municipality. If the figure is high in any city, the number of people in the community at certain times is larger than the total resident population. A business population requires the assignment of police to the business area. This factor is also related to the amount of commercial property for which police protection is required.

A NORM FOR POLICE SERVICE

To establish a base against which police service in any particular community could be compared, an average was computed for nine of the most populous and well-established cities in St. Louis County. One city, which according to recent population estimates ranks in the top nine, was omitted from the computation because its service level is so far below that of the other municipalities; owing to an extremely rapid increase in population, its governmental services have lagged far behind. The nine cities used are University City, Webster Groves, Kirkwood, Overland, Jennings, Clayton, Richmond Heights, Ferguson, and Maplewood. Their populations range from 14,000 to 53,000.

The norm for police service was ascertained by obtaining the average number of policemen employed in these nine County municipalities in terms of each of the foregoing five factors, which were given equal weight:

6.33 per square mile
1.22 per 1,000 population
.64 per $1,000,000 assessed valuation
.42 per mile of streets
.60 per $1,000,000 annual receipts from retail sales and services

The following examples show the computations made to compare two cities against the established norm.

First city:

Area	2.18 sq. miles	× 6.33 = 13.80
Population (in thousands)	12.13	× 1.22 = 14.80
Assessed valuation (in millions)	22.22	× .64 = 14.22
Miles of streets	22	× .42 = 9.24
Annual receipts (in millions)	22.4	× .60 = 13.44
Number of policemen required to meet the norm		= 13.10

In order to meet the proposed norm, this city needs to employ 13.1 policemen. It actually has 13.2 policemen. The fraction is accounted for by the use of some part-time policemen.

Second city:

Area	5.25 sq. miles	× 6.33 = 33.23
Population (in thousands)	16.00	× 1.22 = 19.52
Assessed valuation (in millions)	20.05	× .64 = 12.83
Miles of streets	50	× .42 = 21.00
Annual receipts (in millions)	23.1	× .60 = 13.86
Number of policemen required to meet the norm		= 20.09

The actual number of police employed by this city is 9.5. The community, which is new and rapidly growing, is substantially below the norm established for police service.

MEASURING FIRE PROTECTION

A norm against which the fire protection furnished by any municipality or special fire protection district can be measured was established in a manner similar to that used for police service. Eight of the same nine cities were used in computing the norm. The ninth was omitted since it is included in a special fire protection district and therefore has no municipal fire department. Only three factors assumed to account for the need for fire protection were used. These were area, population, and assessed valuation of property.

Area is an important factor in fire protection because it affects the number of locations of fire-fighting equipment. Experienced fire fighters emphasize the need for having equipment situated as near as possible to property that must be protected. Population shows the number of persons and indirectly the number of pieces of property for which a fire department has responsibility. Using both area and population in establishing a norm takes into account the effect of density. Assessed value of property gives some idea of the total value of property to be protected. It also indicates relative ability to finance fire protection as general property taxes are used in the City and County to support fire departments. The number of miles of streets and value of sales and services, which were utilized in establishing a norm for police protection, were omitted as they did not seem to be directly related to the number of fire fighters needed in a community. Computations on sales and services were made, but this factor was ultimately excluded because it had no substantial effect on the result. The norm for fire protection was determined by taking the average number of firemen employed by the eight cities in terms of the three factors discussed above.

The average number of firemen was:

3.97 per square mile
.75 per 1,000 population
.38 per $1,000,000 assessed valuation

A city and a special fire protection district may be used to illustrate the standard for fire protection.

A city:

Area	$2.18 \times 3.97 = 8.65$
Population	$12.13 \times .75 = 9.10$
(in thousands)	
Assessed valuation	$22.22 \times .38 = \underline{8.44}$
(in millions)	
Number of firemen needed to	
meet the norm	$= 8.73$

To come up to the norm, this city needs to employ 8.73 fire fighters on a full-time basis. The community actually has 9 full-time fire fighters; it thus is practically at the standard for fire protection.

The following example shows the use of the norm for fire protection in a special district that includes a number of small municipalities as well as unincorporated area.

A fire district:

Area	5.36 sq. mi.	× 3.99 = 21.39
Population (in thousands)	25.00	× .75 = 18.75
Assessed valuation (in millions)	28.07	× .38 = 10.67
Number of firemen needed to meet the norm		= 16.94

In order to meet the standard, this district would need to employ the equivalent of 16.9 full-time fire fighters. The number actually employed is equal to 11 full-time men. The difference in the city and the district as shown by the application of this standard is partially substantiated by the ratings for fire insurance purposes established by the Missouri Inspection Bureau. Part of the district has an eight rating; the remainder has a nine. The lowest bureau rating of ten applies to areas with no tax-supported fire protection. The city in this example, on the other hand, which meets the standard developed by the Survey, has a rating of six, the equivalent of what has been assigned to the larger municipalities in the County.

MEASURING PUBLIC EDUCATION

After analyzing data on public education in the City-County area, the Survey decided to include this public service within the scope of its recommendations. This decision necessitated the formulation of units of measure that would make possible significant comparisons of local school districts. Data were readily available on pupil enumeration, enrollment, average daily attendance, number of teachers, teacher qualifications, salaries of teachers, number of graduates, and number of graduates entering college. Financial data were also available on assessed valuation, tax rate, indebtedness, total expenditures, and state and county aid to school districts.

Two generally recognized measures were used in the Survey reports to compare school districts, assessed valuation of property and expenditures, both on the basis of each pupil in average daily attendance. The first is a measure of ability of a district to finance education. Practically all local support for public education in Missouri must be raised through taxes on real and personal property. Therefore, the assessed valuation of taxable property in a district represents the basis of its financial support. Comparisons could be arrived at by computing the total assessed value of property in terms of per pupil enumerated in each district, per pupil actually enrolled, or per pupil in average daily attendance. Enumeration is not a satisfactory unit for comparative purposes in St. Louis City and County because, under state law, it includes age groups that are very unlikely to be in school. The upper age is twenty years, and only infrequently is a twenty-year-old pupil enrolled in the public schools as none of the districts maintains more than a four-year high school program. Enumeration also includes pupils who attend non–tax-supported private and parochial schools. This factor would not be serious if the proportion of those attending private and parochial schools was fairly uniform in the various districts; this situation, however, does not prevail in the County. In some districts a much larger proportion of families send their children to private and parochial schools.

Enrollment is a more satisfactory measure than enumeration for comparative purposes, but it also has certain weaknesses. Every pupil who attends school for even a single day in a school year is included in the enrollment figure. Consequently, districts with a high degree of population instability show larger enrollments than districts where populations are relatively stable. If a family with three pupils resides in a district a few months and then moves, the three children will be included in the annual enrollment figure. If a new family containing three school-age children moves into the house that the first family vacated, their children will also be included. Thus the enrollment figure from this residence would be twice as great as if one family had lived in the house throughout the year.

Average daily attendance is the most useful measure in attempting to make valid comparisons among school districts. Ability to support public schools locally was therefore measured in terms of assessed value of property per pupil in ADA. Comparative figures for all districts were reported in the Survey's first report, *Background for Action,* and demonstrated a wide disparity in financial abilities of school districts. One district has an assessed valuation of only $2,201 per pupil in ADA, whereas another has $37,521. Four districts have assessed valuations per pupil in excess of $20,000; three fall below $5,000.

Another measure used by the Survey was designed to compare current operating costs of the various districts. This was accomplished by computing costs per pupil in ADA in each district.

Expenditures alone are, of course, not an accurate measure of quality of education, but they do give an impression of the kind of educational opportunities offered. Comparative data for all districts relative to this measure were also presented in *Background for Action*. Extensive disparities exist among school districts in the County. One district spends only $112.88 per pupil in average daily attendance—another spends $638.09.

Comparisons of tax rates for school purposes were made to determine whether the low per pupil expenditures existed because of low tax levies. These comparisons revealed that the tax rate in the district with the highest expenditure per pupil in ADA was the lowest in the County. The tabulation presented conclusive evidence that high expenditures per pupil were more directly related to high assessed valuation of property rather than to high tax rates. The conclusion was inescapable that low expenditures per pupil in some districts resulted from an insufficient tax base rather than from an unwillingness of residents to support tax levies.

QUALITY OF EDUCATION

Determining an objective measure of the quality of education available in a school district is extremely elusive, all the more so if the measure is designed to express accomplished results. Even if valid tests were available to measure educational achievement in basic public school subjects, these tests would not present evidence of the success of character and personality development programs. Moreover, in St. Louis County the lack of a uniform testing program prevents any possible comparison of achievement in even the basic required school courses. The Survey, therefore, stopped its efforts to measure objectively the results of the educational programs in the various school districts.

The Survey's attention focused on quantifiable criteria that seemingly measured educational results indirectly. It was assumed, for example, that educational results in a school district are affected by the qualifications of the teachers employed. For this factor, objective measures were readily available. The factors adopted for comparative purposes were (1) per cent of teachers with 150 or more semester hours of college credit, (2) per cent of teachers with ten years or more teaching experience, (3) pupil-teacher ratio, (4) total number of units of high school credits offered, (5) average salaries of teachers, and (6) per cent of high school graduates entering college.

County and City residents are familiar with these factors, which are generally considered to be evidence of good school systems. These factors seemed useful as the purpose of comparisons was to inform local residents of interdistrict differences in types of educational opportunities offered.

A simple form of comparison was used—arranging school districts in rank order for each of the above-listed factors. A composite rank order was then determined by totaling the ranks of each district on all five factors. The high positions of such districts as Clayton, University City, Webster Groves, Maplewood–Richmond Heights, Ladue, and Normandy came as no surprise for these systems are generally recognized as being among the best in the area. Because the tax rate for school purposes in the City, whose school system ranked eighth in the total of twenty-seven districts, was $1.21 for each $100 assessed valuation as compared to a low of $1.68 and a high of $3.58 in the County,

TABLE 49

RANK OF SCHOOL DISTRICTS ON SELECTED FACTORS

School district[a]	Composite rank[b]	Teachers having 150+ semester hours	Teachers having 10+ years experience	Pupils per teacher	Units of high school instruction	Average salary of teachers	Per cent of graduates entering college	Expenditures per pupil in ADA
Clayton	1	1	1	1	4	1	3	1
Maplewood	2	5	2	4	7	3	8	8
University City	3	3	10	8	1	6	1	6
Webster Groves	4	4	9	10	3	7	6	15
Normandy	5	6	3	10	10	5	19	11
Ladue	6	2	25	2	14	10	2	2
Wellston	7	12	8	5	2	4	25	5
Jennings	8	7	14	3	13	11	11	9
St. Louis	9	9	4	23	5	2	18	3
West Walnut	10	8	5	7	21	9	16	16
Kirkwood	11	14	13	14	18	8	4	19
Brentwood	12	15	21	7	12	12	5	7
Hancock	13	11	11	11	11	14	23	20
Affton	14	10	20	15	17	22	9	12
Ritenour	15	19	12	19	6	16	21	23
Berkeley	16	17	16	20	16	13	14	18
Riverview	17	13	22	21	8	15	17	17
Ferguson-Florrisant	18	16	30	18	9	21	10	21
Pattonville	19	25	17	22	15	18	12	24
Bayless	20	23	29	6	19	20	13	14
Eureka	21	20	7	19	22	24	22	22
R-8	22	26	28	9	25	19	7	10
R-9	23	24	24	16	20	23	15	13
Hazelwood	24	21	19	12	23	28	21	4
Valley Park	25	27	23	7	24	27	20	26
Kinloch	26	18	18	24	27	30	18	27
Maryland	27	28	27	19	26	26	24	25

  [a] Three districts that are too small to operate high schools are omitted from the table.
  [b] Equal weights were given to each factor in arriving at the composite rank.

some reflection on the economical operation of the smaller districts in the County seemed in order.

SIZE OF SCHOOL DISTRICTS

Utilizing a standard against which the size of school districts in the County could be compared seemed desirable. The most useful material of this type was compiled in 1948 by the National Commission on School District Reorganization, sponsored by the Rural Educational Project of the University of Chicago and the Department of Rural Education of the National Education Association.

The Commission based its judgments relative to school district size on the principle that a school district maintaining an adequate educational program must have a staff of nonteaching specialists to handle such services as supervision of attendance, instruction, and transportation, school library service, adult education leadership, and physical examination of children. A study of practices in the better school systems in the nation revealed that a staff of thirty to forty persons is required for these special services. The commission therefore concluded that a "school district large enough to permit the employment of such a staff at a cost bearing a reasonable relationship to the total cost of the educational program will need to have an enrollment of from 10,000 to 12,000 pupils." [2]

Recognizing the difficulties involved in universally applying a minimum enrollment size to school districts, especially in view of the need to keep the territorial size reasonable, the commission added modifications that might be satisfactory under certain conditions. It suggested a median modification setting the minimum size of a district at from 5,000 to 6,000 enrollment. It stipulated as a maximum modification districts with enrollments from 1,500 to 1,800 pupils, in which only a small number of supervisory and special service personnel would be possible.

The school district in the City easily meets the standard of adequacy set up by the National Commission on School District Reorganization, but no district in the County does so. Only six of the twenty-nine districts in the County meet the median modification, and twenty-one come up to the maximum modification. The existing twenty-nine districts in the County would have to be

---

[2] *Your School District,* National Commission on School District Reorganization (Washington: National Education Association, 1948), p. 87.

reduced to nine in order to obtain a minimum of 10,000 pupils in each school district.

A STANDARD BASED ON NUMBER OF TEACHERS

All school districts in the County were also compared against a standard based on number of teachers employed. The standard was derived from a research project published by Teachers' College of Columbia University.[3] This study, based on an examination of school districts in Maryland and Connecticut, was designed to compare administrative units on their ability to

1) secure skilled and continuous educational leadership;

2) attain economy in the use of the time of the leadership employed; and

3) make economical use of the funds spent for general (administrative and supervisory) control.

This source indicated a rapid gain in economy as the size of the administrative unit[4] increased up to the range of 70 to 100 teachers. Significant economies were noted as the size increased up to 250 teachers, but no significant economies were detected in districts having more than 250 teachers. Application of this standard in the City-County area revealed that the school district in the City and five districts in the County employ as many as 250 teachers and sixteen employ fewer than 100 teachers.

The Survey's use in its first public report of these two standards in relation to size of school districts attracted considerable newspaper coverage and editorial comment and stimulated wide public discussion of the need for reëxamining many of the existing school districts.

USE OF STANDARDS IN SURVEY'S RECOMMENDATIONS REPORT

On the basis of its comparisons of local school districts and the standards presented in the publications of the National Commission on School District Reorganization and Columbia University, the Survey developed two specific recommendations about

[3] A. O. Briscoe, *The Size of the Local Unit for Administration and Supervision of Public Schools* (New York: Columbia University Teachers' College, Contributions to Education, no. 649, 1935).

[4] The term administrative unit is synonomous with school district and should not be confused with the term "attendance unit," which refers to a single school. An administrative unit may contain a number of attendance units.

school districts in its second report, *Path of Progress*. First, all districts with fewer than 1,500 pupils either should be combined to form larger districts or should be annexed to larger districts. Second, a County-wide tax should be levied to equalize to a greater degree educational opportunities among the districts.

The previously described standards of police and fire protection were used as the basis for specific recommendations in *Path of Progress*. The police standard, it will be recalled, was based on an average of the level of police service maintained in nine of the most populous cities of the County. Application of this standard to each municipality in the County revealed that the actual number of policemen employed in cities with populations of 5,000 or more compares favorably with the standard. Of the fourteen cities with populations of 5,000 or more (not including the nine used in computing the standard), only two have deficiencies of more than one full-time police officer. These cities have experienced exceptionally rapid growth and all their public services have lagged. The significant deficiencies are present in cities with populations below 5,000; only a few cities under 4,000 maintain any full-time police officers.

It became apparent from these comparisons that no serious indictment could be made against the larger municipalities of the County regarding local police service. This certainly was an important determinant in the Survey's decision not to recommend the consolidation of all municipalities in the County, or the creation of a single County-wide police force and the abolition of all municipal police operations. Data collected by the Survey did demonstrate, however, that the very small municipalities were not providing sufficient police protection. Such evidence led to the recommendation that the County police department be responsible for police protection in all cities with populations under 4,000 as well as in unincorporated areas. The adoption of this proposal would permit cities with populations of 4,000 or more to continue to provide their own local police protection so long as it was maintained at a satisfactory level.

The standard for police service served another purpose in the Survey's second report—to show how the recommendations on police service would financially affect each municipality. It was necessary to estimate the additional cost the County would assume in rendering police service in the small municipalities. This estimate, made by applying the standard to the area included in these municipalities, revealed that 102 additional policemen would be required to provide adequate service to the 70 municipalities with populations of less than 4,000. The estimated cost of the additional 102 policemen was determined by using as a conversion factor the average salary of a policeman, $5,000, in the nine large cities of the County upon which the police service standard was based. Additional costs to the County government were therefore estimated to be $510,000. This additional cost could be expressed as a tax rate because the total assessed valuation of property in the County was readily available. Computation revealed that an increase of 4.9 cents on each $100 assessed valuation in the tax rate would be required to pay for this additional County police service.

The standard was also useful in estimating the effect of the Survey recommendations on the larger cities that might choose to furnish their own police service. The recommendations provided that each municipality with a population of 4,000 or more, which maintained police protection at a satisfactory level, would receive a rebate from County tax funds equal to the actual cost of maintaining such service. Each city, however, providing service above the established standard would have to do so from its own funds.

By applying the Survey standard to each municipality and by using the $5,000 conversion figure, the Survey could readily compute the cost for each of them. The total for all such municipalities would constitute the amount of rebates which the County government would have to finance. This expenditure could be converted into a tax rate on the basis of the total County assessed valuation. The computation revealed that a County-wide tax rate of 20.2 cents on each $100 assessed valuation would be required to give rebates to all cities meeting the qualifications. Therefore, the Survey proposal would require an additional County-wide tax of 25.1 cents on each $100 assessed valuation to finance the proposed new police program.

The amount of refund to be expected by each city was determined by computing the cost of maintaining police service at the standard level in each city. The anticipated rebate could be reduced to a tax rate on the basis of the total assessed valuation of property in the city. If this rate proved to be greater than the additional County rate of 25.1 cents required, then the city would profit. According to these computations, only three cities would fail to profit by the proposed changes, and the greatest loss was equal to a rate of only 2.8 cents. One city would gain the equivalent of a tax rate of 50.7 cents on each $100 assessed valuation.

The standard established for fire protection was not used as extensively by the Survey, because recommendations about this service followed a different pattern. It did, however, show a need for more adequate fire protection in most cities in the County and in unincorporated urban areas located in special fire protection districts.

Eleven municipalities, in addition to the eight that the Survey used to establish the standard, maintain fire departments. The remaining seventy-eight municipalities either contract with some other authority for fire protection or are served by one of eighteen special fire protection districts operating in the County. Only three of these districts maintain protection equal to the standard devised by the Survey, and in most which do not meet the standard, the deficiency is substantial.

The existence of special fire protection districts is evidence of public recognition that small municipalities cannot be expected to support adequate fire departments. But application of the standard indicated that the districts as organized were not adequately coping with the needs of these small incorporated centers. This led the Survey to recommend the vesting of authority in the County council to plan, on the basis of study, proposed reorganizations of existing fire districts and the assumption by the County government of certain fire prevention functions on a County-wide basis.

The Survey was aware that the standards on education, police, and fire measured indirectly rather than directly the results achieved by a governmental unit in the performance of services. Although governmental officials voiced some opposition to the specific recommendations about these three services, they did not attack the standards for comparison among the various governmental units.

The measures appear to have several features that make them useful in action-oriented research. They are readily adaptable to other local governmental services. They are based upon actual performance levels in communities well known to most residents of the particular area. Moreover, the information required for computation of standards and for comparisons is available in most instances, and the computation is readily understandable by the public.

16

The Economy of the
St. Louis Metropolitan Area:
An Input-Output Approach

THE SURVEY undertook an input-output analysis in order to gain
a fuller understanding about the economic structure of and relationships within the St. Louis metropolitan area and therefore
to be better able to project economic activities. The particular
framework of analysis is known as an input-output approach.
Consideration is given to the techniques involved in such an approach, its rationale, some methodological problems encountered,
and some results of the study.

AN EXPLANATION OF THE ANALYSIS

The technique known as input-output analysis is relatively
simple in its basic structure. The refinements and details of the
analysis, however, involve many technical problems that are beyond the scope of what is reported here, but it will suffice to indicate the nature of input-output analysis in simplified form.

The basic concept of input-output analysis is that in order
to produce outputs (for example, steel bars), inputs are necessary
(coal, iron ore, manpower, to mention a few). To produce a whole
bundle of outputs, a whole set of inputs is needed. Moreover,
the outputs of one firm become the inputs of another. The output
of a flour mill is an input to a bakery. Further, the output

[369]

of a bakery becomes an input to another industry—households. (Households are conceived of as an industry insofar as they use inputs—food, clothing, shelter, and so on—in order to produce outputs—accountants, mechanics, tailors, and so forth.)

The next step in understanding input-output analysis is to recognize that at least in the short run the various activities are interrelated in a somewhat precise manner. To produce the output, a chocolate cake, requires certain inputs such as flour, chocolate, shortening, and other ingredients. Further, if two chocolate cakes are to be produced, the amounts of each ingredient need to be doubled. The same analysis applies to other goods, airplanes, boxcars, and so forth. Input-output merely takes these relationships and places them together in a useful analytical manner.

The following problem will illustrate the ideas and techniques of input-output analysis and, in addition, permit the identification of some terms used in the analysis.

Suppose consideration is given to a simple economy where only two types of goods are produced, manufactured and agricultural. Further, assume that for every dollar of agricultural outputs, 20 cents of manufactured goods are needed—tractors, wire, tires, and other such goods. How much will the manufacturing industry (sector) sell to agriculture? The answer is 20 per cent of the value of agricultural outputs. The manufacturing sector, in turn, needs inputs from the agricultural sector, such as wheat and cotton, in order to produce its outputs.

Suppose the manufacturers need 50 cents of agricultural inputs for every dollar of output. These interrelations can be shown in the form of a table—technically, a matrix. Reading across the rows, the matrix shows that the output of M (manufactures) goes to A (agriculture) in the amount of .2 dollars for every dollar of

$$
\begin{array}{c}
\text{From} \\
\begin{array}{ccc}
 & \text{M} & \text{A} \\
\text{To} \quad \text{M} & 0 & .2 \\
\text{A} & .5 & 0
\end{array}
\end{array}
$$

agricultural output. Reading down the columns, A needs .2 dollars of inputs for every dollar of output. The .2 and .5 are the production coefficients. (It should be noted in this example that A(M) industries do not need inputs from other A(M) industries. This is assumed in order to keep the example simple; it is not realistic.)

At this point consumers, called "households" (H), are introduced. They demand outputs from both the A and the M sectors. How much do they demand? In this simple model this is not known, but must be given. Assume that outside forces of income, tastes, and so forth yield a consumers' demand for $12 of M goods and $3 of A goods. This information, furnished from outside sources, constitutes part of what is known as the "final demand" sector. (In the St. Louis metropolitan area, final demand includes, for example, exports out of the area. Why? The volume of exports is not determined by the St. Louis area economy, but by outside forces.)

This new information can be added as follows; the household sector (H) is added at the end.

		From		Final demand
		M	A	H
To	M	0	.2	12
	A	.5	0	3

The question now posed is, how much do the A and M sectors need to produce in total in order to give consumers $12 of M and $3 of A? It is not just $12 of M goods; that would not be enough. Part of the $12 will be needed by A in order to produce $3 of A goods. Some amount more than $12 needs to be produced. In other words, consumers' demand and agriculture's demand need to be accounted for. This can be put as a simultaneous system of two equations and two unknowns. Reading across the rows:

$$(1) \quad M = .2A + 12$$
$$(2) \quad A = .5M + 3$$

This can be solved, yielding M = $14 and A = $10. Thus, to provide consumers with $12 (M) and $3 (A) requires a total output of $14 (M) and $10 (A). (Why do so many A goods need to be produced? Recall that every dollar of M output requires .5 dollars of A inputs. A lot of A output is going to the M sector.)

At this point it is possible to ask, what if the (H) demands are increased from $12 (M) to $13 (M)? Again the calculation could be made to indicate the impact of this change on the economy.

If the final demand sector was "exports," not households, the impact would be the same. Moreover, if this was a description of the St. Louis metropolitan economy, the impact of a one-dollar increase in (M) exports on the area's economy could be traced.

What, then, are the basic ingredients of an input-output model?

First, it shows the interrelations, or how sectors are tied together, in the form of production coefficients, often called technical coefficients. Second, it shows the total amount of output needed to satisfy the final demand, that is, the demands given by outside forces. (It should be noted again that this discussion has omitted many qualifications and other points with respect to input-output analysis.)

THE SURVEY'S USE OF INPUT-OUTPUT

In deciding to adopt the input-output approach, the Survey considered alternative methods of examining the area's economic structure. Two other approaches are worth mentioning.

One popular form of analysis of an urban area is the "economic base" approach. Usually dealing in terms of employment, it is similar in many respects to the input-output analysis. Some industries are considered "basic"; they are usually the export industries. The nonbasic industries, such as retail and services, are considered as a second group. The level of activity of the nonbasic sector depends upon the basic sector. Roughly, employment in shoe stores (nonbasic) depends upon employment in the factories (basic) and factories (basic) upon export markets.

For the Survey's purpose, there are two limitations to this type of analysis: (1) it deals in employment and not dollar amounts, and (2) not enough information is spelled out concerning the interrelations of the economy of the St. Louis metropolitan area. This does not, however, invalidate the usefulness of the economic base approach.

A second possible approach would be merely to attempt to analyze the St. Louis area economy in a general way. No specific framework would be employed. The Survey would merely seek to look into important areas such as labor force, kinds of industry, incomes, and population trends. In a sense, this general analysis had to be carried out in order to get the background of the St. Louis area economy, and some results of work along this line were incorporated in an earlier part of this book. The real issue was whether or not to cast all the analysis in this form.

The Survey's decision to undertake an input-output analysis, as opposed to an economic base or general approach study, was based on the following considerations. One, input-output analysis is a relatively new analytical technique. Conceptually, it has great possibilities. Yet, it had never been applied to a major metropolitan area using direct source data, that is, data gathered specifically for that purpose. As an intellectual venture, then, it seemed worthwhile. Two, the information gathered, even though parts of the data might be rough, helps to provide insights into the inter-relations within the area to a greater extent than is possible through an economic base study. Thus, it is possible to indicate how economically dependent the people in one part of a metropolitan area are on those in other parts.

(The following two sections discuss the technical issues in implementing the input-output study. Readers interested only in the findings may skip to page 385.)

ST. LOUIS AREA INPUT-OUTPUT STUDY: DATA AND TECHNIQUE

STUDY AREA

The area used in this study is the St. Louis standard metropolitan area, composed of a city and four counties: St. Louis City, St. Louis County and St. Charles County in Missouri, and Madison and St. Clair counties in Illinois. The area's 1955 population was estimated at 1.8 million. Surrounded by a very sparsely populated and mainly agricultural hinterland, the area is far removed from other metropolitan areas. Very little labor mobility exists between the metropolitan area and adjacent sections. In many respects the St. Louis standard metropolitan area is a distinct, closely interrelated economic entity.

The local metropolitan economy is distinguished by its diversification. There are ten industries, each accounting for more than 4 per cent of manufacturing employment. In employment in 1955, the food and kindred products industry occupied first place, constituting about 14 per cent of the manufacturing total. Second ranking was the transportation equipment industry with about 11 per cent. The area's relatively slow growth is another important characteristic. During the first half of the present century, the population of metropolitan areas in the United States grew on the average about one and one-half times as fast as the population of the St. Louis metropolitan area.

STUDY PERIOD

The St. Louis area input-output relations pertain to the calendar year 1955. While company data were collected for this period, industry output totals were checked against the *1954 United States Census of Manufactures* and the *1954 United States Cen-*

sus of Business. There is evidence that relatively minor changes took place between 1954 and 1955. Some of them, for example, in the steel industry, were measured and adjustments made.

Basically, the reasons for selecting the year 1955 were that it is a recent and a reasonably normal period. No extreme fluctuations took place during this time, and business activity was at a relatively high level.

DATA SOURCES

At least two major sources of data can be used to implement a metropolitan area input-output study. Primary reliance could have been placed upon input-output relationships developed in the national Interindustry Relations Study for 1947.[1] Two assumptions would have had to be made: relations in the St. Louis metropolitan area and the nation are the same, and no major changes have occurred between 1947 and 1955. An alternative approach is to seek the coöperation of the various sectors of the local metropolitan economy. Various activities can be asked to abstract data from their files. Consistent with the theory underlying the model, each unit can complete its own table of inputs and outputs, and this information can be combined to indicate the transactions in the area. It should be remarked that the state and national governments are different and special estimates are needed, as discussed later.

Basically, the second method—developing local data—was used to implement the input-output study of the St. Louis metropolitan area. It was supplemented by Census and trade data in order to derive output totals for industries. For certain industries for which no local primary data could be obtained, 1947 national interindustry relations were used as a point of departure and adjusted on the basis of relevant local information. Fortunately, most of them were relatively unimportant industries.

The Survey realized that the task of preparing a company's input-output table would be a major undertaking for each firm. Consequently, the heads of Washington and St. Louis universities personally invited the presidents of the major companies in the St. Louis area to a meeting. After the project had been explained,

---

[1] W. Duane Evans and Marvin Hoffenberg, "The Interindustry Relations Study for 1947," *The Review of Economics and Statistics*, XXXIV (May, 1952); "Industry Reports: General Explanations," U.S. Bureau of Labor Statistics, *BLS Report No. 9* (Washington: 1953); and "General Explanations of the 200 Sector Tables," U.S. Bureau of Labor Statistics, *BLS Report No. 33* (Washington: 1953).

each industrial leader agreed to assign a key official to work with the Survey staff for a period of approximately three months in preparing the needed information. In this fashion, the active coöperation and participation of virtually all large employers and many smaller ones were secured.

To assure uniformity in reporting, each company representative was given a set of instructions and a booklet into which company input-output data were to be placed. Each company recorded its inputs and outputs as originating from and flowing to fifty industrial sectors and also differentiated between industrial sectors inside and outside the local metropolitan area.

Meetings were held in which these instructions were explained to groups of ten to twelve company representatives and related to their particular industries. About fifteen companies were assigned to a specific staff member, who checked weekly with and assisted each company representative. Questions, answers, and comments were recorded to keep a running account of the data collection phase. Completed input-output tables were checked by the staff for accuracy, completeness, and consistency.

Because the central focus of the Metropolitan St. Louis Survey was governmental organization and operations in the City-County area, extensive field work on its local governments was undertaken early. The City and County contain about 75 per cent of the population of the standard metropolitan area, and the fiscal data collected about its many governments, especially for 1955, were valuable to the Survey's input-output study.

THE CLASSIFICATION SYSTEM

The St. Louis area interindustry flow table (matrix) divides the economy by location of transactions and by economic sectors participating in the transactions. The geographical classification system divides transactions into those that do and those that do not take place within the metropolitan area. This classification helps to distinguish among three types of transactions, which can be summarized as local, export, and import sections. (In theory, there is a fourth section, nonlocal sales to nonlocal sectors. This matrix is of little interest to regional analysis and is virtually beyond implementation.)

The three relevant matrices are defined as follows:

1) The *local matrix* represents local sales to local sectors.

2) The *import matrix* represents nonlocal sales to local sectors.

3) The *export matrix* represents local sales to nonlocal sectors.

In terms similar to the two previous examples (pp. 370–371), this classification may be illustrated as follows:

		From		
		M	A	X
	M	.2	.1	12
To	A	.1	0	3
	I	.4	.1	

This matrix uses exports (X) instead of the households as the final demand sector. It also indicates that part of the needed inputs comes in the form of imports (I). For example, St. Louis area manufactures (M) in producing a dollar's worth of output require, reading down the column, .2 dollars of inputs from other St. Louis area manufactures, .1 dollars of the inputs from the local agricultural sector, and .4 dollars of inputs imported (I) from outside the St. Louis area.

The industrial classification system divides the economy into an appropriate number of identifiable sectors. Economic activity in the St. Louis area was analyzed, consistent with the national Interindustry Relations Study for 1947, whose classification conforms to the *Standard Industrial Classification Manual,* prepared by the Office of Statistical Standards of the United States Bureau of the Budget, and thus to most official national governmental reports. Fifteen manufacturing sectors were identified as sufficiently important to the local metropolitan economy to warrant separate treatment. All additional manufacturing was lumped together into a further sector, miscellaneous manufacturing. Eleven nonmanufacturing sectors were identified, in addition to the household sector, three government sectors—national, state, and local—and gross private capital formation. The industrial classification system used in the St. Louis area input-output study divides the local economy into thirty-three industrial sectors.

Table 50 presents the 33 sectors and relates them to the 50- and 192-industry classifications of the Interindustry Relations Study for 1947. Also the component industries of each sector are given.

TABLE 50

INDUSTRY CLASSIFICATION OF ST. LOUIS METROPOLITAN AREA
AND INTERINDUSTRY RELATIONS STUDY FOR 1947

St. Louis metro. area industry sector number	St. Louis Metro. Area 33-industry classification	BLS industry sector number	BLS 50-industry classification	BLS 192-industry classification
1	Food and kindred products	2	Food and kindred products	Meat packing and wholesale poultry; dairy products; canning, preserving, and freezing; grain mill products; bakery products; sugar; alcoholic beverages; miscellaneous food products
2	Textiles and apparel	4	Textile mill products	Spinning, weaving, and dyeing; special textile products; jute; linen, cordage, and twine; canvas products; apparel and house furnishings and other nonapparel
		5	Apparel	
3	Lumber and furniture	6	Lumber and wood products	Logging; sawmills; planing and veneer mills plywood; fabricated wood products; wooden containers and cooperage; wood furniture; metal furniture; partitions, screens, shades, etc.
		7	Furniture and fixtures	
4	Paper and allied products	8	Paper and allied products	Pulp mills; paper and paperboard mills; converted paper products
5	Printing and publishing	9	Printing and publishing	Printing, publishing, and allied products
6	Chemicals	10	Chemicals	Industrial inorganic chemicals; industrial organic chemicals; plastics materials; synthetic fiber; synthetic rubber; explosives; drugs and medicines; soap and related products; paints and allied products; gum and wood chemicals; fertilizers, vegetable oils; animal oils; miscellaneous chemical industries
7	Products of petroleum and coal	11	Products of petroleum and coal	Crude petroleum and natural gas; petroleum products; coke and products; paving and roofing materials
8	Leather products	13	Leather products	Leather tanning and finishing; other leather products; footwear (except rubber)
9	Iron and steel	15	Iron and steel	Iron ore mining; blast furnaces; steel works and rolling mills; iron and steel forging
10	Nonferrous metals	16	Nonferrous metals	Copper mining; lead and zinc mining; bauxite mining; other metal mining; primary copper; copper rolling and drawing; primary lead; primary zinc; primary metals, n.e.c.; nonferrous metal rolling; aluminum rolling and drawing; secondary nonferrous metals; nonferrous foundries
11	Fabricated metal products	17	Plumbing and heating supplies	Metal plumbing; heating equipment; structural metal products; boiler shop products; tin cans and other tinware; cutlery; tools and general hardware, n.e.c.; metal stampings; metal coating and engraving; lighting fixtures; fabricated wire products; metal barrels, drums, etc.; tubes and foils; miscellaneous fabricated metal products; steel springs; nuts, bolts, and screw machine products
		18	Fabricated structural	
		19	Other fabricated metal products	

TABLE 50 (Continued)

St. Louis metro. area industry sector number	St. Louis metro. area 33-industry classification	BLS industry sector number	BLS 50-industry classification	BLS 192-industry classification
12	Machinery	20	Agricultural, mining, and construction machinery	Farm tractors; farm equipment; construction and mining machinery; oil field machinery and tools; machine tools and metal working machinery; cutting tools, jigs, and fixtures; steam engines and turbines; internal combustion engines; special industrial machinery pumps and compressors; elevators and conveyors; blowers and fans; power transmission equipment; industrial machinery, n.e.c.; commercial machines and equipment; refrigeration equipment; valves and fittings; ball and roller bearings machine shops; electrical appliances
		21	Metal working machinery	
		22	Other machinery (except electric)	
13	Electrical machinery	23	Motors and generators	Motors and generators; radio and related products; wiring devices and graphite products; electrical measuring instruments; transformers; electrical welding apparatus; insulated wire and cable; engine electrical equipment; electric lamps and appliances; tubes; communication equipment; storage batteries; X-ray apparatus
		24	Radios	
		25	Other electrical machinery	
14	Motor vehicles	26	Motor vehicles	Motor vehicles; truck trailers; automobile trailers
15	Other transportation equipment	27	Other transportation equipment	Aircraft and parts; ships and boats; locomotives; railroad equipment; motorcycles and bicycles
16	Miscellaneous manufacturing	1	Agriculture and fisheries	Meat animals and products; poultry and eggs; dairy products; food grains and field crops; cotton; tobacco; oil-bearing crops; vegetables and fruit; all other agricultural; fisheries, hunting, and trapping; tobacco manufactures; tires and inner tubes; miscellaneous rubber products; stone, sand, clay, and abrasives; sulfur; other nonmetallic minerals; glass; cement; structural clay products; concrete and plaster products; abrasive products; asbestos products; other miscellaneous nonmetallic minerals; instruments, etc.; optical, ophthalmic, and photo equipment; medical and dental instruments and supplies; watches and clocks; jewelry and silverware; musical instruments and parts; toys and sporting goods; office supplies; plastic products; cork products; motion picture production; miscellaneous manufactured products
		3	Tobacco manufactures	
		12	Rubber products	
		14	Stone, clay, and glass products	
		28	Professional and scientific equipment	
		29	Miscellaneous manufacturing	
17	Coal, gas, electric, power, and water	30	Coal, gas, and electric power	Coal mining; electric light and power; natural, manufactured, and mixed gas
18	Railroad transportation	31	Railroad transportation	Railroads
19	Other transportation	33	Other transportation	Trucking; other water transportation; air transportation; pipeline transportation; local and highway transportation; warehousing and storage
20	Trade	34	Trade	Wholesale trade; retail trade

TABLE 50 (Continued)

St. Louis metro. area industry sector number	St. Louis metro. area 33-industry classification	BLS industry sector number	BLS 50-industry classification	BLS 192-industry classification
21	Communications	35	Communications	Telephone and telegraph
22	Finance and insurance, real estate and rentals	36	Finance and insurance	Banking, finance, and insurance; real estate and rental
		37	Rental	
23	Business and personal services	38	Business services	Advertising, including radio and television; business services; hotels; laundries and dry cleaning; other personal services; automobile repair services and garages; other repair services; medical, dental, and other professional services; motion pictures and other amusements
		39	Personal and repair services	
		41	Amusements	
24	Medical, educational, and nonprofit organizations	40	Medical, educational, and nonprofit organizations	Nonprofit institutions
25	Undistributed	42	Scrap and miscellaneous industries	Waste products, metal; waste products, nonmetal; undistributed
		43	Undistributed	
26	Eating and drinking	44	Eating and drinking places	Eating and drinking places
27	Capitalized construction and maintenance	45	New construction and maintenance	Construction
28	Households	50	Households	Households
29	Local government	48	Government	State and local government
30	Inventory change	46	Inventory change	Inventory change
31	Federal government	48	Government	Federal government
32	State government	48	Government	State and local government
33	Gross private capital formation	49	Gross private capital formation	Producer durables

For example, sector 2 (textiles and apparel) of the Survey's study is an aggregate of sectors 4 (textile mill products) and 5 (apparel) of the 50-industry classification. They in turn are aggregates of spinning, weaving, and dyeing; special textile products; jute; linen, cordage, and twine; canvas products; apparel and house furnishings and other nonapparel, all industries identified in the 192-industry classification.

In implementing the industrial classification system, four different criteria could be used—commodity, establishment, activity, or process. As in the 1947 study, the establishment criterion was principally used, since it was most applicable to the local situation.

One of the problems in the empirical application of input-output analysis is estimating control totals. In essence, the problem is to estimate the total output of the various sectors given in table 50. In addition, it is necessary to know the disposition of the output. What, for example, is the total output of the food and kindred products sector? How is it distributed among various users of food and kindred products—some in the St. Louis metropolitan area, others outside?

ESTIMATING OUTPUT AND CONTROL TOTALS

Aside from collecting primary financial data from local companies, output totals for each sector were estimated with the help of Census and trade association data. These estimates were designed to (1) check the primary output data and (2) gauge the adequacy of the sample data obtained for a sector in which only part of the firms coöperated in the study.

Estimates of control totals were based on numerous data sources including employment, wages, production, value added by manufacture, sales, and value of shipment. They were gathered from the *1954 United States Census of Manufactures* and the *1954 United States Census of Business*, trade associations, and other sources.

In the absence of Census data for the metropolitan area's value of shipments, one method was used extensively to estimate control totals of the manufacturing sectors. It utilized the ratio of value of shipments (sales) to the value added of a specific industry in Missouri. (Value added is the difference between a firm's sales and the cost of purchases from other firms.) This ratio then was applied to the metropolitan area's value added by manufacture. In this way an estimate was derived of the value of shipments of an industry in the St. Louis metropolitan area.

This method seemingly produced reasonable estimates. It assumes that in 1954 there was no significant difference between Missouri's and the St. Louis area's value of shipments and value added relationships. The overwhelming importance of the St. Louis metropolitan area in the industrial life of the state of Missouri makes this a reasonable assumption. In 1954 the Missouri portion of the St. Louis metropolitan area accounted for more than one-half of Missouri's employment in manufacturing and almost 57 per cent of value added by manufacture. Value added by manufacture in the entire St. Louis metropolitan area amounted to about 75 per cent of that of Missouri.

This method was employed extensively to estimate control totals of the manufacturing sectors, but other sectors required different methods. For instance, agricultural output was estimated from the *1954 United States Census of Agriculture* figure of value of farm products sold. Adjustments for inventory changes and on-farm use were made. (Agriculture is a component of sector 16 in the classification made for the St. Louis area study.)

The *1954 United States Census of Business,* supplemented by trade information on professional services, was the basis for the control total estimate of business and personal services. From the same source, control totals for eating and drinking places were estimated. On the other hand, trade information and publications of the Interstate Commerce Commission were the major sources of information on railroad and other transportation. The calculation of control totals for the final demand sectors as well as households and local governments will be discussed separately in a section dealing with these sectors.

Control totals derived in this manner were compared with aggregate output data prepared by local companies. For some sectors company data covered the entire sector. In others the reporting firm's output had to be "blown up" on the basis of employment data in order to obtain an estimate of the sector's total. The two sets of data were then compared and adjusted to produce a reasonable total.

CONSTRUCTION OF THE INPUT-OUTPUT TABLE

The St. Louis area input-output table is largely a composite of the input-output tables of local firms, with independently derived control totals being used to check and adjust total outputs. The input-output tables of local firms, after careful checking (for instance, against their 1955 annual statements), were aggregated into industrial sector tables. In those sectors in which virtually all firms reported input-output information, a complete sector table was obtained after output totals were compared and, where they did not jibe, reconciled with the independently estimated control totals.

In sectors where some firms did not reply, it was necessary to estimate the entire sector from those who did respond. The estimates were made on the assumption that the reporting firms were representative of all firms in the sector. Although it is difficult to assess the adequacy of this assumption, it appears to be met more by some sectors than by others. For example, there was evidence that the input-output table of one gray-iron foundry could well represent the structural relations of all twenty gray-iron foundries in the area.

In a few subsectors for which no local firms prepared input-output tables, a rather complicated method was used. The production coefficients of these industries, as given in the national input-output table for 1947, were used as the base. They were adjusted in the light of recognizable dissimilarities in the area's production techniques, marketing practices, and industrial differences. In deciding whether inputs originated inside or outside the area, the area breakdown of the same inputs to similar industries was relied upon as a guide. Outputs were treated similarly.

GOVERNMENT SECTOR

Developing relevant data on the combined national, state, and local government sector posed some special problems. Inputs of each government subsector represent the purchases of goods and services by those governments. For all levels of government, new public construction and maintenance were considered to have been purchased from the construction industry.

Local government input data were readily available. A substantial number of representative municipal governments and school districts and one county government prepared input-output tables in great detail.

Current expenditures of state government in the St. Louis metropolitan area were primarily in the form of office operations, maintenance activities, and welfare payments. With the help of state officials, total expenditure figures were estimated and inputs allocated to industrial sectors.

National government inputs were determined by detailed study of the operations and purchases of the national government in the St. Louis metropolitan area. The estimate of payments to households proved to be most difficult, since many federal agencies make such payments without keeping records containing useful geographical breakdowns.

Outputs of the various governments are represented by the total tax bills paid by the different sectors.

Analysis of the tax system and structure of each government sector made possible a separation of the amount of taxes paid by households and nonhouseholds (business and industry). These latter tax payments were allocated according to the sectors' employment. In most cases it was possible to check the output of a specific government sector to a particular industrial sector. The counterpart to this entry was the industrial sector's tax payment to the particular government, information derived from company data.

HOUSEHOLD SECTOR

Another difficult sector is households. Household inputs take the form of personal consumption expenditures, direct personal taxes, and personal savings, which are allocated to gross private capital formation and to government capital formation and current deficits. Household outputs are represented by payments to individuals, including depreciation of businesses and other capital consumption allowances. Specifically, the household output is a composite of wages and salaries (including bonuses and retirement benefits), depreciation, interest, dividends, noncorporate profits, retained earnings, and various subsidy payments.

In the absence of an appropriate consumer purchase study for the St. Louis metropolitan area, the following approach was used to estimate total household input and output, and allocate it to industrial and geographical sectors.

The national Interindustry Relations Study for 1947 was taken as the point of departure. The input percentages of households by industrial sectors were calculated. To estimate total household inputs in the St. Louis metropolitan area, the assumption was made that, in 1947, about 70 per cent of total United States household demand had originated in urban households. On this assumption, 1947 United States urban household inputs were estimated. With the help of an estimate of the percentage of all urban families residing in the St. Louis area, 1947 household inputs in the St. Louis metropolitan area were estimated. This 1947 estimate was adjusted for population growth as well as price and income changes to give a first estimate of 1955 St. Louis area household inputs. This total input estimate was tentatively divided among the various industrial sectors in conformity with the 1947 national relationship.

From the *Study of Consumer Expenditures, Incomes and Savings,* it was learned that in 1950 the annual consumption of a St. Louis area family tended to exceed that of the average urban family by about $100.[2] After this amount was adjusted to reflect income changes between 1950 and 1955, it was distributed among the industrial sectors in which local demand exceeded the average national demand. The total input was accordingly adjusted to produce a refined estimate of 1955 St. Louis area household demand, excluding personal savings.

Inputs were divided as originating inside and outside the St. Louis metropolitan area on the basis of detailed investigations about which goods and services can be locally produced and which have to be imported. The output of St. Louis area households was derived for the different industrial sectors on the basis of sector information on payments to households. Checks were made with the data of the *1954 United States Census of Manufactures, 1954 United States Census of Business,* and the United States Department of Commerce publication, *Personal Income by States Since 1929.*

THE RECONCILIATION PROCESS

Input-output relations require a consistent set of figures. A change in one estimate alters values all the way down the line. The problem of consistency is technically the "reconciliation process." Readers less interested in the technical aspects may skip this discussion.

An input-output table is a double-entry table where every cell stands for an input as well as an output. The same cell can be looked upon as being occupied by an input figure derived from the input pattern of a specific industry stated at the head of the column and an output figure derived from the output pattern of an industry stated at the beginning of the row. The two figures should be the same. Except for a few cases, these two figures in the St. Louis area model are independently estimated and can therefore differ from each other. If there is a difference, reconciliation is needed. About the same problem was faced by the Interindustry Relations Study for 1947.

The reconciliation process is an iterative or repetitive one. Re-

---

[2] Wharton School of Finance and Commerce (Philadelphia: University of Pennsylvania Press, 1957).

vision in any one cell requires reconciliation in many cells of the same row and column. At each stage of revision, the row and column totals have to be equated and made consistent through appropriate adjustments in the unallocated row and column entries. Further adjustments are needed to balance the income and product sides in a gross national product sense.

To start with, sector 1, which consists of food and kindred products, was analyzed. Each input entry of this sector was compared with the recorded output entries of the other industrial sectors flowing into sector 1. The comparison was in terms of both industrial sectors and inside and outside the area detail. In all cases, data based on company records were assumed superior in quality to other types. In addition, discrepancies were checked as to origin, and adjustments were made after careful investigation. Input column 1 was taken up by this method. This was followed by a reconciliation of column 2 data and then row 2 data, and so on. As this process proceeded, the number of cells subject to reconciliation declined until all column and row data were reconciled.

THE 1955 ST. LOUIS METROPOLITAN AREA TRANSACTION STRUCTURE

Appendix table F1 presents the over-all flows for the St. Louis area in 1955. The local relations are presented on pages 460–465, and the exports outside the area are presented on pages 466–471. Consideration of various industries will show the use of this table.

For industry 2, textiles and apparel, reading across the rows, consider the entries under column 6, the chemical industry (p. 461). The entry, $253,000 (000 and the dollar sign are omitted from all entries), signifies that the textile industry in the St. Louis area sold that much of its output to the chemical industry in the St. Louis area. Take another entry. Column 20 (p. 463), reading down, shows how much was spent by the trade sector (such as department and hardware stores) during the year. The second entry, $211,000, indicates that the trade sector purchased this amount from the textile and apparel industry of the area. Farther down column 20, the entry of $481,992,000 denotes the wages paid households for labor services performed for the trade sector. (Households, are treated as an industry.) Other entries are read the same way. (It should not bother the reader if some of the entries are not meaningful, for example, gross private capital formation. Those not acquainted with input-output will have some difficulty in following this type of entry. For present purposes, such an entry may be ignored.)

The advantage of appendix table F1 is that it offers some estimates of the magnitudes involved in the St. Louis area economy. For example, household income of $3.8 billion, the total of row 28 (p. 465), is derived from a number of sources, which can be compared.

Table F1, by a technical process that need not be of concern here, can be converted into a table of technical coefficients, which has been done in appendix table F2. Again, a few examples will indicate the nature of the information contained in this table (pp. 472–476).

By going down the columns, revealing information is provided. Consider food and kindred products. The second entry, .003869, tells that in order to produce a dollar's worth of output, the food and kindred products industry must buy .003869 dollar's worth of inputs (materials of various kinds) from the textile and apparel industry in the St. Louis area. Farther down column 1, the entry .144564 indicates that a dollar's output of food and kindred products requires the use (input) of 14.4564 cents' worth of labor (household). The columns need not add up to one dollar, as imports from outside the metropolitan area are not included in the processing sector data.

By use of another tool, the inverse matrix, appendix table F3 may be derived, giving the direct and indirect requirements to meet a given final demand. Again, the technical aspects may be omitted. In order to see what the table presents, it is necessary to point out one kind of interrelationship that input-output analysis handles.

Suppose final demand for St. Louis area chemicals rises by one dollar, for some reason. Part of this sales dollar received by the St. Louis area chemical industry is paid to clerks as wages. And these workers use their wages to buy more goods, some of which contain chemicals produced in the St. Louis area. Again, part of this is increased wages, and so it goes. It is clear that an increase of one dollar in chemical sales will cause more than a dollar's increase when all these ramifications are taken into account. Appendix table F3 (pp. 477–481) takes them into account, that is, it indicates the direct and indirect effects of a given change in final demand.

Consider the printing and publishing industry, which is row 5.

Suppose its sales to a group of firms in New York go up by one dollar. What is the total impact on the printing and publishing industry in the St. Louis area? Total output will go up at least one dollar, but when all rounds of spending and interactions are taken care of (as in the foregoing chemical industry example), total output will go up another 11.4 cents, as seen from the entry 1.114245 in row 5, column 5.

What happens to the income of households? Row 5, column 28 (p. 481), gives the answer. Income goes up by 87.4 cents. Note that in table F2, not table F3, the entry under column 5, row 28 (p. 473), is 44.7 cents. Thus, the direct impact of the increase in a dollar sale of printing and publishing is 44.7 cents. By the time households get through spending this additional income and the printing and publishing industry has placed further orders for supplies from St. Louis area firms, and they, in turn, have placed further orders, and so on, total income to households has gone up not only by the original 44.7 cents of table F2, but also by an additional amount so that the total is 87.4335 cents—table F3, column 28, row 5. This is a form of income multiplier. Persons interested in the economic base approach will recognize this as a form of the base; that is, an increase in basic activity of 44.7 cents gives rise to a total dollar increase in household income of 87.4 cents—the basic to nonbasic ratio being almost one to one in terms of dollars.

By its very nature, the Survey's input-output study involved enormous statistical calculations and field work. As much of the pay-off for such an undertaking comes at the level of basic research, the methods and problems encountered are well worth reporting.

The study furnishes the means of seeing the impact of industrial change on the St. Louis area economy as a whole and in particular sectors. Through its use the relations of any specific industry or set of industries can be determined. In addition, the information is useful in projections, the subject treated next in this volume.

17

Projections:

Governmental Expenditures, Economic Activity, and Population

BASICALLY, the Survey prepared projections so as to get an indication of the magnitude of growth that can be expected and with which local governments will have to cope. Specifically, estimates of magnitudes for 1965 were made for (1) governmental expenditures, relying in part on the multiple regression technique, and (2) sectors of the economy and the population, largely using input-output techniques.

PROJECTING LOCAL GOVERNMENTAL EXPENDITURES

The first projection is concerned with estimating governmental expenditures in the City-County area in 1965. The reader is asked to recall the basic concepts used in chapter 14 in the multiple regression study of the factors affecting the per capita expenditures for specific functions. Multiple regression analysis is the basis for this projection.

METHOD

Projecting local governmental expenditures on the basis of multiple regression analysis of cross-section data (that is, on the basis of per capita expenditure relations discussed in chapter 14) involves the following steps:

1) The per capita expenditure relations of a recent year are estimated.

2) These relations are adjusted to reflect changes that are expected to come about between the recent period and the period to which expenditures are to be projected.

3) Estimates are made of the values of the independent variables for the period to which the projection is intended—for example, service level to be required in the future and future fiscal ability.

4) By placing these estimates into the expenditure relations, per capita expenditures of a specific service can be projected.

5) To project total expenditures for the specific service, population projections are prepared. These population projections are multiplied by the per capita expenditure projection.

6) By making similar projections for the various local governmental services and aggregating them, a projection of total local governmental expenditures is obtained.

The first five steps will be illustrated briefly in relation to a ten-year projection of expenditure levels for police protection in St. Louis County:

1) The 1955–56 per capita expenditure relations on police protection are given by the following equation:

$$X_1 = -5.248 + 0.030X_5 + 0.0658X_6 + 0.958X_9 + 0.00214X_{10}.$$

(For the technical reader: the inference aspects of the problem are neglected for simplicity's sake. Otherwise, standard errors of prediction and prediction bands would have to be considered.) The meaning of X_1, X_5, X_6, X_9, and X_{10} will become clear in step 3 below.

2) It will be assumed that no major changes in the basic relations and price and wage levels will come about during the period of projection. Thus, the above expenditure relation does not need to be modified.

3) In 1955–56, X_5 = per cent of nonwhites, was 2.0,

X_6 = per cent of population under 25 years of age, was 39.8,

X_9 = index of quality of police protection, was 3.78, and

X_{10} = average per capita assessed valuation of real property, was \$1,750.

A figure for X_1, per capita police expenditures for 1955–56, is obtained by inserting these values into the equation. That figure is \$4.35.

On the basis of demographic and land-use studies, it was concluded that by 1965 the percentage of nonwhites in St. Louis County will decline to about 1.8 per cent and the population under 25 years of age will have increased to 41 per cent. In the expectation that the recommendation of the Metropolitan St. Louis Survey to have the St. Louis County police department render police services to all communities with less than 4,000 inhabitants would be implemented by 1965, the quality of police protection was expected to improve to a rating of 4.1. Finally, on the basis of employment and income projections, average per capita assessed valuation of real property is expected to be $2,200 in 1965.[1]

4) Placing these parameters into the expenditure equation projects the 1965 per capita expenditure level for police protection: $X_1 = -5.248 + 0.030\ (1.8) + 0.0658\ (41) + 0.958\ (4.1) + 0.00214\ (2,200) = \$6.20$. (Compared to the $4.35 per capita expenditure in 1955, the projected $6.20 would mean a 43 per cent increase.)

5) Population projections indicate a 1965 population for St. Louis County of 815,000. Multiplying this population projection by the projected per capita expenditures for police protection results in a projected 1965 expenditure for police protection in St. Louis County of $5,053,000. (Compared to the 1955 total expenditures of $2,392,000, a 111 per cent increase is projected.)[2]

This general method was used to project 1965 current local governmental expenditures for the St. Louis City-County area. These projections indicated the general magnitude of the fiscal problem that will have to be faced by the people of the area. They furthermore pin-pointed the departments where the most serious expenditure increases were to be expected.

Two Approaches

A total of twenty different services were identified. The water department, airport, harbor, and wharves were excluded, since they render self-paying services. Empirical expenditure functions had been derived for only five services in the study of factors

---

[1] The projected assessed valuation assumes no major changes in the present concept and method of assessment.

[2] Instead of a single projection, it is often preferable to make a number of projections, each based upon different assumptions. For instance, separate expenditure projections can be made on the assumption of maximum, minimum, and average population and per capita expenditure levels, respectively. In this fashion at least three projections will be made. The range that comes about this way, however, should not be confused with a confidence interval. These projections are not made in an inference setting.

affecting per capita expenditure levels. These five services, however, accounted for 80 per cent of the governmental expenditures incurred in St. Louis County and 55 per cent in St. Louis City. With such a high percentage of expenditures covered by expenditure functions, two methods recommended themselves to project aggregate expenditures. One method relies upon intuitive projections for each service without an empirical expenditure function. The second method applies the weighted average per capita expenditure change of the five services to the other services for which no expenditure functions are available.

FINDINGS

Table 51 relies largely upon the first approach; per capita expenditures of fifteen services are projected on an intuitive basis. When these projections are combined with those for five services which are based on multiple regression equations, a total ten-year per capita expenditure increase of 19.3 per cent is projected for St. Louis City and of 45.6 per cent for St. Louis County.

The second approach assumes that the per capita expenditure increase for the five services for which multiple regression equations have been computed will hold also for the other services. Based on this approach, an increase of 9.5 per cent for St. Louis City and 39.6 per cent for St. Louis County is projected for 1955–65.

Projections based on the two approaches produce almost identical results for St. Louis County. There is a difference in the projection for St. Louis City, which partly stems from the fact that City expenditures for health, hospitals, and debt service are likely to increase at a much more rapid rate than those for the five services for which multiple regression equations have been computed. Consequently, the per capita expenditure increases in St. Louis City are likely to be closer to 19 per cent than 9 per cent.

Multiplying the per capita expenditures of 1955 by the projected percentage increases yields projections of per capita expenditures for 1965. Relying on the data obtained by the first method, the per capita projections for St. Louis City are $116.44 and for St. Louis County $118.21. In view of projected population figures, total expenditures are expected to be in excess of $96 million for both St. Louis City and St. Louis County by 1965. Compared to the St. Louis City-County area expenditures of $127,595,742 in 1955, the City plus County total of about

TABLE 51

PROJECTION OF CURRENT EXPENDITURES AND DEBT SERVICE FOR SERVICES RENDERED BY LOCAL GOVERNMENTS IN ST. LOUIS CITY AND ST. LOUIS COUNTY (EXCLUDING MAJOR CAPITAL EXPENDITURES),[a] 1955 AND 1965

(In 1955 dollars)

Item	St. Louis City area				St. Louis County area			
	1955 Per capita expenditure	Expected 1965 per capita expenditure[b]	1955 Total expenditure	Expected 1965 total expenditure	1955 Per capita expenditure	Expected 1965 per capita expenditure	1955 Total expenditure	Expected 1965 total expenditure
Police protection	$12.44	$12.81	$10,578,213	$10,630,000	$ 4.35	$ 6.20	$ 2,392,500	$ 5,053,000
Fire protection	6.85	7.06	5,823,472	5,860,000	3.49	3.77	1,919,550	3,073,000
Roads	2.60	5.57	2,208,284	4,620,000	10.05	17.50	5,527,500	14,262,000
Refuse collection	2.67	2.75	2,266,300	2,280,000	3.72	4.05	2,046,000	3,301,000
Library	1.60	1.65	1,358,845	1,370,000	.71	.85	390,500	693,000
Parks and recreation	5.22	5.38	4,433,659	4,470,000	.26	1.00	143,000	815,000
General government	5.59	5.76	4,747,352	4,780,000	4.84	6.00	2,662,000	4,890,000
Judiciary	2.09	2.15	1,778,610	1,780,000	.70	.70	385,000	570,000
Sheriff	.39	.40	331,315	332,000	.58	.58	319,000	473,000
Jail	.61	1.03	515,576	855,000	.09	.20	49,500	163,000
Coroner	.11	.12	96,836	99,600	.05	.05	27,500	41,000
Constable	0.00	0.00	0	0	.45	.45	247,500	367,000
Health and hospital	14.50	20.60	12,323,518	17,100,000	2.94	4.00	1,617,000	3,260,000
Welfare	1.28	1.32	1,086,306	1,100,000	1.00	1.10	550,000	897,000
Sanitation	2.65	2.73	2,252,880	2,270,000	1.09	1.50	599,500	1,222,000
Civil defense	.10	.10	87,001	83,000	.05	.05	27,500	41,000
Building inspection	.54	.77	462,450	639,000	.53	.53	291,500	432,000
Other regulation	2.21	2.28	1,883,824	1,890,000	.04	.04	22,000	33,000
Total City and County current expenses	61.45	72.48	52,234,441	60,158,000	34.94	48.57	19,217,000	39,585,000
City and County debt service	5.62	7.37	4,770,000	6,120,000	2.26	5.25	1,243,000	4,279,000
Total City and County current expenditure, debt service	67.07	79.85	57,004,441	66,278,000	37.20	53.82	20,460,000	43,863,000
Sewer service	.83	2.12	702,119	1,760,000	.11	1.91	62,800	1,557,000
Sewer debt	.18	.63	94,200	523,000	.77	.90	423,000	734,000
Total sewer expenses	1.01	2.75	796,319	2,283,000	.88	2.81	485,800	2,290,000

Education:								
Current expenditure	28.25	29.68[c]	23,995,200	24,630,000	37.73	42.31[c]	20,749,080	34,483,000
Debt service	1.34	1.41[c]	1,138,300	1,170,000	5.39	16.46[c]	2,966,602	13,415,000
Total education	29.59	31.09	25,133,500	25,810,000	43.12	58.77	23,715,682	47,898,000
Over-all total	97.57	116.44	82,934,260	96,640,000	81.20	118.21	44,661,482	96,341,000
		+19.3%		+16.5%		+45.6%		+115.8%

^a Certain services that yield a profit and are not common throughout the area, such as water utilities and airports, are excluded from the analysis. It is based on a County population of 550,000 in 1955 and 815,000 in 1965, and a City population of 850,000 in 1955 and 830,000 in 1965. Services accounted for make up 81 per cent of total expenditures in 1955 including capital outlay and about 88 per cent of total current expenditures plus debt service.

^b An adjustment was made for the 1965 per capita expenditure for the City. Per capita expenditures were increased across the board by 3 per cent to allow for the decrease in population because of doubt that total expenditures would decrease with so slight a decrease in population.

^c The debt service figure was computed by taking the average per pupil in ADA capital outlay per year, retiring 5 per cent per year and assuming a rate of interest of 3.1 per cent for the first five years and 3.2 per cent for the second five years. Total bonded indebtedness was computed for each year and related to debt service costs. Both debt service costs and current costs were computed on a per pupil in ADA basis, using 1965 estimates of total pupils in ADA based on population projections. For the County this means that there will be a slight increase in the proportion of pupils in ADA to total population and for the City a slight decrease. Per pupil in ADA costs for both the City and the County assume an increase in the average level or quality of education offered. This increase, 1955 to 1965, is from 1.05 to 1.20 for the County and .98 to 1.20 for the City. Total costs for the City and County were obtained by multiplying the per pupil in ADA costs by the number of pupils anticipated for the year 1965. Per person costs were then computed by dividing this total by the anticipated 1965 population. These data also assume a slightly increasing ratio of the number of pupils in ADA to the number of persons of school age.

$193 million expenditures expected in 1965 constitutes a 51 per cent increase. These projections of an expenditure increase of almost $66 million assume no change in the 1955 price and wage level. If allowance is made for prospective price and wage level changes, the $66 million figure increases to about $85 million.

In addition to current expenditures and debt service, there are capital outlays that sometimes must be projected. In growing suburban areas capital outlays for school buildings are especially heavy. On the basis of projected needs and financial ability, capital outlays for schools in St. Louis County were projected to add up to $200 million during the period 1955–1965. In comparison to this figure, capital outlays for schools in St. Louis City will be quite small. For this reason, the per capita differential in school expenditures between the City and the County is expected to widen, as shown in table 51.

Of particular interest to the Survey is the vast projected increase in expenditures for roads. With per capita expenditures in the City expected to increase over 100 per cent and those in the County by 75 per cent, serious problems could arise. These large increases in expenditures point up quite vividly the need for City-County coördination in highway construction. Such coördination was one objective of the Survey's recommendations relating to the authority of the metropolitan district government over an area-wide road system.

PROJECTING GENERAL ECONOMIC ACTIVITY

The input-output model of the St. Louis metropolitan area can be used, among other purposes, to attempt economic and population projections. This was accomplished by first projecting the St. Louis area's final demand for 1965 on the basis of detailed industry studies. On the assumption that the technical (production) coefficients will not change from 1955 to 1965—and this admittedly is an assumption which will need to be taken into account when results are appraised—1965 inputs and outputs of each sector can be estimated.

With the help of empirical employment-output relations, which are based on time-series data of local companies as well as 1955 employment-output ratios, projected output was converted into projected employment. After projected employment was adjusted for unemployment and noncivilian labor force to produce an estimate of the total 1965 labor force, a population–labor force ratio was estimated and used to derive a population estimate for 1965. These steps will be discussed in order.

FINAL DEMAND

The input-output relations approach defines final demand sectors that are linked by structural relationships to the processing sectors. Changes in economic activity of the processing sectors are assumed to be generated by changes in final demand. In the Survey's St. Louis area model, final demand is composed of local sales to the following: gross private capital formation, national and state governments, and inventories. Each of the thirty-three nonlocal sectors is another unit. Each local industrial sector, then, faces the final demand of all or part of these thirty-four final demand sectors. For this reason it becomes necessary to estimate the final demand that can be expected to face the various local industrial sectors.

In general, final demand facing a given local industrial sector depends upon (1) national and international demand and (2) the local industry's locational advantages in relation to actual and potential markets.

To project an industry's over-all demand, it was best to start by projecting gross national product, United States population, and imports and exports. Consistent with projections of the United States commerce and labor departments, the Survey assumed a 1965 per capita gross national product of $2,941 and a population of 190.3 million, which are respective increases from 1955 of 25 per cent and 15 per cent. Detailed industry studies were made and the national demand of the industry was projected to be consistent with the gross national product and population assumptions. Key personnel of leading companies in the industry did much of the spade work in projecting their industry's demand. Continuation of the "cold war" atmosphere was assumed, as well as maintenance of United States military forces at their present level, but with rising defense expenditures due to a continued increase in the cost per member of the armed forces at the rate prevailing during the past decade. As a first approximation, continuation of the present international trade relations was assumed.

To help to determine the share of over-all 1965 demand of the St. Louis area industries, three main points were considered: (1) the general pulling powers of metropolitan areas, (2) the hinterland of metropolitan areas, and (3) the comparative advantages of industries in the St. Louis metropolitan area. These three points are considered in turn.

PULLING POWER

There are discernible general forces that tend to favor the emergence of regional economies centered around healthy and vigorous metropolitan areas. Self-sufficient regional economies are emerging within the United States, and metropolitan areas are attracting increasingly larger shares of industry. Relatively few industries still remain primarily raw material–oriented. Except for fuel, raw material costs have been declining in importance in comparison with other costs. Furthermore, with many end products requiring increasingly large numbers of material inputs from different parts of the country, plants can often be located advantageously in a number of regions. Transportation costs appear to have declined in relation to other costs.

Regional economies are also brought about by the increase in the variety of products. Many consumer goods, once offered only in a few staple lines, are today produced in a wide selection of colors, styles, accessories, and packaging. Consequently, large-scale operation is no longer as feasible as it used to be, and inventories and distribution favor manufacturing close to the market. Also, a general movement toward more uniform wages has reduced the labor orientation of industries. Skill-oriented industries are strongly pulled into metropolitan areas. Perhaps most importantly, many regional economies have grown sufficiently to offer in the near future a market large enough to warrant regional plants. In general, it was concluded that many forces are at work which attract industry.[3]

HINTERLAND

With the help of a gravitation formula, the trading region of the St. Louis metropolitan area was delineated. It was found to contain 71 counties in eastern Missouri, 30 counties in southwestern Illinois, 8 counties in northern Kentucky, and 5 counties in northern Tennessee. While these 114 counties constituted the immediate hinterland, St. Louis' industrial products found major markets in the mid-American region composed of Arkansas, Illinois, Iowa, Kansas, Kentucky, Missouri, Nebraska, Oklahoma,

[3] Raymond Vernon, "Production and Distribution in the Large Metropolis," *The Annals of the American Academy of Political and Social Science,* CCCXIV (Nov., 1957), 15–29.

and Tennessee. In general, for many decades the mid-America region has been more agricultural than the United States as a whole. The nine states' share of the national population has declined by about 22 per cent since 1870. Yet during the same period, value added by manufacturing has increased by about 28 per cent.

The present and potential markets for each local industry were investigated. This effort was carried out in conjunction with location studies.

How much of the over-all market can be captured by the local industries depends on locational considerations as well as the readiness of industries to capitalize on their advantages. Commodity experts of leading firms closely coöperated with this study to make a location study for each major industry.

First, an analysis was made of the relative importance of and expected changes in an industry's location considerations in a national setting. The relative importance of the following factors in industrial location decisions was assessed: (a) market considerations, (b) production relationships, (c) availability of material, (d) management relationships, (e) labor (wages, productivity, labor supply, labor-management relations), (f) sites and plant, (g) water rates and supply, (h) industrial fuel rates and supply, (i) electricity rates and supply, (j) waste disposal, (k) transportation facilities, (l) tax considerations, (m) availability of risk capital, and (n) distribution facilities.

Second, with the aid of industry experts, the locational advantages and disadvantages of the main industries in the St. Louis metropolitan area were determined. Here an attempt was made to duplicate the process through which industry proceeds in deciding upon the location of new plants and expansion, contraction, or abandonment of existing ones. Two important explicit assumptions were made in this connection. It was assumed that the recommendations for governmental reorganization made by the Metropolitan St. Louis Survey would be promptly implemented and the St. Louis County council would proceed to prepare a master plan and zoning ordinance which would make available a substantial portion of St. Louis County to industry.

In this fashion, the 1965 final demand facing St. Louis area's 29 processing sectors was projected. It is summarized in column 1 of table 52. In some sectors, for example textiles and apparel, about a 20 per cent decline in final demand is projected for the period 1955 to 1965. In other sectors substantial final demand increases

TABLE 52

1965 FINAL DEMAND, OUTPUT, AND EMPLOYMENT PROJECTIONS
FOR THE ST. LOUIS METROPOLITAN AREA

Industry sector	Projected 1965 final demand (000 omitted)	Projected 1965 input and output (000 omitted)	Projected 1965 percentage output changes	Expected employment per $1,000,000 output in 1965	Projected 1965 employment
	1	2	3	4	5
1. Food	$ 841,753	$1,313,264	16.5	27	35,000
2. Textiles and apparel	88,112	170,935	−5.8	100	17,100
3. Lumber and furniture	35,739	88,428	11.6	91	8,000
4. Paper	44,645	149,004	14.0	66	9,800
5. Printing and publishing	51,609	163,144	15.8	90	15,000
6. Chemicals	572,183	648,780	31.2	43	28,000
7. Products of petroleum and coal	535,321	747,787	13.7	12	9,000
8. Leather	109,342	121,168	−18.5	93	11,000
9. Iron and steel	254,520	375,964	36.6	59	22,000
10. Nonferrous metals	110,237	148,616	−1.7	46	6,800
11. Fabricated metal	99,314	264,764	18.5	108	28,600
12. Machinery (nonelectrical)	177,774	295,599	26.4	86	25,000
13. Electrical machinery	288,496	318,329	56.8	101	32,200
14. Motor vehicles	510,568	757,001	29.4	19	14,000
15. Other transportation equipment	623,715	641,102	118.7	66	42,000
16. Miscellaneous	235,072	507,370	15.1	66	33,000
17. Coal, gas, electric power, and water	44,958	238,917	20.4	67	16,000
18. Railroad transportation	242,901	408,116	10.0	64	26,000
19. Other transportation	87,257	275,112	23.8	112	30,800
20. Trade	145,304	945,414	19.9	201	190,000
21. Communications	18,815	108,193	20.4	95	10,000
22. Finance, insurance, rentals	33,565	810,200	21.3	50	41,000
23. Business and personal services	20,593	463,210	20.8	102	47,200
24. Medical, educational, and nonprofit	38,270	187,116	22.6	221	41,400
25. Undistributed	416,240	698,399	15.1	51	36,000
26. Eating and drinking places	—	215,660	22.2	102	22,000
27. Capitalized construction and maintenance	622,913	856,048	18.3	53	45,000
28. Households	505,454	4,724,689	22.1	—	—
29. Local government	1,674	252,302	21.1	155	39,100
31, 32. Federal and state government					12,000
Total					889,000

were projected. For instance, the final demand for other transportation equipment was projected to increase by about 120 per cent during this period. All projections were made in terms of 1955 prices.

INPUT AND OUTPUT PROJECTIONS

By multiplying the value in each cell of appendix table F3, which shows the direct and indirect requirements per dollar of final demand (see page 477) by the aggregate final demand of the corresponding industrial sector, and horizontally summing the values thus derived, projected 1965 inputs for each local industrial sector were obtained. Because each processing sector's projected input equals its projected output, these input totals are also output totals. They are presented in column 2 of table 52. Column 3 of table 52 shows the projected 1955–1965 percentage changes in the output of the 29 processing sectors.

EMPLOYMENT PROJECTION

Output projections can be converted into employment projections by a number of different methods. Perhaps the simplest method estimates for each sector the output per worker by dividing total employment estimates for each sector into its total gross output. The estimate thus obtained pertains to the base year and not the period for which employment is to be projected. This estimate can be improved with the help of industry specialists who can attempt to project changes and help to give an estimate of the output per worker in the future period.

Another approach relies upon an empirical employment-output function with the regression coefficient indicating the average output per worker. Company data on employment and output are aggregated to represent the entire local industrial sector for a number of years. The output data are deflated—that is, they are represented in 1955 dollars. A regression line is fitted to these time-series data. Industry specialists can help in extrapolating this regression line by indicating expected changes in the future employment-output relationship.

Both methods were used. Column 4 of table 52 presents the expected 1965 St. Louis metropolitan area employment per $1,000,000 output, while column 5 shows the 1965 projected employment of the processing sectors. The 1965 projected employment for the 29 processing sectors totals 877,000. If a 12,000 projected employment by national and state governments is added, a total projected 1965 employment of 889,000 is obtained for the St. Louis metropolitan area.

The employment projections next must be checked against the manpower pool and industrial sites that can be expected to be available in 1965. Past experience indicates that the required labor force could become available. However, there will be enough sites to make possible the projected employment increases, but only if this study's explicit assumption on early completion of a master plan and zoning ordinances to provide sites for industry is met.

POPULATION PROJECTION

An estimate of the 1965 total labor force was obtained by adding projected unemployment and noncivilian labor to the 1965 employment projection. It was not the aim of this study to predict future business cycles—a virtually impossible task—but to project long-run population changes. Thus, it was relevant to stipulate what unemployment percentage was expected in the future. Believing that the Employment Act of 1946 would continue to be implemented effectively in the future, it was assumed that 2.8 per cent of the civilian labor force would be unemployed. Furthermore, it was projected that the noncivilian labor force of the St. Louis metropolitan area would be about 28,000 in 1965.

On these assumptions, a total labor force of 943,000 was projected for the St. Louis metropolitan area for 1965. An estimate of the 1965 population–labor force ratio would make possible the calculation of the 1965 projected population.

According to the *1950 United States Census of Population* the population–labor force ratio in the St. Louis metropolitan area in that period was 2.35. This ratio can be expected to increase slowly in the near future. In 1957, the ratio for the St. Louis area was 2.38 and by 1965, it might be expected to be 2.43.

The projections, together with 1955 data, are presented in table 53. An employment of 889,000 and a 0.972 employment rate were assumed. On this basis a population of 2,290,000 was projected for 1965.

TABLE 53

EMPLOYMENT, LABOR FORCE, AND POPULATION PROJECTIONS FOR THE
ST. LOUIS METROPOLITAN AREA, 1965

Labor force	1950	1955	1965
Employed workers	676,917	746,000	889,000
Employed workers as per cent of civilian labor force	0.960	0.963	0.972
Civilian labor force	705,132	774,700	914,700
Total labor force	716,077	803,700	943,000
Population–labor force ratio	2.35	2.38	2.43
Population	1,681,281	1,913,000	2,290,000

ADJUSTED EMPLOYMENT RATIO METHOD

A number of methods may be used to check and compare projections based on the input-output relations model. One such method takes industry employment data of the metropolitan area from the most recent *United States Census of Population,* and on the basis of national projections calculates what the area's future employment would be if it were to grow at the same rates expected for the rest of the country. These ratio estimates were then modified to take account of the area's location considerations.

The data are presented in table 54, where in column 1 the 1950 United States Census employment data are given. Projections of United States employment changes for the fifteen-year period, 1950–1965, were prepared by a private research firm, and are presented in column 2. By multiplying the 1950 employment figures by the projected national employment change, 1965 ratio estimates were obtained. These estimates, which are based on the assumption that the St. Louis metropolitan area's employment changes will conform to the national ones, are recorded in column 3. On the basis of location studies of the various industries in relation to markets, the ratio estimates were adjusted to reflect the differential growth the area is expected to face; these adjusted estimates are presented in column 4.

The series of employment projections make for a most interesting comparison. It should be pointed out that both were made entirely independently, except that approximately the same information was used to project final demand as was used to modify the ratio estimates. Projected total employment is surprisingly similar regardless of method. However, as was to be expected, there are distinct discrepancies between projections for specific industries.

It must be remembered that the adjusted ratio method projects each industry's output separately. There is no way of knowing whether these employment projections are internally consistent. In other words, the method does not provide for the projected employment of one industry to be consistent with the various detailed demands other industries will make on it. On the other hand, the input-output relations method makes possible internally consistent employment projections. To the extent that an appro-

TABLE 54

EMPLOYMENT PROJECTIONS FOR ST. LOUIS METROPOLITAN AREA, 1965:
ADJUSTED EMPLOYMENT RATIO METHOD

Industry	1950 United States census	Projected 1950–1965 national employment percentage change	1965 ratio estimate	1965 adjusted ratio estimate
	1	2	3	4
Total employment	676,917	+34.3	909,099	888,000
Manufacturing	228,935	+35.7	310,585	297,700
Food and kindred products	32,888	+46.9	48,315	40,000
Textile mill products	2,343	−7.9	2,160	2,200
Apparel	17,115	+31.1	22,438	13,000
Lumber, wood, furniture, and fixtures	5,682	−32.0	3,865	5,500
Printing and publishing	12,709	−11.7	11,225	13,500
Chemicals and allied products	15,605	+52.8	23,838	24,500
Primary metals, fabricated metals, machinery, except electrical, electrical machinery equipment, automobiles, other transportation equipment	90,803	+57.9	143,355	145,000
All other manufacturing	51,790	+6.9	55,389	54,000
Nonmanufacturing	447,982	+33.6	598,514	590,300
Wholesale and retail trade, including auto repair	138,354	+31.5	181,976	179,000
Finance, insurance, and real estate	27,843	+43.4	39,917	39,000
Transportation services, telephone, telegraph, electric power, gas	68,128	+26.3	86,066	85,000
Business and repair services	15,960	+100.0	31,999	29,000
Hotels	6,286	+3.4	6,502	7,000
Personal services	34,014	+11.7	37,980	38,000
Recreation and amusement	6,156	+17.9	7,266	7,300
Professional and related services, government	86,754	+52.8	132,599	132,000
Agriculture, forestry, fisheries	13,398	−18.8	10,877	10,000
Mining	2,933	−3.1	2,843	3,000
Contract construction	35,366	+44.0	50,912	51,000
Miscellaneous	12,790	−25.1	9,577	10,000

priate input-output table and final demand projections are available, the projections will tend to be both reliable and consistent.

ADJUSTED POPULATION RATIO METHOD

Just as the adjusted employment ratio method can help check employment projections derived by the input-output method, the adjusted population ratio method helps check on population projections. To start with, the area's per cent of total United States population was computed as far back as possible. In this study this ratio was calculated from 1900 to 1950. Instead of simply extrapolating this ratio, adjustments to the extrapolated ratio can be made by studying the migration, fertility, and mortality patterns of the metropolitan area in relation to those of the United States. The greatest difficulty usually rests with the estimate of the area's migration pattern. By multiplying the projected ratio for 1965 by the projected 1965 United States population, a population estimate for the metropolitan area was derived.

Ratios for 1900 to 1950 are presented in table 55. The 1965 ratio is estimated to be 1.14 and the projected 1965 United States population is 190.3 million. The 1965 population projection for the St. Louis metropolitan area is 2.17 million. This figure is about 120,000 below the previously derived estimate.

TABLE 55

POPULATION PROJECTIONS FOR ST. LOUIS STANDARD METROPOLITAN AREA, 1965:
ADJUSTED POPULATION RATIO METHOD

Year	United States (000,000 omitted)	Ratio of area population to United States population	St. Louis standard metropolitan area (000 omitted)
1900	76.1	1.05	801
1910	92.4	1.09	1,004
1920	106.5	1.07	1,140
1930	123.1	1.10	1,360
1940	132.1	1.08	1,432
1950	151.7	1.11	1,681
1965	190.3	1.14	2,170

The population ratio method is considered rather crude and not too much faith should be placed in its results. Nevertheless, this method serves a very useful purpose. For example, it indicates that in order for the St. Louis area to have a population of about 2.29 million in 1965, its growth has to be faster than that of the rest of the nation. Furthermore, its share of the United States population will have to increase and the increase will have to be at an accelerated pace.

APPENDIXES

APPENDIX A

Working Outline of the Survey

THIS OUTLINE, prepared at the outset of the Survey's full-time research, was modified through elaborations, additions, and deletions as the work proceeded. For example, the Survey, on the basis of its judgments about the most appropriate form of metropolitan government, later decided to make recommendations about various types of local government.

All items marked by an asterisk refer to hypotheses to be tested by the sample survey of citizen opinion and participation.

I. BASIC ASSUMPTIONS

A. The governmental pattern of the St. Louis metropolitan area, especially the city of St. Louis and St. Louis County:
   1. Impairs effectiveness of services and efficiency of operation;
   2. Dilutes responsibility to the public;
   3. Impedes the orderly and healthy development of the expanding community;
   4. Lacks sufficient flexibility to meet changing conditions resulting from population shifts and economic growth;
   5. Fosters wide local variations between service needs and financial resources or ability.
B. A number of major public needs, both area-wide and local, which government is expected to meet, are not being and cannot be adequately met by the present uncoördinated pattern of government.

II. PURPOSES OF THE PROJECT

A. To prepare proposals for consideration by a City-County board of freeholders to be appointed pursuant to Art. VI, Sec. 30(a) of the Constitution of Missouri to draft a charter designed to adjust intergovernmental relations between St. Louis and St. Louis County. Such charter will become effective upon approval of a majority of the voters of the city of St. Louis and a majority of the voters of St. Louis County participating in separate elections.

B. To furnish, for consideration by citizens in other metropolitan centers:

   1. An evaluation of techniques used to gather information on metropolitan problems;
   2. An analysis of attitudes of residents in a metropolitan area, including their complaints and frustrations pertaining to governmental services and costs, and their reactions to suggested proposals for change;
   3. An analysis of referendum campaign techniques and an assessment of their effectiveness.

C. To aid in the development of a systematic conceptual framework within which research in the general field of metropolitan government may be more meaningfully conducted.

D. To increase the supply of trained research workers in metropolitan government. This end will be accomplished by actual student participation in each phase of the project and by a formal seminar conducted by the senior members of the staff. The students enrolled in the seminar will receive academic credit from one of the two local universities.

III. RESEARCH DESIGN IN RELATION TO WORKING HYPOTHESES

Points A, B, and C of the research design cover the collection of extensive data concerning all governmental units functioning in the St. Louis City-County area: ninety-six municipalities of St. Louis County, eighteen fire districts, the government of the city of St. Louis, the government of St. Louis County, the metropolitan sewer district, the Bi-State Development Agency, and the thirty school districts. The examination of school districts, however, will be confined primarily to (1) their interrelationships with the other governmental units, and (2) the factors prompting and the techniques employed in school district reorganization. Other sections of the metropolitain area will be considered to the extent that they are involved in metropolitan problems.

A. Survey of governmental jurisdictions
1. History and legal basis
2. Scope and limits of authority (legal, geographical, and functional)
3. Governmental organization and structure
4. Areas of overlapping jurisdiction
5. Nature and extent of formal and informal coöperation

HYPOTHESES

a. Widely varying reasons account for the large number of governmental units in the area.
b. Many of these units overlap, in terms of area covered and people served, resulting in conflicts of authority.
c. The multiplicity of special districts hinders annexation and consolidation movements by incorporated communities.
d. * In numerous areas and with respect to particular services, the citizens do not know what public officials to hold responsible.

B. Survey of functional services
1. Police and fire protection
2. Health and sanitation
3. Sewers
4. Streets, roads, and trafficways
5. Transit, traffic control, and parking
6. Public housing
7. Urban redevelopment and urban renewal
8. Parks and recreation
9. Planning
10. Public utilities
11. Libraries and other cultural facilities
12. Building construction supervision

HYPOTHESES

a. Functional services vary widely in their availability, adequacy, and cost among the units in the metropolitan area largely because of the existing governmental pattern.
b. Many people regularly utilize or depend upon services performed by units over which they have no direct control.
c. Many people regularly utilize or depend upon services toward which they make no direct financial contribution.

    d. The failure of particular units to perform adequately certain services adversely affects the performance of such services by other units.

    e. Deficiencies in the performance of various functions by different governments lead to serious inconveniences that are costly and time-consuming to the public.

    f. * A substantial proportion of the population is critical of the inadequate performance of one or more of these functional services.

C. Finance and revenue survey
    1. Tax structure
    2. Tax levies in relation to legal limits
    3. Debt structure
    4. Present debt in relation to legal limit
    5. Expenditure patterns
    6. Property assessments
    7. Grants-in-aid

HYPOTHESES

    a. There is wide variation in the tax burden borne by individuals and corporations on the basis of their location within the area, despite similarity in value of residence or business property.

    b. The tax burden on the individual or corporation is not consistently related to the scope and adequacy of the public services rendered.

    c. In many of the governmental units in the metropolitan area, the tax base is so small that essential public services cannot be sufficiently or economically supported.

    d. Extended services provided by the County government to some unincorporated urban areas represent an unwarranted subsidy to such areas by City residents.

    e. * The number and variety of taxing units, and the lack of correlation between taxes and services, are sources of substantial confusion and adverse criticism among taxpayers.

D. Analysis of population, land-use, and economic developments
    1. Over-all population and economic growth
    2. Population shifts area-by-area
    3. Movements of economic, ethnic, and other groups
    4. Residence and employment location

5. Factors determining industrial and commercial location and movement
6. Land-use pattern

HYPOTHESES

a. The changing social composition of the core city in recent years has diminished its financial resources.
b. The growth of population in the metropolitan area has placed a severe strain on the resources of many communities.
c. Numerous land-use policies are contradictory and uneconomic in terms of sound metropolitan development.
d. Decisions of major private organizations on industrial and commercial location have important governmental and economic repercussions upon the metropolitan area.
e. Local zoning laws have substantially affected the pattern of population movement.

E. Analysis of citizen participation and interest in government
   1. Voting participation in local, state, and national elections
   2. Composition, tenure, and background of membership in local governmental bodies and commissions
   3. Officers, activities, and influence of nongovernmental organizations

HYPOTHESES

a. Size of local government or unincorporated community does not substantially affect popular participation in local public affairs.
b. Politics in local public affairs is not limited to general government.
c. There is no adequate citizen control of metropolitan matters due to lack of any method of area-wide local participation.
d. * The concern over the solution of metropolitan problems ranks high in the value system of many metropolitan residents.

IV. CHRONOLOGY

A. Gather and collate existing data (governmental, economic, and social) selected primarily on the basis of the foregoing hypotheses.
B. Obtain from recognized leaders, groups (business, labor, ethnic, religious, political), and residents of the area their per-

ceptions, definitions, and evaluation of metropolitan problems.

C. Analyze the efforts made in other metropolitan areas to solve such problems, and assess the results.

D. Define the major problems of the St. Louis metropolitan area and formulate possible solutions. Consideration will be given to the financial consequences and political feasibility of the proposals.

E. Arrange meetings with private citizens for discussion of metropolitan problems and their possible solution.

F. Prepare and publish interim and final reports. One of the final reports will contain carefully drafted proposals designed to solve the metropolitan problems; the other will include a consideration of the methodology employed in the project.

G. Upon request, make available to the board of freeholders reports and unpublished data.

H. Make a continuing survey of operations of the board, the pressures on it, and the attitude of residents toward its proceedings.

I. Make a case study of the referendum campaign on the proposals submitted by the board of freeholders.

Summary of Recommendations of the Metropolitan St. Louis Survey

THE ST. LOUIS METROPOLITAN GOVERNMENT

I. A metropolitan government should be established for the St. Louis City–St. Louis County area. This government should have authority to

(1) designate and assume control over arterial roads and streets and related major off-street parking facilities within the area in order to establish an integrated traffic-way system,

(2) regulate all local public transit carriers,

(3) prepare and adopt a comprehensive master plan for the physical development of the area, and require all local zoning to conform substantially to it,

(4) coöperate with private groups in promoting industrial and commercial location in the City and County, and develop industrial and commercial tracts of land for lease or sale to private firms,

(5) exercise the functions—sewerage and drainage—now vested in the Metropolitan St. Louis Sewer District,

(6) assume all civil defense responsibilities in the City-County area, and

(7) take over the function of property assessment now exercised individually by the City and County governments.

II. The legislative authority of the metropolitan government should be vested in a council of twelve elected members, six from the City and six from the County, and two appointed members, one selected by the mayor of the city of St. Louis and one by the County supervisor. Three of the representatives from the City should be chosen in City-wide elections and three in single-member districts. Three members from the County should be selected in County-wide elections and three by district. The terms of office should be four years, and the elections should be on a nonpartisan basis.

III. The executive powers of the metropolitan government should be vested in a president elected at large in a nonpartisan election by the voters of the City-County area. His term of office should be four years.

A City-County board of freeholders, appointed under the provisions of Article VI, Section 30a, of the Missouri Constitution, has authority to draft a governmental plan establishing a multipurpose metropolitan district that can be endowed with the above powers. This plan will become effective when approved by separate majority votes of the people in both St. Louis City and St. Louis County.

THE BI-STATE DEVELOPMENT AGENCY

I. After the establishment of the metropolitan government, the Missouri representatives on the Bi-State Development Agency should include at least two officials of the metropolitan government.

This proposal can be adopted by amending the present state statute authorizing the Governor to appoint the Missouri representatives.

II. The Agency's revenue bonds should be made legal for investment by trusts, estates, and similar funds and the Agency should be granted specific authority to buy bridges.

These recommendations require action by the state legislatures of Missouri and Illinois and the approval of Congress.

THE MUNICIPALITIES OF ST. LOUIS COUNTY

I. The County police department should furnish specialized services to all police departments in the County. These services should include (1) central uniform record-keeping, (2) central dispatching, (3) training programs, (4) a crime detection laboratory, and (5) special criminal investigation service. The County department should also coördinate the efforts of municipal police in emergencies which require a concentration of manpower.

II. The County police department should furnish protection to the unincorporated areas of the County, to all municipalities with populations under 4,000, and to any other city or town that requests such service or fails to provide its own police protection at a minimum level of adequacy. This level should be determined by the County council with technical and professional assistance.

III. Any municipality with a population of 4,000 or more which maintains its police force at or above the minimum standard should be reimbursed by the County in an amount equal to the cost of maintaining its force at the minimum level.

IV. The County health department should extend its environmental sanitation program to all municipalities with populations of less than 15,000. Any city with a population of 15,000 or more which maintains a health program equal to or above a minimum standard should be reimbursed by the County in an amount equal to the cost of maintaining a program at the minimum level. This standard will be determined in the same manner as is provided above for establishing a standard level of police service.

V. The newly created County office of supervisor of fire and accident prevention, in addition to the duties assigned to him in the present ordinance, should be empowered to enforce a uniform safety and fire prevention code in both the incorporated and unincorporated areas of the County. The County council should be authorized to adopt such a uniform code applicable throughout the County.

The above recommendations can be achieved by the passage of a state legislative act enabling the County government (1) to perform police and health services and to enforce a uniform fire safety code within municipalities and (2) to make refunds to cities that meet minimum standards of adequacy in the performance of these services.

An amendment to the Missouri Constitution (Article X, Section 11b) will be required for the County to raise, through property taxes, the revenue required to meet the costs of its expanded services and to make the required refunds to municipalities. An amendment should be adopted which will raise the maximum tax which the County can levy for general purposes. The present maximum is 35 cents on each $100 of assessed valuation.

VI. The state laws relating to disincorporation, annexation, and consolidation should be clarified and simplified to encourage a reduction of the number of municipalities in the County.

(1) The County council should be authorized to set a date upon which each city with a population less than 4,000 would

vote on the question of disincorporation. A similar election should be provided in any city by a petition signed by 2 per cent of the qualified voters. A simple majority vote should be sufficient to accomplish the disincorporation.

(2) The County council should be authorized to propose consolidation of municipalities and to call elections on such proposals. Elections on proposed consolidations should also be required when a petition is signed by 2 per cent of the qualified voters in each municipality involved. A proposed consolidation should become effective if it is approved by both a simple majority of those voting in the area as a whole and a simple majority of those voting within each municipality involved. If a proposal receives a favorable vote in the area as a whole but fails to receive a majority within one or more of the municipalities involved, the County council should have power to (a) declare the proposal defeated, (b) declare the consolidation in effect in the municipalities where it received a favorable vote, or (c) declare the consolidation in effect within the entire area covered by the proposal.

(3) All cities, towns, and villages should be permitted to initiate proceedings to annex adjacent unincorporated territory by resolution or ordinance of their legislative bodies. The present state statute pertaining to declaratory judgments in annexation matters should be made clearly applicable to all cities, towns, and villages. The circuit court should also be permitted to consider the comparative merits of competing annexation actions.

Periodic studies of the fire protection districts in the County should be made to determine if consolidations can provide better coverage and more full-time professional departments. The County council should be given the same responsibility with respect to the consolidation of fire protection districts as has been recommended above for municipalities. A state law will be required to give the County this authority.

THE ST. LOUIS COUNTY GOVERNMENT

I. Basic changes should be made in the administrative organization of the County government.

(1) The elective offices of County clerk, highway engineer, recorder of deeds, sheriff, treasurer, collector, coroner, and public administrator should be abolished and their duties transferred to officials appointed by the chief executive.

(2) The office of chief executive should be strengthened by

extending his supervisory power to the administrative officers that are now popularly elected and by giving him essential management tools. If the County executive is to be popularly elected, as is now the case, he should be authorized to appoint a professional administrator to assist in directing and coördinating the activities of the various departments. As an alternative, the elective office of supervisor could be abolished and the executive could be appointed by the County council.

(3) An integrated department of finance should be provided to centralize the functions now performed by the County clerk, collector, treasurer, auditor, budget officer, and purchasing agent. The director of the department should be appointed by the chief executive.

(4) The four offices of constable should be abolished and their duties assigned to the sheriff's office.

(5) The merit system should be extended to all nonpolicy-forming employees.

These five changes can be accomplished through amendments to the county charter.

II. The powers of the County government should be broadened to permit it to perform municipal-type functions in both incorporated and unincorporated areas. Specific recommendations with respect to the role of the County government in police, fire, and health are made above under the heading "The Municipalities of St. Louis County."

III. The County collector should be responsible for the collection of property taxes for all municipalities. Each city and town is now required to make arrangements for its own collection.

State legislation is required to extend the powers of the County as recommended in II and III.

IV. All municipalities and fire districts should be required to file annual financial reports with the County clerk on forms specified by the County auditor. State legislation is required to effect this recommendation.

SCHOOL DISTRICTS

I. The six school districts in the County which in 1956–57 had enrollments of less than 1,500 should be combined with other districts. This can be accomplished under the present state reorganization act. Initiative for this action rests with the County board of education.

II. The County board of education should have sufficient funds to make continuing studies of reorganization needs. A change in the reorganization law should be made to provide for such expenditures out of the state school fund.

III. The County superintendent of schools should be appointed by the County board of education. At the present time he is popularly elected. An amendment to the County charter is required to make this change.

IV. A standard level of educational opportunity, measured in terms of expenditures per pupil in average daily attendance, should be assured to each school district in the County by a uniform property tax throughout the County. Any district should be permitted to provide an educational program above the standard level by levying additional taxes locally.

This recommendation requires the passage of a state law authorizing the County board of education to establish this standard level and to levy a County-wide tax sufficient to finance it. The law should also assign to the County clerk responsibility for distributing the revenue derived from the tax to local school districts.

THE CITY OF ST. LOUIS

I. The present programs of rehabilitation of slum and blighted areas and of neighborhood improvement should be extended. General municipal services must be maintained at a high level to prevent deterioration of both residential and commercial property. In order to insure sufficient revenue to maintain these programs, a thorough study of the tax structure of the City should be undertaken to determine the best means of meeting the needs.

II. The so-called county offices of the City, which are provided for and governed by state law rather than by the City charter, should be abolished and their duties assigned to City offices provided by City charter or ordinance.

This recommendation can be accomplished by a state law authorizing the City to integrate its "county" functions with its City functions and to assign them in the most efficient manner to a single set of officers.

APPENDIX C

Methodology of the Sample Survey

THE SAMPLE survey is a tool of growing importance for the study of the behavior of large human aggregates. The reason is clear. If all individuals were much alike, one could observe those about him and generalize to "people," and this is, in fact, what "common sense" usually rests upon. But when we must talk about large masses of people who are highly differentiated, then such easy generalizations are of doubtful reliability. The great virtue of the sample survey is the inclusion of all kinds of people in a population within a study group of manageable size.

The procedure is to study a sample as an estimator of a much larger aggregate (called, technically, a universe or population). Insofar as the sample is a good one, certain statistical techniques hold for any kind of universe with a fair degree of confidence. On the basis of the sample, we can describe the existing situation (the distribution of household income in a city, the degree of satisfaction with governmental services); we can also move toward certain explanations (if most objectors to present police protection are Negroes and poorer white people, we have localized the dissatisfaction and are nearer explaining it than when we considered it applicable to the metropolitan population). Perhaps most important, we can test the common-sense generalizations as to their explanatory value for the population as a whole. (We can see if people are overwhelmingly dissatisfied with local government.) We can, therefore, correct, discard, and qualify the notions with which we began.

STEPS IN THE SAMPLE SURVEY

The steps in the collection of sample survey data may be conveniently broken into four groups: the drawing of the sample, construction of the schedule of questions, interview of the respondents, and coding of the information gathered.

THE SAMPLE DRAWN

The sample, to reflect accurately, must be an unbiased selection from the universe of interest; that is, each individual must have an equal chance of being included. Otherwise, the sample distorts the proportion of women, homeowners, or voters, for instance, in the population. Ideally, the goal is a random sample in which each item is assigned an identifying symbol and the sample is then drawn unbiased from among the symbols. Many approximations of the random sample, however, have been invented for use where complete randomization is not practicable.

THE SCHEDULE OF QUESTIONS

The questions asked should have the same meaning to all respondents. We should avoid language peculiar to a certain type of people (say Negroes or academic persons), or any terminology that is ambiguous. Many standard forms of questions have been developed by the United States Bureau of the Census, the various research organizations, and social science investigators. Also, the questions should be pretested on people similar to the respondents in the survey itself.

THE INTERVIEW

The questions may vary considerably if those who ask them are not clearly aware of the sources of bias peculiar to the interview situation itself. Interviewers must be carefully selected and trained. They must be able to follow instructions for selecting the respondent, or the sample itself is biased; they must not prompt the respondent or affect his response by their tone; they must record accurately and fully. And, of course, they must initially elicit the respondent's coöperation in the interview.

THE CODING

The information gathered by the interviewer must be coded numerically before it can be transferred to punch cards and processed by machine. A good code is (1) relevant to the kinds of distinctions demanded by the general direction of inquiry, (2) made up of mutually exclusive categories, and (3) the categories exhaust or almost exhaust the varieties of response elicited by the scheduled questions. Through coding and decoding, the original information must be preserved in a usable form.

There are two types of error to which a sample survey is liable. All the foregoing steps can bring about what is called response error. Also, the very acceptance of a sample as a universe makes a degree of error likely, for different respondents will give different answers, though they should group around the correct answer; this is called sampling error.

PROCEDURE OF THE ST. LOUIS SAMPLE SURVEY OF CITIZEN OPINION AND PARTICIPATION

THE SAMPLE DRAWN

A systematic random sample of dwelling units in St. Louis City and the urban portion of St. Louis County was based on a total listing of all dwelling units, with every 10th, 20th, or 100th chosen as part of the sample.[1]

Because of our concern with the political opinions and governmental agencies of the suburban county, the County was oversampled, as was the Negro population in the central city. The final samples drawn were composed of one in each 400 households in the City (with an extra one in 400 of the 22 heavily Negro census tracts) and one in each 100 households in the County; 627 assignments were drawn in the City, 1,512 in the County, and an additional 129 cases in the 22 Negro tracts.

Within each household, only those 21 years old and over were eligible for interview, consistent with the objectives of the survey. Each adult had an equal chance of being interviewed through the use of a random selection table for choosing the respondent.[2] Although such a sample might be expected to overestimate those from households with fewer adults and underestimate those from larger households, as each household is represented by only one interview, intensive analysis of the effects of weighting by number in the household indicate that this has usually no more than 1 per cent variation.

It would be desirable to check the representative quality of the sample by known characteristics of the total population. However, the 1950 census data were six years old at the time of the survey and not too relevant. One available check involving a stable characteristic is the sex of those 21 years of age and older in the

---

[1] It was our good fortune to have made available to us without charge such a sample of the area, drawn for the St. Louis Origin and Destination Study, undertaken by Wilbur Smith and Associates for the Citizens Metropolitan Transit Committee of St. Louis and St. Louis County. The Origin and Destination sample, based upon a listing of all dwelling units in the population sampled (through the use of real estate maps and field enumeration), provided a frame within which the Metropolitan St. Louis Survey could build the most desirable sample, one to which the statistics of random samples may be applied without correction.

[2] See Leslie Kish, "A Procedure for Objective Respondent Selection within the Household," *Journal of the American Statistical Association* (Sept., 1949), pp. 380–387.

city of St. Louis. In 1950 the per cent male was 46.7; our sample proportion is 45 per cent, and, corrected for household size, 46.2 per cent.

The final sample thus insured coverage of every area within the City and the County.

THE SCHEDULE OF QUESTIONS

The questions may be divided into three categories: (1) occupation, income, education, religion, and other background attributes, (2) social and political participation, and (3) satisfaction and dissatisfaction with governmental services and choice of governmental alternatives.

The schedule drew upon previous studies, particularly for many of the first two types of questions. Many questions were drafted in forms previously found useful for other content. Pretests carried out in five different sections of the City-County area showed wide variance in ethnic composition, social rank, and style of life. From the 154 trial interviews, simple tabulations and intensive reading sifted the questions that elicited the information desired from those that were inadequate. A procedure of reformulation, rapid test, and further reformulation of questions about government and political behavior was necessary. Thus the items on government are the result of several pretests. Their final form seemed to be clearly understood by many different kinds of people and to interest the respondents enough to elicit significant answers.

THE INTERVIEWING

From 200 applicants, 74 interviewers and 7 group leaders were chosen. Each group leader, responsible for 8 to 12 interviewers, edited their completed interviews, counseled them on tactics and problems, and promoted or fired them. Ambiguities arose continually, and the interviewers' first order in case of problems was to call into headquarters: the integrity of the sample required consistent rules.

Although some interviewers had had previous experience, the majority had to be trained by the Survey staff. The training program included three phases: (1) general orientation, (2) practice interviewing, and (3) group leaders' personal instruction and careful editing of the first interviews taken in the main sample. New interviewers were first assigned respondents in the areas known to be easier—the middle-class, suburban neighborhoods of the County.

The City-County area was divided into control sections, in each of which a minimum response rate of 80 per cent was required. The over-all response rate for the total sample was 85 per cent—

less than would be desirable with an unlimited budget, but nevertheless adequate by the conventions of survey research. The response rate varied, however, by control area; 81 per cent of the assignments in the city of St. Louis were completed, compared with 85 to 89 per cent in the more middle-class, nonethnic, and family-oriented areas of the County.

The agreement between the sex distribution of the sample and that of the 1950 census for the city of St. Louis indicates that bias by sex is unimportant, even in the area where interviewing was most difficult. This is evidence that random selection by household and within the household was effective, and the sample interviewed is, like the sample drawn, representative of the total adult population within the limits of sampling error.

The total number of interviews was 2,025, including 1,285 in the County, 515 in the City, and an oversample of 225 taken in order to provide data for more intensive analyses in certain parts of the City-County area.

THE CODING

Each question in the Survey schedule was designated type A, B, or C, indicating the complexity of the code. Type A questions were precoded on the schedule, necessitating only the establishment of residual categories ("don't know," "refused to respond," and the like). Type B questions, requiring a relatively simple code, included facts such as age groupings, census tract designations, and marital status. The most difficult, designated C, were open-end attitude and opinion questions. "Do you think this is a good neighborhood in which to raise children? Why do you think so?" Approximately two-thirds of the questions were types A and B.

The codes were principally constructed from the results of the pretest. Categories for questions not included on the pretest schedule, including many dealing with government and governmental reform, were developed from continued pre-testing, as well as from the first 100 practice schedules turned in by interviewers in training. Responses were recorded for 150 interviews. However, because they were not a perfect sample of the 2,025 interviews coded, some codes had to be changed as the work progressed, usually by adding categories. The resulting set of codes very seldom designated more than 5 per cent of the responses to a question as "all others" or "miscellaneous."

A complete check was made of the coding of the first 200 schedules, and in the instance of four decks with more problem cases, the first 400, and error tallies were kept. The error for the first 117,425 codes assigned totaled 744—or less than six-tenths of one per cent. In view of these very low error rates in coding, the checking was cut down to a systematic 10 per cent random spot check of all code sheets. A further check was made for agreement in coding. The questions having the highest error rates in each category were recoded "blind" by other than the original coders. Because the recoding agreed in 98 per cent of the cases with the original coding, it was felt that coding error had been reduced to a minimum below which it was impractical to aim.

Similarly, the transfer of material from code sheets to punched cards was a point at which much error seemed possible. Therefore, the first 200 interviews punched, some 80,000 punches, were checked against the code sheets. The error rate was substantially less than one-half of 1 per cent; subsequently the 10 per cent random spot check was adopted. Finally, as the first tallies were run, all nonsensical information, such as responses in a column having no code meaning, was carefully traced back to the error in the punch, the code, or the interviewer's recording.

SAMPLING ERRORS

Aside from response error, all sample studies are liable to sampling error because any given sample may underestimate or overestimate the proportion of the total population having a given characteristic. The size of the sampling error to be expected can, however, be derived from techniques applicable to any random sample. Knowing the sampling error, we can indicate upper and lower limits (around the proportion in our sample) within which the true population proportion has a given probability of falling 95 per cent of the time.

For example, we estimate that slightly over 15 per cent of the City-County population had some high school education but no college education. This is based upon the sample of 837 (one in 400 households, City and County), and the sampling error is 2.4 per cent; thus in 95 out of 100 instances the true proportion will be between 17.4 and 12.6 per cent of the entire population of the City-County area. The sampling error varies, then, with the proportion estimated in the sample and the size of the sample. Table C1 in this appendix allows the reader to make a rough estimate of the sampling error for the various estimates reported in this book. To use the table, it is necessary to know (1) the size of the sample or subsample on which the estimate is based and (2) the proportion of the sample having the given characteristic. The upper and lower limits are then calculated by adding the sampling error to the sample proportion (upper limit) and subtracting it from the proportion (lower limit).

It is important to remember that these calculations estimate only the sampling errors. The response errors remain.

DIFFERENCES BETWEEN SUBSAMPLES

We frequently compare subsamples with respect to behavior in which we are interested. Thus, we compare the voting rates of residents in the County and in the central city. If we wish to

TABLES FOR COMPUTATION OF STATISTICAL SIGNIFICANCE

TABLE C1

SAMPLING ERRORS

(In 95 of 100 cases, the true population value will lie in the zone indicated by the sample proportion, plus or minus the number of percentage points shown in the table.)

Sample size	Sampling errors for reported percentages around				
	5 or 95%	10 or 90%	20 or 80%	30 or 70%	50%
50			12%	14%	14%
100		6%	8	9	10
200	4%	5	6	7	7
300	2	3	5	5	6
400	2	3	4	5	5
500	2	3	4	4	4
600	2	2	3	4	4
700	2	2	3	3	4
800	2	2	3	3	4
900	1	2	3	3	3
1,000	1	2	2	3	3
1,200	1	1	2	3	3

TABLE C2

SAMPLING ERRORS OF DIFFERENCES BETWEEN SUBSAMPLES

(In 95 of 100 cases, differences as great as these are statistically significant.)

Part A: Combined Proportion Is About 50 Per Cent

Size of other sub-sample	Size of one subsample										
	50	100	200	300	400	500	600	700	800	900	1,000
50	20%	17%	16%	15%	15%	15%	15%	15%	14%	14%	14%
100		14	12	11	11	11	11	11	10	10	10
200			10	9	9	8	8	8	8	8	8
300				8	8	7	7	7	7	7	6
400					7	7	6	6	6	6	6
500						6	6	6	6	5	5
600							6	5	5	5	5
700								5	5	5	5
800									5	5	5
900										5	5
1,000											4

Part B: Combined Proportion Is About 30 or 70 Per Cent

Size of other sub-sample	Size of one subsample										
	50	100	200	300	400	500	600	700	800	900	1,000
50	18%	16%	14%	14%	14%	13%	13%	13%	13%	13%	13%
100		13	11	10	10	10	10	10	10	10	9
200			9	8	8	8	7	7	7	7	7
300				7	7	7	6	6	6	6	6
400					6	6	6	6	6	5	5
500						6	5	5	5	5	5
600							5	5	5	5	5
700								5	5	5	4
800									4	4	4
900										4	4
1,000											4

Part C: Combined Proportion Is About 10 or 90 Per Cent

Size of other sub-sample	Size of one subsample										
	50	100	200	300	400	500	600	700	800	900	1,000
50	12%	10%	9%	9%	9%	9%	9%	9%	9%	9%	9%
100		8	7	7	7	6	6	6	6	6	6
200			6	5	5	5	5	5	5	5	5
300				5	5	4	4	4	4	4	4
400					4	4	4	4	4	4	3
500						3	3	3	2	2	2
600							2	2	2	2	2
700								2	2	2	2
800									2	2	2
900										2	2
1,000											2

SOURCE: Adapted from Vernon Davies, *Table Showing Significance of Differences between Percentages*, Pullman, Washington Agricultural Experiment Stations, Stations Circular No. 102, 1950.

evaluate the differences associated with residence, we need to know whether they are statistically significant. Would they remain if (1) we had interviewed the entire population or (2) had chosen another sample? In short, we must control for the possibility that the differences simply reflect the random fluctuation attendant upon using a sample to represent a population.

In order to know the significance of a difference, we use the sampling error of differences. If the difference between our two subsamples is greater than the sampling error, then we can be sure 95 per cent of the time that the difference is not simply an artifact of our sample variation.

The sampling error for differences between proportions is given in table C2. To use the table, we need to know (1) the size of the two subsamples, (2) the percentage difference between them, and (3) the proportion of the characteristic found in the two subsamples combined. If the proportion in the combined sub-samples is about 50 per cent, we use Part A of the table; if it is about 10 per cent we use Part C. We then find one sample size on the horizontal line and one on the vertical; their intersection will be the sampling error for samples this size with this combined proportion. If the difference between the two subsamples is greater than the difference in the table, it is a significant difference. If it is smaller, it is nonsignificant and may be due to sampling variation.

In using both tables, the reader must interpolate, and the answer will be approximate in all instances. In constructing the tables, the rule has been to let the benefit of doubt be on the side of nonsignificance.

Supplementary Tables to Part Three—

Citizen Participation and Attitudes

All percentages in tables are rounded to the nearest whole number.

N denotes the number of persons interviewed.

An asterisk denotes a value of less than one-half of 1 per cent.

TABLE D1

MULTIPLE VOTING IN DIFFERENT KINDS OF LOCAL ELECTIONS

	Has voted in					
Type of person	None	One	Two or more	None listed[a]	Ineligible[b]	N
All respondents	28%	11%	53%	3%	5%	837
Those ever voting while in community	. . .	16	80	4	. . .	554

  [a] These respondents reported they have voted in local elections but not in municipal, school, fire district, or County elections. Such respondents could have been mistaken in their answer to the question "Have you ever voted . . . ," could have forgotten in which type of election they had voted, or could have voted in special elections that were not listed.
  [b] Not ascertained, which is less than one-half of 1 per cent, is combined with the ineligibles.

TABLE D2

PARTICIPATION IN LOCAL ELECTIONS AND 1956 PRESIDENTIAL ELECTION

	Local elections	
Presidential election	Did vote	Did not vote
Did vote	66%	13%
Did not vote	4	17
Total		100%[a]

  [a] Total is based upon the weighted sample, less those who said they were ineligible to vote for any local officials. The weighted sample is described in chapter 9, footnote 1.

TABLE D3

RANK ORDER OF LOCAL GOVERNMENTS BY GOOD AND VERY GOOD EVALUATIONS

Rank order by respondents in:	
City	County
1. St. Louis City (59%)	Own County municipality (61%)
2. Metropolitan sewer district (40%)	St. Louis City (58%)
3. County municipalities (28%)	County municipalities (44%)
4. St. Louis County government (21%)	St. Louis County government (42%)
5.[a]	Metropolitan sewer district (40%)

[a] One fewer judgment by City residents since "your own County municipality" is inapplicable.

TABLE D4

EVALUATION OF GOVERNMENTS BY RESIDENTS WITH OPINIONS: CITY AND COUNTY

Specific government	Very good, good	Fair	Poor, very poor	N
St. Louis City government				
City	62%	32%	6%	494
County	63	33	5	1,189
St. Louis County municipalities				
City	47	46	7	301
County	49	44	7	1,144
Own County municipality				
County residents only	72	23	5	825
St. Louis County government				
City	41	46	12	263
County	47	42	11	1,149
Metropolitan sewer district				
City	54	38	8	381
County	52	28	21	985

TABLE D5

OPINIONS OF THE FEDERAL SYSTEM BY PERSONS MOST DISLIKING
THE OTHER ALTERNATIVES

Most disliked change	Opinion of the federal system			N
	Liked	Disliked	Don't know	
Merger	58%	32%	10%	225
Reëntry of City into County	53	39	8	115
Municipal consolidation in County	67	28	4	91
Status quo	68	27	5	241

EXCLUDED: 83 respondents who could not make up their minds.

TABLE D6

DESIRABILITY OF AN ELECTION ACCORDING TO BEST LIKED ALTERNATIVE

	Desirability of an election			
Proposal most liked	Yes	No	Don't know	N
Merger	86%	10%	4%	280
Reëntry of City into County	83	14	3	112
Federal system	79	18	3	128
Municipal consolidation in County	70	26	5	86
Status quo	43	47	10	175

TABLE D7

BELIEF IN PROBABILITY OF GOVERNMENTAL REORGANIZATION,
ACCORDING TO BEST LIKED ALTERNATIVE

	Optimism concerning change			
Proposal most liked	Yes (likely)	No (unlikely)	Don't know	N
Merger	48%	45%	7%	280
Reëntry of City into County	48	41	11	112
Federal system	48	45	6	128
Municipal consolidation in County	50	44	6	86
Status quo	35	49	16	175

TABLE D8

ASSOCIATION BETWEEN VOTING IN ONE TYPE OF LOCAL ELECTION
AND THREE OTHER TYPES: ST. LOUIS COUNTY

	Has also voted in elections of				
Voted in elections	County	Municipality	Fire district	School district	N
County		63%	20%	60%	807
Municipality	84%		16	59	603
Fire district	95	57		80	167
School district	93	68	26		521

TABLE D9

PARTICIPATION IN LOCAL ELECTIONS AND THE 1956 PRESIDENTIAL ELECTION:
CITY AND COUNTY

Voting in 1956 presidential election	Voting in local elections[a]	
	Did vote	Did not vote
Did vote		
City	64%	12%
County	68	15
Did not vote		
City	4%	19%
County	4	13
City N = 495		
County N = 1,196		

[a] Includes only those who said they were eligible to vote in local elections.

TABLE D10

NUMBER OF CHANGES AND IMPROVEMENTS SUGGESTED IN LOCAL COMMUNITY

Residence	No change	One	Two	Three	Four or more
City	21%	34%	27%	15%	3%
County	17	30	29	20	4

The N column is omitted from appendix tables pertaining to City-County comparisons when the entire basic sample (512 in the City and 1,285 in the County) is involved.

TABLE D11

NUMBER OF CHANGES SUGGESTED IN THE CITY-COUNTY AREA

Residence	No change	One	Two	Three or more
City	30%	38%	22%	10%
County	26	36	23	15

TABLE D12

EVALUATION OF LOCAL GOVERNMENTAL SERVICES

Service[a]	Dissatisfied or very dissatisfied	Very satisfied	Fairly satisfied	Don't know	Rank in dissatisfaction	
					City	County
Traffic conditions[b]						
City	45%	13%	37%	5%	1	1
County	57	9	32	2		
Public transportation						
City	34	21	36	9	3	2
County	44	18	26	13		
Condition of street						
City	38	18	43	1	2	4
County	30	29	40	1		
Parks and playgrounds						
City	29	30	33	8	4	3
County	34	26	31	9		
Police protection						
City	20	31	45	3	5	7
County	9	52	37	2		
Sewage disposal						
City	9	42	44	4	8	5
County	26	40	30	4		
Garbage collection						
City	17	38	42	3	6	6
County	11	59	26	4		
Libraries						
City	9	41	28	21	7	8
County	8	50	24	18		
Schools						
City	9	37	41	13	9	9
County	7	51	30	12		
Water supply						
City	7	64	28	*	10	10
County	7	71	22	1		
Fire protection						
City	3	58	34	4	11	11
County	5	59	31	5		

[a] Services ranked by decreasing dissatisfaction in City-County population as a whole.
[b] Relates to conditions in the City-County area as a whole.

TABLE D13

INDIVIDUAL OR AGENCY TO WHICH COMPLAINTS WERE MADE

| | Individual | | | Agency | | | |
Residents	Elected official	Other official	Private party[a]	Local government	Metropolitan Sewer District	Private agency	Other, don't know
City (N = 62)	5%	17%	3%	54%	3%	13%	5%
County (N = 268)	20	16	6	45	7	6	1

[a] Includes political party officials.

TABLE D14

RESULTS OF COMPLAINTS MADE IN CITY AND COUNTY

Residence	Success	Partial success	Failure	Other, don't know	N
City	34%	5%	60%	2%	62
County	36	12	51	1	268

TABLE D15

REASONS GIVEN FOR NOT COMPLAINING BY PERSONS WANTING TO COMPLAIN

Residence	Rational inaction	Naïveté	Ignorance	Cynicism	Don't know	N
City	36%	33%	10%	20%	1%	135
County	38	28	18	15	1	223

TABLE D16

EXCESSIVE NUMBER OF MUNICIPALITIES IN CITY-COUNTY AREA

Residence	Yes	No	Don't know
City	45%	42%	12%
County	59	33	8

TABLE D17

BELIEF IN PROBABILITY OF GOVERNMENTAL REORGANIZATION,
ACCORDING TO BEST LIKED ALTERNATIVE

	Optimism concerning change			
Most liked proposal	Yes	No	Don't know	N
Merger				
City	51%	42%	7%	196
County	41	53	6	337
Reëntry of City into County				
City	51	37	12	67
County	43	47	10	179
Federal system				
City	51	44	5	79
County	44	50	6	195
Municipal consolidation in County				
City	55	36	10	31
County	46	50	4	221
Status quo				
City	36	48	16	97
County	33	50	16	314

TABLE D18

AGE AND VOTING IN LOCAL ELECTIONS

Residence	21–29	30–49	40–49	50–64	65 and over
City	38% (96)[a]	65% (94)	65% (107)	81% (131)	77% (87)
County	37% (228)	67% (363)	75% (302)	79% (278)	76% (114)

[a] The figures in parentheses here and in following similar tables represent the number of interviews in each category. When certain interviews are excluded, the reasons are given in a footnote to the table.

TABLE D19

EDUCATION AND VOTING IN ANY LOCAL ELECTION

Residence	Years of education completed					
	0–7	8	9–11	12	13–15	16 and over
City	61% (113)	64% (125)	71% (114)	66% (103)	71% (28)	72% (29)
County	73% (90)	63% (233)	64% (238)	63% (393)	75% (167)	74% (162)

EXCLUDED: City 3 and County 2 "don't know."

TABLE D20

YEARS IN PRESENT DWELLING UNIT AND VOTING IN ANY LOCAL ELECTION

Residence	Less than 1	1–2	3–4	5–9	10–19	20 or more
City	34%	52%	61%	80%	83%	93%
	(79)	(124)	(64)	(92)	(92)	(61)
County	20%	55%	71%	83%	88%	92%
	(181)	(292)	(202)	(305)	(197)	(100)

EXCLUDED: City 3 and County 8 "don't know."

TABLE D21

AGE AND VOTING IN MUNICIPAL ELECTIONS

Voters	21–29	30–39	40–49	50–64	65 and over
Voted					
City	41%	64%	67%	81%	76%
County	30	60	61	66	56
Have not voted					
City	52	26	30	16	20
County	39	26	19	15	11
Incompetent					
City	7	10	3	2	5
County	30	14	19	19	33
Number					
City	(87)	(89)	(104)	(129)	(86)
County	(141)	(265)	(242)	(233)	(99)

EXCLUDED: City 20 ineligible; County 315 ineligible or living in unincorporated areas.

TABLE D22

HOUSEHOLD INCOME AND VOTING IN MUNICIPAL ELECTIONS

Voters	$0–2,999	$3–4,999	$5–6,999	$7,000 and over
Voted				
City	65%	63%	68%	82%
County	47	49	52	64
Have not voted				
City	29	31	31	17
County	20	27	23	19
Incompetent				
City	7	5	1	1
County	33	23	25	17
Number				
City	(122)	(146)	(113)	(71)
County	(70)	(132)	(252)	(415)

EXCLUDED: City 63 "don't know," "refused," or ineligible; County 416 "don't know," "refused," ineligible, or live in unincorporated areas.

TABLE D23

ETHNICITY AND VOTING IN MUNICIPAL ELECTIONS

Voters	Old American	German	Southern and eastern European	Negro
Voted				
City	62%	81%	79%	61%
County	60	57	49	43
Have not voted				
City	31	19	19	31
County	21	17	34	43
Incompetent				
City	6	0	2	8
County	18	25	18	14
Number				
City	(191)	(118)	(47)	(114)
County	(480)	(323)	(107)	(35)

EXCLUDED: City 45 ineligible, "don't know," or "other"; County 340 ineligible, "don't know," "other," or live in unincorporated areas.

TABLE D24

YEARS IN THE METROPOLITAN AREA AND VOTING IN MUNICIPAL ELECTIONS

Voters	Less than 5	5–19	20 or over	Native
Voted				
City	46%	45%	72%	76%
County	40	53	61	58
Did not vote				
City	42	43	24	21
County	37	24	16	22
Incompetent				
City	12	12	4	3
County	23	22	22	21
Number				
City	(24)	(98)	(166)	(204)
County	(57)	(164)	(268)	(480)

EXCLUDED: City 23 ineligible or "don't know"; County 316 ineligible, "don't know," or live in unincorporated areas.

TABLE D25

YEARS IN PRESENT DWELLING AND VOTING IN MUNICIPAL ELECTIONS

Voters	Less than 1	1–2	3–4	5–9	10–19	20 and over
Voted						
City	39%	56%	62%	80%	79%	90%
County	19	45	56	72	69	68
Did not vote						
City	53	37	33	18	18	5
County	48	34	23	14	9	8
Incompetent						
City	10	7	5	2	2	5
County	33	21	21	14	22	23
Number						
City	(68)	(117)	(64)	(90)	(92)	(61)
County	(102)	(213)	(156)	(253)	(158)	(82)

EXCLUDED: City 23 ineligible or "don't know"; County 321 ineligible, "don't know," or live in unincorporated areas.

TABLE D26

AGE AND VOTING IN SCHOOL ELECTIONS

Voters	21–29	30–39	40–49	50–64	65 and over
Have voted					
City	16%	46%	51%	71%	58%
County	17	41	52	54	50
Have not voted					
City	46	21	38	19	30
County	30	28	22	18	20
Incompetent					
City	38	32	11	10	12
County	52	29	24	24	26
Number					
City	(87)	(89)	(104)	(129)	(86)
County	(185)	(337)	(290)	(272)	(112)

EXCLUDED: City 20 and County 89 ineligible.

TABLE D27
YEARS IN METROPOLITAN AREA AND VOTING IN SCHOOL ELECTIONS

Voters	Less than 5	5–19	20 or more	Native
Have voted				
City	17%	30%	55%	60%
County	20	40	51	44
Have not voted				
City	46	43	29	21
County	29	25	20	25
Incompetent				
City	37	28	16	20
County	51	35	29	31
Number				
City	(24)	(98)	(166)	(204)
County	(70)	(198)	(321)	(604)

EXCLUDED: City 23 and County 92 ineligible or "don't know."

TABLE D28
TYPE OF OCCUPANCY AND VOTING IN SCHOOL ELECTIONS

Voters	Renters	Owners
Have voted		
City	37%	69%
County	29	46
Have not voted		
City	37	21
County	31	23
Incompetent		
City	25	10
County	40	31
Number		
City	(296)	(199)
County	(161)	(1,035)

EXCLUDED: City 20 and County 89 ineligible.

TABLE D29

YEARS IN PRESENT DWELLING AND VOTING IN SCHOOL ELECTIONS

Voters	Less than 1	1–2	3–4	5–9	10–19	20 or more
Have voted						
City	19%	33%	50%	62%	65%	79%
County	14	26	41	54	63	65
Have not voted						
City	47	42	33	24	18	11
County	36	32	25	19	14	16
Incompetent						
City	34	25	17	13	16	10
County	50	41	34	27	23	19
Number						
City	(68)	(117)	(64)	(90)	(92)	(61)
County	(129)	(269)	(197)	(300)	(193)	(100)

EXCLUDED: City 23 and County 97 ineligible or "don't know."

TABLE D30

AGE AND VOTING IN COUNTY AND MUNICIPAL ELECTIONS[a]

Voters	21–29	30–39	40–49	50–64	65 and over
Have voted					
County	44%	67%	73%	76%	68%
City	41	64	67	81	76
Have not voted					
County	39	24	19	16	12
City	52	26	30	16	20
Incompetent					
County	17	9	8	8	20
City	7	10	3	2	5
Number					
County	(185)	(337)	(290)	(272)	(112)
City	(87)	(89)	(104)	(129)	(86)

[a] In this table and the two following, "Voting in County and Municipal Elections" means County residents voting for officials of the County government and City residents voting for municipal officials. Unlike the immediately preceding tables, the County entries appear first because they are the focus of this particular analysis.

EXCLUDED: County 89 and City 20 ineligible.

TABLE D31

EDUCATION AND VOTING IN COUNTY AND MUNICIPAL ELECTIONS

Voters	Years of education completed					
	0–7	8	9–11	12	13–15	16 or more
Have voted						
County	71%	58%	63%	65%	79%	76%
City	61	66	70	71	68	77
Have not voted						
County	15	25	26	26	13	17
City	33	26	27	26	29	23
Incompetent						
County	15	17	11	9	8	6
City	7	7	3	3	4	0
Number						
County	(89)	(220)	(221)	(361)	(150)	(153)
City	(110)	(122)	(110)	(96)	(28)	(26)

EXCLUDED: County 91 and City 23 ineligible or "don't know."

TABLE D32

YEARS IN PRESENT DWELLING AND VOTING IN COUNTY AND MUNICIPAL ELECTIONS

Voters	Less than 1	1–2	3–4	5–9	10–19	20 and over
Voted						
County	30%	56%	67%	78%	83%	79%
City	37	56	62	80	79	90
Did not vote						
County	50	27	24	14	11	10
City	53	37	33	18	18	5
Incompetent						
County	19	16	8	7	6	11
City	10	7	5	2	2	5
Number						
County	(129)	(269)	(197)	(300)	(193)	(100)
City	(68)	(117)	(64)	(90)	(92)	(61)

EXCLUDED: County 97 and City 23 ineligible or "don't know."

TABLE D33

YEARS IN METROPOLITAN AREA AND VOTING IN THE 1956 PRESIDENTIAL ELECTION

Residence	1–4	5–19	20 and over	Native
City	48%	60%	79%	81%
County	61	75	83	84
Number				
City	(31)	(102)	(168)	(211)
County	(97)	(219)	(328)	(637)

EXCLUDED: City 3 and County 4 "don't know."

TABLE D34

YEARS IN PRESENT DWELLING AND VOTING IN THE 1956 PRESIDENTIAL ELECTION

Residence	Less than 1	1–2	3–4	5–9	10–19	20 or more
City	51%	64%	80%	81%	85%	90%
	(79)	(124)	(64)	(92)	(92)	(61)
County	58%	75%	87%	87%	91%	86%
	(181)	(292)	(202)	(305)	(197)	(100)

EXCLUDED: City 3 and County 8 "don't know."

TABLE D35

AGE AND BELIEF IN IMPORTANCE OF LOCAL ELECTIONS

Residence	21–29	30–39	40–49	50–64	65 and over
City	79%	72%	69%	68%	53%
	(96)	(94)	(107)	(131)	(87)
County	85%	86%	80%	78%	70%
	(228)	(363)	(302)	(278)	(114)

TABLE D36

EDUCATION AND BELIEF IN IMPORTANCE OF LOCAL ELECTIONS

	Years of education completed					
Residence	0–7	8	9–11	12	13–15	16 or more
City	46%	65%	78%	82%	79%	83%
	(113)	(125)	(114)	(103)	(28)	(29)
County	71%	71%	82%	86%	81%	88%
	(90)	(233)	(238)	(393)	(167)	(162)

EXCLUDED: City 3 and County 2 "don't know."

TABLE D37

HOUSEHOLD INCOME AND BELIEF IN IMPORTANCE OF LOCAL ELECTIONS

Residence	$0–2,999	$3–4,999	$5–6,999	$7,000 and over
City	52%	69%	80%	84%
	(123)	(155)	(117)	(75)
County	72%	80%	87%	84%
	(98)	(203)	(341)	(510)

EXCLUDED: City 45 and County 133 "don't know" or refused to supply information.

TABLE D38

OCCUPATION AND BELIEF IN IMPORTANCE OF LOCAL ELECTIONS

Residence	Occupation of head of household				
	Operative	Craftsman	Clerical	Professional	Other
City	66%	71%	82%	79%	57%
	(152)	(115)	(66)	(58)	(122)
County	80%	82%	86%	82%	74%
	(193)	(322)	(190)	(433)	(146)

EXCLUDED: City 2 and County 1 "don't know."

TABLE D39

AGE AND NAMING TWO OR MORE LOCAL COMMUNITY CHANGES

Residence	21–29	30–39	40–49	50–64	65 and over
City	44%	55%	49%	38%	40%
	(96)	(94)	(107)	(131)	(87)
County	53%	62%	54%	48%	40%
	(228)	(363)	(302)	(278)	(114)

TABLE D40

AGE AND DISSATISFACTION WITH TRAFFIC CONDITIONS

Residence	21–29	30–39	40–49	50–64	65 and over
City	51%	56%	42%	41%	36%
	(96)	(94)	(107)	(131)	(87)
County	62%	62%	59%	55%	30%
	(228)	(363)	(302)	(278)	(114)

TABLE D41

EDUCATION AND DISSATISFACTION WITH TRAFFIC CONDITIONS

Residence	Years of education completed					
	0–7	8	9–11	12	13–15	16 and more
City	37%	40%	53%	48%	57%	48%
	(113)	(125)	(114)	(103)	(28)	(29)
County	40%	48%	49%	60%	63%	78%
	(90)	(233)	(238)	(393)	(167)	(162)

EXCLUDED: City 3 and County 2 "don't know."

TABLE D42
HOUSEHOLD INCOME AND DISSATISFACTION WITH TRAFFIC CONDITIONS

Residence	$0–2,999	$3–4,999	$5–6,999	$7,000 and over
City	38%	49%	45%	56%
	(123)	(155)	(117)	(75)
County	37%	54%	56%	67%
	(98)	(203)	(341)	(510)

EXCLUDED: City 45 and County 133 "don't know" or refused.

TABLE D43
OCCUPATION AND DISSATISFACTION WITH TRAFFIC CONDITIONS

Residence	Laborer	Operative	Craftsman	Clerical	Professional
City	36%	51%	50%	44%	47%
	(36)	(116)	(115)	(66)	(58)
County	30%	50%	55%	58%	65%
	(27)	(166)	(322)	(190)	(433)

EXCLUDED: City 2 and County 1 "don't know."

TABLE D44
HOUSEHOLD INCOME AND DISSATISFACTION WITH PUBLIC TRANSPORTATION

Residence	$0–2,999	$3–4,999	$5–6,999	$7,000 and over
City	24%	34%	36%	48%
	(123)	(155)	(117)	(75)
County	37%	40%	44%	46%
	(98)	(203)	(341)	(510)

EXCLUDED: City 45 and County 133 "don't know" or refused.

TABLE D45
ETHNIC BACKGROUND AND DISSATISFACTION WITH PUBLIC TRANSPORTATION

Residence	Old American	German	Southern and eastern European	Negro
City	23%	35%	43%	26%
	(200)	(124)	(49)	(116)
County	41%	43%	54%	45%
	(624)	(425)	(147)	(51)

EXCLUDED: City 26 and County 35 "don't know" or "other."

TABLE D46

YEARS IN METROPOLITAN AREA AND DISSATISFACTION
WITH PUBLIC TRANSPORTATION

Residence	Less than 5	5–19	20 or more	Native
City	13%	26%	37%	41%
	(31)	(102)	(167)	(212)
County	33%	46%	46%	43%
	(97)	(219)	(328)	(637)

EXCLUDED: City 3 and County 4 "don't know."

TABLE D47

EDUCATION AND DISSATISFACTION WITH RESIDENTIAL STREETS

	Years of education completed					
Residence	0–7	8	9–11	12	13–15	16 and more
City	40%	36%	47%	33%	39%	31%
	(113)	(125)	(114)	(103)	(28)	(29)
County	43%	36%	34%	30%	24%	20%
	(90)	(233)	(238)	(393)	(167)	(162)

EXCLUDED: City 3 and County 2 "don't know."

TABLE D48

HOUSEHOLD INCOME AND DISSATISFACTION WITH RESIDENTIAL STREETS

Residence	$0–2,999	$3–4,999	$5–6,999	$7,000 and over
City	44%	41%	35%	37%
	(123)	(155)	(117)	(75)
County	39%	33%	33%	27%
	(98)	(203)	(341)	(510)

EXCLUDED: City 45 and County 133 "don't know" or refused.

TABLE D49

ETHNICITY AND DISSATISFACTION WITH RESIDENTIAL STREETS

Residence	Old American	German	Southern and eastern European	Negro
City	38%	33%	31%	51%
	(200)	(124)	(49)	(116)
County	29%	27%	38%	51%
	(626)	(425)	(148)	(51)

EXCLUDED: City 26 and County 35 "don't know" or "other."

TABLE D50

AGE AND DISSATISFACTION WITH PARKS AND PLAYGROUNDS

Residence	21–29	30–39	40–49	50–64	65 and over
City	33% (96)	41% (94)	32% (107)	25% (131)	13% (87)
County	32% (228)	42% (363)	36% (302)	25% (278)	22% (114)

TABLE D51

YEARS IN PRESENT DWELLING UNIT AND DISSATISFACTION WITH PARKS AND PLAYGROUNDS

Residence	Less than 1	1–2	3–4	5–9	10–19	20 or more
City	28% (79)	34% (124)	28% (64)	35% (92)	27% (92)	15% (61)
County	26% (181)	33% (292)	33% (202)	38% (305)	32% (197)	37% (100)

EXCLUDED: City 3 and County 8 "don't know."

TABLE D52

AGE AND COMPLAINTS TO LOCAL GOVERNMENTS

Complainants	21–29	30–39	40–49	50–64	65 and over
Felt like complaining					
City	49% (96)	46% (94)	45% (107)	35% (131)	15% (87)
County	38% (228)	47% (363)	37% (302)	34% (278)	24% (114)
Complained					
City	11% (96)	15% (94)	14% (107)	13% (131)	6% (87)
County	17% (228)	24% (363)	23% (302)	19% (278)	15% (114)
Felt like complaining and complained					
City	23% (47)	33% (43)	31% (48)	37% (46)	38% (13)
County	45% (87)	52% (170)	61% (113)	57% (94)	63% (27)

TABLE D53

EDUCATION AND COMPLAINTS TO LOCAL GOVERNMENTS

Complainants	Years of education completed					
	0–7	8	9–11	12	13–15	16 and over
Felt like complaining						
City	26%	29%	45%	52%	61%	31%
	(113)	(125)	(114)	(103)	(28)	(29)
County	41%	31%	37%	40%	38%	43%
	(90)	(233)	(238)	(393)	(167)	(162)
Complained						
City	8%	8%	12%	17%	29%	10%
	(113)	(125)	(114)	(103)	(28)	(29)
County	22%	13%	18%	21%	27%	29%
	(90)	(233)	(238)	(393)	(167)	(162)
Felt like complaining and complained						
City	30%	28%	27%	33%	47%	33%
	(30)	(36)	(51)	(54)	(17)	(9)
County	54%	42%	49%	51%	72%	67%
	(37)	(73)	(87)	(159)	(64)	(70)

TABLE D54

HOUSEHOLD INCOME AND COMPLAINTS TO GOVERNMENTAL AGENCIES

Complainants	$0–2,999	$3–4,999	$5–6,999	$7,000 and over
Felt like complaining				
City	29%	41%	47%	41%
	(123)	(155)	(117)	(75)
County	33%	31%	43%	42%
	(98)	(203)	(341)	(510)
Complained				
City	8%	10%	14%	23%
	(123)	(155)	(117)	(75)
County	13%	15%	21%	26%
	(98)	(203)	(341)	(510)
Felt like complaining and complained				
City	28%	23%	29%	55%
	(36)	(64)	(55)	(31)
County	41%	48%	49%	62%
	(32)	(63)	(148)	(210)

TABLE D55

ETHNICITY AND COMPLAINTS TO LOCAL GOVERNMENTS

Complainants	Old American	German	Southern and eastern European	Negro
Felt like complaining				
City	34% (200)	32% (124)	41% (49)	54% (116)
County	38% (626)	37% (425)	38% (148)	47% (51)
Complained				
City	13% (200)	13% (124)	6% (49)	13% (116)
County	22% (626)	22% (425)	19% (148)	14% (51)
Felt like complaining and complained				
City	38% (69)	40% (40)	15% (20)	22% (63)
County	56% (239)	59% (158)	49% (57)	29% (24)

TABLE D56

TYPE OF OCCUPANCY AND COMPLAINTS TO LOCAL GOVERNMENTS

Complainants	Renters	Owners
Felt like complaining		
City	41% (312)	34% (203)
County	32% (199)	39% (1,086)
Complained		
City	10% (312)	15% (203)
County	13% (199)	22% (1,086)
Felt like complaining and complained		
City	25% (127)	43% (70)
County	41% (64)	57% (427)

TABLE D57

Years of Residence in Present Dwelling and Complaints to Local Governments

Complainants	Less than 1	1–2	3–4	5–9	10–19	20 or more
Felt like complaining						
City	30%	43%	39%	54%	35%	28%
	(79)	(124)	(64)	(92)	(92)	(61)
County	23%	36%	38%	45%	47%	37%
	(181)	(292)	(202)	(305)	(197)	(100)
Complained						
City	2%	12%	12%	21%	15%	7%
	(79)	(124)	(64)	(92)	(92)	(61)
County	10%	17%	22%	23%	27%	30%
	(181)	(292)	(202)	(305)	(197)	(100)
Felt like complaining and complained						
City	8%	28%	38%	38%	44%	23%
	(24)	(53)	(21)	(50)	(32)	(17)
County	43%	49%	58%	51%	59%	81%
	(42)	(105)	(76)	(136)	(92)	(37)

TABLE D58

Ethnicity and Belief in the Worth of Government: Per Cent Who Agree That Local Taxes Are Too High

Residence	Old American	German	Southern and eastern European	Negro
City	35%	23%	49%	56%
	(200)	(124)	(49)	(116)
County	42%	44%	49%	63%
	(626)	(425)	(148)	(51)

Excluded: City 26 and County 35 "don't know" or "other."

TABLE D59

Age and Awareness of Metropolitan Problems: Proportion Suggesting One or More Changes

Residence	21–29	30–39	40–49	50–64	65 and over
City	73%	80%	75%	67%	54%
	(96)	(94)	(107)	(131)	(87)
County	77%	78%	75%	71%	59%
	(228)	(363)	(302)	(278)	(114)

TABLE D60
EDUCATION AND AWARENESS OF METROPOLITAN PROBLEMS

Residence	Years of education completed					
	0–7	8	9–11	12	13–15	16 or more
City	53%	55%	74%	90%	75%	100%
	(113)	(125)	(114)	(103)	(28)	(29)
County	54%	58%	70%	78%	87%	88%
	(90)	(233)	(238)	(393)	(167)	(162)

EXCLUDED: City 3 and County 2 "don't know."

TABLE D61
HOUSEHOLD INCOME AND AWARENESS OF METROPOLITAN PROBLEMS

Residence	$0–2,999	$3–4,999	$5–6,999	$7,000 and over
City	55%	73%	79%	82%
	(123)	(155)	(117)	(75)
County	57%	72%	74%	82%
	(98)	(203)	(341)	(510)

EXCLUDED: City 45 and County 133 "don't know" or refused.

TABLE D62
AGE AND "LIKING" OF GOVERNMENTAL ALTERNATIVES

Proposal	21–29	30–39	40–49	50–64	65 and over
Merger					
City	49%	48%	55%	68%	59%
County	29	37	36	39	46
Reëntry of City into County					
City	41	46	49	51	44
County	37	42	41	40	41
Federal system					
City	47	56	55	62	54
County	53	50	50	49	54
Municipal consolidation in County					
City	42	56	53	40	46
County	53	50	50	49	54
Status quo					
City	46	37	36	30	38
County	37	42	41	40	41
Number					
City	(96)	(94)	(107)	(131)	(87)
County	(228)	(363)	(302)	(278)	(114)

TABLE D63

SEX AND "LIKING" OF GOVERNMENTAL ALTERNATIVES

Proposal	Female	Male
Merger		
City	49%	66%
County	41	43
Reëntry of City into County		
City	42	53
County	38	43
Federal system		
City	58	52
County	52	48
Municipal consolidation in County		
City	43	52
County	49	57
Status quo		
City	43	30
County	49	33
Number		
City	(283)	(232)
County	(704)	(581)

TABLE D64

EDUCATION AND "LIKING" OF GOVERNMENTAL ALTERNATIVES

Proposal	Years of education completed					
	0–7	8	9–11	12	13–15	16 or more
Merger						
City	55%	55%	57%	58%	61%	62%
County	43	39	37	35	36	33
Reëntry of City into County						
City	58	48	45	38	53	34
County	42	43	40	38	42	39
Federal system						
City	50	59	61	60	43	34
County	49	54	53	47	50	52
Municipal consolidation in County						
City	43	46	49	51	54	45
County	42	48	49	51	57	65
Status quo						
City	46	42	31	34	32	24
County	48	50	45	43	35	23
Number						
City	(113)	(125)	(114)	(103)	(28)	(29)
County	(90)	(233)	(238)	(393)	(167)	(162)

EXCLUDED: City 3 and County 2 "don't know."

TABLE D65

Ethnicity and "Liking" of Governmental Alternatives

Proposal	Old American	German	Southern and eastern European	Negro
Merger				
City	61%	64%	51%	48%
County	37	36	37	43
Reëntry of City into County				
City	45	39	47	60
County	39	41	45	49
Federal system				
City	48	56	55	76
County	50	52	46	57
Municipal consolidation in County				
City	43	48	53	53
County	53	56	48	29
Status quo				
City	33	34	53	37
County	39	41	49	53
Number				
City	(200)	(124)	(49)	(116)
County	(626)	(425)	(148)	(51)

Excluded: City 26 and County 35 "don't know" or "other."

TABLE D66

Farm Background and "Liking" of Governmental Alternatives

Proposal	Farm	Nonfarm
Merger		
City	45%	61%
County	35	37
Reëntry of City into County		
City	51	44
County	41	40
Federal system		
City	52	57
County	56	51
Municipal consolidation in County		
City	42	47
County	47	54
Status quo		
City	42	34
County	46	39
Number		
City	(201)	(313)
County	(395)	(890)

Excluded: City 1 "don't know."

TABLE D67

Type of Dwelling and "Liking" of Governmental Alternatives

Proposal	Single-family	Multiple-family
Merger		
City	66%	52%
County	37	29
Reëntry of City into County		
City	42	49
County	40	43
Federal system		
City	49	59
County	51	46
Municipal consoli-dation in County		
City	43	49
County	53	47
Status quo		
City	31	41
County	41	50
Number		
City	(180)	(335)
County	(1,130)	(155)

TABLE D68

Sex and Preference among Governmental Alternatives

Proposal	Men	Women
Merger		
City	46%	31%
County	32	21
Reëntry of City into County		
City	15	11
County	15	13
Federal system		
City	15	15
County	15	15
Municipal consolidation in County		
City	6	6
County	18	17
Status quo		
City	13	23
County	18	30
Number		
City	(232)	(283)
County	(581)	(704)

Supplementary Tables to Chapter 14—

Factors Affecting Local Governmental Expenditure Levels

Major results of the multiple regression and correlation analysis have been given in text form in chapter 14. The actual statistical results are given here, along with a brief exposition on their interpretation.

The interpretation of multiple regression and correlation analysis is best illustrated by an actual example. Take the multiple regression, using the same equation used in the first analysis of combined services (see pp. 347–348).

$$X_1 = 8.84 + \underline{0.0125X_2} + \underline{0.0711X_3} + \underline{0.00304X_4}$$

$$(0.569) \qquad (0.190) \qquad (0.697)$$

$$R^{*2} = 0.706$$

What does this mean to the nonstatistical reader?

First, the X's must be identified. Here they have the following meanings:

X_1 = the per capita expenditures on fire and police protection, street service, and refuse collection combined. It stands for some number in dollars.

X_2 = the size of the night-time population. It represents a number of people, say 42,329.

X_3 = a service-quality index. The higher the index is, the better the over-all quality of service.

X_4 = the average per capita assessed valuation. It is a dollar figure.

Next consider the numbers 0.0125, 0.0711, and so on. Technically they are the net regression coefficients. The first figure tells, for example, that if the night-time population goes up by one person, there will be, on the average, an increase in the annual per capita expenditures on these four services of 1.25 cents, while the effect of changes in the other two independent variables is held constant. Others are read in the same manner. Those that are underlined are statistically significant.

Moving on to the $R^{*2} = 0.706$, this denotes that about 71 per cent of the variation in X_1 is associated with variations in X_2, X_3, and X_4. In order to understand this term, technically the coefficient of multiple determination, an example is appropriate. Instead of night-time population, a service-quality index, and assessed valuation as independent variables, suppose canned salmon in Alaska, water temperature in Miami, and the total budget of the Metropolitan St. Louis Survey had been used. Here, unless some spurious correlation crept in, R^{*2} would be zero. All the independent variables, in total, have not explained a thing. A perfect explanation would be 1.0.

Finally, consider the numbers in parentheses, (0.569) and so forth. Technically the partial correlation coefficient, these numbers indicate the statistical significance of the relation between the particular independent variable and the dependent variable. Again the number can range from 0.0 to 1.0. How high a number should be in order to be regarded as statistically significant depends on (1) the size of the sample and (2) the level of significance required, that is, the level of confidence desired for prediction, for example.

The statistical data pertaining to the multiple regression equations, the correlation coefficients, and other information are presented in the three accompanying tables.

TABLE E1
Results of Multiple Correlation Analyses[a]

Service analyses	Number of cases used	Coefficient of multiple correlation		Degrees of freedom	Coefficient of multiple determination		Critical significance value of correlation coefficient
	N	R	R* (adjusted)		R^2	R^{*2} (adjusted)	
Individual service analyses:							
Public education analysis[b]	54	.92	.90	54 − 8 = 46	.85	.82	±.28
Fire protection analysis[b]	64	.92	.90	64 − 9 = 55	.84	.82	±.26
First police protection analysis	64	.95	.94	64 − 11 = 53	.91	.90	±.26
Second police protection analysis[c]	63	.94	.93	63 − 5 = 58	.89	.87	±.26
Refuse collection analysis	87	.63	.59	87 − 8 = 79	.40	.35	±.22
Street service analysis	53	.48	.35	53 − 7 = 46	.22	.12	±.28
Combined service analyses:							
Police Fire Refuse Street { First combined analysis	17	.87	.84	17 − 4 = 13	.76	.71	±.51
Second combined analysis[d]	17	.97	.96	17 − 4 = 13	.94	.93	±.51

[a] This table may be interpreted as follows, using public education as the example. Fifty-four cases were used as the sample (N). The coefficient of multiple correlation (R) measures the total relationship between all of the factors inserted that affect per pupil spending for this service. A coefficient of 0.00 would indicate absolutely no relationship, while a coefficient of 1.00 would indicate that all the factors influencing per pupil spending had been accounted for. Column three, R*(adjusted), is the coefficient of multiple correlation adjusted for the reliability or number of cases used in the sample, based on certain assumptions concerning the data.

Column four, degree of freedom, relates to the adjustment of the coefficients obtained where the sample size (N) is not large. Column five is the coefficient of multiple determination which means that 85 per cent of the variations in per pupil spending (or the dependent variable) are explained by the variables tested in this equation. In other words, given the small sample size of 54 cases (N), 82 per cent of the variation in per pupil spending was explained by the variables inserted in this equation. Column seven, significance value, refers to the data given in the following table. A partial correlation coefficient (the measure of association between one independent variable such as total number of pupils in ADA to the dependent variable, per capita cost) must have a value of ± (plus or minus) 0.28 in order to have a significant effect on per pupil spending for public education. Values of less than plus or minus 0.28 cannot be considered as importantly affecting per pupil spending.

[b] Cases from two years were used for the public education analysis (1951–52, 1954–55) and the fire protection analysis (1952, 1955), thus doubling the sample size.

[c] In the second police analysis, fewer variables were used and St. Louis City was deleted.

[d] In this second combined analysis, area was substituted for population as a factor affecting per capita spending.

TABLE E2

Relationship of Various Factors to Per Capita Spending by Local Governments: Partial Correlation Coefficients[a]

Service analyses	Community characteristics									Service quality	Administration	Resources
	Population and its characteristics							Service area				
	Total	Total squared	Per cent increase 1950–1955	Density	Per cent nonwhite	Per cent under 25 years of age	High school as per cent of ADA	Area in square miles	commercial development	Index	Contractual arrangements index	Per capita assessed valuation
Individual service analyses												
Public education analysis	−.09b	.07b	−.03b	−.03b			.36			.41		.68b
Fire protection analysis	−.20	.42	−.14	.00e				−.49e	−.28d	.33		.86
First police protection analysis	−.18	.06		.18	.26	.25		.07e	−.15d .20f	.52		.92
Second police protection analysis	−.08			−.10g	.25	.18			.08f	.62		.93
Refuse collection analysis				−.32h						.43	.22	−.08
Street service analysis	−.10		.08					−.25 .18i		.10		.38
Combined service analyses:												
Police ⎫ First combined	.57j									.19		.70
Fire ⎬ analysis												
Refuse ⎫ Second combined								.66j		.48		.69
Street ⎬ analysis												

[a] The following is the way this table is to be interpreted. Fire protection is used as an example of the net relationships of each variable (such as total population or area) to the per capita expenditure for fire protection. A partial correlation coefficient of .00 means it has no effect or relationship to per capita spending. A coefficient of 1.00 would mean complete association. With the exception of refuse collection, a partial coefficient must have a value of at least ±.26 (see table E1) to be considered significant. The significant relationships are underlined.

Total population, column one, shows a negative association. It is not large enough to be considered significant by itself. Column two shows that the relationship between population and per capita spending is curvilinear. Thus there is a significant relationship. As population increases, per capita spending decreases until a population of approximately 110,000 is reached and then it begins to increase. See the discussion on p. 335 of the Fire Protection Findings.

Population increase and density do not significantly affect per capita spending (columns three and four). Service area in square miles is important, column eight. As service area increases, per capita spending decreases. Commercial development, in this case as measured by total receipts of wholesale, retail, and service establishments in 1954, is negatively correlated with spending (see note d). In other words, as sales and receipts increase, per capita spending decreases.

Column ten, service quality index, is positively correlated. As service level increases, per capita spending increases. Column twelve, per capita assessed valuation, shows a high degree of correlation with spending. Thus, as the per capita resources of the area increase, per capita spending for fire protection also increases. Per capita assessed valuation is also a measure of burnable property.

[b] For public education, total number of pupils in average daily attendance (ADA) was used as a measure of population of the school district.

[c] Dwelling units per square mile used as the measure of density.

[d] Total 1954 receipts of wholesale, retail, and service establishments.

[e] Number of miles of streets as measure of extent of the service area.

[f] Total number of retail, wholesale, and service establishments, 1954.

[g] The number of persons per dwelling unit was used as the second measure of density.

[h] Dwelling units per square mile used as the first measure of density.

[i] Miles of streets in secondary equivalent or adjusted for the relative cost of installing different types of thoroughfares.

[j] Scatter diagrams put the validity of these relationships in doubt. If St. Louis City and Kinloch are eliminated from the sample for the combined analysis, negative relationships are obtained between (1) area served and per capita spending, and (2) population served and per capita spending.

TABLE E3

ANALYSIS OF FIVE SUBCATEGORIES OF PUBLIC EDUCATION

Expenditure category	Multiple coefficient		Partial correlation coefficients							Critical significance value of correlation coefficient
Expenditure per pupil in ADA for:	R² coefficient of multiple determination	R² adjusted	No. of pupils in ADA	No. of pupils in ADA squared	Per cent increase in pupils, 1950–1955	Pupil density per square mile	High school as per cent of ADA	Service-quality index	Per pupil assessed valuation	
Instruction	.82	.79	−.16	.15	−.02	−.03	.42	.59	.40	±.28
Auxiliary services	.76	.72	.21	−.24	−.17	−.29	−.22	−.36	.73	±.28
General control	.63	.57	−.25	.24	−.00	−.07	.05	−.00	.62	±.28
Plant operation and maintenance	.61	.55	.01	−.13	−.21	−.01	.25	.10	.51	±.28
Fixed charges	.52	.45	−.08	−.11	.16	−.06	.23	.12	.34	±.28

For a text explanation of similar columns, see the explanatory notes to tables E1 and E2. Columns two and three in table E3 are similar to columns five and six in table E1, and the last column in table E3 is comparable to the last column in table E1. Columns three through nine in table E3 are similar to the columns in table E2 which contain results of the public education analysis.

APPENDIX F

Supplementary Tables to Chapter 16—
The Economy of the St. Louis Metropolitan Area

TABLE F1

INTERINDUSTRY FLOW OF GOODS AND SERVICES BY INDUSTRY AND AREA
OF ORIGIN AND DESTINATION, ST. LOUIS METROPOLITAN AREA, 1955

	Local sales to local sectors			
Industry	Food and kindred prod. 1.	Textiles and apparel 2.	Lumber and furn. 3.	Paper and allied prod. 4.
1. Food and kindred products	46,302	149		586
2. Textiles and apparel	4,356	15,071	2,760	366
3. Lumber and furniture	554	101	1,894	376
4. Paper and allied products	19,318	1,448	330	15,000
5. Printing and publishing	2,299	44	30	413
6. Chemicals	1,664	587	1,432	585
7. Products of petroleum and coal	2,337	166	318	1,143
8. Leather and leather products	3	86	183	10
9. Iron and steel	232		2,575	
10. Nonferrous metals	60	3		43
11. Fabricated metal products	36,267	47	1,355	276
12. Machinery (except electrical)	329	723	318	355
13. Electrical machinery	476			
14. Motor vehicles	162			17
15. Other transportation equipment				
16. Miscellaneous	21,640	3,418	708	805
17. Coal, gas, electric power, and water	5,487	669	371	1,462
18. Railroad transportation	15,332		1,589	1,895
19. Other transportation	11,958	1,612	1,274	1,983
20. Trade	11,680	5,002	1,485	2,947
21. Communications	2,003	273	157	154
22. Finance, insurance, rentals	3,307	1,717	1,029	700
23. Business and personal services, etc.	13,847	1,396	1,530	826
24. Medical, educational, nonprofit organizations	6	1		158
25. Undistributed	1,884	663	3,351	6,598
26. Eating and drinking places				
27. Capitalized construction and maintenance	3,377	232	173	511
28. Households	162,763	58,110	27,561	34,303
29. Local government	3,654	202	124	254
30. Inventory change	320		293	
31. Federal government	139,957	5,936	3,114	7,948
32. State government	6,284	348	214	436
33. Gross private capital formation				
Total inside St. Louis met. area	517,858	98,004	54,168	80,150
Total outside St. Louis met. area—imports	608,351	83,518	25,050	50,518
Total inputs of St. Louis met. area	1,126,209	181,522	79,218	130,668

Each row shows distribution of output of St. Louis area producing industry named at left. Each column shows input distribution for purchasing industry named at top. All figures are in thousands of dollars.

TABLE F1 (Continued)

Local sales to local sectors							
Printing and publ'g 5.	Chemicals 6.	Prod. of petr. and coal 7.	Leather and leather prod. 8.	Iron and steel 9.	Nonfer. metals 10.	Fab. met. prod. 11.	Mach'y (except elect'l) 12.
	1,293	1,129	285	2		3	
	253	6			163	44	28
2	157	20	3,023	288	108	217	2,460
708	3,685	1,840	1,830	71	676	1,470	731
12,566	979		839	78	95	374	808
530	28,428	6,320	672	814	2,633	307	119
66	61	16,000	119	2,251	1,034	340	109
	18	34	8,364	10	30	35	315
	1,352	178		4,969	598	12,339	6,975
306	3,332	216	3	335	2,459	6,362	255
22	3,939	4,629	1,203	2,313	1,080	7,064	8,611
886	25	127		595	559	3,598	13,066
				263	654	1,083	5,656
	20					519	168
				17			
	677	1,281	103	5,637	1,081	1,159	3,256
633	3,759	5,485	983	3,165	1,790	1,849	1,426
743	9,264	16,022	795	9,083	2,621	1,998	2,828
738	7,970	7,250	528	1,470	980	473	1,368
929	2,917	586	1,969	3,143	3,312	2,531	5,982
852	1,554	890	398	815	146	659	712
1,362	1,881	1,970	1,615	2,218	542	1,133	1,525
1,704	1,815	1,251	1,665	529	396	1,552	2,033
2	21			5	7	1	
6,488	170	22,465	2,312	20,920	9,817		1,279
328	5,391	1,543	942	1,508	1,167	493	2,426
62,736	124,836	50,901	56,348	97,222	40,386	79,648	72,058
233	1,773	2,471	544	851	189	344	707
568	1,575	475	232			49	
6,684	33,881	39,567	10,098	24,901	4,639	9,314	20,290
400	3,049	4,249	935	1,462	326	591	1,217
99,486	244,075	186,905	95,805	184,935	77,488	135,549	156,408
41,337	250,677	470,726	52,882	90,291	73,675	87,941	77,394
140,823	494,752	657,631	148,687	275,226	151,163	223,490	233,802

TABLE F1 (Continued)

INTERINDUSTRY FLOW OF GOODS AND SERVICES BY INDUSTRY AND AREA
OF ORIGIN AND DESTINATION, ST. LOUIS METROPOLITAN AREA, 1955

Industry	Local sales to local sectors			
	Elec. mach'y 13.	Motor vehicles 14.	Other trans. equip. 15.	Miscellaneous 16.
1. Food and kindred products				3,298
2. Textiles and apparel	27	7,598	157	2,893
3. Lumber and furniture	322	706	526	998
4. Paper and allied products	1,318	1,354	155	9,514
5. Printing and publishing	1,445		97	44
6. Chemicals	2,329		540	445
7. Products of petroleum and coal	236	1,272	901	2,212
8. Leather and leather products	61	114	91	85
9. Iron and steel	3,010	12,833	7,317	17,008
10. Nonferrous metals	10,783		295	2,500
11. Fabricated metal products	6,930	15,677	1,130	2,827
12. Machinery (except electrical)	3,567	11,406	469	837
13. Electrical machinery	2,630	397	1,267	
14. Motor vehicles	51	90,304	26	149
15. Other transportation equipment			5,878	1
16. Miscellaneous	797	7,205	541	23,213
17. Coal, gas, electric power, and water	2,403	2,556	1,264	6,477
18. Railroad transportation	1,346	9,357	908	6,226
19. Other transportation	1,375	2,525	744	4,398
20. Trade	416	2,257	1,127	5,729
21. Communications	532	657	591	770
22. Finance, insurance, rentals	905	647	1,325	18,254
23. Business and personal services, etc.	1,779	3,130	273	6,363
24. Medical, educational, nonprofit organizations	5			6
25. Undistributed	166	10,351		26,072
26. Eating and drinking places				
27. Capitalized construction and maintenance	579	1,806	2,287	2,040
28. Households	88,937	96,730	97,076	161,866
29. Local government	220	713	918	1,096
30. Inventory change		287		7,672
31. Federal government	5,384	24,982	11,486	18,119
32. State government	378	1,226	1,579	1,885
33. Gross private capital formation				
Total inside St. Louis met. area	37,931	306,968	138,968	332,997
Total outside St. Louis met. area— imports	65,039	279,312	154,153	107,940
Total inputs of St. Louis met. area	202,970	585,402	293,121	440,937

Each row shows distribution of output of St. Louis area producing industry named at left. Each column shows input distributio n for purchasing industry named at top. All figures are in thousands of dollars.

TABLE F1 (Continued)

			Local sales to local sectors				
Coal, gas, etc. 17.	Railroad trans. 18.	Other trans. 19.	Trade 20.	Commu-nications 21.	Finance, insur., rentals 22.	Bus. and pers. service 23.	Med., educa'l, etc. 24.
28	904	904	2,469	125		1,224	8,586
54	31	30	211		169	269	182
183	157	79	725	295	2,927	18	465
75	97	102	13,213	38	1,935	1,405	777
190	1,054	509	3,682	590	4,653	23,618	2,726
300	3,362	404	956	32	400	625	3,676
15,320	12,241	10,261	3,971	105	12,803	2,348	530
37	10	2	8	17		67	
383	757	1	1,458		291		
114	65	10	19				88
465	257	374	957	16		1,247	502
531	1,220	63	203	694	405	4,092	304
3,326						24	310
497	42	4,895	821	545	45	8,431	
34	488	1,719	186				
557	517	521	1,478	148	2,863	5,966	2,119
6,480	1,110	1,222	1,452	389	77,534	6,777	3,202
3,471	17,273	517	1,961	30	217	670	161
828	4,004	2,735	5,554	101	2,394	885	732
694	880	6,596	4,632	188	13,817	6,339	1,527
252	1,095	1,269	3,659	1,869	2,973	4,352	460
1,438	1,527	7,980	46,824	780	29,113	20,405	253
1,185	7,338	7,026	56,714	293	7,907	19,235	920
3						2,425	3,961 377
201		930				2,177	
		153	2,878		605		930
9,902	34,746	2,967	3,090	2,091	64,762	1,876	2,869
50,709	145,694	96,125	481,992	39,898	225,143	219,198	117,264
5,721	3,289	2,658	7,884	1,484	27,899	2,963	65
							36
16,744	21,912	9,164	53,484	8,992	16,910	13,581	799
9,836	5,656	4,570	13,556	2,552	47,972	5,094	111
129,558	265,726	163,786	724,037	61,272	545,871	357,138	149,971
68,918	105,178	58,406	64,557	28,595	122,131	26,227	2,604
198,476	370,904	222,192	788,594	89,867	668,002	383,365	152,575

TABLE F1 (Continued)

INTERINDUSTRY FLOW OF GOODS AND SERVICES BY INDUSTRY AND AREA
OF ORIGIN AND DESTINATION, ST. LOUIS METROPOLITAN AREA, 1955

	Local sales to local sectors			
Industry	Undis- tributed 25.	Eating and drinking places 26.	Capital- ized constr. & maint. 27.	House- holds 28.
1. Food and kindred products	717	26,622	39	290,063
2. Textiles and apparel	1,600	246	461	34,278
3. Lumber and furniture		15	11,409	15,554
4. Paper and allied products	917	812	2,906	6,228
5. Printing and publishing	13,896	393		20,257
6. Chemicals	169	296		3,475
7. Products of petroleum and coal	24,803	220	15,560	42,692
8. Leather and leather products			8	2,422
9. Iron and steel	5,428		15,360	206
10. Nonferrous metals		29	1,341	61
11. Fabricated metal products		377	28,784	8,123
12. Machinery (except electrical)	37,649	32	9,189	5,588
13. Electrical machinery				6,423
14. Motor vehicles	35,655	21	908	54,676
15. Other transportation equipment				1,283
16. Miscellaneous	22,006	3,346	49,001	65,215
17. Coal, gas, electric power, and water		5,815	777	2,296
18. Railroad transportation		1,687	19,806	10,858
19. Other transportation		1,292	14,425	73,078
20. Trade	22,229	14,128	50,315	485,691
21. Communications		158	1,110	43,930
22. Finance, insurance, rentals		6,098	6,864	470,481
23. Business and personal services, etc.		3,998	24,034	195,636
24. Medical, educational, nonprofit organizations			7	113,701
25. Undistributed	10,371			108,780
26. Eating and drinking places				171,986
27. Capitalized construction and maintenance	6,136	973	178	2,657
28. Households	217,560	61,543	289,818	36,493
29. Local government	24,328	1,561	1,308	113,565
30. Inventory change				
31. Federal government	22,053	14,557	8,297	481,807
32. State government	41,832	2,684	2,248	48,992
33. Gross private capital				530,355
Total inside St. Louis met. area	487,349	146,903	554,153	3,446,850
Total outside St. Louis met. area— imports	119,289	29,649	169,737	421,745
Total inputs of St. Louis met. area	606,638	176,552	723,890	3,868,595

Each row shows distribution of output of St. Louis area producing industry named at left. Each column shows input distribution for purchasing industry named at top. All figures are in thousands of dollars.

TABLE F1 (Continued)

Local sales to local sectors					
Local government 29.	Inventory change 30.	Federal government 31.	State government 32.	Gross private capital formation 33.	Totals
3,101		7,544	702		396,075
129	2,448	517	81		74,428
601	2,362	373	2	9,118	56,035
597	1,083	138	311		90,082
1,358		983	416	1,944	96,380
180	12,751	358			74,389
1,557	2,694	853	1,717		176,240
	1,872	273		172	14,327
156	8,366	239	212		102,243
1	6	23			28,709
344	3,388	1,431	219	2,444	142,298
223	7,955	1,037	158	13,926	120,129
151	5,526		153	7,569	35,908
656	16,456	620	893	122,374	338,951
8			11		9,625
1,977	3,505	7,395	1,911	26,539	266,585
2,206	7,640	865	2,177		169,721
687		10,865	936	10,052	159,198
2,397	1,119	2,695	3,174	3,722	165,781
958	2,691	559	197	49,455	712,908
778		1,468	1,023		75,559
6,140	1	2,409	817	13,780	655,040
1,829		3,051	2,384	1,275	372,914
1,273		23,877	1,734		147,570
				134,684	369,679
					176,552
29,846		34,452	73,858	428,684	723,890
147,326		349,379	44,165	34,807	3,868,595
				1,395	208,413
					11,507
				15,182	1,049,782
				2,400	212,082
					530,355
204,479	79,863	451,404	137,251	879,522	11,631,950
3,934		216,425	4,160	35,101	3,995,460
208,413	79,863	667,829	141,411	914,623	15,627,410

TABLE F1 (Continued)

INTERINDUSTRY FLOW OF GOODS AND SERVICES BY INDUSTRY AND AREA
OF ORIGIN AND DESTINATION, ST. LOUIS METROPOLITAN AREA, 1955

Industry	Local sales to nonlocal sectors			
	Food and kindred prod. 1.	Textiles and apparel 2.	Lumber and furn. 3.	Paper and allied prod. 4.
1. Food and kindred products	92,765	1,053	615	7,435
2. Textiles and apparel		14,013	306	
3. Lumber and furniture		240		
4. Paper and allied products	5,800	1,219	369	15,000
5. Printing and publishing				
6. Chemicals	19,650	377	3,860	15,522
7. Products of petroleum and coal	453	1,518	3,290	1,888
8. Leather and leather products	89			
9. Iron and steel	412		6,686	
10. Nonferrous metals		2,788	83	2,316
11. Fabricated metal products		50	1,355	
12. Machinery (except electrical)		695	316	
13. Electrical machinery				
14. Motor vehicles		41	51	
15. Other transportation equipment				
16. Miscellaneous	3,523	8,973	1,429	721
17. Coal, gas, electric power, and water				
18. Railroad transportation	7,338		17,369	16,770
19. Other transportation	2,761	1,457	5,096	1,718
20. Trade		9,188	1,654	1,175
21. Communications				
22. Finance, insurance, rentals				
23. Business and personal services, etc.		2,925	534	53
24. Medical, educational, nonprofit organizations	8			84
25. Undistributed	1,884	663	3,351	6,597
26. Eating and drinking places				
27. Capitalized construction and maintenance				
28. Households				
29. Local government				
30. Inventory change				
31. Federal government				
32. State government				
33. Gross private capital formation				
Total inside St. Louis met. area	134,683	45,200	46,364	69,279

Each row shows distribution of output of St. Louis area producing industry named at left. Each column shows input distribution for purchasing industry named at top. All figures are in thousands of dollars.

TABLE F1 (Continued)

Local sales to nonlocal sectors							
Printing and publ'g 5.	Chemicals 6.	Prod. of petr. and coal 7.	Leather and leather prod. 8.	Iron and steel 9.	Nonfer. metals 10.	Fab. met. prod. 11.	Mach'y (except elect'l) 12.
7	9,049						
379	209		450				59
250	3,213	550	1,168	20	200	847	480
4,188							
97	301,992	26,149	690	51	435		1,491
78	15,574	216,312		38,448	1,323	718	1,671
			67,085				126
	44	967			2,102	15,907	22,934
997	2,375	951		16	61,811	2,860	559
	45,252	9,048				824	
				214		1,709	13,066
							51,743
						794	1,104
	7,861		1,020			2,100	1,349
	3,609	8,419		13,635	2,943	1,369	1,111
			178	1,770		450	
	1,412			1,986	11	2,734	1,322
48	903			857		8	728
1	55	7					8
6,488		22,465	2,312	20,920	19,190		1,279
12,533	391,548	284,868	72,903	77,917	88,105	30,320	99,030

TABLE F1 (Continued)

INTERINDUSTRY FLOW OF GOODS AND SERVICES BY INDUSTRY AND AREA
OF ORIGIN AND DESTINATION, ST. LOUIS METROPOLITAN AREA, 1955

	Local sales to nonlocal sectors			
Industry	Elec. mach'y 13.	Motor vehicles 14.	Other trans. equip. 15.	Miscellaneous 16.
1. Food and kindred products	2			51,561
2. Textiles and apparel	309	5,678		
3. Lumber and furniture				
4. Paper and allied products	707	400	188	384
5. Printing and publishing				
6. Chemicals	4,320		1,071	29,844
7. Products of petroleum and coal	774	219		23,237
8. Leather and leather products	10			
9. Iron and steel	2,350	5,608	51,543	6,351
10. Nonferrous metals	571	538	6,299	1,847
11. Fabricated metal products	6,929			5,286
12. Machinery (except electrical)			4,610	348
13. Electrical machinery	40,441	37,444		
14. Motor vehicles	441	90,303		4,447
15. Other transportation equipment				
16. Miscellaneous	7,740		47	23,743
17. Coal, gas, electric power, and water				
18. Railroad transportation				73,643
19. Other transportation				22,487
20. Trade	3,122		801	28,778
21. Communications				
22. Finance, insurance, rentals				
23. Business and personal services, etc.				1,517
24. Medical, educational, nonprofit organizations				4
25. Undistributed		10,350	997	26,072
26. Eating and drinking places				
27. Capitalized construction and maintenance				
28. Households				
29. Local government				
30. Inventory change				
31. Federal government				
32. State government				
33. Gross private capital formation				
Total inside St. Louis met. area	67,716	150,540	65,556	299,549

Each row shows distribution of output of St. Louis area producing industry named at left. Each column shows input distribution for purchasing industry named at top. All figures are in thousands of dollars.

TABLE F1 (Continued)

			Local sales to nonlocal sectors				
Coal, gas, etc. 17.	Railroad trans. 18.	Other trans. 19.	Trade 20.	Commu-nications 21.	Finance, insur., rentals 22.	Bus. and pers. services 23.	Med., educa'l, etc. 24.
	855		4,564			1,609	
	16			20			
12							3,000
20	30	30	3,960	10	683	410	345
				131		26,109	
			10,654			2,661	783
7,339	748	15,477	5,651		25,443	705	1,868
	4	3	8,798				
1							
	165					2,018	
	30	246					
						833	
		481				34,828	
		96,823					
6						9,464	1,834
18,832	1,578		6,741				
7,682	50,330		739				
1,405			6,235		68		
255			579		797	9,162	
				2,087		8,000	
					11,173	1,789	
					625	284	
					2,052		536
						2,177	3,434
35,552	53,756	113,060	47,921	2,248	40,841	100,049	11,800

TABLE F1 (Continued)

INTERINDUSTRY FLOW OF GOODS AND SERVICES BY INDUSTRY AND AREA
OF ORIGIN AND DESTINATION, ST. LOUIS METROPOLITAN AREA, 1955

| | Local sales to nonlocal sectors | | | |
Industry	Undis-tributed 25.	Eating and drinking places 26.	Capital-ized constr. & maint. 27.	House-holds 28.
1. Food and kindred products		9,698		548,102
2. Textiles and apparel	1,599			82,224
3. Lumber and furniture				15,266
4. Paper and allied products	916	230	875	1,870
5. Printing and publishing				12,311
6. Chemicals				
7. Products of petroleum and coal	24,803	502	14,122	74,546
8. Leather and leather products				67,050
9. Iron and steel	5,428		42,892	
10. Nonferrous metals			29,942	8,298
11. Fabricated metal products		12		8,821
12. Machinery (except electrical)	37,649			22,286
13. Electrical machinery				36,601
14. Motor vehicles	35,654	20	569	73,690
15. Other transportation equipment				
16. Miscellaneous	22,007		1,202	65,215
17. Coal, gas, electric power, and water	1,604			
18. Railroad transportation			6,749	
19. Other transportation		2,072	6,562	4,152
20. Trade		11,150		1,560
21. Communications				4,221
22. Finance, insurance, rentals				
23. Business and personal services, etc.				1,969
24. Medical, educational, nonprofit organizations				2,250
25. Undistributed				108,780
26. Eating and drinking places				
27. Capitalized construction and maintenance				
28. Households				
29. Local government				
30. Inventory change				
31. Federal government				
32. State government				
33. Gross private capital formation				
Total inside St. Louis met. area	129,660	23,684	102,913	1,139,212

Each row shows distribution of output of St. Louis area producing industry named at left. Each column shows input distribution for purchasing industry named at top. All figures are in thousands of dollars.

TABLE F1 (Continued)

Local sales to nonlocal sectors						
Local govern-ment 29.	Inventory change 30.	Federal govern-ment 31.	State govern-ment 32.	Gross private capital formation 33.	Totals	Total output of St. Louis met. area (local sales to local and nonlocal sectors)
129		2,514	176		730,134	1,126,209
120		1,549	163		107,094	181,522
		757		3,908	23,183	79,218
		412			40,586	130,668
305		983	416		44,443	140,823
		716			420,363	494,752
1,262		1,705	1,717		481,391	657,631
					134,360	148,687
		954			172,983	275,226
		202			122,454	151,163
		1,432			81,192	223,490
116		1,037	158	31,193	113,673	233,802
		2,478			167,062	202,970
657		186,673	893		246,451	585,402
		15,013			283,496	293,121
468			637		174,352	440,937
					28,755	198,476
					211,706	370,904
					56,411	222,192
					75,686	788,594
					14,308	89,867
					12,962	668,002
					10,451	383,365
					5,005	152,575
					236,959	606,638
						176,552
						723,890
						3,868,595
						208,413
						11,507
						1,049,782
						212,082
						530,355
3,057		216,425	4,160	35,101	3,995,460	15,627,410

TABLE F2

TECHNICAL COEFFICIENTS: DIRECT PURCHASES PER DOLLAR OF OUTPUT,
ST. LOUIS METROPOLITAN AREA, 1955

Industry	Food and kindred prod. 1.	Textiles and apparel 2.	Lumber and furn. 3.	Paper and allied prod. 4.
1. Food and kindred products	.041125	.000821		.004485
2. Textiles and apparel	.003869	.083026	.034970	.002801
3. Lumber and furniture	.000492	.000556	.023997	.002878
4. Paper and allied products	.017158	.007977	.004181	.114795
5. Printing and publishing	.002042	.000242	.000380	.003161
6. Chemicals	.001478	.003234	.018144	.004477
7. Products of petroleum and coal	.002076	.000914	.004029	.008747
8. Leather and leather products	.000003	.000474	.002319	.000077
9. Iron and steel	.000206		.032626	
10. Nonferrous metals	.000053	.000017		.000329
11. Fabricated metal products	.032212	.000259	.017168	.002112
12. Machinery (except electrical)	.000292	.003983	.004029	.002717
13. Electrical machinery	.000423			
14. Motor vehicles	.000144			.000130
15. Other transportation equipment				
16. Miscellaneous	.019220	.018830	.008971	.006161
17. Coal, gas, electric power, and water	.004873	.003686	.004701	.011189
18. Railroad transportation	.013618		.020133	.014502
19. Other transportation	.010621	.008880	.016142	.015176
20. Trade	.010374	.027556	.018815	.022553
21. Communications	.001779	.001504	.001989	.001179
22. Finance, insurance, rentals	.002937	.009459	.013038	.005357
23. Business and personal services	.012299	.007691	.019385	.006321
24. Medical, educational, nonprofit organizations	.000005	.000006		.001209
25. Undistributed	.001673	.003652	.042458	.050494
26. Eating and drinking places				
27. Capitalized construction and maintenance	.002999	.001278	.002192	.003911
28. Households	.144564	.320126	.349205	.262520
29. Local government	.003245	.001113	.001571	.001944

Each entry shows direct purchases from St. Louis area industry named at left by industry named at top per dollar of output by latter.

TABLE F2 (Continued)

Printing and publ'g 5.	Chem. 6.	Prod. of petr. and coal 7.	Leather and leather prod. 8.	Iron and steel 9.	Nonfer. metals 10.	Fab. met. prod. 11.	Mach'y (except elect'l) 12.
	.002622	.001718	.001920	.000007		.000013	
	.000513	.000009			.001078	.000197	.000120
.000014	.000318	.000030	.020363	.001046	.000714	.000971	.010522
.005048	.007472	.002800	.012327	.000258	.004472	.006579	.003127
.089594	.001985		.005652	.000283	.000628	.001674	.003456
.003779	.057643	.009617	.004527	.002958	.017418	.001374	.000509
.000471	.000124	.024347	.000802	.008179	.006840	.001522	.000466
	.000036	.000052	.056340	.000036	.000198	.000157	.001347
	.002741	.000271		.018054	.003956	.055223	.029833
.002182	.006756	.000329	.000020	.001217	.016267	.028473	.001091
.000157	.007987	.007044	.008103	.008404	.007145	.031615	.036830
.006317	.000051	.000193		.002162	.003698	.016103	.055885
				.000956	.004326	.004847	.024191
	.000041					.002323	.000719
				.000062			
	.001373	.001949	.000694	.020481	.007151	.005187	.013926
.004513	.007622	.008347	.006622	.011500	.011842	.008275	.006099
.005297	.018784	.024381	.005355	.033002	.017339	.008942	.012096
.005262	.016161	.011032	.003557	.005341	.006483	.002117	.005851
.006624	.005915	.000892	.013263	.011420	.021910	.011327	.025586
.006075	.003151	.001354	.002681	.002961	.000966	.002949	.003045
.009711	.003814	.002998	.010879	.008059	.003586	.005071	.006523
.012149	.003680	.001904	.011216	.001922	.002620	.006946	.008695
.000014	.000043			.000018	.000046	.000004	
.046259	.000345	.034185	.015574	.076010	.064943		.005470
.002339	.010931	.002348	.006345	.005479	.007720	.002206	.010376
.447300	.253126	.077457	.379563	.353244	.267169	.356461	.308201
.001662	.003595	.003760	.003665	.003092	.001250	.001540	.003024

TABLE F2 (Continued)

TECHNICAL COEFFICIENTS: DIRECT PURCHASES PER DOLLAR OF OUTPUT,
ST. LOUIS METROPOLITAN AREA, 1955

Industry	Elec. mach'y. 13.	Motor vehicles 14.	Other trans. equip. 15.	Misc. 16.
1. Food and kindred products				.007612
2. Textiles and apparel	.000133	.012985	.000536	.006677
3. Lumber and furniture	.001586	.001207	.001794	.002303
4. Paper and allied products	.006494	.002314	.000529	.021959
5. Printing and publishing	.007119		.000331	.000102
6. Chemicals	.011475		.001842	.001027
7. Products of petroleum and coal	.001163	.002174	.003074	.005105
8. Leather and leather products	.000301	.000195	.000310	.000196
9. Iron and steel	.014830	.021932	.024962	.039255
10. Nonferrous metals	.053126		.001006	.005770
11. Fabricated metal products	.034143	.026793	.003855	.006525
12. Machinery (except electrical)	.017574	.019494	.001600	.001932
13. Electrical machinery	.012958	.000678	.004322	
14. Motor vehicles	.000251	.154335	.000089	.000344
15. Other transportation equipment			.020053	.000002
16. Miscellaneous	.003927	.012314	.001846	.053577
17. Coal, gas, electric power, and water	.011839	.004368	.004312	.014949
18. Railroad transportation	.006632	.015992	.003098	.014370
19. Other transportation	.006774	.004315	.002538	.010151
20. Trade	.002050	.003857	.003845	.013223
21. Communications	.002621	.001123	.002016	.001777
22. Finance, insurance, rentals	.004459	.001106	.004520	.042131
23. Business and personal services	.008765	.005349	.000931	.014686
24. Medical, educational, nonprofit organizations	.000025			.000014
25. Undistributed	.000818	.017691		.060176
26. Eating and drinking places				
27. Capitalized construction and maintenance	.002853	.003087	.007802	.004708
28. Households	.438178	.165318	.331181	.373596
29. Local government	.001084	.001219	.003132	.002529

Each entry shows direct purchases from St. Louis area industry named at left by industry named at top per dollar of output by latter.

TABLE F2 (Continued)

Coal, gas, etc. 17.	Railroad trans. 18.	Other trans. 19.	Trade 20.	Communications 21.	Finance, insur., rentals 22.	Bus. and pers. services 23.	Med., educ'l., etc. 24.
.000141	.002435	.004069	.003131	.001391		.003193	.056287
.000272	.000084	.000135	.000268		.000253	.000702	.001193
.000922	.000423	.000356	.000919	.003282	.004382	.000047	.003048
.000378	.000262	.000459	.016755	.000423	.002897	.003665	.005094
.000957	.002842	.002291	.004669	.006565	.006966	.061607	.017871
.001512	.009064	.001818	.001212	.000356	.000599	.001630	.024099
.077188	.033003	.046181	.005036	.001168	.019166	.006125	.003475
.000186	.000027	.000009	.000010	.000189		.000175	
.001930	.002041	.000005	.001849			.000759	
.000574	.000175	.000045	.000024				.000577
.002342	.000693	.001683	.001214	.000178		.003253	.003291
.002675	.003289	.000284	.000257	.007723	.000606	.010674	.001993
.016758						.000063	.002032
.002504	.000113	.022030	.001041	.006065	.000067	.021992	
.000171	.001316	.007737	.000236				
.002806	.001394	.002345	.001874	.001647	.004286	.015562	.013892
.032649	.002993	.005500	.014522	.004329	.116069	.017678	.020991
.017488	.046570	.002327	.002487	.000334	.000325	.001748	.001055
.004172	.010795	.012309	.007043	.001124	.003584	.002309	.004799
.003497	.002373	.029686	.005874	.002092	.020684	.016535	.010011
.001270	.002952	.005711	.004640	.020797	.004451	.011352	.003016
.007245	.004117	.035915	.059377	.008679	.043582	.053226	.001659
.005970	.019784	.031621	.071918	.003260	.011837	.050174	.006031
.000015					.003630	.010322	.002471
.001013		.004186				.005679	
		.000689	.003650		.000906		.006097
.049890	.093679	.013353	.003918	.023268	.096949	.004894	.018808
.255492	.392808	.432621	.611204	.443967	.337039	.571774	.768748
.028824	.008867	.011962	.009998	.016513	.041765	.007729	.000426

TABLE F2 (Continued)

TECHNICAL COEFFICIENTS: DIRECT PURCHASES PER DOLLAR OF OUTPUT,
ST. LOUIS METROPOLITAN AREA, 1955

Industry	Undist. 25.	Eating and drinking places 26.	Cap. constr. 27.	Households 28.	Local gov't. 29.
1. Food and kindred products	.001182	.150788	.000054	.074979	.014879
2. Textiles and apparel	.002637	.001393	.000637	.008861	.000619
3. Lumber and furniture		.000085	.015761	.004021	.002884
4. Paper and allied products	.001512	.004599	.004014	.001610	.002865
5. Printing and publishing	.022907	.002226		.005236	.006516
6. Chemicals	.000279	.001677		.000898	.000864
7. Products of petroleum and coal	.040886	.001246	.021495	.011036	.007471
8. Leather and leather products			.000011	.000626	
9. Iron and steel	.008948		.021219	.000053	.000749
10. Nonferrous metals		.000164	.001852	.000016	.000005
11. Fabricated metal products		.002135	.039763	.002100	.001651
12. Machinery (except electrical)	.062062	.000181	.012694	.001444	.001070
13. Electrical machinery				.001660	.000725
14. Motor vehicles	.058775	.000119	.001254	.014133	.003148
15. Other transportation equipment				.000332	.000038
16. Miscellaneous	.036275	.018952	.067691	.016858	.009486
17. Coal, gas, electric power, an water		.032936	.001073	.000593	.010585
18. Railroad transportation		.009555	.027361	.002807	.003296
19. Other transportation		.007318	.019927	.018890	.011501
20. Trade	.036643	.080022	.069506	.125547	.004597
21. Communications		.000895	.001533	.011356	.003733
22. Finance, insurance, rentals		.034539	.009482	.121615	.029461
23. Business and personal services		.022645	.033201	.050570	.008776
24. Medical, educational, nonprofit organizations			.000010	.029391	.006108
25. Undistributed	.017096			.028119	
26. Eating and drinking places				.044457	
27. Capitalized construction and maintenance	.010115	.005511	.000246	.000687	.143206
28. Households	.358632	.348583	.400362	.009433	.706894
29. Local government	.040103	.008842	.001807	.029356	

Each entry shows direct purchases from St. Louis area industry named at left by industry named at top per dollar of output by latter.

TABLE F3

DIRECT AND INDIRECT REQUIREMENTS PER DOLLAR OF FINAL DEMAND, ST. LOUIS METROPOLITAN AREA, 1955

Industry	Food and kindred prod. 1.	Textiles and apparel 2.	Lumber and furn. 3.	Paper and allied products 4.
1. Food and kindred products	1.075363	0.008768	0.003046	0.024828
2. Textiles and apparel	0.058831	1.098091	0.004812	0.017065
3. Lumber and furniture	0.069734	0.048205	1.029818	0.013834
4. Paper and allied products	0.061255	0.010974	0.007467	1.136783
5. Printing and publishing	0.078225	0.010128	0.005609	0.014807
6. Chemicals	0.048709	0.006485	0.003811	0.014187
7. Products of petroleum and coal	0.021509	0.002688	0.001599	0.005792
8. Leather and leather products	0.068896	0.009435	0.026944	0.022447
9. Iron and steel	0.065537	0.008807	0.005970	0.008404
10. Nonferrous metals	0.057244	0.008936	0.006028	0.012856
11. Fabricated structural prod.	0.063556	0.008491	0.005835	0.015079
12. Machinery (except electrical)	0.062743	0.008731	0.016229	0.012020
13. Electrical machinery	0.074836	0.009863	0.007250	0.016256
14. Motor vehicles	0.040351	0.022156	0.004771	0.008513
15. Other transportation equipment	0.052623	0.007361	0.005694	0.006348
16. Miscellaneous	0.084371	0.017853	0.008380	0.035396
17. Coal, gas, electric power, and water	0.052780	0.007153	0.005721	0.007104
18. Railroad transportation	0.075616	0.009553	0.007168	0.009129
19. Other transportation	0.081748	0.010437	0.006267	0.009982
20. Trade	0.107511	0.013630	0.008583	0.030608
21. Communications	0.072002	0.009202	0.008817	0.008199
22. Finance, insurance, rentals	0.076855	0.010405	0.012093	0.013233
23. Business and personal services	0.108223	0.014599	0.007953	0.016932
24. Medical, educational, nonprofit organizations	0.179149	0.016937	0.011669	0.020340
25. Undistributed	0.075316	0.013616	0.006380	0.012180
26. Eating and drinking places	0.231365	0.011800	0.005844	0.018563
27. Capitalized construction and maintenance	0.083900	0.012499	0.022492	0.017172
28. Households	0.138595	0.017469	0.009235	0.013920
29. Local government	0.135137	0.016350	0.013698	0.017601

Each entry shows, per dollar of deliveries to final demand by industry named at left, the total dollar production directly and indirectly required from St. Louis area industry named at top.

TABLE F3 (Continued)

DIRECT AND INDIRECT REQUIREMENTS PER DOLLAR OF FINAL DEMAND,
ST. LOUIS METROPOLITAN AREA, 1955

Industry	Printing and publ'g 5.	Chemicals 6.	Prod. of petr. and coal 7.	Leather and leather prod. 8.
1. Food and kindred products	0.009378	0.003377	0.013713	0.000331
2. Textiles and apparel	0.011353	0.006087	0.018717	0.001110
3. Lumber and furniture	0.015639	0.023129	0.028801	0.003221
4. Paper and allied products	0.016044	0.008080	0.031146	0.000648
5. Printing and publishing	1.114245	0.007552	0.025519	0.000760
6. Chemicals	0.010815	1.063406	0.015694	0.000483
7. Products of petroleum and coal	0.004748	0.011615	1.034456	0.000252
8. Leather and leather products	0.019683	0.008291	0.021886	1.060398
9. Iron and steel	0.014130	0.006337	0.033105	0.000683
10. Nonferrous metals	1.013161	0.021584	0.029999	0.000785
11. Fabricated structural prod.	0.013849	0.004979	0.021879	0.000819
12. Machinery (except electrical)	0.016497	0.004037	0.021031	0.002162
13. Electrical machinery	0.021875	0.016570	0.024758	0.001089
14. Motor vehicles	0.008417	0.002149	0.017019	0.000691
15. Other transportation equipment	0.009612	0.004258	0.018908	0.000846
16. Miscellaneous	0.016869	0.004962	0.034432	0.000973
17. Coal, gas, electric power, and water	0.011319	0.005084	0.099433	0.000724
18. Railroad transportation	0.017717	0.013421	0.059276	0.000742
19. Other transportation	0.018955	0.005612	0.072210	0.000764
20. Trade	0.028714	0.005666	0.038112	0.001013
21. Communications	0.019839	0.003170	0.021894	0.000895
22. Finance, insurance, rentals	0.023153	0.004575	0.055410	0.000772
23. Business and personal services	0.090422	0.006592	0.039758	0.001217
24. Medical, educational, nonprofit organizations	0.040880	0.030539	0.039115	0.001151
25. Undistributed	0.039427	0.003940	0.065018	0.000823
26. Eating and drinking places	0.018640	0.005396	0.028178	0.000721
27. Capitalized construction and maintenance	0.018112	0.004565	0.049703	0.000894
28. Households	0.023165	0.004982	0.037056	0.001305
29. Local government	0.029093	0.006037	0.046647	0.001158

Each entry shows, per dollar of deliveries to final demand by industry named at left, the total dollar production directly and indirectly required from St. Louis area industry named at top.

TABLE F3 (Continued)

Iron and steel 9.	Nonfer. metals 10.	Fab. met. prod. 11.	Mach'y (except elect'l) 12.	Elec. mach'y. 13.	Motor vehicles 14.	Other transp. equip. 15.	Miscel- laneous 16.
0.005002	0.001595	0.038671	0.004193	0.001711	0.009471	0.000338	0.032954
0.004014	0.000740	0.006686	0.009575	0.001878	0.015513	0.000475	0.040917
0.040109	0.001516	0.026649	0.013969	0.002468	0.022036	0.000649	0.036656
0.004578	0.001162	0.009394	0.011935	0.002052	0.019151	0.000550	0.028784
0.004847	0.003244	0.008790	0.017013	0.002616	0.023861	0.000580	0.027716
0.006268	0.008055	0.014287	0.004235	0.001561	0.012378	0.000481	0.017762
0.002605	0.000902	0.010204	0.004567	0.000845	0.007915	0.000266	0.010655
0.005039	0.001008	0.016617	0.006933	0.002148	0.018643	0.000497	0.024146
1.024627	0.002443	0.016748	0.013294	0.003342	0.022421	0.000607	0.047290
0.010945	1.018046	0.017331	0.014445	0.006635	0.019800	0.000492	0.034354
0.062657	0.031012	1.041139	0.023616	0.007720	0.019706	0.000475	0.028700
0.039681	0.004601	0.048987	1.066498	0.028224	0.018134	0.000511	0.038621
0.022425	0.056742	0.045154	0.026205	1.016442	0.020228	0.000580	0.030429
0.032398	0.001658	0.038689	0.030231	0.002943	1.194896	0.000352	0.031492
0.029236	0.001987	0.010223	0.006197	0.006160	0.013649	1.020847	0.020154
0.048101	0.007338	0.016796	0.013574	0.002865	0.025330	0.000643	1.086829
0.007170	0.002439	0.011883	0.008739	0.019259	0.017142	0.000619	0.025046
0.008833	0.001357	0.013028	0.011094	0.002332	0.019826	0.002014	0.032820
0.005576	0.000991	0.011858	0.007997	0.002528	0.046367	0.008536	0.030268
0.007575	0.001131	0.012767	0.009488	0.003410	0.029671	0.001005	0.037823
0.004679	0.000790	0.008954	0.014276	0.002334	0.025302	0.000487	0.026537
0.007692	0.001387	0.013482	0.009047	0.004471	0.020792	0.000608	0.038728
0.008322	0.001487	0.016224	0.022032	0.003902	0.054686	0.000738	0.053107
0.007398	0.002341	0.018655	0.011876	0.005956	0.030608	0.000857	0.055700
0.019104	0.001387	0.013601	0.075133	0.003958	0.090121	0.000528	0.066844
0.005705	0.001359	0.016070	0.006992	0.002957	0.020258	0.000622	0.049082
0.032485	0.004445	0.051825	0.022092	0.003120	0.024888	0.000796	0.101068
0.006121	0.001155	0.013298	0.009934	0.003873	0.034609	0.000913	0.043335
0.011297	0.001817	0.020800	0.012761	0.004535	0.034911	0.000970	0.059584

TABLE F3 (Continued)

DIRECT AND INDIRECT REQUIREMENTS PER DOLLAR OF FINAL DEMAND,
ST. LOUIS METROPOLITAN AREA, 1955

Industry	Coal, gas, electric power, and water 17.	Railroad transportation 18.	Other transportation 19.
1. Food and kindred products	0.017356	0.019983	0.021542
2. Textiles and apparel	0.024393	0.007021	0.026852
3. Lumber and furniture	0.030328	0.031902	0.038266
4. Paper and allied products	0.032289	0.024710	0.034302
5. Printing and publishing	0.030733	0.015020	0.028396
6. Chemicals	0.023597	0.026991	0.031201
7. Products of petroleum and coal	0.015913	0.029361	0.017880
8. Leather and leather products	0.030007	0.014494	0.023840
9. Iron and steel	0.034254	0.043936	0.025307
10. Nonferrous metals	0.032177	0.028513	0.025569
11. Fabricated structural prod.	0.030729	0.020026	0.021441
12. Machinery (except electrical)	0.029216	0.023303	0.025643
13. Electrical machinery	0.037581	0.018204	0.029470
14. Motor vehicles	0.019544	0.026666	0.017842
15. Other transportation equipment	0.021610	0.010370	0.018025
16. Miscellaneous	0.047169	0.027667	0.034275
17. Coal, gas, electric power, and water	1.052703	0.029114	0.022171
18. Railroad transportation	0.027623	1.061179	0.035000
19. Other transportation	0.036053	0.013522	1.036043
20. Trade	0.056295	0.015175	0.037644
21. Communications	0.027367	0.009031	0.021926
22. Finance, insurance, rentals	0.151325	0.015717	0.029572
23. Business and personal services	0.059538	0.015544	0.033578
24. Medical, educational, nonprofit organizations	0.059488	0.016586	0.040498
25. Undistributed	0.026066	0.013058	0.023689
26. Eating and drinking places	0.065089	0.022374	0.031868
27. Capitalized construction and maintenance	0.032989	0.041857	0.046442
28. Households	0.040845	0.013776	0.038518
29. Local government	0.052389	0.021754	0.049189

Each entry shows, per dollar of deliveries to final demand by industry named at left, the total
dollar production directly and indirectly required from St. Louis area industry named at top.

TABLE F3 (Continued)

Trade 20.	Communications 21.	Finance, insur., rentals 22.	Business and pers. services 23.	Medical, educa'l, nonprofit organ. 24.	Undistributed 25.	Eating and drinking places 26.
0.064574	0.007896	0.059849	0.042498	0.011362	0.017495	0.016287
0.123512	0.011791	0.109826	0.059090	0.020207	0.028583	0.029338
0.135424	0.014714	0.133599	0.081661	0.024409	0.076039	0.035229
0.118245	0.011299	0.102050	0.056894	0.020829	0.081593	0.028274
0.134736	0.020262	0.141960	0.079081	0.027386	0.082951	0.039677
0.081290	0.011465	0.081669	0.043777	0.016013	0.019799	0.023179
0.034563	0.005030	0.036793	0.019716	0.006819	0.044105	0.009838
0.122917	0.014577	0.124740	0.069473	0.023389	0.045128	0.033856
0.120221	0.014480	0.119217	0.058413	0.022756	0.106746	0.033071
0.121732	0.011256	0.102206	0.055368	0.019924	0.092019	0.028915
0.115786	0.014317	0.112950	0.061542	0.022191	0.032525	0.032234
0.130217	0.014619	0.115130	0.065262	0.021904	0.035522	0.031784
0.124936	0.015867	0.130520	0.072303	0.026160	0.036450	0.037957
0.072376	0.008694	0.070561	0.041903	0.014045	0.041175	0.020352
0.088939	0.011129	0.092689	0.044904	0.018344	0.022938	0.026724
0.141374	0.015579	0.175489	0.082113	0.026720	0.100519	0.038429
0.091682	0.010779	0.097186	0.053115	0.018381	0.025454	0.026367
0.126464	0.016135	0.128829	0.086272	0.025595	0.030983	0.036888
0.156040	0.019815	0.170183	0.100686	0.027341	0.037273	0.039855
1.174615	0.023475	0.238575	0.162529	0.037010	0.042643	0.056111
0.116499	1.033307	0.126878	0.062521	0.024642	0.028266	0.035730
0.151867	0.018551	1.177921	0.083075	0.030565	0.032811	0.039374
0.186759	0.039696	0.233810	1.142031	0.047305	0.052261	0.052866
0.203218	0.023638	0.201648	0.106856	1.044050	0.049047	0.066692
0.158605	0.013353	0.127739	0.065920	0.025693	1.054178	0.037168
0.202446	0.014795	0.167138	0.094538	0.026074	0.031670	1.037535
0.206699	0.017070	0.158609	0.111828	0.029306	0.041560	0.042252
0.219835	0.023029	0.228290	0.112057	0.048285	0.053102	0.070558
0.206429	0.024661	0.232349	0.114283	0.047827	0.049217	0.060574

TABLE F3 (Continued)
DIRECT AND INDIRECT REQUIREMENTS PER DOLLAR OF FINAL DEMAND, ST. LOUIS METROPOLITAN AREA, 1955

Industry	Cap. construct. and maint. 27.	Households 28.	Local government 29.
1. Food and kindred products	0.016916	0.357935	0.019748
2. Textiles and apparel	0.021692	0.644351	0.029676
3. Lumber and furniture	0.030387	0.774638	0.038076
4. Paper and allied products	0.027014	0.620820	0.032209
5. Printing and publishing	0.030308	0.874335	0.041460
6. Chemicals	0.030266	0.510358	0.026315
7. Products of petroleum and coal	0.013569	0.216499	0.015393
8. Leather and leather products	0.031001	0.745325	0.037052
9. Iron and steel	0.033201	0.728076	0.038379
10. Nonferrous metals	0.089281	0.635200	0.032290
11. Fabricated structural prod.	0.027385	0.709879	0.032788
12. Machinery (except electrical)	0.035126	0.698488	0.034467
13. Electrical machinery	0.302772	0.836826	0.037536
14. Motor vehicles	0.020347	0.448201	0.022244
15. Other transportation equipment	0.026129	0.589133	0.028432
16. Miscellaneous	0.039164	0.845026	0.044473
17. Coal, gas, electric power, and water	0.076046	0.580716	0.055670
18. Railroad transportation	0.124161	0.812688	0.044651
19. Other transportation	0.045193	0.860392	0.051380
20. Trade	0.046251	1.155186	0.062640
21. Communications	0.049202	0.787818	0.050395
22. Finance, insurance, rentals	0.139899	0.844534	0.084015
23. Business and personal services	0.047497	1.162033	0.061071
24. Medical, educational, nonprofit organizations	0.058091	1.335543	0.057593
25. Undisturbed	0.041592	0.816533	0.076676
26. Eating and drinking places	0.039083	0.820197	0.048226
27. Capitalized construction and maintenance	1.033682	0.925460	0.043939
28. Households	0.041321	1.557196	0.064242
29. Local government	0.185586	1.333529	1.058433

Each entry shows, per dollar of deliveries to final demand by industry named at left, the total dollar production directly and indirectly required from St. Louis area industry named at top.

Index